Connected Worlds
History in Transnational Perspective

Connected Worlds
History in Transnational Perspective
Co-edited by Ann Curthoys and Marilyn Lake

E PRESS

Published by ANU E Press
The Australian National University
Canberra ACT 0200, Australia
Email: anuepress@anu.edu.au
Web: http://epress.anu.edu.au

National Library of Australia
Cataloguing-in-Publication entry

Connected worlds : history in trans-national perspective.

Includes index

ISBN 978 1 920942 44 1
ISBN 1 920942 45 9 (online)

1. Historiography. 2. World history. 3. Australia - Historiography. I. Curthoys, Ann, 1945- . II. Lake, Marilyn.

907.2094

All rights reserved. No part of this publication may be reproduced, stored in a retrieval system or transmitted in any form or by any means, electronic, mechanical, photocopying or otherwise, without the prior permission of the publisher.

Copyedited and indexed by Robin Ward.
Cover design by Brendon McKinley.
The cover image was taken from Jacob Roggeveen (et al.), *Dagverhaal der ontdekkings-reis van Mr. Jacob Roggeveen : met de Schepen den Arend, Thienhoven en de Afrikaansche Galei, in de jaren 1721 en 1722 / met toestemming van Zijne Excellentie den Minister van Kolonien uitgegeven door het Zeeuwsch Genootschap der Wetenschappen*, (Middelburg: Gebroeders Abrahams, 1838), held in the Menzies Library rare book collection, The Australian National University, Canberra.

This edition © 2005 ANU E Press

Table of Contents

Acknowledgements: v
Contributors: vii
1. Introduction: *Ann Curthoys and Marilyn Lake* 5
Different Modes of Transnational History 21
    2. Putting the nation in its place?: world history and C. A. Bayly's
    The Birth of the Modern World: Tony Ballantyne 23
    3. Paths not yet taken, voices not yet heard: rethinking Atlantic
    history: *Michael A. McDonnell* 45
    4. Postcolonial histories and Catherine Hall's *Civilising Subjects: Angela
    Woollacott* 63
Migration and Other Voyages 75
    5. Steal a handkerchief, see the world: the trans-oceanic voyaging of
    Thomas Limpus: *Emma Christopher* 77
    6. Revolution and respectability: Chinese Masons in Australian
    history: *John Fitzgerald* 89
    7. 'Innocents abroad' and 'prohibited immigrants': Australians in
    India and Indians in Australia 1890–1910: *Margaret Allen* 111
    8. Postwar British emigrants and the 'transnational moment':
    exemplars of a 'mobility of modernity'?: *A. James Hammerton* 125
Modernity, Film and Romance 137
    9. 'Films as foreign offices': transnationalism at Paramount in the
    twenties and early thirties: *Desley Deacon* 139
    10. Modern nomads and national film history: the multi-continental
    career of J. D. Williams: *Jill Julius Matthews* 157
    11. The Americanisation of romantic love in Australia: *Hsu-Ming
    Teo* 171
Transnational Racial Politics 193
    12. Transcultural/transnational interaction and influences on
    Aboriginal Australia: *John Maynard* 195
    13. From Mississippi to Melbourne via Natal: the invention of the
    literacy test as a technology of racial exclusion: *Marilyn Lake* 209
Postcolonial Transnationalism 231
    14. Islam, Europe and Indian nationalism: towards a postcolonial
    transnationalism: *Patrick Wolfe* 233
Index 267

Acknowledgements

Many people have assisted in the preparation of this book.

First, we wish to thank all those people involved in the conference, entitled the Trans-National History Symposium, which formed the basis of the present volume. While discussion of transnational history has been going on for some time in the United States, this was the first time transnational history had been discussed explicitly and in detail at a conference of historians in Australia. The Symposium, featuring some twenty participants, was held on 10 and 11 October 2004 at the Humanities Research Centre at the Australian National University and attracted a lively audience from around Australia and overseas.

For their funding and administrative support we especially wish to thank the HRC, its Director Ian Donaldson and conference administrator, Leena Messina; the ANU National Institute for the Humanities and Creative Arts, its convener Adam Shoemaker and administrator, Suzanne Knight, and the Faculty of Humanities and Social Sciences at La Trobe University. We also wish to thank those colleagues who presented stimulating papers which do not appear in this collection: Joanna Bourke, Laurence Brown, Georgine Clarsens, Liz Conor, Joy Damousi, Cassandra Pybus, Amanda Rasmussen and Pierre-Yves Saunier. We thank our contributors for their responsiveness to editorial suggestions and deadlines and in particular Desley Deacon and John Fitzgerald for reading and providing useful feedback on the introduction.

Finally, we thank ANU E Press for its encouragement and support.

Ann Curthoys and Marilyn Lake

Contributors

Margaret Allen is Associate Professor in Gender Studies at the University of Adelaide. Her research interests are focused within fields of feminist and postcolonial histories. She is working on a biographical study of the Australian writer Catherine Martin (1848–1937), on whom she has published many articles. She co-edited *Fresh Evidence, New Witnesses, Finding Women's History* (South Australian Government Printer, 1989), and has edited many journal special issues including *Gender in the 'Contact Zone', Australian Feminist Studies*, vol. 16, no. 34, 2001. She is interested in locating Australians within the racialised hierarchies of Empire, publishing 'White Already to Harvest': South Australian Women Missionaries in India', *Feminist Review*, vol. 65, no. 1, 2000. Currently she holds an ARC grant to investigate links between India and Australia 1880–c.1930 within a broader imperial focus.

Tony Ballantyne. Before assuming his current position as Senior Lecturer in History at the University of Otago, Tony Ballantyne taught at the University of Illinois, Urbana-Champaign and the National University of Ireland, Galway. His research focuses on the production of colonial knowledge in South Asia and the Pacific as well as the institutional and discursive 'webs' that underpinned the British empire. His publications include *Orientalism and Race: Aryanism in the British Empire* (Basingstoke: Cambridge Imperial and Post-Colonial Studies Series, Palgrave-Macmillan, 2002) and *Bodies in Contact: Rethinking Colonial Encounters in World History* (Durham, NC: Duke University Press, 2005), which he co-edited with Antoinette Burton. In 2006 Duke University Press will also publish his study of the intersections between religion, empire and migration, *Between Colonialism and Diaspora: Sikh Cultural Formations in an Imperial World*.

Emma Christopher is a postdoctoral fellow in the School of Historical Studies at Monash University, Melbourne. Originally a scholar of the transatlantic slave trade, she gained her PhD at University College, London in 2002 and subsequently taught for a year at the University of Toronto. Her book *Slave Trade Sailors and their Captive Cargoes* is forthcoming with Cambridge University Press, New York in 2006. Having more recently turned her attention to convict transportation, she is currently working on a book about the British felons who were sent to West Africa in the years prior to the settlement of Australia. She has published several articles on both the slave trade and convict transportation, and is also the co-editor (with Marcus Rediker and Cassandra Pybus) of *Other Middle Passages*, a collection exploring the global exportation of non-free persons, which will be published by the University of California Press in 2006.

Ann Curthoys is Manning Clark Professor of History at the Australian National University. She writes about many aspects of Australian history, including Aboriginal-European relations, the development of the White Australia Policy, journalism, television and feminism, as well as more generally about the past and future of historical writing. Her book, *Freedom Ride: A Freedomrider Remembers* (Crows Nest, NSW: Allen and Unwin, 2002) was awarded the Stanner Prize by the Australian Institute of Aboriginal and Torres Strait Islander Studies. Written jointly with John Docker, her most recent book is *Is History Fiction?* (Sydney and Ann Arbor, MI: University of New South Wales Press and University of Michigan Press, 2005). She is currently working with Ann Genovese, Larissa Behrendt, and Alex Reilly on a study of the ways historical expertise is used by the law in cases involving Indigenous litigants.

Desley Deacon is Professor of Gender History in the History Program of the Research School of Social Sciences at the Australian National University. She is author of *Elsie Clews Parsons: Inventing Modern Life* (Chicago, IL: University of Chicago Press, 1997) and the forthcoming *Mary McCarthy: Four Husbands and a Friend* (Chicago, IL: University of Chicago Press) (the friend is Hannah Arendt). The lives of these women, and teaching for many years in the American Studies Department at the University of Texas in Austin, stimulated her longstanding interest in internationalism and transnational history. Her interest in the history of film was stimulated by her research on McCarthy's first husband, Harold Johnsrud, who worked for MGM in the early 1930s, and will be continued in her new project 'Judith Anderson 1897–1992: Voice and Emotion in the Making of an International Star'.

John Fitzgerald worked at the Australian National University, in the Australian Federal Parliament, and in the History Department of the University of Melbourne before moving to La Trobe University in 1992 and taking up the Chair in Asian Studies there in 1995. In 1998, his book *Awakening China: Politics, Culture and Class in the Nationalist Revolution* (Stanford, CA: Stanford University Press) was awarded the Joseph Levenson Prize for Twentieth Century China by the US Association for Asian Studies. His recent books include John Fitzgerald, R. Jeffrey, and Tessa Morris-Suzuki, *Maximizing Australia's Asia Knowledge: Repositioning and Renewal of a National Asset* (Bundoora, Vic: Asian Studies Association of Australia, 2002); K. L. Billy, John Fitzgerald, Huang Jianli and James K. Chin (eds) *Power and Identity in the Chinese World Order: Festschrift in Honour of Professor Wang Gungwu* (Hong Kong: Hong Kong University Press, 2003); and *Rethinking China's Provinces* (editor, New York, NY: Routledge, 2002). He has recently taken up the position of Director of the International Centre of Excellence in Asia-Pacific Studies at the ANU.

James Hammerton, before his recent retirement, was Associate Professor of History and Head of the School of Historical and European Studies at La Trobe University. His publications include: *Emigrant Gentlewomen: Genteel Poverty and Female Emigration, 1830-1914* (London: Croom Helm, 1979), *Cruelty and Companionship: Conflict in Nineteenth Century Married Life* (London:

Routledge, 1992), and [with Eric Richards], *Speaking to Immigrants: Oral Testimony and the History of Australian Immigration* (Canberra, ACT : History Program and Centre for Immigration and Multicultural Studies, Research School of Social Sciences, Australian National University, 2002). His current research focuses on the emigration of the British since World War II; the first volume to flow from this research, *'Ten Pound Poms': Australia's Invisible Migrants*, co-authored with Alistair Thomson, was published in 2005 by Manchester University Press.

Marilyn Lake has an Australian Professorial Fellowship, based at La Trobe University, and is also an Adjunct Professor in the Humanities Research Centre, Australian National University. Between 2001 and 2002, she held the Chair in Australian Studies at Harvard University. Her most recent book is *Faith: Faith Bandler, Gentle Activist* (Crows Nest, NSW: Allen and Unwin, 2002), winner of the 2002 Human Rights award for non-fiction. Her research interests include Australian history; nation and nationalism; gender, war and citizenship; femininity and masculinity; history of feminism; race, gender and imperialism; global and transnational history. She is currently working on a study of the emergence of the idea of the white man's country in a transnational context, that looks at intellectual and political developments linking Africa, America, Asia and Australasia in the late nineteenth and early twentieth centuries. She has recently edited *Memory, Monuments and Museums*, to be published by Melbourne University Press in 2006.

Jill Julius Matthews is a Reader in History at the Australian National University. She has written extensively in Australian social and cultural history, and in the fields of feminist history, history of popular culture, and history of sexuality. Her publications include *Good and Mad Women. The Historical Construction of Femininity in Twentieth-Century Australia* (Sydney: George Allen & Unwin, 1984), *Sex in Public: Australian Sexual Cultures* (editor, St Leonards, NSW: Allen & Unwin, 1997), and *Dance Hall and Picture Palace. Sydney's Romance with Modernity* (Sydney: Currency Press, 2005).

Michael A. McDonnell has recently been appointed to a new post in Atlantic History at the University of Sydney after teaching for several years at the University of Wales, Swansea. He has a book forthcoming entitled *The Politics of War: Race, Class, and Conflict in Revolutionary Virginia* (University of North Carolina Press for the Omohundro Institute of Early American History and Culture), and has published several articles on the American Revolution in the *William and Mary Quarterly*, the *Journal of American History*, the *Journal of American Studies*, and the *Australasian Journal of American Studies*. He is currently working on a new project entitled 'Beyond Borders: Indians, French, and Métis in the Great Lakes 1700-1850'.

John Maynard is an Australian Research Council post-doctoral fellow with Umullilko Centre for Indigenous Higher Education Research at the University of Newcastle. His traditional roots lie with the Worimi people of Port Stephens, New South Wales. He was the recipient of the Aboriginal History (ANU) Stanner Fellowship for 1996 and the New South Wales Premiers Indigenous History Fellowship for 2003–2004. He has worked with and within many Aboriginal communities, urban, rural and remote. He is the author of *Aboriginal Stars of the Turf: Jockeys of Australian Racing History* (Canberra, ACT: Aboriginal Studies Press, 2003) and a number of articles on the history of Aboriginal protest movements in New South Wales.

Hsu-Ming Teo teaches in the Department of Modern History, Macquarie University. She is currently researching the culture of romantic love in Australia and finishing another project on British colonialism, race and the mass-market romance novel. She co-edited *Cultural History in Australia* (Sydney: University of New South Wales Press, 2003) and has published articles on travel history, romance and imperialism. In 1999 she won The Australian Vogel Literary Award for her first novel, *Love and Vertigo*. Her second novel, *Behind the Moon*, was published in 2005.

Patrick Wolfe is an ARC Research Fellow at the Europe-Australia Institute, Victoria University of Technology. He is the author of *Settler Colonialism and the Transformation of Anthropology : The Politics and Poetics of an Ethnographic Event* (London and New York, NY: Cassell, 1999) and a number of articles on race, colonialism and the history of anthropology. His current research project is a comparative international study of racial discourse.

Angela Woollacott is Professor of Modern History at Macquarie University. Her books include *Gender and Empire* (Palgrave, 2006); *To Try Her Fortune in London: Australian Women, Colonialism and Modernity* (Oxford and New York, NY: Oxford University Press, 2001); and *On Her Their Lives Depend: Munitions Workers in the Great War* (Berkeley, CA: University of California Press, 1994). She has also co-edited two anthologies: Mrinalini Sinha, Donna J. Guy and Angela Woollacott (eds) *Feminisms and Internationalism* (Oxford and Malden, MA: Blackwell Publishers, 1999) and Miriam Cooke and Angela Woollacott (eds) *Gendering War Talk* (Princeton, NJ: Princeton University Press, 1993).

For John Docker and Sam Lake

1. Introduction

Ann Curthoys
Marilyn Lake

For some years, historians have been pointing to the significance and implications of history's complicity with the nation state. History as a professional discipline was constituted to serve the business of nation building, and has accordingly very often seen its task as providing an account of national experience, values and traditions, thus helping forge a national community. The question historians are now asking is: has history as handmaiden to the nation state distorted or limited our understanding of the past? And if so, can a transnational approach help develop new and more adequate forms of historical writing?[1]

This collection of essays addresses these questions and also seeks to demonstrate in practice what transnational history looks like. It investigates with an enthusiastic, if critical eye the potential of transnational approaches to develop new understandings of the past by highlighting historical processes and relationships that transcend nation states and that connect apparently separate worlds. Our aim is both theoretical, for instance considering the claims of 'postcolonial', 'regional', or 'world history' approaches to illuminate historical analysis, and practical, presenting historical case studies that demonstrate how transnational approaches can produce new and exciting forms of historical knowledge. We particularly focus on ways in which expertise in 'Australian history' can contribute to and benefit from transnational histories, though a number of important essays in this collection do not touch on Australia at all.

Defining transnational history

So, what is transnational history? We can define it in a number of ways, but put simply, it is the study of the ways in which past lives and events have been shaped by processes and relationships that have transcended the borders of nation states. Transnational history seeks to understand ideas, things, people, and practices which have crossed national boundaries. It is generally in a complex relation with national history; it may seek to interrogate, situate, supersede, displace, or avoid it altogether. In their reaction against what they see as rigid and confining national histories, many of those enthusiastic about transnational

---

[1] See Ann Curthoys 2003, 'Cultural History and the Nation', in Hsu-Ming Teo and Richard White (eds), *Cultural History in Australia* (Sydney: University of New South Wales Press), pp. 22-37; Marilyn Lake 2003, 'White Man's Country: The Trans-National History of a National Project', *Australian Historical Studies*, vol. 34, no. 122, pp. 346-63; Marilyn Lake c2003, 'History and Nation', in Robert Manne (ed.), *Whitewash* (Melbourne: Black Inc.), pp. 160-73.

history reach for metaphors of fluidity, as in talk of circulation and flows (of people, discourses, and commodities), alongside metaphors of connection and relationship.

How does transnational history differ, if at all, from other kinds of history which also transcend national boundaries: world, regional, and comparative history? World history seeks to understand the world as a whole; at its best, as Tony Ballantyne puts it in his chapter in this collection, it 'pays close attention to "bundles of relationships" … and is sensitive to the complex interplays between different layers of the analysis: the local, the regional, the inter-regional, the national, the continental, and the global'.[2] Regional histories, sometimes organised around oceanic formations – the Pacific Rim or the Atlantic World, whose historiography is discussed in this collection by Michael McDonnell – also insist on the necessity of locating nations in larger economic and political networks. Comparative history is a form of history which crosses national borders by taking two or more societies (cities, regions, nations) and comparing aspects of their history. Such approaches are valuable but they very often keep the idea of the nation both central and intact. Comparative histories are also notoriously difficult to execute well, so large is the sheer quantity of scholarship that is normally required, and so hard is it to translate the conceptual framework developed by and for one national or regional history into that of another.

Transnational histories, then, can take many forms. They may be studies of international organisations, taking as their subjects already constituted bodies such as the Pan-African Congress or the League of Nations, and charting their historical development. Or they may be individual biographies, as exemplified in a forthcoming collection called *Colonial Lives across the British Empire*.[3] Transnational biographies are represented in this volume in Emma Christopher's account of transported convict, Thomas Limpus; Desley Deacon's discussion of film-maker, Walter Wanger; and Jill Matthews's evocation of the varied career of film entrepreneur, J. D. Williams. Other forms of transnational history include imperial histories, and histories of land and maritime exploration, ideas, political movements, migration, voyaging, and environments.[4]

Transnational history has, then, many departure points and follows many lines of enquiry. Whatever form it takes, transnational history suggests that historical understanding often requires us to move beyond a national framework of

---

[2] Ballantyne, this volume, p. 23.

[3] David Lambert and Alan Lester (eds) 2006, *Colonial Lives across the British Empire: Imperial Careering in the Long Nineteenth Century* (Cambridge: Cambridge University Press).

[4] See, for example, Bernard Klein and Gesa Mackentheun (eds) 2004, *Sea Changes: Historicizing the Ocean* (New York, NY: Routledge).

analysis, to explore connections between peoples, societies and events usually thought of as distinct and separate.

Transnational historiography

The interest in transnational history has grown rapidly during the 1990s and 2000s, and there is now a significant literature discussing what it is, why we need it, and how to do it. One major source of this enthusiasm has been from historians of the United States. Ian Tyrrell, one such scholar working in Australia, is an early and persistent advocate of transnational approaches. His target in 'American Exceptionalism in an Age of International History' (1991) was a form of American history writing which focused on the idea of the United States as '"outside" the normal patterns and laws of history', and especially as different from Europe.[5] Despite an interest in relating the United States to the rest of the world and a strong tradition in comparative history, he argues, historians of the United States failed to 'transcend the boundaries of nationalist historiography'. As an alternative, he suggested that 'the possibilities of a transnational history must be considered'.[6] Instead of assuming American exceptionalism, historians could ask *why* it has been such a focus for historians of the United States, and by way of contrast depict United States history 'as a variation on transnational themes'. He pointed out that there was another American historical tradition that offered an alternative to nationalist exceptionalism, one which saw the United States as a prime site for cosmopolitan exchange. Key advocates of American cosmopolitanism had included feminist Jane Addams in her *Newer Ideals of Peace* (1907) and Randolph Bourne in his neglected essay, 'Trans-National America' (1916), whose importance is noted by Desley Deacon in this volume, where she explores the the hopes that the new American film industry in the 1920s and 1930s would become a major source of 'world acquaintanceship'. Tyrrell also noted other forms of transnational history: regional approaches on the model of the French *Annales* school, and global and world history informed by world systems theory and other approaches to conceptualising world history as a whole. Histories of the environment and of international movements and organisations were also subjects that clearly required the transcending of national boundaries.[7]

---

[5] Ian Tyrrell 1991, 'American Exceptionalism in an Age of International History', *American Historical Review*, vol. 96, pp. 1031-55; these quotes on pp. 1031 and 1032.

[6] ibid., p. 1033.

[7] ibid., pp. 1038-54. The movements he had in mind might be organised around class, race, gender, or religion, and examples he gave included the Woman Christian Temperance Union, the Industrial Workers of the World, the United Society for Christian Endeavor, and Marcus Garvey's Universal Negro Improvement Association.

The term 'transnational' caught on, and enthusiasm for it grew quickly in the United States. In a special issue of the *Journal of American History* on transnational history the following year, David Thelen suggested that a transnational approach could 'enrich historical understanding by providing other pasts and presents to compare with the American past and present'.[8] Eight years after the appearance of his original article, Tyrrell developed his earlier argument further. He now demonstrated in greater detail that the national history he was criticising had become dominant in the United States only during and after World War I; before then, a transnational approach had coexisted with nation-centred professional history, and indeed had flourished. In particular, he noted, a broad transnational approach had been taken by women's historians such as Jane Addams and African American historians such as W. E. B. Du Bois and C. L. R. James.[9]

The latter point was expanded upon in the same issue of the *Journal of American History* by Robin Kelley, who argued that Black history in the United States had *always* been transnational. Early black historians had had a diasporic sensibility, shaped by their antiracist and anti-imperialist politics; they had consistently opposed the racist assumptions of their white counterparts, who constituted the mainstream historical profession in America, but in turn found their work generally dismissed by that profession as ideological rather than truly historical. In the Cold War context, black intellectuals had intensified their internationalism. In contrast to other kinds of history, Kelley argued, the transnationalism of African American intellectuals was born not in the academy but in 'social movements for freedom, justice, and self-determination'.[10]

During the 1990s, an interest in transnational history also came from quite another quarter – the revived interest in British imperial history. Although critical of the cultural emphasis of the new imperial history, A. G. Hopkins was important in calling for a reintegration of national postcolonial histories into a broader imperial framework. In the world of historiography, the response to decolonisation in the 1960s and after had been the separate development in each postcolonial nation of a professional, academic, national history. It was time, Hopkins argued in 1999, to bring these postcolonial histories back into

---

[8] David Thelen 1992, 'Of Audiences, Borderlands and Comparisons: Toward the Internationalisation of American History', *The Journal of American History*, vol. 79, issue 2, pp. 432-62.

[9] Ian Tyrrell 1999, 'Making Nations/Making States: American Historians in the Context of Empire', *The Journal of American History* (special issue entitled 'The Nation and Beyond: Transnational Perspectives on United States History'), vol. 86, issue 3, pp. 1015-44.

[10] Robin D. G. Kelley 1999, '"But a Local Phase of a World Problem": Black History's Global Vision', *Journal of American History*, vol. 86, pp. 1054-77.

conversation with one another and with Britain, this time, 'without deference'.[11] Furthermore, as historians like Catherine Hall and Antoinette Burton pointed out, renewed attention to histories of imperialism considered not only the impact of 'Europe' on its colonial possessions, but also the impact of imperialism on metropolitan societies. Imperial powers not only had dramatic impact on the lives of the peoples they colonised, but were also themselves in important ways constituted by the colonising experience. As Burton put it, scholars like Edward Said, Paul Gilroy, Stuart Hall, and others had provoked 'a critical return to the connections between metropole and colony, race and nation'.[12]

Both the American and the British enthusiasm for new kinds of transnational history were consonant with a growing focus on comparative histories of white settler societies, those forms of colonial society which had displaced indigenous peoples from their land. This was a form of colonialism distinguished from others by its relative lack of interest in 'native' labour, and hence very often, in keeping the 'native' alive at all. Most of the European colonial empires included settler colonies; in the English-speaking world, the modern societies sharing this history include the United States, Canada, Australia, New Zealand, and in a limited sense, South Africa. There was a revived interest in comparing the histories of these societies in the 1990s; Daiva Stasiulis and Nira Yuval-Davis's edited collection, *Unsettling Settler Societies* (1995), was important in re-popularising the term.[13] Historians began once again to develop expertise in the history of more than one settler society: Alan Lester and Elizabeth Elbourne, for example, have demonstrated how settler societies were interconnected in the nineteenth century as a result of British imperial policy, especially on matters of Aboriginal policy and settler practice.[14] Julie Evans, Patricia Grimshaw, David Phillips, and Shurlee Swain have provided a detailed comparison of the political rights and statuses of Indigenous peoples in settler societies of the British Empire: Australia, Canada,

---

[11] A. G. Hopkins (ed.) 2003, *Globalization in World History* (London: Pimlico).

[12] Antoinette Burton 2003, 'Introduction', in Antoinette Burton (ed.), *After the Imperial Turn: Thinking with and through the Nation* (Durham, NC: Duke University Press), p. 2.

[13] Deborah Montgomerie 1997, 'Beyond the Search for Good Imperialism: The Challenge of Comparative Ethnohistory', *New Zealand Journal of History*, vol. 31, no. 1, pp. 153-68.

[14] Alan Lester 2002, 'British Settler Discourse and the Circuits of Empire', *History Workshop Journal*, no. 54, p. 26; Alan Lester 2002, 'Colonial Settlers and the Metropole: Racial Discourse in the Early Nineteenth Century Cape Colony, Australia and New Zealand', *Landscape Research*, vol. 27, no. 1, pp. 39-49; Elizabeth Elbourne 2003, 'The Sin of the Settler: The 1835-36 Select Committee on Aborigines and Debates over Virtue and Conquest in the Early Nineteenth Century British White Settler Empire', *Journal of Colonialism and Colonial History*, vol. 4, no. 3, accessed 10 November 2005, http://muse.jhu.edu/journals/journal_of_colonialism_and_colonial_history/v004/4.3elbourne.html

New Zealand, and South Africa.[15] There has been a substantial contribution to this scholarship by Australian feminist historians such as Anne Keary, Kat Ellinghaus, and Ann McGrath, all of whom have compared aspects of Indigenous people's histories in Australia and the United States.[16]

American historians of the United States have been much less likely to include their country in this category than Australian or Canadian or New Zealand historians do, partly because the history of African slavery complicates and to some degree obscures the history of Native American displacement and erasure and partly because their achievement of political independence through revolution is seen to mark a sharp break from their history as a settler colony. Ian Tyrrell is among those who have argued strongly that the United States *should* be included in this analytical framework. Reorienting American history to transnational themes would be incomplete, he observed in 2002, if the focus remained on connections with Europe. Comparisons between the United States and the other British settler societies, he pointed out, were taken for granted by nineteenth century commentators such as Froude, Trollope, Dilke, Jebb, Seeley, and Bryce, but had fallen out of favour with the rise of nationalism during and after World War I. It was time, he suggested, for historical analysis to return to these connections.[17]

Gaining new insights: the transnational history of black political movements

The gains, then, seem very clear. As historians we all belong and have obligations to an international interpretative historical community as well as to our own societies. Taking a transnational approach enables us to take fuller advantage of the insights of this world of international professional scholarship. We can trace connections between people, ideas, and political movements that are lost

---

[15] Julie Evans, Patricia Grimshaw, David Phillips, and Shurlee Swain 2003, *Equal Subjects Unequal Rights: Indigenous People in British Settler Colonies, 1830–1910* (Manchester: Manchester University Press).

[16] Patrick Wolfe 2001, 'Land, Labor, and Difference: Elementary Structures of Race', *American Historical Review*, vol. 106, no. 3, pp. 866-905; Anne Keary 2002, Translating Colonialism: Missionaries and Indigenous Peoples in Eastern Australia and Northwestern America, paper delivered to American Historical Association Annual Meeting, San Francisco, 3-6 January; Katherine Ellinghaus 2002, 'Margins of Acceptability: Class, Education and Interracial Marriage in Australia and North America', *Frontiers: A Journal of Women Studies*, vol. 23, no. 3, pp. 55-75; Ann McGrath forthcoming, *Entangled Frontiers: Marriage and Sex Across Colonizing Frontiers in Australia and North America* (New Haven, CT: Yale University Press).

[17] Ian Tyrrell 2002, 'Beyond the View from Euro-America: Environment, Settler Societies, and the Internationalization of American History', in Thomas Bender (ed.), *Rethinking American History in a Global Age* (Berkeley, CA: University of California Press), pp. 168-92; these quotes on p. 169.

to vision when a firmly national framework is held in place. These possibilities seem to be especially important in the study of movements protesting against racial inequality and exploitation. John Maynard's chapter, for example, demonstrates hitherto little-known links between Marcus Garvey's United Negro Improvement Association and Aboriginal political struggles in New South Wales in the early decades of the twentieth century. In our own recent research, we have both independently found that connections between Black civil rights movements in the United States and campaigns for Aboriginal rights in Australia are important to understanding the latter's political dynamics. A transnational perspective offers insight into the interconnectedness of political movements and ideas.

In Marilyn's research for her biographical study of Faith Bandler, one of the leading campaigners for the 1967 Referendum on Aboriginal citizenship, it became clear that Faith's Pacific Islander family's strong identification with the National Association for the Advancement of Colored People and with cultural heroes, such as the singer Paul Robeson encouraged her to take a stand against racial discrimination and segregation in Australia. Inspiration came from many quarters. In 1951 as a delegate to the Youth Cultural Congress in Berlin and a member of the Margaret Walker Dance Company, Faith performed the lead part in 'The Dance of the Little Aboriginal Girl', a ballet which (despite its name) was based on a Black American poem, 'The Merry-Go Round', written by Harlem Renaissance poet, Langston Hughes, to combat racial prejudice in the playgrounds of the South. When Faith first spoke at a public meeting in Sydney in the early 1950s, it was in protest at the gaoling in the United States of the left-wing writer and suspected Communist Howard Fast, whose novel *Freedom Road*, a tribute to the Black freedom ushered in by Radical Reconstruction after the Civil War, was based on W. E. B. Du Bois' historical study, *Black Reconstruction*. Faith endorsed their ideal of Blacks and Whites living and working together and espoused it in subsequent life-long campaigns for Aboriginal rights in Australia, and in her work for the Federal Council for the Advancement of Aborigines and Torres Strait Islanders, that culminated in the passage of the 1967 referendum.[18]

Ann's book on the Australian Freedom Ride of 1965, published in the same year, 2002, was initially conceived as a national, or even local, history project. Her aim was to explore a very specific political movement – its antecedents, multiple character, tensions, and effects. The Freedom Ride was a two week event in which university students, mainly non-Indigenous but with an Indigenous leader, Charles Perkins, travelled around country towns in New South Wales protesting against discrimination against Indigenous people. In the ensuing public debate, urban public knowledge of racial discrimination grew, some

---

[18] Marilyn Lake 2002, *Faith: Faith Bandler, Gentle Activist* (Sydney: Allen and Unwin).

soul-searching went on in the country towns, racial segregation was challenged and in some cases ended, and alternative ideas of inclusion, equality, and full citizenship rights were much debated. Along with many other events and campaigns, the Freedom Ride contributed to the holding and passing of the referendum of 1967.

Freedom Ride was conceived around the time of the Bicentennial of the British colonisation of Australia, in 1988, that key moment when debate over Aboriginal history emerged as significant in national public discourse. It was researched in the 1990s as national public discourse dealt successively with a series of major issues concerning Indigenous people and Indigenous rights: the Royal Commission into Aboriginal Deaths in Police Custody of 1991, the *Mabo* decision of 1992, Native Title legislation in 1993, the Wik decision of 1996, and the Stolen Generations report of 1997. It was written in 2001, in the contexts of the History Wars over frontier violence and the rapid growth of an anti-Aboriginal rights agenda within national politics and discourse.

But in the research and writing, the question of the international context of the Australian Freedom Ride was always an issue. In particular, Ann was aware, having been a participant, of the importance of the influence of the United States Civil Rights movement, and to a lesser extent of the context of worldwide adjustment to decolonisation in Africa and Asia. As she researched the book she delved further into the question of the influence of American developments, tracing the Australian students' awareness of the United States Freedom Rides of 1961, of Martin Luther King's ideas of non-violence, and so on. Research explored the Australian press coverage of the United States Civil Rights movement, and interviews with former Freedom Riders elicited further information. When asked what influenced their thinking on racial issues, a significant number mentioned African American influences – Paul Robeson's visit to Australia in 1960 when they were teenagers, the press images of dogs and hoses being directed at children in Birmingham, Alabama, Martin Luther King's 'I Have a Dream' speech in Washington, August 1963, and so forth.

But there was always a worry about stressing United States influence, about any suggestions that these movements were 'mere imitations', slavish copies of movements that originated elsewhere. There was also the fear of a radical nationalist response: in stressing United States influences you are demeaning what we did, you are reducing us to mere imitators of United States forms of activism. And indeed, if national political movements are understood purely in terms of overseas influences and connections, then it is true, one does lose the sense of the distinctiveness of the political movement in its particular Australian context. One reaches the point where one is asked, as Ann was recently by a visiting American historian, 'where did the idea for the Tent Embassy come from? I can't think of anything like that in the US'. Allied with this desire not to drown Australian history in an ocean of overseas influence was the aim to write Australian history as a story important in itself, and not merely as an epiphenomenon of events elsewhere. This desire has been important in Australian historiography since the 1970s, as historians reacted against earlier views of Australian history as purely a product of British history, the transplantation of British people in a distant and alien land.

In thinking about ways in which to conceptualise outside influences on national histories, we found an article by Sean Scalmer to be especially helpful. Entitled 'Translating Contention: Culture, History, and the Circulation of Collective Action',[19] it treats the Freedom Ride as an example of the active connection, translation, and circulation between local movements and societies. He replaces the idea of imitation with the concepts of networks and circulation. Borrowing is never mere imitation, he suggests, as local movements select only those actions from elsewhere that fit their own normative standards and which have been made meaningful in local discursive and political frameworks. This is a useful way of emphasising the power of the local as well as the importance of the global. And it is also helpful in making sense of the circulation of technologies such as the literacy test, used by self-styled white men's countries at the end of the nineteenth century as an instrument of racial exclusion, the subject of Marilyn's chapter in this volume. As it moved between the United States, South Africa and Australia, the literacy test changed its form from the requirement to write one's name, to fill out a form in English, to understanding the constitution, to writing out, at dictation, a passage of fifty words in a European language. The test changed as the people targeted for exclusion changed, from Blacks, to Italians, to Indians to Japanese.

The dangers of transnational history

It is clear, then, that historical understanding requires us to move beyond the national frames of analysis that so often blinker our view of the past. But in repudiating national stories history also risks losing relevance for a national audience. In response to Tyrrell's original article advocating transnational history, Michael McGerr worried that too strong a turn to the transnational might lead to 'estrangement from our audiences, which, at least in the United States, still seem intensely nationalistic'.[20] In this volume, Jill Matthews draws attention to this issue. Speaking of Australia specifically, but it could apply in many other societies as well, she writes:

---

[19] Sean Scalmer 2000, 'Translating Contention: Culture, History, and the Circulation of Collective Action', *Alternatives*, vol. 25, pp. 491-514.

[20] Michael McGerr 1991, 'The Price of the "New Transnational History"', *The American Historical Review*, vol. 96, no. 4, pp. 1056-67; this quote on p. 1066.

> There is something sacrosanct about certain aspects of culture ... that triggers the protective, exclusive, mutual embrace; that constitutes a settled 'us' against the nomadic hordes of 'them'. And film history as a genre has been seduced, or recruited, to tell that story.

In their cultural nationalism, film historians are expressing a much wider phenomenon, and Matthews concludes that a transnational approach will not be welcome 'until the larger political discourse changes'.

There is little sign that political discourse will, at least in the short to medium term, abandon cultural and other forms of nationalism in which history and historians play a significant part. In their recent collection, *Partisan Histories*, Max Paul Friedman and Padraic Kenney point to the role history plays in national contexts. In national politics, groups seek support 'by presenting themselves as the only true representatives of the nation through historical narratives that support that claim: the rationale for nationalism is always sought in history'.[21] Indeed, history 'can influence such momentous decisions as whether or not to go to war'.[22] This is as true in Australia as anywhere else; the importance of defining and mining national historical traditions for political purposes is clearly evident in Prime Minister John Howard's relentless espousal of the virtues of Australia's military tradition.[23]

Given the intensely local and national relevance of history, then, it seems to us that there are dangers in transnational histories becoming disconnected from local audiences and by extension national political debates. The issue may not seem so pertinent for historians writing about societies other than the one in which they live and work, but for those who write histories about their own society, and who are thus used to dealing with questions of history's political relevance and sensitivity, the problem of losing relevance and readers can be quite acute. The temptation to write purely for an international scholarly audience can lead to histories which concentrate on showing local material only when it illuminates international scholarly concerns. It often also means publishing only in specialised journals or in expensive books which are little known and often of little interest to local audiences. As a result, there is the danger that the people whose history we write will know little of our work;

---

[21] Max Paul Friedman and Padraic Kenney (eds) 2005, 'Introduction', in *Partisan Histories: The Past in Contemporary Global Politics* (New York, NY: Palgrave Macmillan), p. 4.
[22] ibid., p. 1.
[23] Marilyn Lake 2005, 'The Howard History of Australia', *The Age*, 20 August.

even if they do know it, they recognise that we are not really talking to them. Our gaze has moved elsewhere.[24]

The implications of the tension between national histories and transnational scholarship are especially evident in the example of the history of Indigenous peoples. Such histories provide an excellent illustration of both the promise and the problems that attend transnational approaches. The promise is an enhanced understanding of the interactions between Indigenous and settler peoples and specifically of Indigenous people's political struggles, as John Maynard's chapter here so ably demonstrates. The danger is disconnection from local audiences and politics, the very connections that have made Indigenous histories so important and vibrant in the first place. Historians of Indigenous peoples, whether we are Indigenous or not, can thus find ourselves pulled between engaging in a national debate, in which our professionalism and scholarship is directly connected to ongoing political issues concerning Indigenous rights and politics, and contributing to a worldwide historians' conversation concerning new ways of conceptualising historical processes such as colonialism.

Australian perspectives

The enthusiasm for transnational history often expresses something of the character of the national histories against which it is rebelling. If the United States interest was prompted by an objection to United States exceptionalism and the British interest by a return to the vexed question of the imperial past, the Australian version has been influenced by a desire to break out of historiographical marginality and isolation.

It is perhaps significant that this collection is edited by two historians who have both worked in the fields of Australian feminist history and race relations history, each of which has been a prime site for the development of more transnational approaches. Feminist history has long been more internationalist in its approach than many other fields of history, as the common project of studying women's history and developing gendered perspectives on the past generally has led feminist historians into international conversations even while structuring their own histories within fairly conventional national boundaries. The tri-annual Berkshire Conferences on Women's History and the International Federation of Research into Women's History have both been important sites for this international exchange. The practice of contributing national studies to multi-authored international collections of essays on a common theme, a kind of half-way house on the way to transnationalising history, is particularly evident

---

[24] Ann Curthoys 2003, 'We've Just Started Making National Histories, and You Want Us to Stop Already?', in Burton (ed.), *After the Imperial Turn*, pp. 70-89; Ann Curthoys 2002, 'Does Australian History have a Future?', *Australian Historical Studies*, vol. 33, no. 118, pp. 140-52.

in feminist historical scholarship.[25] Race relations history has also been in the forefront of new developments in transnational history.

Despite their inherent cross-cultural and crossing-borders character, studies of race relations have too often, however, been narrowly and nationally focused, as Mary Dudziak has observed for the United States.[26] There is a growing body of work which attempts to compare not only the race-based political movements discussed earlier, but also the transnational character of racial thinking and racial policies. Patrick Wolfe, for example, has explored racial thinking in Australia, the United States, and elsewhere, while Marilyn Lake is engaged in exploring the transnational dynamics of the formation of self-styled 'white men's countries'.[27]

It isn't only feminist and race relations historians who have sought to go beyond national boundaries. In the case of Australian historiography, Donald Denoon, with various collaborators, has long sought to place Australian history within Pacific regional history.[28] Historians of convict transportation, exemplified in this volume by Emma Christopher, have begun to insist that their subjects cannot be understood within the narrow confines of an Australian historiography.[29]

---

[25] See for just some examples, Ulla Wiklander, Alice Kessler-Harris and Jane Lewis (eds) 1995, *Protecting Women: Labor Legislation in Europe, the United States, and Australia, 1880–1920* (Urbana, IL: University of Illinois Press); Marilyn Lake 1996, 'Female Desire: The Meaning of World War 2', reprinted in Joan Scott (ed.), *Feminism and History* (Oxford: Oxford University Press); Marilyn Lake 1998, 'The Inviolable Woman: Feminist Theories of Citizenship, Australia 1900–1945', in Joan Landes (ed.), *Feminism, the Public and the Private* (Oxford University Press, Oxford) and 'Australian Frontier Feminism and the Marauding White Man', in Clare Midgley (ed.), *Gender and Imperialism* (Manchester: Manchester University Press). See also Fiona Paisley 1999, '"Unnecessary Crimes and Tragedies": Race, Gender and Sexuality in Australian Policies of Aboriginal Child Removal', in Antoinette Burton (ed.), *Gender, Sexuality and Colonial Modernity* (New York, NY: Routledge), pp. 134-47; Patricia Grimshaw, Katie Holmes, and Marilyn Lake (eds) 2001, *Women's Rights and Human Rights: International Historical Perspectives* (Basingstoke: Palgrave); special issue of *Australian Feminist Studies*, vol. 16, no. 36.

[26] Mary L. Dudziak 2000, *Cold War, Civil Rights: Race and the Image of American Democracy* (Princeton, NJ: Princeton University Press).

[27] Marilyn Lake 2004, 'The White Man under Siege: New Histories of Race in the Nineteenth Century', *History Workshop Journal*, vol. 58, no. 1, pp. 41-62.

[28] Donald Denoon and Philippa Mein-Smith, with Marivic Wyndham 2000, *A History of Australia, New Zealand and the Pacific* (Oxford, U.K.; Maiden, Mass.; Blackwell); Donald Denoon, with Marivic Wyndham 2000, 'Australia and the Western Pacific', in Roger Louis and Alaine Low (eds), *The Oxford History of the British Empire* (Oxford and New York: Oxford University Press).

[29] Hamish Maxwell-Stewart and Cassandra Pybus 2002, *American Citizens, British Slaves* (Melbourne: Melbourne University Press); Cassandra Pybus 2002, 'The World is All of One Piece: The African

David Goodman has compared the gold rush experience in Victoria and California and Kirsten McKenzie the history of scandal in Sydney and Cape Town.[30] Ian Tyrrell has compared environmental reform movements in Australia and California while Tom Griffiths and Libby Robin have brought together environmental historians of a number of settler societies.[31] This volume seeks to add significantly to this growing body of work, even as we recognise the continuing importance of engaging a local audience and joining local debates about Australian historical experience, values and traditions.

This volume

We hope to advance the historiographical debates of the last decade, and to that end the volume begins with three historiographical essays. The first, by Tony Ballantyne, places an examination of C. A. Bayly's *Birth of the Modern World 1780–1914: Global Connections and Comparisons* (2004) within the context of a brief and illuminating history of world history. He praises Bayly's breadth, his attention to the Islamic world and South Asia, his clarity on the connections between race, empire, and violence, but draws attention to his relatively thin treatment of subjectivity and colonial modernity. Michael McDonnell outlines the explosion of interest in the history of the Atlantic world, drawing attention to its continuing Anglo-American centrism and suggesting that, despite recognition of the Black Atlantic, Atlantic history 'is in danger of becoming a neo-imperial form of history; one dominated by the rise of the British Empire, and the birth of the United States'. In its place he advocates a more genuinely pan-Atlantic approach, comparing and combining studies of North and South America. He warns, though, of the danger that such approaches might become so encompassing and all-embracing that they end up with no audience, no clear narrative, and much confusion. Angela Woollacott concludes this section by defining the characteristics of postcolonial histories, and analysing Catherine Hall's *Civilizing Subjects* as a justly celebrated example of postcolonial history at its best. Her work, says Woollacott, 'stands out for its political commitment to drawing attention to the continuing negative consequences of imperialism and colonialism'. She argues, though, that the book does not take full advantage

---

Diaspora and Transportation to Australia', in Ruth Hamilton (ed.), *Routes of Passage: Rethinking the African Diaspora* (Ann Arbor, MI: Michigan University Press).

[30] Kirsten McKenzie 2004, *Scandal in the Colonies: Sydney and Cape Town, 1820–1850* (Melbourne: Melbourne University Press); David Goodman 1994, *Gold-Seeking: Victoria and California in the 1850s* (Sydney: Allen and Unwin).

[31] Ian Tyrrell 1999, *True Gardens of the Gods: Californian-Australian Environmental Reform, 1860–1930* (Berkeley, CA: University of California Press); Tom Griffiths and Libby Robin (eds) 1997, *Ecology and Empire: Environmental History of Settler Societies* (Keele: Keele University Press).

of postcolonial scholarship, such as that offered by the Subaltern Studies historians; nor does it sufficiently place its study within a broad imperial framework.

The second section explores voyages and migrations to and from Australia in a wide variety of places (Britain, China, the United States, and India) and periods (from the late eighteenth century to the present). Emma Christopher focuses on the larger context of convict transportation to New South Wales, tracing through the experiences of one man, Thomas Limpus, three different but connected voyages – to West Africa, to the slave city of Baltimore (though he mutinied and escaped before the ship arrived), and finally to Botany Bay. John Fitzgerald takes us on a wonderful journey between colonial New South Wales and China, as he explores the early history of the New South Wales branch of the international Hung League, or Chinese Masonic Society, attempting to sort intriguing history from fascinating legend. Margaret Allen contrasts the Australian missionary women who travelled freely to India in the first half of the twentieth century with the experiences of the growing number of middle class Indian travellers who sought to visit Australia. White Australian expectations of mobility are contrasted with the White Australia Policy's construction of Indians as having no rights to mobility. 'The mobility of modernity', she concludes, 'was reserved for those deemed white'. Finally, Jim Hammerton explores the migration of the 'Ten Pound Poms', the million British people who came to Australia in the two decades or so after World War II. He points out that many of them regarded their migration, initially at least, as a move 'simply "from one part of Britain to another"', and draws attention to the ease of movement the Empire and its aftermath brought to British citizens. Yet along with privilege went many painful personal experiences of migration, and he considers the changing ways in which family relationships were maintained, if weakened, over very long distances.

The mobility of white modernity evoked by Allen and Hammerton is also the theme for the third section, entitled 'Modernity, Film, and Romance'. Desley Deacon explores Walter Wanger's idea of film as fostering cosmopolitanism and transnationalism, film as a kind of 'foreign office' enabling one culture to understand another. In this spirit Paramount developed nature documentary on the one hand and bright sophisticated New York movies on the other. Jill Matthews traces the career of J. D. Williams, a film entrepreneur who worked in the emerging film industry in three continents. Starting in the United States, he was successful in developing the film industry in Australia, Britain, Canada, and again in the United States. She points out that although parts of this career are known to the national film historians of each country, the career as a whole – and its interconnections – has not been understood previously by any of them. Also focusing on modernity, Hsu-Ming Teo explores the ways in which particular ideas about and practices of romantic love have become increasingly transnational because of the global reach of Anglophone culture and the impact of American advertising and marketing industries. In examining the transformation of Australian understandings of romance, she also points to the gendered time-lag in the embrace of commodified dating culture.

The questions of race introduced in parts one and two reappear in a different form in part four. John Maynard explores the hitherto little-known influence on the Australian Aboriginal activists of the 1920s of Marcus Garvey's Universal Negro Improvement Association, formed first in Jamaica and then spreading through the United States and carried across the world often by working seamen. He also points out that Aboriginal Australians, though closely attached to their own country and for many decades denied freedom of movement, have also travelled abroad, and in the process developed new insights into their situation at home. International travel made some of them aware that 'others around the globe had shared similar tragedy under the weight of colonisation'. Marilyn Lake points out that in their focus on nations as imagined communities, historians have too often forgotten the importance of transnational racial identifications. She draws attention to W. E. B. Du Bois' 1910 recognition of the 'new religion' of whiteness that was sweeping the world in the early twentieth century. She also argues that a key instrument of whiteness was the literacy or dictation test, and whereas previous studies of the White Australia Policy have recognised the influence of Natal in this regard, they have not noticed the American precedents in Mississippi in 1890 and the American Immigration Act of 1896. Such tests, she argues, worked to consolidate understandings of 'race' in terms of a dichotomy of whites and non-whites around the world.

The volume ends with an extended essay on Islamic India and its repression in nationalist Indian historiography. Given its origin and existence as an alternative to or critique of national history, transnational history as an idea and a practice has tended to be of particular interest to historians of the modern era, where the nation has been such an important organising principle, both intellectually and pedagogically. Yet, as Tony Ballantyne points out in his essay, it has also been important for historians of earlier periods in its stimulus to the study of large regions, most notably 'Eurasia', (including India, China, Central Asia and Europe), the Atlantic world (Africa, Europe, the Americas and the Caribbean) and the societies around the Indian Ocean (East Africa, South and Southeast Asia). The pre-modern aspect of transnational history is represented here in Patrick Wolfe's contribution, which emphasises the long historical connections between Europe, the Mediterranean Islamic world including Muslim Spain, and Islamic India. Transnational approaches, broadly conceived, he reflects, can help us be wary of false homogenised images of Europe, or Islam, or India. 'Europe', he argues, cannot be seen as entirely distinct from Hindu or Islamic culture – they were intricately connected and mutually influencing. As a result, when Europe in the nineteenth century confronted Muslim India, it was also 'returning to its own repressed', a tradition of repression that has been perpetuated in both British and Indian nationalist historiography.

One final comment. This book is being published by ANU E Press, a new press focusing on online publication with print-on-demand book copies also available. Since the technology of access means many readers can read chapters singly, rather than in book form, we have endeavoured to ensure that each chapter can stand alone. What may be lost in the conversations *between* chapters will be made up, we hope, in the easy and open and inexpensive access to this work around the world. And that is transnational in spirit indeed.

Different Modes of Transnational History

2. Putting the nation in its place?: world history and C. A. Bayly's *The Birth of the Modern World*

Tony Ballantyne

History writing and the nation state have a symbiotic relationship. From the eighteenth century, the development of professional historical writing has been entwined with the elaboration and consolidation of national identity. Professional historians have typically worked in archives created, funded and policed by the state and have been employed by institutions that are either financed or regulated by the state. The stories that historians have most often told are national ones; the nation state remains a key, probably *the* key, unit for historical analysis and narrative. This is true not only in the 'West', where history has been a primary intellectual tool for nation-makers over the last two centuries, but also in most 'non-Western' contexts. An intimate relationship between history and the nation – which Sudipta Kaviraj identifies as a 'narrative contract' – has characterised the development of history as a discipline in Asia, Africa, Latin America and the Pacific, where history has been central in both anti-colonial nationalism and in postcolonial debates over the intersections between ethnicity, religion, and the nation.[1] In those parts of Asia that were not colonised, history has also become a potent servant of the nation as long-established genres of historical writing were re-crafted under modernity to produce national narratives.[2]

As teachers, professional historians also frame their classroom narratives and arguments around the nation. National surveys – 'Australian History', 'Indian History' or 'The History of the United States' – remain the staple of undergraduate curricula. Even though history departments might offer their undergraduates various thematic courses – medical history, environmental history, or women's history – that seemingly break away from national histories, many of these courses are delimited by a focus on a particular national experience or present narratives in which nation states are the key actors. Moreover, while post-graduate students pursue finely-grained archival research, often relating

---

[1] Sudipta Kaviraj 1992, 'The Imaginary Institution of India', in Shahid Amin and Gyanendra Pandey (eds), *Subaltern Studies VII* (Delhi), pp. 1-39.

[2] Prasenjit Duara 1995, *Rescuing History from the Nation: Questioning Narratives of Modern China* (Chicago, IL: University of Chicago Press); Brian Moloughney 2001, 'Nation, Narrative and China's New History', in Roy Starrs (ed.), *Asian Nationalism in an Age of Globalization* (Richmond: Japan Library), pp. 205-22; Stefan Tanaka 1993, *Japan's Orient: Rendering Pasts into History* (Berkeley, CA: University of California Press).

to a very particular place and time, they are frequently encouraged to think about where their material fits within the national 'story' and agonise over how representative their research is of the national 'pattern'. Upon completion of their doctorates, these students enter job markets that remain predominantly organised around national histories, as most history departments continue to search for experts in particular national fields. When job searches are shaped more thematically, for example around gender history or the history of science, the fine print of the job advertisement typically stresses the desirability of a particular national focus.

Thus, the centrality of the nation to historical practice is reaffirmed at every significant stage in the training and professionalisation of historians. Not surprisingly, this constant reiteration encourages historians to see the nation as the normative, even natural, site for historical analysis and to formulate their own professional identity in reference to the nation state. This is strikingly clear when historians get together at workshops or conferences, where they typically define themselves by their national expertise ('Hi, I'm Pat and I'm a historian of Ireland').

However there are, of course, important forms of historical analysis that use analytical frameworks other than the nation state, many of which are explored or demonstrated in this volume. This essay examines one long-established form of writing history that has produced a range of narratives that transcend the nation state: world history. In exploring world history's distinctive approach to the past – one that examines the encounters, exchanges, networks and institutions that bring communities into contact, co-dependence and conflict – this essay is divided into three parts. The first part offers a short and general overview of the development of world history as a research field. It begins by briefly discussing a popular variety of world history in the early twentieth century, when efforts to create historical narratives that went beyond the nation were enthusiastically received by a large international readership, but were rejected by professional historians. I then trace the emergence of new and professionalised versions of world history after World War II and map a range of important frameworks for historical analysis that were developed from the 1950s. This section of the essay then concludes by discussing the ways in which more recent world history research has offered new challenges to Eurocentric histories and fashioned a vision of a multi-centred world. In the second part of the essay, my focus shifts to examine one important and lauded work of world history: C. A. Bayly's *The Birth of the Modern World* (2004). Here I examine how Bayly's vision of modern history works within the framework of recent world history research and highlight his volume's key innovations that push world history as a field in new and important directions. The final and briefest part of the essay offers a critique of two significant aspects of Bayly's volume (his use of the body as a site of analysis and the 'geography of modernity' that shapes key points of his argument), before assessing the relationship between world history and postcolonial histories of the kind examined in Angela Woollacott's chapter.

***

At the dawn of the twentieth century, a point when national history traditions were well established within Europe and were calcifying in many European colonies as well as in much of Asia, a diverse group of historians were searching for new models of historical writing that reflected the strong sense of global interconnectedness that was a key product of the nineteenth century. H. G. Wells, Oswald Spengler and Arnold Toynbee produced world histories within an intellectual and political context charged by the global reach of European imperial power and a widespread conviction that the 'West' was both modernity's natural location and the key vector for its transmission. Within this milieu and given the locations where these authors wrote from, it is hardly surprising that these texts played a central role in consolidating Europe and North America at the heart of understandings of global history. Wells and company articulated powerful narratives that moulded the complex, fragmentary and heterogeneous nature of the human past into striking accounts of the creation, consolidation and extension of the power of the 'West' and the crisis 'Western Civilisation' faced in the early twentieth century.[3] While this narrative appealed to a broad readership, 'world history' had little intellectual authority in universities and among university-based historians.[4] As a result of world history's marginal position in academic culture in the first half of the twentieth century, Michael Geyer and Charles Bright have noted that world history was typically seen as an 'illegitimate, unprofessional and therefore foolish enterprise' associated with dilettantes and figures at the margins of academic life.[5]

After World War II, world history slowly and unevenly began to gain in credibility. In the wake of global war and the conflicts surrounding decolonisation and the onset of the Cold War, the project of world history took on new relevance. UNESCO formulated a plan to produce a six-volume set of

---

[3] Oswald Spengler 1922, *The Decline of the West* (London: Allen and Unwin); Arnold J. Toynbee 1934–1954, *A Study of History*, 10 volumes (Oxford: Oxford University Press); H. G. Wells 1920, *Outline of History* (London: Cassell). Spengler certainly recognised the significance of non-Western civilisations, but for him only 'Western Civilisation' had fulfilled its potential and the crisis that he diagnosed in the early twentieth century reflected the instability born out of the decline of 'Western Civilisation'.

[4] Gilbert Allardyce 1990, 'Toward World History: American Historians and the Coming of the World History Course', *Journal of World History*, vol. 1, no. 1, p. 25.

[5] Michael Geyer and Charles Bright 1995, 'World History in a Global Age', *American Historical Review*, vol. 100, no. 4, p. 1034.

textbooks to serve as standard texts for international education. This collection, UNESCO hoped, would record the richness of the civilisations that had shaped the world and rematerialise the common bonds that united humanity.[6] Under the editorship of the Yale historian Ralph E. Turner, the UNESCO project was dedicated to turning history into an instrument for peace and cross-cultural understanding. The UNESCO history was not to be simply a history of 'Western Civilisation' masquerading as global history, but rather a truly collaborative effort drawing upon scholars from all corners of the world and committed to the equitable treatment of the world's various cultural traditions. As Gilbert Allardyce has argued, as an exercise in history writing by committee, the UNESCO project was riddled with conflict.[7] Arriving at a consensus over interpretations of previous international conflicts was difficult and there was widespread dispute over the weight to be attached to certain historical events and actors. This was made abundantly clear when the University of Chicago's Louis Gottschalk suggested that his volume on the 1300–1775 period should be entitled *The European Age*. This title was rejected by the UNESCO Commission that oversaw the project and the Commission president, Pablo E. DeBerredo Carneiro of Brazil, reminded Gottschalk that 'world history' was not simply 'European' history writ large but rather that all global regions, not just Europe, were central to understanding any given period of the global past. Gottschalk's work, like the other volumes in the series, was the product of extensive collaboration and consultation with over 350 scholars, religious authorities, and national representatives reading either part or whole of his text. As Gottschalk searched for compromises, his analysis was weakened and his work became increasingly descriptive.[8] In turn, the revisions he settled on alienated other scholars and when his work finally appeared in 1969 it received hostile reviews.[9] By the late 1960s, the limitations of the UNESCO project became clear: no historian could produce a narrative that would please all scholars, let alone all religious, ethnic and national communities. In struggling to produce a vision of the past that sought to attach equal weight to all societies and to use history as a tool for peace, the UNESCO world history in fact revealed the centrality of conflict in human history and made it clear that historical writing is as likely to produce enmity as amity.

While many reviewers dismissed the UNESCO volumes as lacking coherence and attaching too much weight to the 'Third World', the vision of world history developed by W. H. McNeill was warmly received by 'general readers' and

---

[6] Leonard Wooley 1963, *History of Mankind: Cultural and Scientific Development: Vol. I: The Beginnings of Civilization* (London: George Allen and Unwin), pp. xvii-xxiii.

[7] Allardyce 1990, 'Toward World History', pp. 23-76.

[8] ibid., pp. 28-39.

[9] See Franklin L. Ford 1972, review in *American Historical Review*, vol. 77, no. 5, pp. 1406-7.

began to gain some academic respectability for world history. McNeill produced a punchy rendering of the global past that was organised around two key arguments. Firstly, McNeill suggested that it was encounters with strangers that provided the main impetus for change in human history. In focusing on cross-cultural encounters as conduits for the transmission of ideas and technology, McNeill formulated a vision of history that in many ways was an updated rendering of older cultural diffusionist arguments. Secondly, he suggested that the key story in world history was the emergence of Europe and its rise to dominance in the early modern period. In 1963, McNeill published his paradigmatic *The Rise of the West,* a work that had sold over 75 000 copies by 1990, which continues to be popular with the public and is still widely used in tertiary classrooms. The subtitle of McNeill's work (*A History of the Human Community*) reduced human history to a narrative of the 'rise of the west', a model that he now recognises as 'an expression of the postwar imperial mood' and a 'form of intellectual imperialism'.[10] McNeill was working in the wake of Toynbee (he later produced a biography of the pioneering world historian), but in comparison to Toynbee's work, he produced a secular rendering of world history with a stronger and clearer argument. In many ways, McNeill's vision of the 'rise of the west' actually marked a retreat from the detailed and often nuanced analysis of Toynbee. Where Toynbee saw nineteen civilisations acting as meaningful units in world history, McNeill's work was built around just four civilisations: Europe and the Mediterranean, China, India and the Middle East. Other societies, such as the pre-Columbian Americas, the islands of the Pacific and most of Africa were of little importance in this framing of global history. Even in the 1990s, when McNeill recognised that his *Rise of the West* gave 'undue attention to Latin Christendom' and was blind to the 'efflorescence of China', he continued to assert that 'sub-Saharan Africa . . . remained peripheral to the rest of the world, down to and including our own age'.[11]

McNeill's narrative quickly provided an influential and remarkably durable framework for understandings of the global past in undergraduate lecture halls, graduate seminar rooms, and faculty lounges. From the 1970s, sociologists and area studies specialists cemented the centrality of the 'West' in world history, for although world system and dependency theories offered staunch critiques of capitalism they confidently located Europe and North America as the 'core' of the modern world.[12] But we must guard against seeing world history between

---

[10] McNeill 1990 and 1998, reflects critically upon the 'rise of the West' model in his essays 'The *Rise of the West* after Twenty-five Years', *Journal of World History*, vol. 1, no. 1, pp. 1-22 and 'World History and the Rise and Fall of the West', *Journal of World History*, vol. 9, no. 2, pp. 215-36.

[11] McNeill 1990, 'The *Rise of the West* after Twenty-five Years', pp. 5, 7.

[12] Wallerstein's work can be read as Eurocentric critique of capitalism. Mignolo notes that the essential difference between world systems theory and dependency theory was that 'Dependency theory was

1950 and 1990 as an intrinsically Eurocentric approach because of the prominence that McNeill enjoyed; other analytical traditions emerged alongside and in competition with the 'rise of the west' model. While a careful reconstruction of the transnational production of world history as a research field is beyond the scope of this essay, here we might note three significant clusters of research that have taken shape since World War II and have helped to establish the foundations of world history as a serious and respected field of study: histories of 'Eurasia', 'Atlantic History', and work on the 'Indian Ocean World'. These larger regional or oceanic units have been the prominent structures in shaping research within the field of world history; while much teaching within the field is conducted on a truly global canvas, research is more typically organised around a particular set of networks and exchanges within a regional, imperial or oceanic unit of analysis.

From the 1950s, historians working on a range of issues began to explore the unity of Eurasian history, moving beyond narrow national, civilisational, and continental frameworks. This work on Eurasia roamed over a wide range of sites and periods. Whether the research focused on the development of long-distance trade, the expanding reach of Islam, Buddhism, and Christianity, the interaction between nomadic and sedentary peoples, or the rise and fall of empires, historians of Eurasia highlighted the porousness of the boundaries that supposedly marked 'India', 'China', 'Central Asia' and 'Europe' and the interdependence of these regions prior to the growth of European maritime empires during the early modern period. Marshall S. Hodgson's work was particularly significant in formulating the history of 'Eurasia' as a meaningful and important unit of analysis. Hodgson, a leading Chicago-based historian of Islam, was critical of the common tendency to see 'the modern West' as the 'only significant end point of progress' and saw world history as a powerful instrument to be deployed against Eurocentrism.[13] Hodgson warned against any privileging of Europe and the tendency of history as a discipline to naturalise European perceptions and intellectual traditions. He instead insisted that for the period between 1000 BCE to 1800 CE, 'Afro-Eurasia' was a more appropriate and particularly powerful

---

a political statement for the social transformation of and from Third World countries, while world-system analysis was a political statement for academic transformation from First World countries.' Walter D. Mignolo 2002, 'The Geopolitics of Knowledge and the Colonial Difference', *South Atlantic Quarterly*, vol. 101, no. 1, p. 63. Key entry points into world systems and dependency theory are: Immanuel Wallerstein 1974–1989, *The Modern World System*, 3 volumes (New York, NY: Academic Press); Andre Gunder Frank 1971, *Capitalism and Underdevelopment in Latin America: Historical Studies of Chile and Brazil* (Harmondsworth: Penguin).

[13] Marshall G. S. Hodgson 1993, *Rethinking World History: Essays on Europe, Islam, and World History*, Edmund Burke III (ed.) (New York, NY: Cambridge University Press), p. 290. Also see his 1974–1977, *The Venture of Islam*, 3 volumes (Chicago, IL: University of Chicago Press).

frame of analysis. While it was possible to identify distinctive civilisational traditions within 'Afro-Eurasia' – Europe, the Middle East, India and East Asia – Hodgson suggested that the 'cleavages' between these had been overestimated and that it made more sense to conceive of them as 'a single great complex of historical developments' underpinned by complex inter-regional connections and the gradual growth of a common store of human knowledge.[14] These connections and unities have been subsequently explored by many historians, including those based in the former Soviet Union and China. While significant bodies of scholarship have focused on the silk roads and the role of religion in the integration of Eurasia, it is widely accepted that the cohesiveness of Eurasian history reached its apogee under the Mongol Empire. According to this scholarship, the Mongol Empire was characterised by a remarkable cosmopolitanism and multi-ethnic make-up; in the imperial capital, Chinese and Scandinavian traders rubbed shoulders with Uighur scribes, Parisian goldsmiths and Afghani administrators.[15] As a massive land-based Empire that reached from eastern Europe to China, the Mongol state enabled the economic, demographic and even biological integration of Eurasia and established political and cultural patterns that profoundly shaped the subsequent development of East, South and Central Asia. The substantial body of work that has highlighted the pivotal role of the Mongols in shaping the history of Eurasia underpinned Janet Abu-Lughod's influential work on the 'world system' between 1250 and 1350 as well as S. A. M. Adshead's provocative assessments of European-Chinese relationships and the place of Central Asia in world history.[16]

Where this work on Eurasia has focused on the movement of missionaries and pilgrims, caravan routes, and the elaboration of imperial structures that integrated the disparate societies of Europe and Asia before 1500, 'Atlantic History' is structured around the ocean. Its key structures are the shipping routes, markets, and communication networks that connected Africa, Europe, the Americas and the Caribbean into a highly interactive system from the late fifteenth century through to the early nineteenth. 'Atlantic History' is now perhaps the best established variation of 'world history' and enjoys particular standing in the United States, but as a field it slowly took shape out of research on both sides of the Atlantic. A key spur was the work of the *Annales* school, especially Braudel's research on the Mediterranean, together with Pierre Chaunu's

---

[14] Hodgson 1993, *Rethinking World History*, p. 10.

[15] Thomas T. Allsen 1997, 'Ever Closer Encounters: The Appropriation of Culture and the Apportionment of Peoples in the Mongol Empire', *Journal of Early Modern History*, vol. 1, no. 1, pp. 2-23.

[16] S. A. M. Adshead 1993, *Central Asia in World History* (New York, NY: St Martin's Press); Adshead 1988, *China in World History* (New York, NY: St Martin's Press); and Adshead 1997, *Material Culture in Europe and China, 1400–1800* (New York, NY: St Martin's Press).

pioneering work on both the place of Seville and Latin America in the Atlantic. This French research produced models that demonstrated the richness of work organised around large regional units, even oceans, and foregrounded the relationship between history and geography.[17] In North America, Bernard Bailyn, perhaps the key American figure in the emergence of 'Atlantic History', was precocious in his engagement with the *Annales* school.[18] Bailyn's research on migration and political culture within 'colonial America' placed the American colonies within a larger north Atlantic frame. Bailyn's enlarged vision of the early history of United States was also moulded by work on early modern British history. Of particular importance here was the work of historians such as David Beers Quinn and Nicholas Canny which examined British rule in Ireland and mapped how models of rule and colonisation developed in Ireland were subsequently transplanted to North America.[19] Of course, historians of the African diaspora and the Caribbean have also played a pivotal role in shaping this field, which is not surprising as slavery is frequently identified as the key institution that undergirded the 'Atlantic world'. But the history of the 'black Atlantic' is not simply a history of slavery: C. L. R. James' *The Black Jacobins* stands at the head of an important sequence of work on resistance and revolutions within the Atlantic and has provided a touchstone for many scholars who have tried to push Atlantic history into a stronger engagement with cultural history and critical theory.[20] While Africa, especially sub-Saharan Africa, disappeared from McNeill's vision of world history, it is a central presence in Atlantic history

---

[17] Pierre Chaunu 1955–1960, *Séville et l'Atlantique (1504–1650)*, 12 volumes (Paris: SEVPEN); and Chaunu 1953, 'Économie atlantique, économie mondiale', *Cahiers d'historie mondiale*, vol. 1, no. 1, pp. 91-104.

[18] Bernard Bailyn 1951, 'Braudel's Geohistory. A Reconsideration', *Journal of Economic History*, vol. 11, pp. 277-82; and Bailyn 1977, 'Review Essay', *Journal of Economic History*, vol. 37, pp. 1028-34.

[19] Nicholas P. Canny 1999, 'Writing Atlantic History; Or, Reconfiguring the History of Colonial British America', *Journal of American History*, vol. 86, no. 3, pp. 1093-114; Canny 1978, 'The Permissive Frontier: Social Control in English Settlements in Ireland and Virginia 1550–1650', in K. R. Andrews, Nicholas P. Canny, and Paul Edward Hedley Hair (eds), *The Westward Enterprise: English Activities in Ireland, the Atlantic and America, 1480–1650* (Liverpool: Liverpool University Press), pp. 17-44; and Canny 1973, 'The Ideology of English Colonization: From Ireland to America', *William and Mary Quarterly*, 3rd series, vol. 30, no. 4, pp. 575-98; David Beers Quinn 1958, *Ireland and Sixteenth Century European Expansion* (Tralee: The Kerryman); Quinn 1991, *Ireland & America: Their Early Associations, 1500–1640* (Liverpool: Liverpool University Press).

[20] C. L. R. James 1938, *The Black Jacobins: Toussaint L'Ouverture and the San Domingo Revolution* (London: Secker & Warburg); Paul Gilroy 1993, *Black Atlantic: Modernity and Double Consciousness* (Cambridge, MA: Harvard University Press).

and Atlantic historians have revealed the centrality of Africa and Africans in the making of both the Americas and Europe since the fifteenth century.

Scholarship on the Indian Ocean is long-standing and although some American and European-based scholars have been prominent in this sub-field, many of its leading practitioners have been based in South Asia and Australia. The historiography of the Indian Ocean explores the complex interactions of empires, merchants, and communities from East Africa to Southeast Asia and China. This scholarship has stressed the historical importance of the long-established trading systems that developed across the Indian Ocean long before the intrusion of Europeans at the end of the fifteenth century. In tracing this 'traditional' world of trade, scholars have reconstructed some of the histories of merchant communities that thrived in the region's port cities and the complex flows of prized commodities along its shipping lanes.[21] One of the real challenges posed by Indian Ocean as a unit of analysis is the sheer diversity of significant agents in its modern history: from the sixteenth century on, scholars are confronted by Portuguese, Dutch, French, English, and Danish agents as well as merchants from East Africa, the Islamic World, Gujarat, the Malabar and Coromandel coasts, Bengal, Southeast and East Asia. Perhaps the most influential model of this work is K. N. Chaudhuri's *Trade and Civilisation in the Indian Ocean*, which communicated a strong sense of the interconnections created by travel, commerce, and intellectual engagement from 700 CE to 1750 CE. After reconstructing the intricate threads that linked communities around the rim of the Indian Ocean in the wake of the rapid expansion of the Islamic world, Chaudhuri's volume traced the comparatively late entry of Europeans into this cosmopolitan world and the gradual emergence of European power in the middle of the eighteenth century. This identification of the mid-eighteenth century as a point of rupture reflects one abiding concern of the scholarship on the Indian Ocean, the very slow initial growth of European power before 1700 but the fundamental shifts in the structure and culture that accompanied the growth of European territorial empires in the late eighteenth century. From the late 1940s, Holden Furber produced a crucial sketch of the nature of European enterprise in the region and his work on imperial competition complemented C. L. R. Boxer's landmark studies of both Dutch and Portuguese enterprise in the region.[22] More recent work by Sugata Bose and Mark Ravinder Frost has begun to reshape the field, stressing the persistence of crucial trans-oceanic connections into the early

---

[21] Colin G. F. Simkin 1968, *The Traditional Trade of Asia* (London: Oxford University Press).

[22] Holden Furber 1948, *John Company at Work: A Study of European Expansion in India in the Late Eighteenth Century* (Cambridge, MA: Harvard University Press); Furber 1976, *Rival Empires of Trade in the Orient, 1600–1800* (Minneapolis, MN: University of Minnesota Press); C. R. Boxer 1965, *The Dutch Seaborne Empire, 1600–1800* (New York, NY: Knopf); and Furber 1969, *Portuguese Seaborne Empire, 1415–1825* (London: Hutchinson).

twentieth century and the important role of various non-European elites in creating expansive political and cultural networks across the ocean within a context of colonial modernity and the rise of the nation state.[23] Equally importantly, Tansen Sen and Sanjay Subrahmanyam as well as Joseph Fletcher have produced arguments that have reconstituted some of the key connection between the Indian Ocean world and the broader history of Eurasia.[24]

Even the most cursory reading of any of these bodies of scholarship quickly reveals the limitations of 'national' histories, particularly when they are projected back into the period before the emergence of nation states. The best work in world history pays close attention to 'bundles of relationships' that shape any given object of study and is sensitive to the complex interplays between different layers of the analysis: the local, the regional, the inter-regional, the national, the continental, and the global. The nation state is not cast aside entirely, at least for the modern period, but rather it is put firmly in its place, as *one*, albeit an often significant, structure that governs human action and cross-cultural engagements.

Moreover, in interrogating 'Europe' and its place in the world, recent work in the field has also exposed some of the older models of analysis that are organised around European exceptionalism or the 'rise of the west'. Since early 1980s, world historians have explicitly challenged the primacy attached to Europe or the 'West' as the prime historical agent of cross-cultural integration, a project whose political and intellectual significance must not be overlooked.[25] Janet

---

[23] Sugata Bose 2002, 'Space and Time on the Indian Ocean Rim: Theory and History', in Leila Fawaz and C. A. Bayly (eds), *Modernity and Culture: From the Mediterranean to the Indian Ocean, 1890–1920* (New York, NY: Columbia University Press); Mark Frost 2002, '"Wider Opportunities": Religious Revival, Nationalist Awakening and the Global Dimension in Colombo, 1870–1920', *Modern Asian Studies*, vol. 36, no. 4, pp. 937-67; and Frost 2004, 'Asia's Maritime Networks and the Colonial Public Sphere, 1840–1920', *New Zealand Journal of Asian Studies*, vol. 6, no. 2, pp. 63-94.

[24] Joseph F. Fletcher 1985, 'Integrative History: Parallels and Interconnections in the Early Modern Period, 1500–1800', *Journal of Turkish Studies*, vol. 9, pp. 37-58; Sanjay Subrahmanyam 1992, 'Iranians Abroad: Intra-Asian Elite Migration and Early Modern State Formation', *Journal of Asian Studies*, vol. 51, no. 2 , pp. 340-63; and Subrahmanyam 1997, 'Connected Histories: Notes Towards a Reconfiguration of Early Modern Eurasia', *Modern Asian Studies*, vol. 31, no. 3, pp. 735-62; Tansen Sen 2003, *Buddhism, Diplomacy, and Trade: The Realignment of Sino-Indian Relations, 600–1400* (Honolulu, HI: University of Hawai'i Press).

[25] As Micol Seigel has suggested, the 'radical social context' of world history is obscured by the conservatism of the World History Association (established in 1982) and the *Journal of World History*. Micol Seigel 2004, 'World History's Narrative Problem', *Hispanic American Historical Review*, vol. 84, no. 3, p. 432.

Abu-Lughod's *Before European Hegemony*, for example, called into question the belief that Europeans were central in driving cross-cultural exchanges, by drawing attention to the complex circuits of long-distance trade that integrated Eurasia in the thirteenth and fourteenth centuries.[26] The particular weight Abu-Lughod attached to the dynamism and significance of central Asia – an important blow to the notion that world history is the story of the development and significance of 'civilisations' – has been extended by other scholars who have identified the 'Mongol explosion' in this period as marking the emergence of the first truly 'world empire'.[27] Most importantly, however, it has been work on China and its connections with inner Asia, Southeast Asia, the rest of East Asia, and Europe which has radically transformed our understandings of the basic pattern of world history. China had emerged as the key centre of 'civilisation' within Eurasia and its economic hub for most of its history before 1700 CE: the key markers of Europe's modernity – urbanisation, intensified production, complex bureaucratic state structures, and print culture – were well established in China by 1000 CE. At the same time, work on the economic history of South Asia has both revised the long-dominant image of a corrupt and weakening Mughal Empire, an understanding inherited from British colonial discourse, and has emphasised that the Indian Ocean was the centre of a series of interlocking commercial networks that reached out as far as East Africa and Indonesia. It was only as a result of the militarisation of trade during the eighteenth century and the growing colonial aspirations of European East India Companies after the British East India Company became a territorial power in 1765, that Europeans gradually came to dominate the long-established markets and commercial hubs around the Indian Ocean.

In effect, this work on Asian economic history and Asia's trade with Europe has both called into question the exceptional status so frequently accorded to Europe and recast our understandings of the chronology of world history.[28] One of the

---

[26] Janet L. Abu-Lughod 1989, *Before European Hegemony: The World System A. D. 1250–1350* (New York, NY: Oxford University Press).

[27] Adshead 1988, *China in World History*; Adshead 1993, *Central Asia in World History*; David Christian 1998, *A History of Russia, Central Asia, and Mongolia* (Oxford: Blackwell).

[28] Much of this work is synthesised in the *Cambridge History of China*. For a collection of work that explores the connections between the development of the Chinese economy and global trade see Dennis O. Flynn and Arturo Giráldez (eds) 1997, *Metals and Monies in an Emerging Global Economy* (Aldershot: Variorum). Also see the provocative arguments forwarded in Dennis O. Flynn and Arturo Giraldez 1995, 'Born with a "Silver Spoon": The Origin of World Trade in 1571', *Journal of World History*, vol. 6, no. 2, pp. 201-21; on South Asia and the Indian Ocean see Satish Chandra 1987, *The Indian Ocean: Explorations in History, Commerce and Politics* (New Delhi: Sage); K. N. Chaudhuri 1985, *Trade and Civilisation in the Indian Ocean: An Economic History from the Rise of Islam to*

key debates that continues to exercise world historians is the relationship between Europe's rise to global dominance, empire building and the emergence of global capitalism. While some historians, such as David Landes, continue to attribute Europe's rise to power to supposedly intrinsically European cultural qualities ('work, thrift, honesty, patience, tenacity'), recent research has tended to underscore the centrality of imperialism in the new world in both allowing Europe to escape from its ecological constraints and constituting the very nature of European culture itself.[29] Moreover, where McNeill might have given shape to history by discerning the rising dominance of the 'West', what has emerged out of recent world historical research is an image of a multi-centred world during the period between 1250–1800, where China was perhaps the single most powerful region. In the century from 1800, it seems that Europe did exercise increasing power at a global level as a result of the military-fiscal revolution which consolidated its military advantage over non-European nations, its harnessing of its natural resources – especially coal – to its industrial revolution, and a sustained period of imperial expansion beginning from the 1760s.[30] But the thrust of much recent work has shown that although European ascendancy profoundly transformed the world, particularly through its imperial projects, it was short-lived. The United States, Russia and Japan emerged as both industrial forces and imperial powers around the turn of the twentieth century, while Tokyo, Shanghai, Singapore, and Bombay emerged as new commercial, cultural, technological and migratory centres. World history research on migration, economics, empires and ideologies suggests that history cannot be imagined as an inexorable march to Western dominance and global homogeneity, but rather as a more complex and ambiguous set of interwoven and overlapping processes driven from by diverse array of groups from a variety of different locations.[31]

1750 (Cambridge: Cambridge University Press); Kenneth McPherson 1993, *The Indian Ocean: A History of People and the Sea* (Delhi: Oxford University Press).

[29] David Landes 1998, *The Wealth and Poverty of Nations: Why Some are So Rich and Some So Poor* (New York, NY: W. W. Norton), p. 523.

[30] Kenneth Pomeranz 2000, *The Great Divergence: China, Europe, and the Making of the Modern World Economy* (Princeton, NJ: Princeton University Press); Kenneth Pomeranz and Steven Topik 1999, *The World That Trade Created: Culture, Society, and the World Economy, 1400–the Present* (Armonk, NY: M. E. Sharpe); and the essays in the forum on the 'great divergence' in *Itinerario*, vol. 24, nos 3/4, 2000.

[31] e.g. Arjun Appadurai 1996, *Modernity at Large: Cultural Dimensions of Globalization* (Minneapolis, MN: University of Minnesota Press); Michael Geyer and Charles Bright 1995, 'World History in a Global Age', *American Historical Review*, vol. 100, no. 4, pp. 1034-60; Akira Iriye 1989, 'The Internationalization of History', *American Historical Review*, vol. 94, no. 1, pp. 1-10; Adam McKeown 2001, *Chinese Migrant Networks and Cultural Change: Peru, Chicago, Hawaii, 1900–1936* (Chicago, IL: University of Chicago Press).

***

This vision of world history provides the basic framework for C. A. Bayly's *The Birth of the Modern World, 1780–1914: Global Comparisons and Connections*. This volume, which was greeted with tremendous enthusiasm and acclaim on its publication early in 2004, is shaped by Bayly's expertise as both a leading South Asianist and an influential historian of the British Empire and extends the provocative vision of world history he had sketched in earlier publications.[32] At the heart of Bayly's *The Birth of the Modern World* is the emergence of 'global *uniformities* in the state, religion, political ideologies, and economic life' between 1780 and 1914.[33] According to Bayly, these uniformities manifested themselves in numerous ways, from the emergence of the census as a key technology of governance for almost every state by 1914 to the international popularity of the Western-style suit as a marker of sobriety, seriousness and status, or from the rise of municipal government at a global level to the profound transformations enacted by the rigorous time-keeping central in the 'industrious revolution'.[34] At the same time, however, Bayly traces the ways in which various forms of connection worked to 'heighten the sense of *difference*, and even antagonism, between people in different societies', highlighting how 'those differences were increasingly expressed in similar ways'.[35] The most obvious example of this paradox was what Bayly terms the age of 'hyperactive nationalism' after 1890 which witnessed the consolidation of European nation states, the emergence of settler nationalism within the British Empire, the rise of the significant anti-colonial movements in Egypt, India, French North Africa and Indochina as well as the emergence of the 'Young Turk' movement within the Ottoman Empire and the Chinese revolution of 1911.[36] Each of these nationalist movements stressed the distinctiveness of their own community, yet the symbolic repertoire and historical vision of these imagined communities were in many ways remarkably similar.[37] This reminds us that despite the fact that each nation is defined by its supposedly unique character, nationalisms share powerful characteristics and that they are also produced transnationally. For Bayly,

---

[32] C. A. Bayly 1998, 'The First Age of Global Imperialism, c. 1760–1830', *Journal of Imperial and Commonwealth History*, vol. 26, no. 2, pp. 28-47; Bayly 2002, '"Archaic" and "Modern" Globalization in the Eurasian and African Arena, ca. 1750–1850', in A. G. Hopkins (ed.), *Globalization in World History* (New York, NY: Norton), pp. 45-72.

[33] C. A. Bayly 2004, *The Birth of the Modern World, 1780–1914: Global Connections and Comparisons* (Malden, MA: Blackwell), p. 1.

[34] ibid., pp. 13-4, 474, 478.

[35] ibid., pp. 1-2.

[36] ibid., p. 462.

[37] ibid., pp. 199-244, 462-4.

however, nation states were not the sole anchor of identity even in an age of 'hyper-active nationalism'; rather he insists one of the markers of modernity was the range of identities, often overlapping and frequently competing, that were produced out of a range of collectivities: class, ethnicity, race and religion.

At the heart of *The Birth of the Modern World* are two theses. The first of these asserts that a central precondition for the emergence of modernity was the growth of internal complexity within most societies between 1780 and 1914. Bayly argues that during this period we can trace a significant shift in most large scale societies as professionals of various types began to displace older knowledge traditions and geographies of expertise. Networks of kinship and marriage-alliance were jostled aside by professional associations and interest groups. During the nineteenth century distinct legal professions, for example, emerged in many colonised lands, in Japan and in the Chinese Treaty Ports. At the same time, Western medicine was increasingly globalised and doctors trained in Western methods enjoyed increased social influence even as increasingly systematised forms of non-Western medicine retained significant cultural authority in the Islamic World, South and East Asia. In the economic domain, Bayly argues, it is in this period that we see 'specialist bodies of managers, accountants and insurers' becoming a key feature of the global economy as they spread out to major urban centres across the globe from London, Amsterdam, and Paris.[38] In terms of economic production, global industrialisation reshaped long established labour patterns as a 'kind of international class structure was emerging', where workers in Europe, the Americas, India or Japan were subjected to similar pressures and began to articulate increasingly shared aspirations.[39]

Bayly's second thesis is that during the long nineteenth century there was a shift towards 'outward uniformity' at a global level. In other words, the profound differences that marked off originally disparate cultural formations were softened and even undercut due to the integrative work of imperial political systems, global technological change, and the globalisation of religion and race as 'universal' languages. Between 1780 and 1914, for example, Hinduism, which had confounded many early European observers with its innumerable gods, devotional paths, and little traditions, was increasing systematised and outwardly, at least, began to look like other 'religions' (like Islam and Christianity). This transformation, Bayly suggests, was by no means unique, as during the long nineteenth century many 'traditions which had once been bundles of rights, shamanistic practices, rituals and antique verities' were reshaped into coherent 'religions' with 'their own spheres of interest and supposedly uniform characteristics'. For Bayly, the World Parliament of Religions held in Chicago

---

[38] ibid., p. 21.
[39] ibid.

in 1893 is a potent symbol of the outcome of these systematising processes. This event would have been incomprehensible a century before, as in the late eighteenth century the notion of 'religion' remained largely unknown outside the West and Europeans had a limited understanding of Hinduism, a thin grasp of Islamic traditions in Southeast Asia, and virtually no knowledge of Buddhism. Over the following century the power of print, the reforming efforts of elites in the Pacific, Asia and Africa, and the entanglement of various devotional paths with imperial power meant that 'the claims of the great standardizing, religions were much more widely known and acted on' by 1914.[40]

Bayly develops these arguments on a truly global scale over a wide range of different domains – the economic, the political, the social, the cultural and so on – and they are underpinned by a growing body of work within world history that has questioned the Eurocentrism of social theory as well as Europe's privileged position in both historical and theoretical accounts of modernity. The long-established tendency to treat European patterns as either 'natural' or 'universal' (in the way that say Marx, Talcott Parsons, or David Landes have done) and thereby reducing China or India, or the Islamic world to being cases of failed or stagnated development has been undercut by recent work on economics and state building within Eurasia. Most importantly, Kenneth Pomeranz and R. Bin Wong have demolished many of the arguments that have been used to highlight European exceptionalism (whether we are talking about patterns of agricultural production, fertility patterns and family structures, the development of transportation networks, or the workings of the market or 'culture'). Wong traces a broad set of similarities within 'Eurasian' economic history as well as a key set of divergences in the history of European and Chinese state-making, especially in terms of the capacities they developed and both the internal and external threats they faced. His work suggests the particular rather than universal nature of European models and has been central in reorienting ongoing debates over the history of the state, the path of capitalist development and the nature of Chinese history itself.[41] In a similar vein, Pomeranz suggests that Europe enjoyed little or no advantage over East Asia before 1800. The 'great divergence' that emerged between Europe and Asia during the nineteenth century was ultimately the product of 'windfalls' from the New World (precious metals, but also slave labour, food plants and various commodities) and the tapping of Europe's, but especially Britain's, coal deposits to maximise production and save the land.[42]

---

[40] ibid., pp. 364-5.

[41] R. Bin Wong 1997, *China Transformed: Historical Change and the Limits of European Experience* (Ithaca, NY: Cornell University Press).

[42] Pomeranz 2000, *The Great Divergence*, pp. 57-62 and 264-97.

The work of Wong and Pomeranz are key elements of the overall scaffolding of Bayly's work, shaping, in particular, his rendering of the world around 1800. In their wake, Bayly recognises both the connections between China and Europe and some of the key similarities between their economic and social development. Bayly suggests that modernity was the product of a 'complex parallelogram of forces' that were driven from a variety of different centres, not just the 'West'.[43] This vision of a multi-centred world certainly echoes Pomeranz's argument and the drive of the last generation of world historians to break away from the rather mechanistic approach of world systems theory. In fact, in this regard the core arguments articulated in *The Birth of the Modern World* could be read as a response to R. Bin Wong's warning that 'History often seems to reach non-western peoples as they come into contact with Europeans …. modern histories are conventionally constructed along the axis of native responses to Western challenges.'[44]

But it is important to recognise that in several important ways Bayly's vision of world history is significantly different from not only the work of Wong and Pomeranz but recent research within the field more generally. In contrast to the Sinocentrism of Pomeranz and Wong, Bayly's vision of modernity places particular emphasis on both the Islamic world and South Asia. This is not surprising given the trajectory of Bayly's research: his early work reconstructed the transformation of the economic fortunes and social lives of north Indian towns and merchant dynasties in the 1770–1870 period and it still stands as a crucial contribution to a heated debate over the transformation of South Asia during the late Mughal period.[45] In addition, his under-appreciated *Imperial Meridian* (1989) located the rapid expansion of the British Empire between 1780 and 1830 in the 'hollowing out' of the great Muslim Empires – the Ottomans, the Safavids and the Mughals – as the result of peasant resistance to taxation regimes, the rise of religious revivalism, the growing power of regional rulers, religious conflict and factional disputes at the imperial courts. *Imperial Meridian* was not simply a rehabilitation of the Robinson-Gallagher thesis (which suggested that the British Empire grew rapidly during the nineteenth century as a result of a succession of local crises in the periphery), but rather the provocative marriage of new perspectives on the rise of the military-fiscal state in eighteenth-century Britain with a nuanced understanding of the culture and politics of the Islamic world.[46]

---

[43] Bayly 2004, *The Birth of the Modern World*, p. 7.

[44] Wong 1997, *China Transformed*, p. 1.

[45] Most importantly: C. A. Bayly 1983, *Rulers, Townsmen and Bazaars: North Indian Society in the Age of British Expansion, 1770–1870* (Cambridge: Cambridge University Press).

[46] C. A. Bayly 1989, *Imperial Meridian: The British Empire and the World, 1780–1830* (London: Longman).

It is also not surprising given Bayly's prominence in debates over both the Mughal and British Empires that the *Birth of the Modern World* places empire building at the heart of modernity. This sets Bayly apart from the Sinocentric vision of much recent world history. Imperialism is not a problematic that is central in the work of Wong and Pomeranz, in part because European empires struggled to maintain anything more than a fingertip grasp on China and in part because both Wong and Pomeranz frame their studies as comparative economic histories of Europe and China. Where empire building does intrude, in Pomeranz's 'new world windfalls' for example, it is framed in essentially economic terms rather than as a larger set of unequal power relations.[47] For Bayly, however, there is no doubt that empire building is profoundly entangled with, and deeply suffuses, modernity. Not only was the new age of global imperialism that emerged in the late eighteenth century one of the engines that transformed various 'old regimes' across the globe, but during the nineteenth century empires played a central role in reshaping material culture, in moulding the modern state, in the crafting of new visions of nations and ethnicities, in dictating the food people consumed and the languages they spoke.

What is also striking and salutary about Bayly's vision of empire is that he does not shy away from confronting the violence of imperial orders. Where Niall Ferguson and David Cannadine have downplayed the significance of race in the world of empire and underplayed imperialism's violence and human cost, Bayly is clear on the connection between race, empire, and violence.[48] Chapter 12 of the *Birth of the Modern* is entitled 'The Destruction of Native Peoples and Ecological Depradation' and it traces the ravages visited upon indigenous peoples by Eurasian diseases, the 'white deluge' of migration, and the deployment of 'sheer violence' of colonialism, as well as the profound changes wrought by broader shifts in technology, communication networks, and global markets.[49] Given the brute power of European empire building, Bayly suggests that the nineteenth century did witness the rise of north-western Europe to global dominance. This dominance might have been contested, provisional and fleeting

---

[47] A significant body of scholarship has begun to emerge over the past few years: James L. Hevia 1995, *Cherishing Men from Afar: Qing Guest Ritual and the Macartney Embassy of 1793* (Durham, NC: Duke University Press); and Hevia 2003, *English Lessons: The Pedagogy of Imperialism in Nineteenth-century China* (Durham, NC: Duke University Press); Lydia H. Liu 2004, *The Clash of Empires: The Invention of China in Modern World Making* (Cambridge, MA: Harvard University Press).

[48] David Cannadine 2001, *Ornamentalism: How the British Saw Their Empire* (London: Oxford University Press); Niall Ferguson 2003, *Empire: How Britain Made the Modern World* (London: Allen Lane). Also see *From Orientalism to Ornamentalism: Empire and Difference in History*, special issue of *Journal of Colonialism and Colonial History*, vol. 3, no. 1, 2002.

[49] Bayly 2004, *The Birth of the Modern World*, pp. 432-50, quote is at p. 440.

in many areas, but in Bayly's view it did mark a key moment when the multi-centred world invoked by Pomeranz was reconfigured. In suggesting that 'efficiency in killing other human beings' was an important element of Europe's, and especially Britain's rise, Bayly is a long way from Cannadine's bloodless and deracinated vision of empire or Ferguson's identification of the British Empire as an exemplary model of global governance.[50]

Here we can identify one further concern that places Bayly's work at odds with much recent work within world history. Throughout *The Birth of the Modern World* he locates his narrative of connection, convergence and conflict in the social and cultural domains as well as in the world of economics that remains the chief concern in world history research. In particular, Bayly puts a good deal of emphasis on what he terms 'bodily practice': dress, bodily decoration and grooming, food and drink, sport and leisure. While it is true that Bayly's discussion of the history of the body supplements rather than transforms his approach, there is no doubt that it marks an important challenge to traditional approaches to world history. Key works within world history over the past twenty years have been grounded in economic history or have adopted an explicitly materialist approach to the past (most obviously: Janet Abu-Lughod's *Before European Hegemony*; Philip Curtin's, *Cross-Cultural Trade in World History*; K. N. Chaudhuri's *Asia before Europe*; Crosby's *Ecological Imperialism* and *The Columbian Exchange*; Andre Gunder Frank's *ReOrient*; Pomeranz's *Great Divergence*; Wong's *China Transformed*; and David Christian's *Maps of Time*). The title of Pomeranz's collection of essays co-authored with Steven Topik, *The World That Trade Made*, is particularly indicative of the outlook of world history: that modernity is essentially the product of a particular set of economic innovations and structures.[51] These concerns remain the stock in trade of the *Journal of World History*, which has been a crucial site for these ongoing debates over global trade and the history of capitalism. In a recent essay, Antoinette Burton and I have argued that the *Journal of World History* and world history more generally seems to have functioned as a redoubt against the cultural turn.[52] One of features that sets world history apart from either postcolonial studies, or the new transnational research within the humanities, is that it has not systematically engaged with questions of race or more particularly gender and sexuality.

***

---

[50] ibid., p. 468.

[51] Pomeranz and Topik 1999, *The World That Trade Created*.

[52] Tony Ballantyne and Antoinette Burton 2005, 'Postscript: Bodies, Genders, Empires: Reimagining World Histories', in Ballantyne and Burton (eds), *Bodies in Contact: Rethinking Colonial Encounters in World History* (Durham, NC: Duke University Press), pp. 409-10.

In this regard, Bayly's stress on 'bodily regimes' is a welcome innovation that begins to break down the economistic tendencies of world history. However, the way in which Bayly deals with these 'bodily regimes' feeds my major reservation about this volume – the constancy of its gaze on the macro, on the global overlay, on the big processes. While this analytical gaze certainly helps us appreciate the 'big picture' of the shaping of modernity, it produces a relatively thin treatment of subjectivities and meaning making. These questions are frequently occluded in the writing of world histories, especially big synthetic histories like this one. But knowing the richly detailed work Bayly has produced on the encounter between British and South Asian knowledge traditions and the emphasis he places on bodily regimes in the introduction to *The Birth of the Modern World*, I had hoped that the 'big' stories that are at the heart of the volume – empire building, international trade, the rise of the nation state and so on – would be given texture and nuance through some detailed discussion of particular movements, locations, and individuals.

There is no doubt that *The Birth of the Modern World* strives to be comprehensive, to present a rich analysis of the making of our world. As a result, however, individual actors (especially women), marginal social groups, and dissenting voices are either ignored or folded into the grand narrative at the heart of the volume. Unfortunately, his treatment of 'bodily regimes', which might have provided one key space for exploring 'small' stories or voices, does not offer a distinctive level of analysis. Where Kathleen Canning has argued that the 'body as method' offers a challenging and distinctive site for historical analysis, for Bayly the history of the body is simply another domain, no different in kind from economics or politics, where he can trace the emergence of modernity.[53] In other words, Bayly's analytical position and focus remains essentially fixed and unmoving throughout the volume – the *Birth of the Modern World* offers an assured and masterful analysis of the making of global modernity, but at times its lacks the texture and richness that a more rigorous examination of the history of the body might have given the text.

One other aspect of *The Birth of the Modern World* that is troubling is what we might term its 'geography of modernity'. Bayly's account of modernity diverges markedly from the visions of colonial modernity that have been produced out of some of the best new work on empire. Even though Bayly stresses that modernity was shaped from a variety of centres and was fashioned out of encounters between a wide range of peoples, *The Birth of the Modern* nevertheless tends to encode modernity as the product of an unproblematised Europe. Modern financial services, science, medicine, and even the nation state emanate from

---

[53] Kathleen Canning 1999, 'The Body as Method? Reflections on the Place of the Body in Gender History', *Gender & History*, vol. 11, no. 3, pp. 499-513.

Europe, from where they disseminate outwards, often conveyed by agents of empire. In stressing the coterminous history of the 'great acceleration' of modernity and the rise to global dominance of European empires in the after 1820, Bayly's vision of the geography of modernity is very traditional. In effect, Bayly frequently frames European modernity and global modernity in a segregated and neatly sequential relationship. Here *The Birth of the Modern World* resolutely ignores one of the key insights of postcolonial criticism: that slavery and empire building were central in the very creation of 'Europe' prior to modernity and that these entanglements in many ways provided the very basis for Europe's modernity. This, of course, has been a particular thrust of the 'imperial turn' in British historiography, where the research produced by James Walvin, Kathleen Wilson, Catherine Hall, Mrinalini Sinha, Antoinette Burton, and Angela Woollacott has undercut the rigid distinction between the history of the imperial metropole and Britain's various colonies. In this regard, Bayly also elides some of the important recent work on colonial modernities that stresses both the particularity of, and in-process nature of, specific formations of modernity in various colonial sites.[54]

Of course, much of the recent work on 'colonial modernity' is inflected by postcolonialism. In the past Bayly has been quite critical of postcolonialism, not least in part because he sees it as marking the 'Americanisation' of British and British imperial history. However, he does recognise that the weight of postcolonial criticism and the cultural turn has necessitated the creation of new forms of historical writing. He has recently suggested that:

> the postmodern and post-colonial [sic] writers who have dominated the last decade or more have tended to be sceptical of 'grand narratives' such as these, arguing instead for the study of the 'fragment', the individual resister or subaltern. But ironically, the postcolonial sensibility has had the countervailing effect of requiring the construction of a new type of world history to replace the old histories of 'Western civilisation' in that greatest of academic marketplaces, the United States.[55]

In fact, we should see Bayly's volume as a response to this need for new narratives. Even though Bayly's vision of modernity is not as decentred as recent postcolonial writing suggests, *The Birth of the Modern World* produces a powerful analysis of the global nineteenth century that will challenge undergraduates and maybe please scholars sympathetic to postcolonialism. After all, this is a world history that places empire at the heart of modernity and violence at the heart of empire building, two points that seem particularly apposite at this moment in global politics. More broadly, in *The Birth of the Modern World* Bayly

---

[54] e.g., Antoinette Burton (ed.) 1999, *Gender, Sexuality and Colonial Modernities* (London: Routledge).

[55] C. A. Bayly 2004, 'Writing World History', *History Today*, vol. 54, no. 2, pp. 36-40.

attaches significant weight to South Asia and the Islamic world, draws upon the recent historiography on China, and certainly escapes from any tendency to see the European experience as normative. R. Bin Wong has recently argued that 'we should exceed the limitations of historical explanations derived from European experiences' by exploring '[t]he plurality of historical pasts' and expanding 'the capacities of social theory through a more systematic grounding in multiple historical experiences'.[56] Bayly's volume is a very significant contribution to that vital project.

---

[56] Wong 1997, *China Transformed*, p. 293.

3. Paths not yet taken, voices not yet heard: rethinking Atlantic history

Michael A. McDonnell

Of late, scholarly journals in the discipline of history have been filled with arguments stressing the need to break with traditional historiographic boundaries. In particular, we are told that in this global age, we must move 'beyond the nation' in our research and in our teaching. In the early modern history of Europe and the Americas, these arguments for thinking 'transnationally' have of late coalesced around a call to focus on the Atlantic World as a new conceptual framework.

Yet, for all these exhortations and good intentions, and a proliferation of conferences and edited collections with titles evoking 'transnational' or more specifically 'Atlantic World' history, few scholars have yet been able to produce work that truly reflects or represents just such an approach. In part, this is because the conceptual insights of Atlantic History have not been matched by the development of appropriate methodological tools. But nationally-based historiographic traditions also make comparative or transnational approaches difficult and are only compounded by institutional barriers at the departmental, University and national levels that often curtail rather than encourage non-national approaches to research and teaching.

This chapter will examine the rise of Atlantic History in recent historiography and its apparent limits. I will argue that the fruits of Atlantic History can only be enjoyed to their full extent if we recognise these problems, begin to think beyond the often Anglo-American Atlantic World, and use the conceptual insights of Atlantic History to create narratives that extend beyond imperial and national boundaries, and across traditional chronologies that support the national narratives that sustain those boundaries.

The essay will conclude by looking at some of the ways in which we might do this by looking beyond the traditionally defined borders of race, nation, and empire, and examining the Atlantic World from different, and eastward facing perspectives, from the bottom-up, and across older imperial and newly created national borders. The challenges of doing so are substantial, but the potential rewards include the possibility of a radically revised Atlantic World history that dynamically fuses the best of recent historical scholarship to an emergent and exciting conceptual advance in transnational history.

A quick scan of new publications in the back pages of the *American Historical Review*, the conference calls on H-Net and the contents pages of just about any leading journal that deals with early modern European or American history will reveal the extent of the dynamic explosion of interest in Atlantic history over the past few years. Conferences, journals, seminars, book prizes, textbooks, courses, graduate programmes, and now, dedicated academic positions in Atlantic history have blossomed. Fired by the possibilities of a new kind of open, empirical agenda (and those jobs), and by encouragement from notable scholars such as John Elliott who wrote recently that Atlantic history was 'one of the most important new historiographical development of recent years', scholars young and old have redefined their own work in a collective effort to reconceptualise the early modern world of Europeans, Africans, and Americans. As David Armitage wrote in 2002 in his introduction to *The British Atlantic World*, it seems 'we are all Atlanticists now'.[1]

The pace of the increasing institutionalisation of Atlantic history has been matched only by the possibilities it has raised and the questions asked of it, particularly about what it encompasses. Atlantic history has, most obviously, something to do with the ocean itself. But is that the North Atlantic, or South, or both? Is it about the sailors and ships that plied that ocean, or about the

---

[1] David Armitage and Michael J. Braddick (eds) 2002, *The British Atlantic World, 1500–1800* (New York, NY: Palgrave Macmillan), pp. 11. For attempts to survey and define the field and trace its lineage, see Bernard Bailyn 1996, 'The Idea of Atlantic History', *Itinerario*, vol. 20, no. 1, pp. 19-44; and more recently, Bailyn 2005, *Atlantic History: Concept and Contours* (Cambridge, MA: Harvard University Press); John Thornton 1992, 'Introduction', in *Africa and Africans in the Making of the Atlantic World, 1400–1800* (Cambridge: Cambridge University Press); Daniel W. Howe 1993, *American History in an Atlantic Context: An Inaugural Lecture Delivered before the University of Oxford on 3 June 1993* (Oxford: Clarendon); Nicholas Canny 1999, 'Writing Atlantic History; Or, Reconfiguring the History of Colonial British America', *Journal of American History*, pp. 1093-114. For some challenges to these ideas and other approaches, see A. T. Bushnell (ed.) 1995, *Establishing Exceptionalism: Historiography and the Colonial Americas* (Brookfield, VT: Variorum); David Brion Davis 2000, 'Looking at Slavery from Broader Perspectives', *American Historical Review*, vol. 105, no. 2, pp. 452-66, and comments by Peter Kolchin, Rebecca J. Scott, and Stanley L. Engerman, pp. 467-84; John H. Elliott 1987, 'Introduction: Colonial Identity in the Atlantic World', in Nicholas Canny and Anthony Pagden (eds), *Colonial Identity in the Atlantic World, 1500–1800* (Princeton, NJ: Princeton University Press), pp. 3-13; J. H. Elliott 1994, *Britain and Spain in America: Colonists and Colonized* (Reading: University of Reading); J. H. Elliott 1998, *Do the Americas Have a Common History?: An Address* (Providence, RI: Published for the Associates of the John Carter Brown Library). See also the forum at *History Compass*, 1 (2003) NA 026, 001-010, www.history-compass.com, especially Jorge Cañizares-Esguerra 2003, 'Some Caveats about the "Atlantic" Paradigm', in *History Compass*, 1. For older attempts to envision the Atlantic, see H. E. Bolton 1933, 'The Epic of Greater America', *American Historical Review*, vol. 38, no. 3, pp. 448-74; R. R. Palmer 1959–1964, *The Age of Democratic Revolution: Political History of Europe and America, 1760–1800*, 2 volumes (Princeton, NJ: Princeton University Press); and John Elliott 1970, 'The Atlantic World', in Elliott, *The Old World and the New, 1492–1650* (Cambridge: Cambridge University Press), pp. 79-104.

myriad people who depended upon them to cross it – in chains or with chests, with fear or with hope – or is it about the people those ships connected? Is it about the places that the ocean connected – Lisbon, Madeira and Rio de Janeiro – or the goods that travelled between those places – the beaver pelts trapped by Ottawa Indians that ended up on the heads of wealthy Parisians, or the silver mined by drafted indigenous mit'a workers in Peru that fuelled European expansion in the early modern period?

And, where exactly does the Atlantic begin and end? Is it at the mouth of the St Lawrence River, or at the Nipigon River on the north shore of Lake Superior? Does it include the Niger River in sub-Saharan Africa along which raiders enslaved Yoruba peoples, or the colonial town of Quito, high in the Ecuadorian Andes, reached only via ports off the Pacific Ocean? Does it begin with the voyages of Columbus, or Portuguese raiding and trading along the West African coast? And did this Atlantic World come to an end with the independence movements that rocked the western hemisphere in the late eighteenth and early nineteenth centuries, or with the abolition of slavery in Cuba and Brazil as late as 1888? Finally, is the Atlantic more about the old world or the new, or is it perhaps merely more a construction of European thinkers, or modern historians, than about the peoples who inhabited it?

Atlantic history is, of course, about all of this and potentially so much more. In summing up recent trends and setting an agenda for new work, Armitage cautiously and correctly chose to embrace an open-ended approach to Atlantic history, noting that it is best used as a field that 'links national histories, facilitates comparisons between them, and opens up new areas of study', ultimately pushing historians 'towards methodological pluralism and expanded horizons'. Depending on how it is defined, Armitage concludes, the field is fluid, "in motion, and potentially boundless," like the Atlantic itself. This is, Armitage concludes, 'the most one can ask of any emergent field of study'.[2]

The great promise of Atlantic history, then, is that it will lead us to think about all kinds of new connections, but above all, that it will be transnational in scope. Even for the pre-national early modern era, colonial historians, and particularly,

---

[2] David Armitage 2002, 'Three Concepts of Atlantic History', in Armitage and Braddick, (eds), *British Atlantic World*, pp. 26-7. For other, similarly open-ended definitions of Atlantic history, see Alan L. Karras 1992, 'The Atlantic World as a Unit of Study', in Karras and J. R. McNeill (eds), *Atlantic American Societies: From Columbus Through Abolition, 1492–1888* (London: Routledge), pp. 1-18; Marcus Rediker and Michael F. Jiménez 2001, 'What is Atlantic History?' *CPAS Newsletter: The University of Tokyo Center for Pacific and Asian Studies* (October), also available at www.marcusrediker.com/Articles/what_is_atlantic _history.htm; Thomas Benjamin, Timothy Hall, David Rutherford 2001, 'Introduction', to their edited collection, *The Atlantic World in the Age of Empire* (Boston: Houghton Mifflin), pp. 1-10.

though not exclusively, colonial American scholars, have been decidedly wedded to a teleological agenda that is designed to explain the emergence of the nation above all else. In a globalising world, Atlantic history has the potential to liberate us from more narrow, and mostly nationalist views of the past, and from an historical agenda that has at its heart the education of a patriotic citizenry dedicated to the principles and values of a single state. In this context, Atlantic history pushes us to examine the more fundamental glue that connected and held people together in pre-national communities, as well as the problems and conflicts that made people aware of their differences, and pulled them apart. In short, Atlantic History is about raising exciting new issues and questions about the interconnections between Africans, Americans, and Europeans – citizens of, quite literally, a new world – quite independent of the nations in which they may or may not have ended up.

As exciting as these new possibilities are, already there seem to be limits emerging, at least in practice. For one thing, despite all the exhortations and good intentions, and a proliferation of conferences and edited collections with titles evoking 'transnational' or more specifically 'Atlantic World' history, the actual steps taken by scholars thus far have seemed tentative, cautious, and circumscribed. In short, few scholars have yet been able to produce good empirical work that reflects or represents a truly Atlantic approach to the early modern period.

What scholars have so far produced tend to be what Armitage has called cis-Atlantic history – the study of particular places or locations in relation to the wider Atlantic World. Indeed, there has been a wonderful explosion of literature on topics ranging from the Atlantic-influenced political and legal culture of Buenos Aires, Argentina, to the cultural lives of African slaves in the early colonial Portuguese world, to the dynamic interactions between Natives, Dutch and English in the early New York region, and finally to the massive upheaval of the Haitian Revolution.[3] But so far, with several important

---

[3] See Jeremy Adelman 2002, *Republic of Capital: Buenos Aires and the Legal Transformation of the Atlantic World* (Stanford, CA: Stanford University Press); James H. Sweet 2003, *Recreating Africa: Culture, Kinship, and Religion in the African-Portuguese World, 1441–1770* (Chapel Hill, NC: University of North Carolina Press); Faren R. Siminoff 2004, *Crossing the Sound: The Rise of Atlantic American Communities in Seventeenth-Century Eastern Long Island* (New York, NY: New York University Press); Laurent Dubois 2004, *Avengers of the New World: The Story of the Haitian Revolution* (Cambridge, MA: Belknap Press of Harvard University Press). See also April Lee Hatfield 2004, *Atlantic Virginia: Intercolonial Relations in the Seventeenth Century* (Philadelphia, PA: PENN/University of Pennsylvania Press); Herman L. Bennett 2003, *Africans in Colonial Mexico: Absolutism, Christianity, and Afro-Creole Consciousness, 1570–1640* (Blacks in the Diaspora) (Bloomington, IN: Indiana University Press); and the edited collections, Bradley G. Bond (ed.) 2005,

exceptions discussed below, there has been relatively little work so far that is truly transatlantic (comparative) or circum-Atlantic (that is, 'the history of the Atlantic as a particular zone of exchange and interchange, circulation and transmission').[4]

As Armitage notes, it may just be a matter of time before an accumulation of cis-Atlantic histories lend themselves to more expansive trans- and circum-Atlantic histories. In the meantime, though, there is a danger that such initial efforts might actually be limiting in the long run. For while historiographers thus far have embraced an open-ended definition of Atlantic history and run ahead of the pack to announce the possibilities that lie ahead, most historians have had to proceed from what they know. And what many 'Atlantic' historians know best is the Anglo-Atlantic World. Thus so far, with some important exceptions, the bulk of the work in Atlantic history has really been about the Anglo-Atlantic World.[5] Armitage and Braddick's path-breaking work, several recently published readers and many of the new and forthcoming

---

French Colonial Louisiana And The Atlantic World (Baton Rouge, LA: Louisiana State University Press); Robert Applebaum and John Wood Sweet (eds) 2005, *Envisioning an English Empire: Jamestown and the Making of the North Atlantic World* (Philadelphia, PA: University of Pennsylvania Press).

[4] Armitage 2002, 'Three Concepts', pp. 16-25.

[5] Examples are many, but see especially the fine work done by people such as Alison Games 1999, *Migration and the Origins of the English Atlantic World* (Harvard, MA: Harvard University Press); Ian K. Steele 1986, *The English Atlantic, 1675–1740: An Exploration of Communication and Community* (New York, NY: Oxford University Press); Alison G. Olson 1992, *Making the Empire Work: London and American Interest Groups, 1690–1790* (Cambridge, MA: Harvard University Press); Andrew Jackson O'Shaughnessy 2000, *An Empire Divided: The American Revolution and the British Caribbean* (Philadelphia, PA: University of Pennsylvania Press); Carla Gardina Pestana 2004, *The English Atlantic in an Age of Revolution, 1640–1661* (Cambridge, MA: Harvard University Press); David Hancock 1995, *Citizens of the World: London Merchants and the Integration of the British Atlantic Community, 1735–1785* (Cambridge: Cambridge University Press); Patrick Griffin 2001, *The People with No Name: Ireland's Ulster Scots, America's Scots Irish, and the Creation of a British Atlantic World, 1689–1764* (Princeton, NJ: Princeton University Press); Joyce E. Chaplin 2001, *Subject Matter: Technology, the Body, and Science on the Anglo-American Frontier, 1500–1676* (Cambridge, MA: Harvard University Press); and recently published edited collections such as Eliga H. Gould and Peter S. Onuf (eds) 2004, *Empire and Nation: The American Revolution in the Atlantic World* (Baltimore, MD: Johns Hopkins University Press); Elizabeth Mancke and Carole Shammas (eds) 2005, *The Creation of the British Atlantic World* (Baltimore, MD: Johns Hopkins University Press), both of which are in a new Johns Hopkins University Press series entitled Anglo-America in the Trans-Atlantic World.

books with 'Atlantic World' in their title are, on closer inspection, about the Anglo-American Atlantic World.[6]

Now, the desire to place European colonies in an Atlantic setting is admirable, as is the push to integrate those colonies into histories of the metropole, but surely in the colonial context, this is what we should have been doing all along. Perhaps this historiographical turn is only natural given that the history of colonial British America is probably the field that has the most catching up to do when it comes to breaking down modern conceptual and political borders. As John Elliott has noted, Atlantic History in the Anglo-American world has been, when seen especially in a broader Atlantic context, and in particular, by Latin American historians, remarkably bifurcated. Whereas the history of Spanish America during the colonial period has conventionally been regarded as a 'natural concomitant of the history of metropolitan Spain, and vice versa', the same cannot be said of general histories of England, nor for that matter, of the British colonies in America, where historians of the latter have been strongly preoccupied with teleological and exceptionalist assumptions about the kind of society into which they were to evolve.[7]

So, there is good reason to celebrate the recent outpouring of monographs and books on both sides of the Atlantic that have transformed Anglo-American history and that have already culminated in the publication of new textbooks such as T. H. Breen and Timothy Hall's, *Colonial America in an Atlantic World* (New York, Nyand London: Pearson Longman, 2004), and Alan Taylor's remarkably rich and Atlantic-minded *American Colonies: The Settling of North America* (London: Penguin, 2001). These books collectively enrich the history of colonial America while they illuminate transatlantic networks of exchange, migration, ideas and labour. They also tell us a good deal about Britain as well, and the impact empire had on the development of the British 'nation', 'national identity', and even newer ideas of empire too.[8] In short, Atlantic history has

---

[6] Or, as Cañizares-Esguerra has put it, they are usually about the '*North* Atlantic' (see his 2003 essay, 'Some Caveats about the "Atlantic" Paradigm', in *History Compass*, 1. Even works that at first glance promise a more pan-Atlantic approach are often more focused on the Anglo-Atlantic World on closer inspection. See, for example, Mary Sarah Bilder 2004, *The Transatlantic Constitution: Colonial Legal Culture and the Empire* (Cambridge, MA: Harvard University Press); and Peter A. Coclanis 2005, *The Atlantic Economy During the Seventeenth and Eighteenth Centuries: New Perspectives on Organization, Operation, Practice, and Personnel* (The Carolina Lowcountry and the Atlantic World Series) (Columbia, SC: University of South Carolina Press).

[7] John Elliott 2002, 'Afterword', in Armitage and Braddick (eds), *British Atlantic World*, pp. 238.

[8] See, for example, Eliga H. Gould 2000, *The Persistence of Empire: British Political Culture in the Age of the American Revolution* (Chapel Hill, NC: University of North Carolina Press); Andrew Fitzmaurice 2003, *Humanism and America: An Intellectual History of English Colonisation, 1500–1625*

thus far helped in telling a much more multifaceted, three-dimensional and integrated tale of the British imperial and the colonial American experience.

But at their worst, these 'new' Atlantic history books tend to replicate and enhance older teleological assumptions about the growth of the United States and the rise of Britain, albeit now with an enriched and broader Atlantic World context. Even the latest, and in many ways very admirable, attempt at placing the colonial American experience in a wider Atlantic perspective – Alan Taylor's, *American Colonies: The Settling of North America* fails to break from an ultimate adherence to explaining the origins of the United States. Presumably, this has much to do with publishers' desires to fill a textbook market for University courses that still revolve around the rise of the United States, albeit a more multicultural United States. It is here that intellectual developments have run far ahead of departmental, institutional, and market forces, needs, and biases.

Quite apart from the inherent limitations in this more traditional approach, if we do not break free from these particular national, or even imperial paradigms, Atlantic history is in danger of becoming a neo-imperial form of history; one dominated by the rise of the British Empire, and the birth of the United States. Bernard Bailyn, for example, has been at the forefront of efforts to invigorate the field of Atlantic history. But in Bailyn's own Atlantic World, Britain is clearly at the centre, and the British Empire and the Anglo-American world radiates outward – throughout the 'entire inter-hemispheric system'. Suddenly British traders are crowding the ports of the Caribbean and British goods are flooding into French ports. And 'England's population moved about the Atlantic World as the people of no other European nation.' Bailyn wants to place Britain and America into a larger Atlantic context, but seems only interested in reading that context through British eyes – the impact of Britain on the Atlantic, rather than the Atlantic impact on Britain. Atlantic history, for Bailyn, is about linking 'European history with the history of the western hemisphere'.[9]

A celebration of Atlantic history in this context suddenly sounds at best suspiciously like older notions of the 'Western civilisation' programme out of which, at least in part, Atlantic history grew. Bailyn himself traces those origins

---

(Cambridge: Cambridge University Press); David Armitage 2000, *The Ideological Origins of the British Empire* (Cambridge: Cambridge University Press); Linda Colley 1992, *Britons: Forging the Nation, 1707–1837* (New Haven, CT: Yale University Press); Michael J. Braddick 2000, *State Formation in Early Modern England, c. 1550–1700* (Cambridge: Cambridge University Press); and the illuminating essays in the special forum on 'The New British History in Atlantic Perspective', *American Historical Review*, vol. 104, no. 2, 1999, pp. 426-500.

[9] Bernard Bailyn 2002, Preface, in Armitage and Braddick (eds), *British Atlantic World*, pp. xv, xvi-xvii.

to Walter Lippmann's influential essay in *The New Republic* in February 1917, when he argued for the preservation of the

> profound web of interest which joins together the western world. Britain, France, Italy, even Spain, Belgium, Holland, the Scandinavian nations, and Pan-America are in the main one community in their deepest needs and their deepest purposes .... What we must fight for is the common interest of the western world, for the integrity of the Atlantic Powers.

And most proponents of Atlantic history recognise its ideological roots in the defensive posturing of the Cold War.[10]

But at worst, this kind of approach also threatens to become something more than a rewarming of the Western civilisation programme. Most recently, Bailyn tipped his hand as to what he meant by Atlantic History when, at the end of an essay detailing the radiating influence of American constitutionalism through the Atlantic World in the early nineteenth century, he wrote of contemporary challenges to that 'classic formulation for the world at large of effectiveness and constraint in the humane uses of power' by people with 'other values, other aspirations, other beliefs in the proper uses of power' and by people who 'emphatically challenge Jefferson's belief that it is America's destiny to extend to other regions of the earth what he called "the sacred fire of freedom and self-government".' What these 'other' values, aspirations and beliefs are, Bailyn leaves up to one's imagination. But in this new era of post-September 11th fears, Atlantic history may yet become a casualty of a Western-oriented new political agenda.[11]

With these caveats aside, and in the spirit of the idea that Atlantic history should be liberating, not limiting, let me suggest several possible directions in which

---

[10] *The New Republic*, February 17, 1917, pp. 60, quoted in Bailyn 1996, 'The Idea of Atlantic History'. More recently, Bailyn has downplayed the Cold War origins of Atlanticism. Atlantic history was, 'essentially' in his view, a result of the 'force of "inner" developments within scholarship itself: the propulsion of expanding knowledge and the perception of hitherto unremarked filiations' (2002, Preface, pp. xvii).

[11] See Bernard Bailyn 2003, *To Begin the World Anew: The Genius and Ambiguities of the American Founders* (New York, NY: Knopf), pp. 149. For similar warnings of this kind, see the essays by Cañizares-Esguerra 2003, 'Some Caveats about the "Atlantic" Paradigm', and Jack P. Greene 2003, 'Comparing Early Modern American Worlds: Some Reflections on the Promise of a Hemispheric Perspective', in *History Compass*, 1, NA 026, 001-010, at www.historycompass.com, in which Greene worries about Atlantic history becoming the latest example of 'Yankee imperialism', while Cañizares-Esguerra notes that such suspicions grow when it is noted that 'Atlantic' history has not extended past the colonial period, when Latin America becomes less about Spain and more about histories, politics, and poverty that challenge 'aseptic and celebratory definitions of the West as the cradle of "democracy", "reason", "prosperity", and "freedom"'.

we should think carefully about how best to use this conceptual tool: by thinking across borders, and especially imperial borders, by facing east as much as we face west, and by taking a bottom-up approach at least as much as a top-down approach. By using Atlantic history along with the best of other new methodological and conceptual advances, we have a real opportunity now of radically reframing Atlantic history and pushing it far beyond what R. R. Palmer and his intellectual heirs had in mind.[12]

One of these is to really move beyond borders. It is of course extremely useful to think about the multicultural origins of the United States, or to reconnect the colonial experience with the European nations that spawned those colonies. And, Atlantic history has helped illuminate a great deal *within* the older imperial systems as a whole. But Atlantic historians need to look further than their imperial borders, too. We need more discussion of comparisons and connections *across* imperial systems. Relatively few scholars have begun to compare and contrast the labour systems of Spanish and English America, to take one example, or even to compare the cultivation of gentility in Portuguese Brazil and French St Domingue. As John Elliott has observed, Anglo-American historians are not the only ones who have focused on a single system; French, Dutch, Portuguese, or Spanish Atlantic history, is still usually 'divided into neat national packages' as Elliot has put it.[13]

This requires everyone, of course, to undertake the rather difficult task of breaking free from the different systems they study, however large they are already. But once we have a more integrated view, and once we give equal weight to the voices of French, Dutch, Portuguese, Spanish and even West Indian

---

[12] Here I draw inspiration from the thoughts of Jiménez and Rediker, 'What is Atlantic History', at http://www.marcusrediker.com/Articles/what_is_atlantic_history.htm

[13] J. H. Elliott 2002, 'Atlantic History: A Circumnavigation', in Armitage and Braddick (eds), *British Atlantic World*, p. 235. Indeed, surveying at least the most recent English-language publications, the study of imperial systems in isolation of each other is not limited to Anglo-American historians. See, for example, the otherwise path-breaking work by Tamar Herzog 2003, *Defining Nations: Immigrants and Citizens in Early Modern Spain and Spanish America* (New Haven, CT: Yale University Press); Roleno Adorno and Kenneth Andrien 1991, *Transatlantic Encounters: Europeans and Andeans in the Sixteenth Century* (Berkeley, CA: University of California Press): Ida Altman 2000, *Transatlantic Ties in the Spanish Empire: Brihuega, Spain & Puebla, Mexico, 1560–1620* (Stanford, CA: Stanford University Press); James Pritchard 2004, *In Search of Empire: The French in the Americas, 1670–1730* (Cambridge: Cambridge University Press); and Kenneth J. Banks 2002, *Chasing Empire across the Sea: Communications and the State in the French Atlantic, 1713–1763* (Montreal and Kingston: McGill-Queen's University Press); and most recently, Laurent Dubois 2004, *A Colony of Citizens: Revolution and Slave Emancipation in the French Caribbean, 1787–1804* (Chapel Hill, NC: University of North Carolina Press).

historians weighing into the discussion about the Atlantic, we can potentially radically reconfigure our narratives, rather than just incorporate scholarship on the so-called 'borderlands' in a sometimes tokenistic way. We can let, for example, the truly multicultural experience of New Spain drive the agenda of our interpretive framework as easily as American constitutionalism seems to drive the current agenda. Too many Anglo-Americans, myself included, too often try to 'fit' Spanish experiences into Anglo models, rather than the other way around, or comparing them equally.[14]

Integral to this effort to move beyond borders will be the need to take up the call of Michael Jiménez and Marcus Rediker and others to completely 'reframe the political and intellectual style of early Atlanticism' and refashion Atlantic History – away from Robert R. Palmer's male upper- and middle-class actors in national politics, and more towards a common and/or comparative social history – towards a new class history, for example. Indeed, as Jiménez and Rediker note, 'we possess considerably more knowledge of previously ignored workers and peasants, women, and peoples of many nations, races, and ethnicities – in intensively studied regions, villages, and neighbourhoods throughout the Atlantic World'. This exciting research has put us in a unique position – not only to produce more enriching scholarship on the comparisons and connections, the similarities and differences, between ordinary people throughout the Atlantic World, but also to write a fundamentally new kind of history. The constellation of the emergence of the new Atlantic history with so many other 'new' histories – on gender, race, and ethnicity in colonial, imperial and postcolonial studies – means that we have a better chance than ever of breaking free from Palmer and others and writing even a new kind of political history, but one which involves a significant 'reworking of the liberal and modernization paradigms which lay at the heart of the earlier Atlantic project'.[15]

There are several very exciting developments in this direction. Rediker and Peter Linebaugh's own work, *The Many Headed Hydra* is of course one of these, but so too is Camilla Townsend's fascinating comparison of early republic Baltimore, Maryland and Guayaquil, Ecuador, in *Tales of Two Cities: Race and Economic Culture in Early Republican North and South America*. And, of course, this is what many Africanists and historians of slavery are and have always been doing. From Philip Curtin to David Eltis and Paul Gilroy, Africanists have been

---

[14] Cañizares-Esguerra 2003, 'Some Caveats about the "Atlantic" Paradigm', 1. And see Jorge Cañizares-Esguerra 2001, *How to Write the History of the New World: Histories, Epistemologies, and Identities in the Eighteenth Century Atlantic World* (Stanford, CA: Stanford University Press), for one example of the potential fruits of doing so.

[15] Jiménez and Rediker, 'What is Atlantic History', at http://www.marcusrediker.com/Articles/what_is_atlantic_history.htm

the best Atlanticists, and pan-Atlanticists at that, and the outpouring of so many outstanding works on African slavery and the slave trade, especially over recent decades, has opened up what Elliott has called 'exciting perspectives that suggest the dawn of a new era of Pan-Atlantic history'. Given this, it is perhaps no surprise that path-breaking work by scholars of the Black Atlantic have helped inspire significantly the proponents of Atlantic history.[16]

Some fields, of course, lend themselves to a more pan-Atlantic approach.[17] But surprisingly, other subjects that might have been at the forefront of such a movement have apparently been left behind. I'm teaching a new course this semester on natives and newcomers in the Atlantic World focused squarely on the experiences of indigenous peoples in the Americas between 1400 and 1800.

---

[16] Elliott 2002, 'Atlantic History', pp. 235. The literature on the Black Atlantic and slavery is, of course, extensive, but see especially, John Thornton 1992, *Africa and Africans in the Making of the Atlantic World, 1400–1800* (Cambridge: Cambridge University Press); P. E. Russell 1995, *Portugal, Spain, and the African Atlantic, 1343–1490* (Brookfield, VT: Variorum); Philip D. Curtin 1990, *The Rise and Fall of the Plantation Complex: Essays in Atlantic History* (Cambridge: Cambridge University Press); Philip D. Curtin 1969, *The Atlantic Slave Trade: A Census* (Madison, WI: University of Wisconsin Press); Paul E. Lovejoy and David V. Trotman (eds) 2003, *Trans-Atlantic Dimensions of Ethnicity in the African Diaspora* (London and New York, NY: Continuum); Paul E. Lovejoy and David Richardson 1999, 'Trust, Pawnship, and Atlantic History: The Institutional Foundations of the Old Calabar Slave Trade', *American Historical Review*, vol. 104, no. 2, pp. 333-55; Robin Law and Kristin Mann 1999, 'West Africa in the Atlantic Community: The Case of the Slave Coast', *William and Mary Quarterly*, vol. 56, no. 2, pp. 307-34; David Eltis 2000, *The Rise of African Slavery in the Americas* (Cambridge: Cambridge University Press); David Eltis 1993, 'Europeans and the Rise and Fall of African Slavery in the Americas: An Interpretation', *American Historical Review*, vol. 98, no. 5, pp. 1399-423; Stanley L. Engerman and Joseph E. Inikori (eds) 1992, *The Atlantic Slave Trade: Effects on Economies, Societies, and Peoples in Africa, the Americas, and Europe* (Durham, NC: Duke University Press); Michael L. Connif and Thomas J. Davis (eds) 1994, *Africans in the Americas: A History of the Black Diaspora* (New York, NY: St Martin's Press); Richard Price 1996, *Maroon Societies: Rebel Slave Communities in the Americas*, 3rd edition (Baltimore, MD: Johns Hopkins University Press); and Frank Tannenbaum's (1946) classic comparative work, *Slave and Citizen: The Negro in the Americas* (New York, NY: Knopf).

[17] Exciting new developments in British imperial history on gender in the colonial world also point to possibilities: see, for example, Anne McClintock 1995, *Imperial Leather: Race, Gender, and Sexuality in the Colonial Contest* (New York, NY: Routledge); and Jennifer L. Morgan 2004, *Laboring Women: Reproduction and Gender in New World Slavery* (Philadelphia, PA: University of Pennsylvania Press). Other works that have taken a pan-Atlantic approach are those that look at early encounters, such as Patricia Seed 1995, *Ceremonies of Possession in Europe's Conquest of the New World, 1492–1800* (Cambridge: Cambridge University Press); and Anthony Pagden 1995, *Lords of All the World: Ideologies of Empire in Spain, Britain and France c1500–c1800* (New Haven, CT: Yale University Press).

I was astonished to find how little there has been published that pushes beyond the artificial national and imperial boundaries Europeans erected and which were often meaningless to indigenous peoples. There are in fact a bewildering array of survey texts on Native Americans in Canada, the United States, and sometimes of Canada and the United States, and many now regularly incorporate Florida and the south-west to accommodate the Spanish dimension to Native American experiences. But there are almost no books that make sustained comparisons and connections *between* the experiences of indigenous peoples throughout the Americas in the face of what was, by and large, a common experience to all. Atlanticists thus also need to pay attention to the insights of those in other fields, like the new Indian history, and 'face east' as much as they normally face west.[18]

The important thing to note here, I think, is that we should strive to think as much about the peripheries as the centres in Atlantic history. We especially need to keep our eyes on the impact that the small politics of local communities had on the larger politics of imperial rule and nation building. The lines of force so often run in multiple directions, but few scholars in taking an Atlantic approach have put the so-called peripheries at the centre of the larger imperial story. But if we really want to think global, we need to watch the local. We need to tell stories from the bottom-up, facing east (as well as north and south), and from gendered perspectives as often, if not more, than we tell stories from the top-down, facing westwards from Europe, and from a single, usually, male-oriented perpsective. Only when we do this can we fully appreciate the

---

[18] See Daniel Richter 2001, *Facing East from Indian Country: A Native History of Early America* (Cambridge, MA: Harvard University Press). John Kicza 2003 recently undertook such an effort in *Resilient Cultures: America's Native Peoples Confront European Colonization, 1500–1800* (Upper Saddle River, NJ: Prentice Hall). A much less successful attempt can be found in Jayme A. Sokolow's (2002) *The Great Encounter: Native Peoples and European Settlers in the Americas, 1492–1800* (Armonk, NY: M. E. Sharpe). The potential fruits of such comparisons and connections are evident in Alison Games' revealing aside that in contrast to historians of North American Indians, historians of Latin American have often considered indigenous peoples, and especially labourers, as migrants. Characterising the experiences of North American Indians as migrants helps us make sense of the tremendous movement of Indian communities in the face of the European invasion. See Alison Games 2002, 'Migration', in Armitage and Braddick (eds), *British Atlantic World*, pp. 44, where she draws on the work of scholars of the Andes, especially Nicolás Sánchez-Albornoz 1978, *Indios y Tributos en el Alto Peru* (Lima: Instituto de Estudios Peruanos) and Karen Viera Powers 1995, *Andean Journeys: Migration, Ethnogenesis, and the State in Colonial Quito* (Albuquerque: University of New Mexico Press). At least some of the essays in Christine Daniels and Michael V. Kennedy (eds) 2002, *Negotiated Empires: Centers and Peripheries in the Americas, 1500–1820* (New York, NY: Routledge) do attempt to balance a westward-eastward perspective.

real and highly contingent nature of the 'negotiated empires' – and their cultural, social, economic, and political dimensions – at the heart of Atlantic World.[19]

Well, how do we do this? Not everyone can hope to emulate the brilliance of Joseph Roach in *Cities of the Dead: Circum-Atlantic Performance* (New York, NY: Columbia University Press, 1996), the virtuosity of Paul Gilroy in *The Black Atlantic: Modernity and Double-Consciousness* (Cambridge, MA: Harvard University Press, 1996), or the erudition and wide-reading of Peter Linebaugh and Marcus Rediker in *The Many-Headed Hydra: Sailors, Slaves, Commoners, and the Hidden History of the Revolutionary Atlantic* (Boston, MA: Beacon Press, 2000) – three works that have helped us believe that such truly transnational and circum-Atlantic histories are possible. And even if we had the creative imagination to offer such interpretations, there are some more mundane and practical problems standing in the way of producing solid empirical work on such topics. Comparative history requires a mastery of at least two or more discrete historiographies, archival systems, and often, and ideally, different languages. But circum-Atlantic history (like any good transnational history) demands even more – often and again, ideally, transcending national and imperial borders and boundaries and the traditional periodisation of the historical narratives that sustain those borders. How then, does one begin archival work on subjects that defy easy categorisation, that are elusive in the records, that ignore the border controls that now separate historical resources?

Some good edited collections have begun to push us forward in this respect. Most offer discrete essays that allow us to make some useful comparisons, such as Nicholas Canny and Anthony Pagden (eds), *Colonial Identity in the Atlantic World, 1500–1800* (Princeton, NJ: Princeton University Press, 1987), Michael A. Morrison and Melinda S. Zook, *Revolutionary Currents: Nation Building in the Transatlantic World* (Lanham, MD: Rowman & Littlefield Publishers, 2004), Franklin W. Knight and Peggy Liss (eds), *Atlantic Port Cities: Economy, Culture and Society in the Atlantic World, 1650–1850* (Knoxville, TN: University of Tennessee Press, 1991), Wim Klooster and Alfred Padula, *The Atlantic World : Essays on Slavery, Migration and Imagination* (Upper Saddle River, NJ: Pearson/Prentice Hall, 2005), Elaine G. Breslaw (ed.), *Witches of the Atlantic World: An Historical Reader and Primary Sourcebook* (New York, NY: New York University Press, 2000), Paul E. Lovejoy and Nicholas Rogers (eds), *Unfree Labour in the Development of the Atlantic World* (Ilford, Essex: Frank Cass, 1994), and David P. Geggus, *The Impact of the Haitian Revolution in the Atlantic World*

---

[19] Some important steps towards the achievement of this goal have been taken by the contributors to Daniels and Kennedy (eds) 2002, *Negotiated Empires*.

(Columbia, SC: University of South Carolina Press, 2001).[20] Moreover, a forthcoming volume edited by Bailyn and drawn from his Harvard-based International Seminar on the Atlantic World entitled *Cultural Encounters in Atlantic History, 1500–1825: Passages in Europe's Engagement with the West* (Palgrave Macmillan, 2005), promises the same (though note the revealing and eastward facing subtitle).

So far, it seems, biographical or prosopographical approaches have worked with some success. Two recent path-breaking works, for example, explore the fascinating worlds of several Africans in the Atlantic World. Randy J. Sparks, *The Two Princes of Calabar: An Eighteenth-Century Atlantic Odyssey* (Cambridge, MA: Harvard University Press, 2004), and Jon F. Sensbach, *Rebecca's Revival: Creating Black Christianity in the Atlantic World* (Cambridge, MA: Harvard University Press, 2005) both demonstrate not only the extent to which Africans were enmeshed in this new Atlantic World, but also how vital they were in creating it. Such biographies help break down borders. In crossing colonial or national boundaries, researchers at least find themselves on less certain footing when making comparisons between diverse peoples or institutions across time and/or places. But while modern researchers may draw back from the uncertainties beyond their historiographic borders, their subjects rarely did.[21]

Non-elite studies of these kinds of people have the biggest potential to transform the field. Communities like the Métis of the Great Lakes, for example, do not really fit into existing narratives and approaches. They were French, and Indian, after all, in an expanding Anglo-American world. But they lived lives that extended much further than the confines of nation-based narratives to which historians have long been bound. Their lives transcended the traditional periodisation to which nation-bound scholars adhere to give coherence to their own narratives. They crossed imperial borders with impunity and they slipped through and across the ethnic, racial, and linguistic categories we have so often imposed on the past. In short, they lived transnational Atlantic lives that defy easy categorisation. In effect, their stories have been fragmented and lost by historians who have been teleologically wedded to tracing the development of new nations.[22] It may take a little more fleet-footed archival work to piece

---

[20] Even student readers are helpful in making the initial connections we need to spur new ideas. See, for example, Timothy J. Shannon 2004, *Atlantic Lives: A History of the Atlantic World* (New York, NY: Pearson Longman).

[21] See also the suggestive and illuminating biographies collected in David G. Sweet and Gary B. Nash (eds) 1981, *Struggle & Survival in Colonial America* (Berkeley, CA: University of California Press), which despite its title, covers all of the Americas.

[22] Richard White's (1991) masterful study *The Middle Ground: Indians, Empires, and Republics in the Great Lakes* (Cambridge: Cambridge University Press), recognises these artificial borders, but

together such lives – from their origins in southern France and the northern Great Lakes, to their scattered communities across Wisconsin, Michigan, and southern and northern Ontario – but the potential rewards are enticing.[23]

Of course, as exciting as all of this sounds, we also need to be aware that this might be difficult, and the task of synthesising such work virtually impossible. It seems hard enough to please a national audience without attempting to synthesise the histories of four continents bordering the Atlantic ocean over three centuries, and our unfamiliarity with so many aspects of the histories contained within the Atlantic World in the early modern period.[24] And, as Atlantic history is a 'history without borders' – a story told from no one vantage point and about no single representative place; no nation states, no single narratives, but instead multiple and often conflicting narratives presented from different perspectives – it can be particularly confusing.

Moreover, in the end we might, as Jack Greene has noted, be not only taken aback at the difficulties of comparative history, but also by a sense of the often vast differences between the different imperial worlds. And not only between the Catholic Iberian-American polities and the Protestant Anglo-American polities established much later, but also within those sprawling entities – particularly between Spanish Peru and Mexico where huge concentrations of imperial indigenous populations combined with mineral resources to produce societies there like nowhere else.[25]

Finally, such an overview, over such a long period, may not be entirely satisfactory – it's a bit more like jet-setting rather than backpacking. We'll see the broader outlines from the air, but rarely get sweaty exploring the forests up close; we'll see patterns of mobility and analyse large groups of people who make up the Atlantic World, but not mingle enough with the locals to perhaps feel like we know what is really going on. And, like jet-setters, we might be in danger of over-emphasising the commonalities and continuities. As we explore the Atlantic World on the same planes, via similar airports, stay in the same luxury chain hotels, and drink coke and bottled water, we'll see superficial

---

White's study, like many others, begins to come to an end with the American Revolution, and we lose sight of his subjects in both the new republic and early Canada.

[23] Others, have successfully focused on the biography of a product, like sugar or tobacco to explore the pan-Atlantic dimensions of the early modern economy. See, for example, Stuart B. Schwartz 2004, *Tropical Babylons: Sugar and the Making of the Atlantic World, 1450–1680* (Chapel Hill, NC: University of North Carolina Press).

[24] For a warning of the dangers and difficulties of undertaking such work, especially comparative histories, see especially Greene 2003, 'Comparing Early Modern American Worlds', pp. 3.

[25] Greene 2003, 'Comparing Early Modern American Worlds', pp. 5-6.

differences in the countries we visit, but remark generally and pithily on the shrinking size of the global village.

But a truly Atlantic approach ultimately allows us to ask – and begin to answer – some significant questions, and to interrupt so many dominant Eurocentric and Anglo-centric historical narratives and trajectories. For example, an Atlantic approach makes it quite clear that the expansion of any kind of European concept of 'liberty' was quite literally and figuratively carried to the New World on the backs of unfree labour. An Atlantic perspective allows us to move beyond endless debates within colonial historiographies about the relative prosperity and opportunity of different colonists and put the system as a whole under the microscope. As David Brion Davis has noted, when put in that broader perspective, there can be no doubt that the history of the entire New World has been dominated by the theme of slavery and freedom. In the 320 years from 1500 to 1820, he writes, two African slaves for every European immigrant arrived in the New World: 'It was African slaves and their descendants who furnished the basic labour power that created the dynamic New World economies and the first international mass markets for such consumer goods as sugar, rice, tobacco, dyestuffs, and cotton.'[26] This seems an obvious fact but one which, if acknowledged properly, helps undermine a Eurocentric 'rise of the West' narrative particularly since the history of North America in particular, but also Europe and the West in general, has long since been predicted upon the idea of progress, of the march of liberal democratic ideas and ideals.

And, we may also be able finally to move beyond the deceit, usually implicit in many studies, but explicitly stated as recently as 1992 by J. R. McNeill that Europeans 'created and controlled' the Atlantic World.[27] Certainly, from the perspective of London, Paris, Madrid, or even of colonists in Philadelphia, Mexico, or Rio de Janeiro, this might have seemed true, but when viewed from the perspective of the motley crew of privateers who shaped so much of the history of the Caribbean in particular, and the Atlantic in general, such a statement rings hollow. And, when viewed from the perspective of the newly emergent Araucanian nation in southern Chile, or the Six Nations of eastern

---

[26] Davis 2000, 'Looking at Slavery from Broader Perspectives', pp. 455. Moreover, the revolutions and movements for independence that ended the first phase in the history of the Atlantic world have always been acquainted with the drive for liberal democratic governments. But does the history of the Atlantic World in this period bear those assumptions and ideas out? Or was, as Edmund Morgan famously postulated for the American Revolution, slavery absolutely – though paradoxically – essential for the development of republican ideas in the New World. See Edmund S. Morgan 1976, *American Slavery, American Freedom: The Ordeal of Colonial Virginia* (New York, NY: Norton).

[27] See J. R. McNeill 1992, 'The End of the Old Atlantic World: America, Africa, Europe, 1770–1888', in Karras and McNeill (eds), *Atlantic American Societies*, pp. 265.

North America, both of whom successfully limited European advances for centuries while in turn profiting from the newcomers, it becomes quite clear that the Atlantic World was a 'negotiated' world. From the start, most Europeans got a foothold along the coasts of western Africa and the Americas via a series of negotiations, invitations, and sought after alliances amongst African and Americans, and all new Atlantic identities were forged from an amalgamation of sustained and intense European, African, and American contact, conflict, and cooperation.[28] If the Atlantic World is to be about anything meaningful, we must start, rather than end, with these premises.

---

[28] For illuminating and suggestive thoughts on this front see especially Donald J. Weber 2002, 'Bourbons and Bárbaros: Center and Periphery in the Reshaping of Spanish Indian Policy', in Daniels and Kennedy (eds), *Negotiated Empires*, pp. 79-104, and Thomas Benjamin 2001, 'Alliances and Conquests', in Benjamin, Hall, and Rutherford (eds), *Atlantic World in the Age of Empire*, pp. 81-7. On identities, see the collected essays in Nicholas Canny and Anthony Pagden (eds) 1987, *Colonial Identity in the Atlantic World, 1500–1800* (Princeton, NJ: Princeton University Press). All of this, then, would help us understand the magnitude of the lines of force that ran the other way through the Atlantic, transforming our understanding of Old World societies too.

4. Postcolonial histories and Catherine Hall's *Civilising Subjects*

Angela Woollacott

As with any area of scholarship, there is much slippage in the terminology of transnational histories. Scholars inflect the terms 'global history', 'world history' and 'postcolonial history' differently. Yet even if these terms inevitably lack precision and completely consensual meaning, there are differences to be descried in their general usage – at least, to my mind, between the terms 'world history' and 'postcolonial history', particularly the kind of world history most associated with the *Journal of World History* and the World History Association. My task here is to posit some of the characteristics and contributions of postcolonial histories as a transnational approach, and to this end to focus on Catherine Hall's monograph *Civilising Subjects: Metropole and Colony in the English Imagination 1830–1867* published by Polity Press and the University of Chicago Press in 2002.

Let me begin with some thoughts about what characterises postcolonial histories.

I would suggest that postcolonial approaches to transnational history are distinguished by:

- political engagement with the operation of imperialism and colonialism;
- a concern with power structures and hierarchies;
- an interest in the historical construction of race (one such hierarchy) and often, an interest in the interconstitution of race, gender, class and sexuality;
- an impetus to interrogate knowledge structures, to ask how categories, taxonomies and language have structured imperial relations and hierarchies;
- a recognition that political, economic, social and cultural structures were constructed at once in colonies and their metropoles; that things did not happen originally or independently in London, Paris or Lisbon, rather they happened in multiple parts of an empire in interconnected and interconstitutive ways – including between colonies; and
- a concern with the contingencies and specificities of historical change within particular imperial and/or colonial frames.

    Further, let me suggest specifically that, among these characteristics, the distinctions between postcolonial histories and the kind of world history one is most likely to find in the pages of the *Journal of World History* consist in:
- postcolonialism's interest in the historical construction of race and its interconstitution with other categories such as gender and sexuality;
- the impetus to interrogate knowledge structures and their regimes;

- the emphasis on cultural interconstitution as well as economic interdependence; and
- the concern with the specificities of historical change, importantly as opposed to any universalist approach.

It is readily apparent that no one work in postcolonial history totally fulfills any such list of characteristics – whether it's my list or a list that another scholar might compile. Yet there is value, I think, in considering how a significant, substantial and influential work such as Catherine Hall's *Civilising Subjects* corresponds to such a set of characteristics. Arguably, *Civilising Subjects* bears evidence of all six of the characteristics of postcolonialism I have listed, but it demonstrates some much more than others. The ways in which it exemplifies some fully, and others only minimally, become telling about both the book and the field of postcolonialism.

The great strengths, in postcolonial terms, of Hall's magnum opus include her concern with the specificities and contingencies of historical change; her compelling insistence on the interconstitutive connections between colony and metropole; her interest in the historical construction of race and its connections to gender and class; and perhaps above all, her political engagement with the operation of imperialism and colonialism and their legacies. The fact that, despite its heft and the time it took to produce, this is far from a universalist history is signaled immediately by Hall's disarming introduction, the first sentence: 'The origins of this book lie in my own history'[1] – and this contrast with a universalist approach is despite her discussion of the influence of humanist universalism on her intellectual development. By making clear the ways in which her own life shaped the project, and the questions she asks, Hall shows both her belief in the subjective nature of history writing, and the political commitments that underscore the book. The history of her family, and her own life, as well as nineteenth-century British politics and culture have been shaped by the interconstitution of the British midlands and Jamaica, in specific ways which she fully delineates.

In his review of the book, published six months before his death, Edward Said makes plain its contemporary political importance. Referring to the Baptist missionaries at the heart of Hall's study, Said closes his review with the sobering observation: 'George Bush's main constituency, as he sets out first to punish and then to remake the world with American power, are seventy million evangelical and fundamentalist American Christians, many of whom are Southern

---

[1] Catherine Hall 2002, *Civilising Subjects: Metropole and Colony in the English Imagination 1830–1867* (Chicago, IL: University of Chicago Press), p. 1.

Baptists'.² Said argues that since the 1960s and 1970s, there has been a disturbing swing in academic and intellectual views of empire, away from the days and views of the anti-Vietnam war movement and support for the anti-colonial nationalists of Asia and Africa. He charts a groundswell of intellectual reaction in the 1980s and 1990s up to the time of his writing, condemning writers from V. S. Naipaul to Niall Ferguson for a revisionist approach that has found redeeming features in the histories of the European empires and, for some at least, has come to consider current American imperialism as an enlightened global force. Passionately advocating a postcolonial approach that interrogates the 'intertwined histories' of the two sides of the imperial divide, Said called for continuing recognition of the enormous and ongoing legacies of imperialism – the as-yet continuing consequences of slavery and the other depredations of imperial regimes both economic and moral. '[T]he legacy of empire', Said says, 'sits like a menacing and metastasising cancer just beneath the skin of our contemporary lives'.³

Not surprisingly, then, Said finds much value in Hall's *Civilising Subjects*, lauding her personal investment in her topic, and her finely detailed account of the changing nature of British imperialism as seen through the actions and words of her protagonists, particularly the shift from the paternalist idealism of the Baptist missionaries in the post-emancipation era of the 1830s and 1840s, to the articulated racism of the 1850s and 1860s. Said admired above all Hall's preparedness, while demonstrating the contingent and evolving nature of imperialism, to show that the empire was fundamentally about the subordination of the colonised to the interests of their English rulers.

One of the historians whom Said contrasts with Hall is David Cannadine. I do not wish to discuss *Ornamentalism* at great length because it has been widely reviewed and discussed in recent years, but for the very same reason I do not want to pass it over. Cannadine sees postcolonialism and the critique of Orientalism as wrongheaded in their emphasis on the imperial construction of racial difference and otherness.⁴ Despite his avowed support for the project of putting 'the history of Britain back into the history of empire, and the history of the empire back into the history of Britain',⁵ he advances the former more than the latter process. He sees the empire as having been cast in the mould of British class hierarchy – and thus as a social extension of the British metropole,

---

[2] Edward Said 2003, 'Always on Top', *London Review of Books*, vol. 25, no. 6, 20 March, p. 14 of web version.

[3] ibid., p. 6.

[4] David Cannadine 2001, *Ornamentalism: How the British Saw their Empire* (Oxford: Oxford University Press), p. xix.

[5] ibid., p. xx.

built more on affinities than on difference. Further, he argues that the empire was 'based more on class than on colour'[6] and was run on collaboration between local elites and British imperial rulers. While he is correct to remind us of such collaboration, several commentators have suggested that the book carries a whiff of nostalgia for empire, implying that its success is a signal of the political shift to which Said pointed. Indeed, it would seem that the book's success reflects the resistance to postcolonialism that is widespread in contemporary British and British Empire historiography. It must also be said that the book's success is in good part a product of its considerable merits: its gracious prose, compelling descriptions of the elaborate structures and ceremonies that upheld imperial rule, and its geographical breadth.

In a context of resistance to postcolonial work on race, and of a lack of interest in the perspectives of the colonised, Hall's book stands out for its political commitment to drawing attention to the continuing negative consequences of imperialism and colonialism, and thus, I think, exemplifies the politics inherent to postcolonialism. Antoinette Burton has laid out the political and intellectual stakes in British historiography's resistance to postcolonialism, specifically to the argument that Britain itself was shaped by the Empire:

> Clearly the persistent conviction that home and empire were separate spheres cannot be dismissed as just any other fiction. Because history-writing is one terrain upon which political battles are fought out, the quest currently being undertaken by historians and literary critics to recast the nation as an imperialized space – a political territory which could not, and still cannot, escape the imprint of empire – is an important political project. It strikes at the heart of Britain's long ideological attachment to the narratives of the Island Story, of splendid isolation, and of European exceptionalism.[7]

Not surprisingly, in her review of Hall's book in a forum in *Victorian Studies*, Burton has pointed to its importance in undermining the hegemonic fiction of Britain's separation from empire; she calls it 'a model of British history in a genuinely transnational frame'.[8]

Equally unsurprisingly, not least because Hall chose to reprint Burton's essay that lays out the political stakes of British historians' investment in the nation in her *Cultures of Empire* reader, Hall agrees in her response to Burton that

---

[6] ibid., p. 171.

[7] Antoinette Burton 2000, 'Who Needs the Nation? Interrogating "British" History', in Catherine Hall (ed.), *Cultures of Empire: A Reader: Colonizers in Britain and the Empire in the Nineteenth and Twentieth Centuries* (New York, NY: Routledge), p. 140.

[8] Antoinette Burton 2003, 'Book Review Forum', *Victorian Studies*, vol. 45, no. 4, p. 700.

challenging the national frame was a central goal of the book. 'One of my imperatives in *Civilising Subjects*', Hall notes, 'was to demonstrate the ways in which the well-established narrative of British history, the national history, the one taught in schools and universities, needs to be rethought through the frame of empire'.[9] Hall goes on to agree with Burton that 'the debate in Britain over the impact of empire is extremely contentious and the stakes are high'. Interestingly, she continues 'Indeed, I have come to think of these debates as Britain's version of "the history wars" – the controversies over interpretations of colonial history that have mobilized historians in hostile camps in Australia, New Zealand, Canada, and elsewhere'.[10] It is hardly worth adding that the work of those who consider themselves global or world historians is far less likely to provoke such political debate in Britain or elsewhere, for the reason that most of it does not engage with contemporary political issues – certainly not issues of race relations and the moral and political questions of the legacies of colonialism.

Despite her central concern with demonstrating the interconnections between Jamaica and Birmingham, Hall does not address broader imperial connections or connections between Jamaica and other colonies beyond Edward John Eyre's career in Australia and New Zealand. Edward Said notes this with the comment that Hall 'mystifyingly doesn't draw' on the work of the Subaltern Studies group[11] – and by implication suggests that Hall's work would have been enriched both by the theoretical insights of Subaltern Studies and a comparative consideration of the interconstitution of India and the metropole in the same period.

It might be suggested that, because of the near absence of a broader imperial view in Hall's book, it does not fully reflect what some scholars of postcolonialism have come to consider an important revision of the image of empire as centre and periphery, the old image of a spoked wheel. Tony Ballantyne has suggested the far better metaphor of a spider web, a metaphor that forces us to keep in mind the constant traffic between and interconstitution of multiple imperial sites, especially between colonies.[12] (I should add that Hall refers to Ballantyne's web metaphor in the *Victorian Studies* forum on her book.)[13] Of course, a reasonable response is that Hall's interest lies in the relationship between Britain

---

[9] Catherine Hall 2003, 'Book Review Forum', *Victorian Studies*, vol. 45, no. 4, p. 723.

[10] ibid., p. 724.

[11] Said 2003, 'Always on Top', p. 13.

[12] Tony Ballantyne 2002, *Orientalism and Race: Aryanism in the British Empire* (Houndmills, Baskingstoke: Palgrave), pp. 14-15.

[13] Hall 2003, 'Book Review Forum', p. 722.

and Jamaica, and therefore she had no empirical reason, beyond Eyre's career, to look at other colonial sites.

While this absence of a broader imperial context might be considered a shortcoming of the book, it also signals, I think, one of the characteristics of postcolonial history – which is that while postcolonialism necessarily means a transnational or transimperial view of history, it does not mean a global or universal view. Traditional world history practitioners claim a global framework, and a less traditional world historian like C. A. Bayly in his *The Birth of the Modern World* also takes the planet as his canvas. Importantly, postcolonial history is not big history or macro history, despite the global significance of its concern with imperialism and colonialism. Postcolonial histories use specific transnational or imperial or transcolonial frameworks, to demonstrate interconstitutive histories with particular substance and detail.

For the purposes of this anthology, it is worth briefly considering other examples of such a specifically postcolonial approach – that is, an approach framed both chronologically and geographically, and based solidly on archival sources – to transnational history. One study that has revealed important constitutive dynamics of gender and race stretching between the imperial metropole and the white-settler dominion of Australia is Fiona Paisley's book on privileged Australian feminists' activism on the status of Aboriginal people, especially Aboriginal women, in the 1920s and 1930s.[14] Paisley's study presents a detailed analysis of what literary critic Simon Gikandi has termed 'the mutual imbrication of both the colonizer and the colonized in the making of modern social and cultural formations'.[15] Using postcolonial perspectives in her analysis of race relations within Australia as colonialism, Paisley underscores the importance of white Australian feminists' international activism. She examines their strategic use of London as an imperial staging ground for feminist critiques of Australian policy on Aborigines, and their deployment of internationalism and the specific humanitarian principles laid out by the League of Nations to focus on Australian governments' failure to deal adequately with the plight of Aboriginal people.

Paisley argues that white Australian feminists' concern with their own citizenship status and their maternalism merged with humanitarian and internationalist impulses in the interwar decades in a historically significant episode of activism on behalf of Aboriginal people. As she shows, interwar feminists' critiques of prevailing assimilationist policies, especially the policy of separating Aboriginal children from their mothers in order to raise them in white society, prefigured

---

[14] Fiona Paisley 2000, *Loving Protection? Australian Feminism and Aboriginal Women's Rights 1919–1939* (Carlton South: Melbourne University Press).

[15] Simon Gikandi 1996, *Maps of Englishness: Writing Identity in the Culture of Colonialism* ((New York, NY: Columbia University Press), p. 20.

the recent controversy in Australia over the legacies of forced child removal, and the debates over how to make amends to Aboriginal people – debates that provoked Australia's current Prime Minister John Howard to decry what he labelled derisively 'black armband history'. Like Hall, Paisley is very conscious of the current political significance of her historical work. She points out that the feminists who mounted this critique of racial policy in the 1920s and 1930s were a small but vociferous group, who used the platforms of mainstream Australian feminist organisations with sizeable memberships to speak at local, national and international levels. They became witnesses for Aboriginal reform at three major inquiries: a Royal Commission on the Constitution, a federal government conference on Aboriginal welfare, and a Royal Commission on the status of Aborigines in Western Australia. Their other important victory was the success they had drawing Australian and metropolitan media attention to the deplorable status of Aboriginal people.

Paisley most directly invokes postcolonial theory in her conclusion, where she points out the limitations to these white feminists' racial analysis, and the ways in which they were the products of their own times, contemporary racial assumptions, and their positioning within Australian structures of colonialism. There she acknowledges that rather than enabling Aboriginal people to speak for themselves, white feminists assumed the right to speak for them and thus effectively contributed to their silencing. Paisley's book exemplifies what I see as several of the key aspects of postcolonial history. It has a transnational focus central to its story: white Australian feminists needed London, the international stage and their own status as modern 'citizens of the world' to conduct their political work. At the same time, Paisley's focus is very much on developments within Australia's shores, the impact of the feminists' activism, and multiple aspects of the political and cultural context. Her study is chronologically focused, based solidly in archival records and contemporary print materials, and fully cognizant of the current political significance of its findings. Constructions of race and gender, shaped by Australian colonialism, are integral to her subject matter.

While Paisley's work illuminates white-settler colonialism through an analysis of political activism and travel between Australia and the metropole, other postcolonial histories examine transnational dynamics that are rather less tangible. Dipesh Chakrabarty's study of the social practice of *adda* in nineteenth- and twentieth-century Calcutta focuses on that particular colonial and post-independence city, but his analysis foregrounds the transnational dynamics of modernisation and urbanisation, and the transnational quest to find both home and subjectivity within the turbulence of modernity. Chakrabarty defines *adda* as a cultural practice of idle and wide-ranging conversation among groups that met regularly, often tied to specific urban sites and settings, and usually consisting exclusively of men. He shows *adda*'s roots in earlier Bengali village life and traditions, yet demonstrates in clear and specific ways its emergence as a cultural practice of modernity. The earliest recorded instances of what became this idiosyncratically Bengali practice (despite its similarity to social practices in other places, such as Cairo) are set in the 1820s, suggesting the rise of the practice, along with that of the Bengali capital itself, under British colonialism. Different versions of the practice occurred through the nineteenth century, some – better known as *majlish* – being associated with wealth and the patronage of a particular elite man. *Adda*s, by contrast, at first carried innuendos of marginal groups who indulged in drugs, but increasingly came to signify democratic gatherings where each member paid for his own refreshments and class distinctions were supposedly irrelevant to the exchange of ideas.

The social practice of *addas* grew along with the expansion of the middle class and education, becoming associated with high school and university groups of young men. They reached their full flowering, Chakrabarty suggests, in the early twentieth century, the period of late colonialism when nationalist politics meshed with a high period of Bengali literary production and publishing. These conversational groups were products of urban modernity in that they were held not only in private homes, but in public spaces such as teashops, coffee houses and public parks. The open access to such spaces combined with the philosophy of egalitarianism within *addas* to nurture democratisation, along with radical and nationalist politics and the growth of literary culture. Despite their Bengali particularity, *addas* forged an intellectual culture linked to cosmopolitanism, and thus helped to create a modern sense of global citizenship – a linking of global culture to local practice.

Chakrabarty acknowledges, and to some extent analyses, the exclusion of women from *addas*. A few women were admitted to some groups by the middle decades of the twentieth century, but their late admission and their sparsity only highlight the fact of this being a homosocial practice that privileged men in their relations to one another as well as in their access to urban spaces and the worlds of literature and politics. In this sexual exclusion *addas* were representative of much else in global modernity, even as they were at times the site of debate in Bengal about gender divisions and definitions. Chakrabarty's history and analysis of this ethnically and locally specific practice thus demonstrates the interconnections among urbanisation, capitalism, education, print culture, masculine homosocial culture, and global consciousness under the aegis of colonial modernity. His narrative of a particular social practice based especially in one city is thus a transnational history, illustrating the focus of a postcolonial approach on combined economic and cultural analysis, on the operations of discourse and cultural practice, and, again, on hierarchies of gender and class.[16] Both Paisley and Chakrabarty give evidence of being aware of wider imperial contexts and significance of their work, yet the projects are both bounded in specific geographic and temporal ways, as well as being tied to archival and contemporary print sources. Postcolonial histories then can be seen as *not* global, even as they address issues of global import – not least, of course, the larger project of provincialising Europe, to use Chakrabarty's phrase.

Hall's interests lie far more in historical contingency and in the developments and legacies of nineteenth-century politics and culture than they do in theory, postcolonial or otherwise. It is not the case that she is theoretically unaware, yet the theory is worn lightly and its elaboration or revision is not a particular goal of the book. This allows reviewers to make comments such as Anthony Pagden's quip that 'Despite some initial obeisance to the household deities of Post-Colonial and Subaltern Studies, *Civilising Subjects* is a work of traditional social history'.[17] The density of detail in Hall's book, as well as the cast of characters that emerges, and the mix of religious, political and economic history, are reasons why more than one reviewer has likened *Civilising Subjects* to E. P. Thompson's *The Making of the English Working Class*, including no less a commentator than Roy Porter. Porter gave Hall's book the following very high praise: *Civilising Subjects* 'does for colonial history what E. P. Thompson's *The Making of the English Working Class* did for social history'.[18] I cannot help but wonder, however, whether some scholars of colonialism and imperialism had not thought that the field of colonial studies had already been launched well before the publication of *Civilising Subjects,* and that Porter's comment is thus somewhat surprising.

Here again the boundedness of Hall's project reflects distinct features of postcolonialism as compared with other approaches to transnational history. Like *The Making of the English Working Class*, *Civilising Subjects* is closely tied to its archival sources and their parameters, for all of its significance. Hall's project's solid archival foundations, what Pagden identifies as the characteristics of traditional social history, form a basis for a detailed and nuanced analysis of the changing interconnections between religious thought, the legal and material conditions of black Jamaicans, racial thinking, and gendered and raced notions of British citizenship. The book reflects the attachment of most postcolonial historians to the archives, and the central place of narrative in their work. Like

---

[16] Dipesh Chakrabarty 2000, '*Adda*: A History of Sociality' in his *Provincializing Europe: Postcolonial Thought and Historical Difference* (Princeton, NJ: Princeton University Press), pp. 180-213.

[17] Anthony Pagden 2003, 'Flog and Hang and Burn', *TLS*, 14 February, p. 8.

[18] Cited in a review of Hall's book by Lorenzo Veracini 2002, *Journal of Australian Studies*, Issue 10, November. It seems very poignant yet fortunate for Hall that her book received high praise from both Roy Porter and Edward Said before their untimely deaths.

other postcolonial scholars, Hall's questions are at once cultural, political and economic – a contrast to the dominant economic approach of many who identify themselves as world historians, as is, probably needless to say, her fine-grained analysis of historically evolving ideologies of masculinity.

To return to the overarching question of postcolonialism as a specific approach to transnational histories: obviously, scholars influenced by postcolonialism are far from being the only transnational historians who bring a critical or materialist political approach to their work. Adherents to schools of thought such as World Systems Theory include those motivated by the desire to reveal the historical roots of current global inequalities, the dependence of so-called Third World countries on the overdeveloped states, and the evolving historical role of capitalism in the creation of poverty, dependency and environmental 'disasters'. Historians who find value in postcolonialism are distinguished not so much by politics of the left, but rather by their added concern to link political questions to historical specificities, and to contingency rather than large-scale narratives or social-scientific paradigms. Further, they typically are concerned with the relationship between culture and politics, as well as the ideological work performed by constructed categories of race, gender and sexuality.

It is important to note that there are historians who might be thought of as writing postcolonial transnational history but who eschew such a theoretical label. Barbara Bush's study of connections between Britain, West Africa and South Africa in the interwar decades, specifically of British imperial attitudes and the development of anti-colonial nationalisms, bears hallmarks of postcolonial history. It is a bounded study concerned with historical specificities and change, that considers the power relations of imperialism as constituted through policy, cultural productions and material relations, and that examines colonial links between race and gender. Yet in her preface to the book Bush voices her worries about the 'weaknesses of post-colonialism, particularly the high jargon and mystifying dense prose of much post-colonial writing'.[19] Bush's distancing of herself from postcolonialism is a reminder of how careful we must be in applying both labels and judgements. The legacies of Marxism, of course, continue to inflect various areas of history-writing, including histories of colonialism. While the fields of Subaltern Studies and postcolonialism bear such legacies, so too does much work in sub-Saharan African history. Yet historians in that field do not often espouse postcolonial theory, and are more likely to invoke cultural anthropology and Gramscian-derived theory on cultural hegemony. These areas of work are both connected and crosscut by lines of differentiation, necessitating careful distinctions. If some world historians share some of the materialist politics

---

[19] Barbara Bush 1999, *Imperialism, Race and Resistance: Africa and Britain, 1919–1945* (London: Routledge), p. xiii.

of postcolonialism, so too do other historians share much of its agenda while being wary of its theoretical roots, or preferring to align themselves with other schools.

Conversely, some world historians espouse the term 'transnational history' and see little if any difference between the fields. Moreover, there is evidence that the field of World History, represented by the *Journal of World History*, is becoming increasingly reflexive, and more inclined to question its own biases and exclusions. In the editorial manifesto published in the inaugural issue of the journal in 1990, Jerry H. Bentley outlined the field as one that 'transcends national frontiers' and studies the history of topics such as 'population movements, economic fluctuations, climatic changes, transfers of technology, the spread of infectious and contagious diseases, imperial expansion, long-distance trade, and the spread of religious faiths, ideas, and ideals'.[20] Despite the evidence of greater self-reflexivity and questioning within world history, it would seem that the field has for much of its organised life been driven by the demographic, economic, technological, and biological interests in Bentley's original list. Cultural history, issues of gender and race, and even some of the more traditional concerns of class-driven social history, are still not equally represented in the field. Their prevalence in postcolonial history, by contrast, continues to be a distinguishing feature between these two variants of global or transnational history.

In my own latest project on the ways in which historiographical understanding of the British Empire in the nineteenth and twentieth centuries has been shaped by feminist scholarship, I constantly found myself returning to evidence of the mobility of imperial culture.[21] Colonial rulers, colonised subjects, and specific vehicles of popular imperial culture circulated not only *from* the metropole, but *to* the metropole and between multiple imperial sites. Thus whether I was working on my chapter on the narratives of interracial sexual assault that were attached to crises of imperial rule in the latter nineteenth century and early twentieth century, or that on the connections between constructions of boyhood, masculinity and imperial wars, or that on the gendered politics of anti-colonial nationalisms, I kept seeing the ways in which events and narratives from one colonial site affected those in another. For my current work, then, a focus on the transnational is ineluctable. But whether we focus on the transnational as that which moved from colony to colony (or nation to nation), or that which belies constructed national boundaries by operating *within* their imagined parameters but not simply because of them, we must be clear about what

---

[20] Jerry H. Bentley 1990, 'A New Forum for Global History', *Journal of World History*, vol. 1, no. 1, p. iv.

[21] Angela Woollacott 2006, *Gender and Empire* (Basingstoke: Palgrave).

questions we are asking, why we are asking them, and what are our own investments in them.

And it is here that Ania Loomba's definition of postcolonialism is so relevant. Loomba points out, as have other critics, that colonialism is a continuing process that has survived declarations of political independence and nationhood. We need to be very clear that in many parts of the world 'the inequities of colonial rule have not been erased' and therefore 'it is perhaps premature to proclaim the demise of colonialism'.[22] Therefore, Loomba suggests, it is useful to see postcolonialism as 'the contestation of colonial domination and the legacies of colonialism', or 'a *process* of disengagement from the whole colonial syndrome'.[23] Catherine Hall's book stands out for its subjective honesty, and its clarity of personal investment and political purpose, qualities that I see as directly linked to its postcolonial transnational framework. At base, as *Civilising Subjects* exemplifies, postcolonial historical scholarship continues to be marked by the imperative to investigate the workings of colonialism in the past, and to expose their legacies for the present.

---

[22] Ania Loomba 1998, *Colonialism/Postcolonialism* (London: Routledge), p. 7.

[23] ibid., pp. 12, 19.

Migration and Other Voyages

5. Steal a handkerchief, see the world: the trans-oceanic voyaging of Thomas Limpus

Emma Christopher

In Geoffrey Blainey's seminal work *The Tyranny of Distance* the idea is present even in the title. For the early Europeans in Australia, he argues, their distance from their homeland was the 'tyranny' of their position, and that distance obviously involved the miles between land masses. The sea, by implication, was a void, a barrier to be crossed to another 'real' location. What is more, Blainey is uninterested in the experiences which had led the convicts across that watery non-place to their new home. It had apparently been covered as if in the blink of an eye. Distance was something that had just been imposed on them from above, rather than the seas being a space they had themselves inhabited directly before their appearance on the shores of Port Jackson. The journey was not a process which had informed their knowledge of the distance and established their new lives as residents of a new land, it was simply an abyss.[1]

This view of the sea as lacking any history of its own is currently being challenged in many fields of historiography. Derek Walcott's much-quoted line 'the sea is history' has become the clarion cry to avoid the kind of formulation unconsciously used by Blainey.[2] Increasingly the ocean is seen as the arena in which much transnational history was lived, rather than simply being the means by which internationalism was achieved. One recent edited collection, Bernhard Klein and Gesa Mackenthun's *Sea Changes: Historicizing the Ocean*, sets its task as moving 'beyond outworn patterns of historical causality and explanation ... to recover in the history of the sea a paradigm that may accommodate various revisionary accounts ... of the modern transnational experience of contact zones'.[3] The designation of the seas as 'other' in historical study is increasingly regarded, just like the 'othering' of groups of people throughout history, as unconstructive and subjective.[4] Yet much Australian convict scholarship seemingly remains

---

[1] Geoffrey Blainey 1968, *The Tyranny of Distance: How Distance Shaped Australia's History* (Melbourne: Macmillan).

[2] Derek Walcott 1979, 'The Sea is History', originally published in *The Star-Apple Kingdom* (New York, NY: Farrar, Straus and Giroux).

[3] Bernhard Klein and Gesa Mackenthun (eds) 2004, *Sea Changes: Historicizing the Ocean* (New York, NY: Routledge), p. 3.

[4] Philip E. Steinberg 2001, *The Social Construction of the Ocean* (Cambridge: Cambridge University Press), pp. 35-8.

tied to the idea that the long voyage out merely delivered – largely unchanged – British and Irish people to their new home in the southern hemisphere.

This is problematical, not just because of this current global focus on the sea as a historical arena, but also because of the realities of the early British settlement in Australia. It was, after all, a peculiarly maritime arrangement, ruled by the only naval governor who presided on land in the British realm. Early Sydney was a 'sailortown'.[5] What this suggests is that the protracted voyage to this settlement was hardly a non-time, but was rather a formative and transformative experience for those who were forced to make it to atone for their crimes. Time, life, experiences, these things did not stop while the voyage was made; the sea was not a watery chasm to be crossed to another 'real' place. It was, rather, the site of adjustment and alteration. To use rhetoric often utilised by the historiographies of other forms of non-free migration, the long voyage southward was the convict settlement's roots as well as the convicts' route.

This nautical characteristic of the early settlement was also one of the traits which set it apart from earlier sites of convict transportation, and this factor changed essentially the nature of the voyage felons embarked upon to reach it. Historicising the oceans in terms of convict studies reveals that it was not simply the destination that changed with the British settlement of New South Wales in 1788, but also the purpose of the voyage by which criminals were banished. The familiar discussions of the origins of European Australia – the loss of the American colonies, the attempts to find an African site for a penal settlement, plus various attempts to re-start the American trade – were not merely theoretical posturing, but were lived as experiences which preceded the First Fleet voyage for some of Australia's founding convicts. Their enforced transnationalism was enacted largely at sea, their familiarity with seagoing then becoming an integral part of the sailortown identity of early Sydney.

In this chapter I want to explore what the convict voyage across the sea meant to one man who, astonishingly, made three very different versions of it. Thomas Limpus is of interest because he was in many ways the archetypal convict – he was a handkerchief thief – but also because his experiences as a transported convict covered the whole realm of events which led to New South Wales. Of all the places commonly mentioned as background to the founding of the penal settlement – locations as diverse as North America, West Africa, and even the peripheral Honduras Bay settlement – Limpus had either been sent there or had narrowly escaped that fate. His route to Australia mirrored the complex twists debated by historians of 'the Botany Bay decision' but he *lived* these destinations;

---

[5] Alan Atkinson 1997, *The Europeans in Australia* (Melbourne: Oxford University Press), volume 1, pp. 37, 57, 110-115; Grace Karskens 1997, *The Rocks: Life in Early Sydney* (Melbourne: Melbourne University Press), pp. 183-94.

to him they were not merely abstract decisions imposed on Britain's miscreants from on high. He arrived in New South Wales not as a newly deported Briton, but as a man who – probably unbeknownst to him at that time – had just ended a segment of his life in which he had constantly been cast away from land. Life had already displayed to him that convict voyages could take many forms, that the sea was both punishment and escape, and that it was a place in which he could negotiate space for himself as an individual.

Thomas Limpus's first convict voyage

Thomas Limpus was in many ways a typical First Fleet convict. He had been sentenced to three years hard labour in 1777 at the age of fifteen for the theft of a handkerchief, so beginning his criminal career banished to an area between sea and land.[6] After the rebellion of the American colonies, hulks anchored on the Thames were established as a stop gap arrangement on which convicts were employed in moving gravel and filling pits, driving in posts to support new wharves, digging ditches and building drains. Although skilled prisoners might be put to other tasks, for the majority the work was monotonous and extremely arduous.[7] Unable to find a place 'beyond the seas' to which to banish the felons, the British government chose to at least settle them on the river, a space which was neither truly land nor sea. At the age of 15, Thomas Limpus's life as a man cast beyond the littoral had begun.

Three years later, back on dry land, he was again at the Old Bailey charged with stealing another handkerchief. It was probably the violence he showed at his arrest that set him on his destiny as international voyager. A witness to the theft said that he heard the watchman, Mr. Collins, 'halloo out Stop thief!' and heard Limpus swear 'damn his eyes, he would cut his bloody ... life out'. Knives were drawn, and Limpus had allegedly tried to cut the watchman. It was evidence enough to ensure that he was sentenced to be transported away from Britain's shores for a period of seven years.[8]

Limpus was sentenced to this particular punishment at a peculiar moment of penal history. With the American colonies already lost (though hope of them accepting British felons was not yet totally despaired of) the government was searching for a new place to receive the reprobates it wished to export. It turned to the outposts of British authority on the West African coast, principally in those years engaged in transatlantic slave trading. Although the leaders of the African Company and slaving merchants had vehemently resisted convicts being

---

[6] Mollie Gillen 1989, *The Founders of Australia: A Biographical Dictionary of the First Fleet* (Sydney: Library of Australian History), p. 221.

[7] Duncan Campbell Letterbooks, Mitchell Library, Sydney, A3230 f. 29a.

[8] Old Bailey Sessions Papers [hereafter OBSP] T17830910-41.

sent to their forts, they were perennially short of labour because of the catastrophic death rates among the white fort soldiers and guards. Eventually the British government circumvented their objections by sending several hundred convicts not as transported felons but by giving them respites to join the British Army. As such they had no different status to the regular soldiers and the African Company could offer no objection. Despite the fact that the army expedition was a total disaster, which ended with the majority either dying or deserting to the supposed enemy and their commander charged with murder, the British government continued its plans to transport convicts to West Africa.[9]

Thus Thomas Limpus had the misfortune to be convicted at the Old Bailey to seven years transportation, not merely to the unstipulated 'places beyond the seas', but to go specifically to Africa. He was to go to West Africa not as a soldier but simply as a transported felon, although what role he was supposed to fulfil there was unclear. Others who went aboard the same ship were to be soldiers at the African Company forts.[10] Moreover, the settlement at which Limpus disembarked had plenty of convict soldiers. Its governor, Joseph Wall, who would later be hanged for having some of those soldiers whipped to death by black slaves, described those he ruled over as 'generally regiments in disgrace for mutiny, deserting their colours, riot or some other cause'. 'Their ranks', he complained, were 'usually recruited by desperadoes, picked up from convicts from our gaols, or incorrigibles in our military prisons.'[11] Regardless, it was not Limpus's fate to be a fort soldier.

Strangely enough, at this point Limpus's story intersects with that of the twelve million plus captive Africans who were transported to the Americas. Searching for a vessel to take the convicts sentenced to Africa, a deal was struck with the owners of the *Den Keyser*, which would continue its voyage transporting Africans to be sold into slavery in perpetuity once the convicts had been delivered.[12] So Limpus was embarked with about forty other convicts 'chained two and two together' aboard one of the notorious slave trading fleet operating out of London at that time.[13] Among his shipmates were two other men who would later be First Fleeters to the colony of New South Wales. John Ruglass and Samuel Woodham had been part of a group of ten or so people who had robbed and

---

[9] The story of these convicts will be told in much more detail in my forthcoming book on this subject.

[10] John Petty, John Prime and John Soons went out on the *Den Keyser* to be soldiers at Commenda Fort. Papers of the Royal African Company for 1784, T 70/1550, National Archives of the UK, London [hereafter NA UK, formerly the PRO].

[11] *The Genuine and Impartial Memoirs of the Life of Governor Wall* (London: 1802), p. 9.

[12] David Eltis, David Richardson, Stephen D. Behrendt and Herbert S. Klein 1999, *The Trans-Atlantic Slave Trade: A Database on CD-ROM* (Cambridge: Cambridge University Press), voyage ID 80980.

[13] OBSP t17830910-41.

beaten a sailor who was newly arrived home from sixteen long years at sea, a crime for which they had originally been sentenced to death.[14] Another First Fleeter, John Martin, described as 'a negro' at his trial, narrowly escaped departing on the *Den Keyser* when he was returned to gaol too sick to travel.[15]

This, then, delivered to a slave ship anchored in the Thames, chained by the legs to another convict, was Thomas Limpus's first experience of convict transportation. Perhaps the convict to whom he had originally been chained had been the black man John Martin. Of course it is not possible to push this analogy too far: British convicts were never slaves. Yet in the uncertainties inherent in their destination, and a lack of knowledge of what was expected of them, there were some strange parallels. Even the fact that their position was temporary rather than theirs to suffer ceaselessly had little reality when very few British men survived for seven years in West Africa. 'Beware beware the Bight of Benin, for one that comes out, there's forty go in' said the seamen's ballad. The *Den Keyser* was not delivering its white cargo to the Bight of Benin, but that was probably little comfort to Limpus, even if he was aware of it.

Beyond these shared experiences, however, it is evident that there is no comparison between the nature of the voyage endured by Limpus and his fellow convicts, and that made by the 300 or so African slaves the ship would transport later on its voyage.[16] The difference was not chiefly the humanity shown (or rather the lack thereof) but in the very purpose of the voyage. In fact, while the *Den Keyser* was a slaving vessel, the function of convict and slave voyages had actually been more similar during the period of transportation to the American colonies when the captain and crew of a ship had a financial interest in the labour of banished British felons. On this occasion, the rationale behind sending the convicts to Africa was ambiguous, and while a fiscal deal had been struck between the British government and the ship's owners and contractors, the crew of the ship were told merely that the shackled passengers were felons who had to go to Africa. John Townsend, who worked for Akerman the keeper of Newgate, later recounted that he had been one of the men who took the prisoners to the port to board their vessel. Once they had 'delivered them safe, and they ironed them, and put them in the hold' the entire duties of the crown and its employees was seemingly discharged.[17] This was truly the moment at which the convict voyage was itself intended as punishment, with each nautical mile covered representing the entire purpose of the venture.

---

[14] OBSP t17810425-49; OBSP t17810530-52; PCOM 2/169 and PCOM 2/170 NA UK.

[15] OBSP T17820703-5.

[16] Eltis et al. 1999, *Trans-Atlantic Slave Trade*, voyage ID 80980.

[17] OBSP t17830910-41.

This uncertainty about the nature of the *Den Keyser's* voyage to Africa was evident in events after arrival, for it delivered convicts to at least three locations to fulfil vastly different roles. Thomas Limpus and about nineteen other convicts were the first to be disembarked, leaving the ship not at Cape Coast Castle, the centre of British slave trading on the West African coast and the destination of most of the transported convicts, but rather in the Senegambia region, probably at Fort St Louis. Exactly where the notorious governor Joseph Wall was when Limpus and the others disembarked is uncertain, but his harsh, chaotic rule is certainly evident behind stories of what happened next. Captain Lacey, who appears to have been as antagonistic to others as his superior officer, having already been challenged to a number of duels, ordered the convicts to be 'drawn up in a circle on the parade'.[18] According to Thomas Limpus, he then 'told us we were all free men, and that we were to do the best we could, for he had no victuals'. John Ruglass said simply that Lacey 'had sent them off' and they were forced to go and fight for their survival as best they could.[19] The uncertainty inherent in the purpose of the voyage, apparent from the moment John Townsend had delivered them with no instructions other than to take them to Africa, had reached its logical conclusion. The voyage had achieved no objective other than to remove the men from Britain, and that, and abandonment, was to be their punishment.

Limpus turned his face back towards the seas. With few other options, he went on board a British ship that was in the river at that time. Going ashore several times he did some work for Governor Wall but ultimately chose to sail away with the ship when she weighed anchor rather than stay behind. It was still wartime, and the French and Dutch, were all around the coast. As he plaintively later put it, 'I did not chuse to go into the hands of the enemy'.[20] Limpus had learned what many before him also had, that the sea could provide escape as well as incarceration. His words also suggest another truth: ships were small outposts of the mother country. They could return him to his homeland, but they also, in another sense, were part of that country floating on the deep blue sea.

John Ruglass and Samuel Woodham also decided on a similar step to Limpus. Having originally been sentenced together, they very probably escaped together, almost certainly also taking passage on a ship that arrived in the area. They may well have had seafaring experience despite being very young, as they had lived and committed their original crime among London's seafaring community.[21]

---

[18] CO 267/20 ff. 373, National Archives, UK; OBSP T17830910-41; OBSP S17841208-1.
[19] Ibid.
[20] Ibid.
[21] OBSP t17810530-52.

Ironically it could well have been a slave ship (or ships) that took away all three men, for they often stopped in the Senegambia region on their way down to the larger slave trading ports of the coast and often needed additional hands to replace seamen who were already dead. So the men who had been despatched from their homelands on a slave ship learned the vagaries of the seafaring life. It was a fact many a seaman – falling foul of his captain or being taken a prisoner of war – had also learned. The gap between chained captive and useful crew member could be very slim indeed.

Unfortunately for Limpus, his freedom was to be short lived. While the ship was temporarily docked in London he was seen by men who knew him to be a banished felon and he was sentenced for having returned from transportation. When he was charged at the Old Bailey, he said that he had only returned to England temporarily and unavoidably; he had planned on to go back to sea with the same captain that had enlisted him in Africa.[22] Indeed, his pleas were not unreasonable. The exact nature of what was expected of a transported convict was in dispute for long after the 1780s, and technically a man did just have to leave the shores of Britain for the term imposed. Of course he should not have been in London, but a seaman's life was clearly reconcilable with the idea of banishment for long periods. Convicts had in recent history been offered respites to serve in the Royal Navy, and occasionally even the merchant marine.[23] Perhaps Limpus had been held in Newgate with men who had exchanged their death sentences for the seafaring profession. Whatever the reasons for his plea, clearly the man who had been loaded on a slave ship, chained by the ankles to a companion, had come to regard the sea as a potential refuge as well as a fate to be endured. He hoped that banishing himself not to a 'place beyond the seas' but to the seas themselves would mollify the British government.

The second voyage

It was not to be. He was sentenced to death for returning from transportation, a fate which was then commuted to transportation for life. This time, as before, there was a specific destination mentioned, but this time it was America.[24] Part of a defiant attempt to get the Americas to again accept British offenders, Limpus was embarked on the *Mercury,* a ship which, following in the wake of the earlier *Swift*, would try to disembark convicts in the rebellious colonies. The subterfuge was that they claimed to be destined for Nova Scotia, but would then put in to Baltimore, Maryland, announcing that they were too short of water or provisions

---

[22] OBSP t17830910-41.

[23] See, for example, HO 42/1 f.475; HO 42/12 f.260; HO 42/35 f.351 NA UK. There are also countless examples in the Duncan Campbell letterbooks, Mitchell Library, Sydney.

[24] OBSP T17830910-41.

to make the more northerly destination.[25] And so Thomas Limpus again embarked on a ship, this time not as a working member of the crew as he had hoped and planned, but once more as a captive held below decks.

This voyage was an attempt by the British government to return to the past, to revert to paying private contractors to remove convicts sentenced to transportation who would then have a fiscal stake in their labour power. Before the American Revolution, banished criminals had been privately owned by masters in the Americas, with many convict ships selling their labour power to the highest bidder after arrival. Although their situation was never directly akin to that of African and African-American slaves, there was far more similarity in the intention of the voyages. Both convict transports and slave ships transported men, women and children to labour elsewhere, and sold them after arrival to those needing labourers.[26] For those engaged as captain and crew of such vessels, part of their job was to deliver the 'goods' in such a condition that they would return the best price.

The contractor for the *Mercury,* George Moore, had the same scheme in mind. He had arranged to take the prisoners, Limpus included, with the idea of profiting financially from their export. In fact it was to prove a gross miscalculation, with the *Mercury* not permitted to disembark its prisoners at any of its intended ports of call. The authorities in Maryland were still smarting from an earlier attempt to pass off convicts from the *Swift* as indentured servants and refused to let it land its passengers.[27] It then sailed for the Honduras Bay settlement in Central America, where despite an acute need for additional labour, the convicts were once again unwanted, the settlers fearing that they 'would damage the credit and character of the country'.[28] Moore's gamble had not paid off, but for those who sailed on the *Mercury* their experiences of the voyage, until its disastrous

---

[25] Bob Reece 2001, *The Origins of Irish Convict Transportation to New South Wales* (Hampshire: Palgrave), pp. 67-9.

[26] Jed Martin 1975, 'Convict Transportation to Newfoundland in 1789', *Acadiensis*, vol. 5, no. 1, pp. 84-99; Eugene I. McCormac 1904, *White Servitude in Maryland, 1634–1820* (Baltimore, MD: Johns Hopkins Press), pp. 42, 61, 99; Kenneth Morgan 1985, 'The Organization of the Convict Trade to Maryland: Stevenson, Randolph and Cheston, 1768–1775', *William and Mary Quarterly* 3rd series, vol. XLII, pp. 201-7; Stephen Nicholas and Peter R. Shergold 1988, 'Transportation as Global Migration', in Stephen Nicholas (ed.), *Convict Workers: Interpreting Australia's Past* (Cambridge: Cambridge University Press), pp. 29-38; F. H. Schmidt 1986, 'Sold and Driven: Assignment of Convicts in Eighteenth-Century Virginia', *Push from the Bush*, vol. 23, October, pp. 2-27.

[27] A. Roger Ekirch 1984, 'Great Britain's Secret Convict Trade to America, 1783–1784', *American Historical Review*, vol. 89, no. 2, pp. 1285-91.

[28] John Alder Burdon 1931, *Archives of British Honduras* (London: Sifton, Praed and Co.), vol. 1, pp. 146-8.

end, would have been similar to earlier generations of criminals sent to the Americas. The sea crossing was designed to deliver much needed workers and to create a profit for the contractors. The punishment was in the loss of control over their personal autonomy and the fruits of their future toil, and for this they had to be prepared for their 'sale' to a master.

For Thomas Limpus, however, whatever his experiences as a man being prepared for the sale of his labour power, they were short lived. He had in fact left the ship long before it reached Maryland and the Honduras Bay settlement. Only four days after the ship departed from England some of the convicts had mutinied and temporarily captured the vessel from the captain and crew. It is not clear what part Limpus took in these proceedings, but it is possible that his previous work aboard ships had given him just the kind of knowledge, and even possibly anti-authoritarian spirit, which the mutineers needed. The rebels first steered for Ireland and then Spain before finally coming to rest in Devon. There the majority, including Limpus, escaped.[29]

Quickly recaptured, Limpus, along with many other of his fellow *Mercury* escapees, was provisionally imprisoned in Exeter gaol. However, this was not designed to take such a large sudden influx of inmates and was sorely overcrowded. Fearing that 'infectious Distempers' would break out, or that they would attempt a mass escape, and unsure where to banish them to, they were removed to the *Dunkirk* hulk.[30] Limpus was again at sea, if this time anchored just offshore.

The government, of course, had not finished trying to banish Thomas Limpus. By a strange twist of fate, the place they had in mind was the one from which he had already escaped. Yet the experiences of Limpus and his fellow transports in Africa had obviously not gone completely unnoticed, because by this time transportation to Africa was considered to be a far worse fate than America. As the admiralty itself put it, 'in the routine of Punishment' Africa was 'considered as next in degree to that of Death'.[31] Even the authorities baulked at the punishment, questioning whether they should suffer 'so severe a sentence as Transportation thither'.[32] The problem, therefore, was clear. If convicts taken to Africa simply died, as so many had, or escaped, there was no justifiable objective. As Limpus's earlier voyage on the *Den Keyser* had illustrated, there was nothing constructive in merely dumping men and women onto another

---

[29] Ekirch 1984, 'Great Britain's Secret Convict Trade to America'; Reece 2001, *Irish Convict Transportation*, p. 69; HO 42/4 f.166 NA UK.

[30] Letter from Lord Sydney, 29 May 1784, ADM 1/1451, NA UK; Letter of J. P. Bastard to Admiralty, 5 November 1784, ADM 1/1451, NA UK.

[31] Admiralty to John Nicol, Mayor of Plymouth, 29 December 1784, HO 42/5, ff.461-2, NA UK.

[32] ibid.

continent. A sea crossing was not, in itself, what the convicts were sentenced to, the government had obviously decided. It had to be a means to an end; it had to be fulfilling part of a larger aim. In the end the admiralty advised the Mayor of Plymouth that a general sentence of banishment 'beyond the seas' would be the best solution for the recaptured *Mercury* mutineers like Limpus.[33]

The third voyage: the First Fleet

Ultimately, of course, the Botany Bay proposal was adopted and once it was embraced the former *Mercury* mutineers waiting on the *Dunkirk* hulk were among the first to be earmarked for the new scheme. Once again, Limpus was among those chosen. For transportation to his third intended continent of banishment he was sent aboard the *Charlotte* in early 1787. Many other *Mercury* veterans were also embarked on the vessels of the First Fleet. Among them were Robert Sidaway who would later part-own Sydney's first theatre; the youngest of the male convicts on the First Fleet, John Hudson, who had been only nine years old when convicted at the Old Bailey in 1873; and James Cox, who would later daringly escape Sydney with the Bryant party.[34] Also embarked on the First Fleet vessels were John Ruglass and Samuel Woodham, Limpus's old *Den Keyser* shipmates who had avoided the *Mercury* fiasco but now were again in chains awaiting shipment.

It is only at this point, then, that Thomas Limpus fits into the usual stories of early Australia. Yet this was clearly not a man who shrieked with fear at the noises of the First Fleet weighing anchor, or who necessarily lamented his homeland fearing he would never return. So how was the long First Fleet voyage experienced by a man like Thomas Limpus? Firstly, it becomes clear that the differences the Botany Bay scheme had from earlier plans, such as the idea to form a settlement in the Gambia River at Lemane Island, were not merely abstract arguments. Certainly to those like Limpus, Ruglass and Woodham, and probably also to many who had narrowly escaped the fate of being abandoned in the Honduran backwoods, it would have been apparent from the outset that this scheme was different. They would not just be deserted, for if that was the plan, surely the British government would not have gone to so much trouble outfitting the fleet, and providing personnel for it. Among the arguments as to whether the penal colony in the southern hemisphere was founded for strategic reasons or merely as a place to get rid of the convicts crowding the gaols, few would

---

[33] ibid.

[34] Gillen 1989, *Founders of Australia*, pp. 434-5; Robert Jordan 2002, *The Convict Theatres of Early Australia, 1788–1840* (New South Wales: Currency House), pp. 250-5; Robert Holden 1999, *Orphans of History: The Forgotten Children of the First Fleet* (Melbourne: Text Publishing), pp. 77-85, 205.

disagree that before the felons embarked on their vessels, the plan had become one of colonisation.[35]

The scale of the arrangements for the First Fleet undoubtedly gave Thomas Limpus a view of this venture different from that of his two earlier convict voyages. It would have been apparent in the time spent outfitting the fleet, the presence of soldiers and even the fact that there were women convicts, that this was a different type of venture. New South Wales was, to be sure, an unknown quantity and was much further away than Africa or America, but from the first the experience must have been different to being put on a slave ship where the crew had no instructions but to dump them where they could. Compared to being abandoned to Africa's deadly disease-ridden environment and feared native peoples, Thomas Limpus's role in the new venture perhaps seemed oddly certain. He was, at least, wanted alive, and his labour power had value.

The organisation, peopling, medical care and victualling of the First Fleet were in large part due to Arthur Phillip, who clearly intended the voyage of the First Fleet ships to have a very different function from oceanic passages made in earlier eras of convict transportation. He aimed to deliver men and women as potential colonists, people who would be useful to Britain from afar. This approach was the origin of the horror at the time of the arrival of the Second Fleet in 1790 – a fleet infamously outfitted by slave traders. Phillip's complaint at the condition of the Second Fleet is telling, for his objections were practical as well as humanitarian. 'Many of those now received are in such situation from old complaints, and so emaciated from what they have suffered in the Voyage, that they never will be capable for any Labour', he wrote.[36] At a time when the fledgling colony desperately needed supplies and a fresh input of workers, he was greatly alarmed that the merchants and captains of the Second Fleet had misunderstood what was required of convict transportation. Its primary function, he seemed to be saying, was not to punish men and women, but to deliver workers.

What this meant on an individual level was that because the nature of the voyage was different to his prior experiences as a transported felon, Limpus could almost certainly negotiate a different space for himself than he had previously. Neither the kind of freedom he had claimed after his abandonment in Africa, nor the slack control which had allowed the mutiny on the *Mercury* would be found during the First Fleet's journey, but there were other advantages. In a colony which would depend on those who were sent off in chains, men like Thomas

---

[35] Alan Atkinson 1990, 'The First Plans for Governing New South Wales, 1786–87', *Australian Historical Studies*, vol. 24, no. 94, pp. 22-40; Alan Frost 1980, *Convict and Empire: A Naval Question* (Melbourne: Oxford University Press), pp. 34-40.

[36] Phillip to the Admiralty, 13.7.1790, T 1/694, NA UK.

Limpus who had seafaring experience were perhaps the most immediately useful of all. Throughout the era convict men were repeatedly put to work in assisting the seamen during the long voyage to Australia. The skills Limpus had gained, or honed, during the years of his banishment were now of use in the new settlement.

In negotiating these particularised spaces, a new 'Australian' culture began to be formed. It had roots between the wooden walls of the convict transports as they crossed the seas, and it borrowed from seafaring culture, not abandoning those traits when it reached the shore. This was partly because of Phillip's rule, for as a naval man he knew that seamen's ethics could not be overlooked. But maritime culture was also adopted by the convicts, among whom those who had been seamen often had positions of privilege or esteem.[37] Seafaring skills would be a nexus through which status could be bargained and which could often grant personal latitude on the edges of the close control of the new settlement, and former convicts with seafaring skills were often put in places of authority.

Thomas Limpus did not succeed in returning to his homeland a third time – he died on Norfolk Island prior to 1801 – but we can suspect that he never gave up hope that he might.[38] Certainly his trans-oceanic voyages as a British convict had not been blank periods of time; rather they had been part of his formative experiences. He embarked on the First Fleet vessel *Charlotte* not as a landlubber forced to sea for his trifling crimes, but as a man who had already experienced two other convict voyages which were destined not only for separate continents, but which had different intentions altogether. By the time he arrived in Botany Bay he could well have learned to use the sea as a site of refuge, a means of rebellion, and to see seafaring culture as a source of alternative authority. He was one of those who ensured that New South Wales was a sailortown in its earliest years. Far from having descended on Port Jackson to forever lament the distance of his homeland, the salt water which rushed through the heads and lapped the shores of Sydney harbour had been his home for some time and he had carved out for himself a status at sea. To Thomas Limpus, the sea definitely had a history, for it was an integral part of his own life story. It is time that historians of the convict trade examined the extent to which that maritime life story was replicated in various ways throughout the early colony. In so doing they might begin the process of unlocking the sea's untold history.

---

[37] Atkinson 1990, *Europeans in Australia,* especially chapter 6.

[38] Gillen 1989, *Founders of Australia*, p. 221.

6. Revolution and respectability: Chinese Masons in Australian history

John Fitzgerald

> The Chinese now are all Freemasons, and form one brotherhood. The old Emperor and his son are Chinese Tartars, and the new emperor intends to carry out all one brotherhood.
>
> – Howqua, Chinese interpreter, Melbourne 1855.[1]

Introduction

In 1911 a lodge of the international Hung League opened an impressive building in Mary Street, Sydney, looking west along Campbell Street towards Paddy's Markets where many of its members earned their livelihood. The Hung League – or Triads as they are often known in English – had grown over the five decades since setting foot in colonial Australia from a loose affiliation of rural clubs into an organised social network with a prominent urban profile. With the opening of its new headquarters in Sydney, the New South Wales Hung League put on a respectable public face under the English title impressed on the building's façade: Chinese Masonic Society.

Mounting a respectable public face was a considerable achievement for an organisation that all 'decent' people were inclined to deride as thieves, thugs, and opium addicts. Not long before the Sydney Masonic Hall was opened, members of the more respectable See Yup native-place association[2] in Victoria took objection to the criminal behaviour and stand-over tactics of the Hung League in Melbourne and established a rival league to do battle with the triad fraternity. Gangs took to fighting one another in the streets. Sydney also had its share of Tong Wars but these were well behind it when the Hung League

---

[1] 'Commission appointed to enquire into the conditions of the goldfields of Victoria', (1855). Reprinted in Ian McLaren (ed.) 1985, *The Chinese in Victoria: Official Reports and Documents* (Melbourne: Red Rooster Press), pp. 6-14, especially p. 14.

[2] Native place associations were established by people migrating within China or overseas to Southeast Asia, Australasia and the Americas to provide common sites of worship, enduring social networks, and practical assistance to members. Membership was based on a migrant's town, county, or district of origin. The See Yup Association was the largest native place organisation in Victoria embracing natives from four districts ('see yup' in Cantonese) south of the provincial capital of Canton.

announced it was emerging in public as a Masonic Society.[3] The Chinese Masonic Society of NSW was working to become the kind of organisation that respectable men would consider joining.

The ideal of respectability was one of the most powerful forces working for social transformation among immigrant communities in federation Australia. Drawing on the work of British social historians, Janet McCalman has observed that a cluster of social traits associated with the idea of respectability (including self-reliance, independence, and self-discipline) were popularised among all classes in the industrial revolution before being transplanted to Australia 'by immigrants hoping for dignity and prosperity in a new land'.[4] The struggle for respectability crossed class, gender and ethnic lines among the inner-urban communities that staffed and ran the factories, utilities, wharves, warehouses and markets of early twentieth century Australian cities. Immigrants who did not harbour aspirations for modern respectability before they arrived were not long in acquiring them after arrival. Children of immigrants from the pre-industrial counties of Ireland, for example, struggled to escape the stigma that attached to the name 'Bog Irish'. Incentives for achieving respectability were particularly strong in societies where migrating settlers from England, Scotland, and Ireland mixed with one another (and with the occasional Russian or Chinese) to a degree rarely replicated in their countries of origin. Opportunities beckoned not only for prosperity but also for achieving equal recognition for themselves, their families, and their particular religious and ethnic communities.[5]

Despite its attempts to achieve respectability the Hung League has yet to gain recognition that its growth and transformation were in any sense comparable to those of other community organisations transplanted to Australia in the nineteenth and twentieth centuries. This chapter questions both Australian and Chinese historiography, and uses a transnational approach to develop a new interpretation of the origins, history, and significance of the Hung League. In seeking explanations for the organisation and conduct of Chinese secret societies it is tempting to look to China for motives and precedents; certainly the rules, rituals, hierarchies, and patterns of internal organisation of secret societies were similar from one place to another. But when the New South Wales (NSW) Hung

---

[3] C. F. Yong 1977, *The New Gold Mountain: The Chinese in Australia 1901–1921* (Richmond, SA: Raphael Arts); Shirley Fitzgerald 1997, *Red Tape, Gold Scissors: The Story of Sydney's Chinese* (Sydney: NSW State Library Press).

[4] Janet McCalman 1985, *Struggletown: Public and Private Life in Richmond 1900–1965* (Carlton: Melbourne University Press), p. 22.

[5] Charles Taylor 2004, *Modern Social Imaginaries* (Durham and London: Duke University Press). For an excellent summary see his 2004 article 'Modern Social Imaginaries', *Public Culture*, vol. 14, no. 1, pp. 91-124.

League went public under the title Chinese Masonic Society it was responding to forces at work not in China but in Sydney, and possibly also in Auckland and San Francisco. The NSW League sought recognition of the rightful place of a Chinese community organisation in a European settler country and it sought acknowledgment that the working men of the Hung League were no less decent than the Chinese-Australians who looked down on them. By focusing on the distinctive local features of secret societies in Australia, rather than turning to China for generic explanations, we gain some sense of what was 'Australian' about Chinese-Australian communities, and we open a window on federation Australia that goes beyond the spectre of a closed and autarkic European enclave that wanted, above all, to keep Chinamen out.

The argument of this chapter is not entirely consistent with Chinese historiography of secret societies either. The role ascribed to secret society networks in China's republican revolution is circumscribed by two common assumptions. One is that secret societies were essentially social in their aims, character and activities. The other is that their limited political aspirations never rose above atavistic notions of imperial restoration, as is suggested in Howqua's deposition to the Victorian commission in 1855, which begins this chapter, specifically referring to the overthrow of the Manchu 'Tartars' and the substitution of a native Han Chinese emperor who could realise the League's aspirations for egalitarian brotherhood. It follows from both these assumptions that if and when secret societies were to come out on the side of the republican revolution they needed to be prodded along by Sun Yatsen's republican movement, which introduced modern nationalism to the Hung League and converted its members into proto-revolutionary allies for the republicans' assault on the Qing Empire.

The notion that modern revolutionary ideologies needed to be imported into overseas secret society networks from outside the networks themselves is not borne out by the Australian case. To be sure, the Chinese Masonic Society of New South Wales is not generally known for engaging in partisan political activities. By reputation it is a community organisation that provides social support for its members, that takes a patriotic stand on current events in China, and that occasionally engages in stand-over tactics against those who deny its authority. A similar reputation attaches to national branches of the Hung League in North America and Southeast Asia. In the Australian colonies, however, members of the Hung League appear to have been capable of politicising and depoliticising themselves, and to have borrowed as freely from Anglo-Australian institutional networks as they did from Sun Yatsen's Chinese nationalist organisations. The Chinese Masonic network of New South Wales had an indigenous revolutionary history long before it adopted a respectable public face. Further, there is reason to believe that the Australian Masonic network was *deradicalised* by the time Sun Yatsen's nationalist movement rose to prominence. In New South Wales, when republican nationalists called upon local lodges of the Hung League to support their revolution, they confronted not atavistic notions of imperial restoration but rather an organisation that had shrugged off a revolutionary past and had come to embrace the Australian ethic of egalitarian respectability.

Evidence for this argument is summoned from two sets of sources. The first includes an oral legend about an early leader of the NSW Hung League who died in 1874 and the historical records of his followers in south China later in that century. The second set relates to the consolidation of a statewide Chinese Masonic network early in the twentieth century and to its links with English, Scottish and Irish Freemasonry.

History and legend

Today the triangle of lanes that encloses the Chinese Masonic building at the eastern end of Campbell Street has been left behind in Sydney's conversion into a world city. At the western end, Paddy's Market now encases a three-star hotel, a four-star university, and a five-star residential development emblazoned with advertisements in Chinese characters. When the building opened in 1911 the eastern end was almost as prosperous as the west. A parade of storehouses, restaurants, and civic associations bearing Chinese characters ran along Campbell Street between the new Masonic Hall and the brick colonnades of Paddy's Markets. Just around the corner from the new building, at the eastern tip of Campbell Street, sat the small but popular Chinese Christian mission church of the Rev. John Young Wai. The opening of the Mary Street headquarters placed the Chinese Masonic Society at the heart of Chinese-Australian community life in the recently federated states of Australia.

Today the Masonic Hall stands as a monument to a time when the Hung League was an organisation of some standing in the community – a time when Chinese-language newspapers were edited and printed on its ground floor, when business was transacted over Oolong Tea on the second, and when secret rituals were enacted and vendettas plotted in the closeted chambers of the third floor. None could cross the threshold to the third floor but sworn brothers who had vowed to keep the secrets of the fraternity and to defend each other's honour unto death. The ground floor reception hall of the Mary Street headquarters bears little trace of the partitioned offices and printing presses that once marked out its busy floor plan. The floorboards have been resurfaced, the walls repainted, and tables and chairs are laid out to welcome guests. But a number of old images pinned to the walls still bear messages conveying the spirit of solidarity, justice, patriotism, masculinity, and egalitarian defiance that characterised the Chinese Masonic network from its earliest days in Australia.

To the right of the reception hall hangs a framed photograph of General Cai Tingkai, the general who defied Generalissimo Chiang Kaishek when he took on battalions of Japanese military invaders in 1931 and founded an independent People's Government in Fujian in 1934. The Australian Masonic Society invited General Cai to tour Australia in March 1935 and meet with Chinese-Australians who shared his contempt for Chiang Kaishek's strategy of fighting Communists in preference to resisting Japanese invaders. The photograph on the wall bears a signed message from General Cai thanking the Sydney Masonic headquarters for its assistance in arranging his visit.

To the left hangs a large framed watercolour of the legendary 108 outlaws of the Liangshan marshes, one of the many fabulous sources to which Chinese lodges trace their eclectic liturgy of beliefs and rituals. Legend has it that seven centuries ago this band of outlaws professed principles of loyalty and justice while upholding an ideal of universal brotherhood – that 'all men are brothers' to borrow the title of Pearl Buck's popular translation of the legend.[6] The 108 outlaws swore oaths of loyalty to one another that they would struggle for justice in the face of corrupt authority.

Like their outlaw heroes, members of the Chinese Masonic network were partial to the trappings of higher orders albeit domesticated into ritual hierarchies of honour and loyalty to which any member could aspire. They also practised collective discipline. A member found guilty of breaking the code of conduct was liable to receive 108 beatings with a cane, a form of punishment that was possibly more familiar to colonial readers of court columns in nineteenth century Australian newspapers than it is to kung-fu movie fans today. In 1896, for example, Victorian newspapers closely followed a case involving 108 beatings which came before the local bench in Bendigo, Victoria, after a certain Lee Fook gave evidence for the prosecution in a criminal case against a sworn brother. For this violation of the code Lee was allegedly summoned before a meeting of 200 brothers and sentenced to a punishment of 108 lashes.[7] Similar punishment was possibly inflicted in ritual spaces on the third floor of the Sydney headquarters. The painting of 108 heroes of Liangshan which hangs prominently on the ground floor serves as a reminder to members of the egalitarian and heterodox values that bound them together and of the punishments that awaited them if they violated the code.

On the far wall, facing the entrance, hangs a set of framed scrolls boldly scripted in large characters. Two vertical scrolls hang left and right, the one on the right reading 'Exert effort for the Hung League through commitment to loyalty and justice', and the one on the left, 'Sacrifice personal interests for the common

---

[6] Pearl Buck, translator, 1937, *All Men Are Brothers* (London: Methuen).

[7] *Bendigo Advertiser*, 17 April and 10 August 1896.

good in working for the Lodge'. Between the two vertical scrolls hangs a large horizontal work of calligraphy framed behind glass. It reads:

> Our history can be traced to the two Grand Lodges
> Our prestige reaches out forever through branches overseas
> Hung League brothers are all loyal and just
> With one heart protecting the Chinese Masonic Lodge [*Zhigongtang*][8]

Tracing the history of the Australian Chinese Masonic network to the 'Two Grand Lodges' in China leaves unanswered many of the questions we might like to ask about the arrival and expansion of the network in colonial and federation Australia. For this we need to consult local legend and Australian historical records.

Legend has it that the precursor of the Chinese Masonic Association, known variously as the Yee Hing or Gee Hing Company as well as the Hung League, came to Australia in the trail of the Taiping and Red Turban rebellions that shook south China in the middle of the nineteenth century. One fable that circulated in Melbourne, Victoria, tells of a Taiping leader by the name of Tock Gee (Huang Dezhi) who fled with his followers in a fleet of small boats from South China to Darwin, before leading them south to seek their fortunes on the goldfields of western Victoria. Tock Gee was known colloquially in Melbourne as the King for Pacifying the South in the Chinese rebel forces.[9] In the Victorian version of the legend Tock Gee is remembered as founder of the southern goldfields chapters of the order in Australia. Another legend emanating from New South Wales tells of an anti-Qing leader by the name of Loong Hung Pung (Long Xingbang) who led hundreds of his comrades to goldfields in the western districts of the colony and there laid the foundations for the NSW lodge of the fellowship.

Historians are properly sceptical of legend. In the Victorian case, there was certainly a man by the name of Tock Gee who passed under the nickname of King for Pacifying the South within the Melbourne Masonic organisation. But there is little evidence to support the claim that Tock Gee led rebel forces in south China before migrating to Australia. Historians are also sceptical of the NSW legend of Loong Hung Pung. In a path-breaking study of Chinese-Australian history, C. F. Yong noted in passing that a certain Loong Hung Pung was

---

[8] The characters for the three scrolls hanging in the main hall are transcribed on the opening page of *Aozhou zhigong zongtang yibai wushinian jinian tekan* [Special commemorative publication marking the 150th anniversary of the General Headquarters of the Chinese Masonic Association of Australia] (Sydney: Chinese Masonic Association, 2004), p. 1.

[9] Alfred Grieg Papers, Royal Historical Society of Victoria. Sophie Couchman brought this written version of the legend to my attention. Oral versions of the legend are still recounted among elderly members of Melbourne's Chinese community.

rumoured to have headed a group of anti-Manchu revolutionaries in Australia in the 1850s and to have cultivated a group of devoted followers who oversaw the development of the underground NSW network over the second half of the nineteenth century. There Yong leaves the legend much as he found it. Loong Hung Pung rates no further mention in his history of Australian Chinese communities in the late nineteenth and early twentieth centuries.[10] In Yong's view 'better documented accounts' confirm the pedigree of two other leaders, John Moy Sing (Mei Dongxing) and James A Chuey (Huang Zhu), as founders and organisers of the brotherhood in New South Wales from the 1850s to the 1920s.[11]

To date, the founding of the parent lodge in nineteenth century New South Wales has been attributed to these two community leaders who brought the underground rural network into the open in Sydney and built the grand Masonic Hall in Mary Street over the first decade of the twentieth century. Around the turn of the century the NSW Masonic network went under the name of the Hongshuntang (Hung obedience hall) which was derived from the title of the Cantonese Lodge in China.[12] Within a decade, we noted, the organisation ventured into the wider English-speaking arena under the English title of Chinese Masonic Society.[13] In June 1916, the Hongshuntang adopted another Chinese title, the *Zhonghua minguo gonghui* (Chinese Republican Association) to keep pace with a similar change of name on the part of the organisation's general headquarters in Hong Kong.[14] Three years later, the Sydney office adopted yet another Chinese name, the Chee Kong Tong (Exert Public Benefit Lodge) in keeping with the title adopted some years earlier by the United States branch

---

[10] Yong 1977, *New Gold Mountain*, pp. 157-8.

[11] The Sydney lodge supports the leadership sequence but not the timing of succession set out in Yong's work. The official genealogy reads as follows: John Moy Sing (1854–1898), James Chuey (1898–1930), Yu Bin (1930–1957), Guo Zilin (1957–1960), Lau Ting (1960–1993), Stephen Huang (1993–). See *Aozhou zhigong zongtang yibai wushinian jinian tekan* [Special commemorative publication marking the 150th anniversary of the General Headquarters of the Chinese Masonic Association of Australia] (Sydney: Chinese Masonic Association, 2004), pp. 26-7.

[12] *Hongshantang* was the name of the Guangdong Lodge of the Hung League network, distinguishing it from the Fujian Lodge or *Qingliangtang* (Green Lotus Hall) and other provincial lodges of the network. See Irene Lim 1999, *Secret Societies in Singapore* (Singapore: National Heritage Board). The first appearance of the title *Hongshantang* in Australian public life is unclear. The name was used in newspaper publicity by the 1910s. See for example *Minguo bao* [Chinese Republic News], 12 November 1916.

[13] Yong 1977, *New Gold Mountain*, p. 160.

[14] *Minguo bao* [Chinese Republic News], 12 November 1916.

office based in San Francisco.[15] Despite these changes to its formal Chinese designation, the organisation retained its informal titles of Hung Men and Yee Hing in colloquial Chinese parlance and retained its formal English title of Chinese Masonic Society without interruption.

These changes in the English and formal Chinese titles of the Masonic network coincided with the leadership transition from Moy Sing to James Chuey, who between them oversaw the transformation of the network from a loose rural affiliation of secret-society lodges into a more tightly focused urban institution with a prominent public profile. Moy Sing is credited with founding the parent organisation around the mid-nineteenth century. C. F. Yong regards Moy Sing as the founder of the organisation from its establishment in 1858 to his retirement in 1913, when James Chuey is assumed to have succeeded him in office.[16]

Elsewhere I have questioned the claim that Moy Sing was the sole founder of the NSW Chinese Masonic network and have pressed a rival (or complementary) claim for the legendary figure of Loong Hung Pung.[17] Put simply, I have suggested that a number of loosely-related lodges were founded at different goldfield sites and tin mines from the middle of the nineteenth century. Moy Sing certainly played a key role in consolidating these rural lodges into a statewide network based at his Sydney headquarters over the federation period. Indeed he based the lodge at his private home for a spell before the Mary Street headquarters was completed.[18] There is little evidence to suggest that any significant lodges operated in Sydney before this time. There were however a number of lodges in rural NSW. Up to the 1880s almost ninety percent of Chinese immigrants lived in rural settlements and regional townships in the Australian colonies. They based their lodges at the same rural sites.[19] The early history of the Masonic network is bound up with the experience of these rural community

---

[15] The term Zhigongtang refers to a four-character expression of the Masonic organisation, "zhi li wei gong" ("exert strength for public benefit"). The abbreviated term Zhigongtang means 'Lodge for Exerting Public Benefit'.

[16] The timing of leadership succession in Yong's account differs from the formal Masonic record published in 2004. According to the latter, Moy Sing led the organisation from 1854 to 1898 and James Chuey from 1898 to 1930. See note 7 above.

[17] John Fitzgerald 2005, 'Legend or History? The Australian Yee Hing and the Chinese Revolution', *Studies on Republican China*, no. 8, pp. 87-111.

[18] I would like to thank Kuo Mei-fen for bringing the role of Moy Sing's private home to my attention.

[19] C. Y. Choy 1975, *Chinese Migration and Settlement in Australia* (Sydney: Sydney University Press), pp. 28-9. Rural sites in NSW for which we have irrefutable evidence of Hung League lodges include Bathurst (site of the Loong Hung Pung legend), Albury, and Tingha. See Janis Wilton 2004, *Golden Threads: The Chinese in Regional New South Wales* (Armidale, NSW: New England Regional Art Museum in association with Powerhouse Publishers).

networks, an experience readily overlooked in retrospective reconstructions of leadership genealogies constructed from the perspective of the metropolis. Without retrieving something of the diversity of this early history it is difficult to appreciate the equally varied political and social history of the movement.

Political history of the Masonic network

Accounts that place Moy Sing at the centre of Chinese Masonic history in Australia make little mention of his politics. Moy Sing's achievements, it appears, were largely administrative. He consolidated the lodges into a statewide network and elevated the status of the old brotherhood to something akin to freemasonry in Australia; that is, respectable, formidable, and above sectarian politics. Loong Hung Pung, by contrast, is identified in legend as the founder of a revolutionary tradition in Australia that long predated the Sydney consolidation and which extended the local Masonic network well beyond Australia.

In 1958, two Taiwanese scholars published an unsourced account of Loong Hung Pung's place in the history of the greater Chinese revolution in the period preceding Sun Yatsen's arrival on the scene. In a chapter of their book on Chinese-Australian history, Liu Daren and Tian Xinyuan state that Loong Hung Pung was the inspiration behind a radical movement based in Australia that helped to set up the earliest of Sun Yatsen's revolutionary organisations, the Revive China Society (*Xingzhonghui*). Loong Hung Pung, they reported, 'was the head of the secret societies in Australia, and advocated opposition to the Manchus and restoration of the Han people while advocating fairness and freedom'. Liu and Tian trace a revolutionary genealogy that bears out many of the claims made for Loong Hung Pung in other sources that recount his influence on the radicalisation of nineteenth century Chinese-Australian communities. These include the claim that Loong inspired Chow Toong Yung and others to set up a revolutionary organisation which was to form a pillar for the erection of the revolutionary Revive China Society in Hong Kong in the 1890s.[20]

In 1933 the serving Grand Master of the Chinese Masonic movement, writing under the cryptic title of '19 1/2', published a eulogy for 'The Great Leader' Loong Hung Pung in the Shanghai magazine *United China*.[21] Loong, he wrote,

---

[20] Liu Daren and Tian Xinyuan (eds) 1958, *Aozhou huaqiao jingji* [Chinese-Australian Economy] (Taipei: Haiwai chubanshe), p. 131. I wish to thank Kuo Mei-fen for this reference.

[21] Grand Master of the Chinese Masonic Lodge 1933, 'Lung Hung Pung "The Great Leader"', *United China*, vol. 1, no. 11, p. 433. In the same article Grand Master '19 1/2' notes cryptically that his curious numerical title was chosen out of respect for Loong Hung Pung. In all likelihood the title '19 1/2' relates to the numerical hierarchies of Hung League leadership in which Grand Masters of regional lodges were ranked as '21'. By implication, it appears succeeding leaders declined to rank themselves at 20 or 21 out of respect for Loong.

was the embodiment of the literary and artistic genius of his race. His writings and speeches were 'faithful to the noblest traditions of the ancients'. At the same time they were highly original, making a lasting 'contribution towards the enrichment of the general mass of mankind, and towards the creation of a New China in the New World'. This reference to Loong's writings touches a treatise associated with his name and known in English as 'The Reconstruction of China as a Modern State'. A pamphlet under this title is reported to have circulated internationally among anti-Manchu activists in the nineteenth century and to have reached Sun Yatsen some time before Sun penned his famous Three Principles of the People. Assuming it ever existed, the text is no longer extant. According to one not wholly reliable source, Sun Yatsen drew upon Loong's work in drafting his famous Three Principles: 'Sun Yatsen procured a copy of Loong's great masterpiece … and started to copy and transpose it. He was unlucky to lose his copy in a fire, and could not procure another, though he tried hard.'[22]

The source for this claim, an Australian journalist by the name of Vivian Chow, proceeded to the less credible claim that Sun tried to pass off as his own what he recalled of Loong's work from memory. 'Thus we have the pot-pourri of the Great Leader, Loong Hung Pung, advanced under the name of Sun Yatsen, "The Three Principles of the People".' Although tendentious this claim finds indirect support in Sun's own writings. Sun Yatsen complained at one point that he could not access his collection of books and manuscripts when he drafted the Three Principles of the People in 1924 because his library had been recently destroyed in a fire.[23] Still, the key claim that Sun passed off Loong's writings as his own is unverifiable. It is worth noting all the same that Sun included in his final manuscript a curious Australian story about a land speculator who made his fortune by bidding for property at auction, in Melbourne, while gesturing aimlessly in a drunken stupor. The moral of this Australian tale was that the state should capture increases in property values because land speculation was an immoral source of wealth.[24] To this day, the source for the Melbourne episode in Sun's Three Principles remains a mystery.

Loong was reputed to have been an organiser and strategist as well as a revolutionary pamphleteer. Vivian Chow credited him with organising 'great expeditions … numbering thousands per contingent' to the Australian goldfields, and with cultivating the major 'goldfields commanders' including Yeng Lee, Yik

---

[22] V. Y. Chow 1933, 'Sun Yatsen's "Fatherhood" of New China', *United China*, vol. 1, no. 11, p. 427.

[23] Sun Yatsen [1924], *San Min Chu I, The Three Principles of the People*. Translated by Frank W. Price. Edited by L. T. Chen 1943, (Chungking: Government Printing House), Author's Preface.

[24] Sun Yatsen [1924], *San Min Chu I*.

Bow, Way Lee, and Kai Koon, who was placed 'in charge of goldfields affairs'. Some of these names are difficult to trace today; Way Lee as we shall see was an early Freemason as well as Chinese Mason, and Kai Koon was naturalised as a British subject in Grafton in 1857.[25] Much of this early Hung League activity seems to have centred on the town of Grafton and neighbouring townships in northern NSW. Loong's organisation was also said to have had members in China to whom it sent funds from the goldfields to support anti-Manchu activities.[26]

By one account their contacts in China let the Australian organisers down. Exposure of mismanagement and waste of the funds remitted from the goldfields to brothers in China appears to have shaken and transformed the NSW Masonic leadership. Corruption of the network in China was exposed through an inquiry into the movement undertaken over the period following Loong's death. The results of this inquiry led to a decision to cease remitting funds to China and encourage instead direct intervention by Chinese-Australians in the anti-Manchu revolution in China. Loong Hung Pung's successors were directed to leave Australia and carry their ideals back to China.[27]

The decision to commit people rather than funds to the cause in China appears to explain why one activist, John See, returned to China in the 1880s. If so, it also accounts for the involvement of his children James and Thomas See in the avant-garde reform and revolutionary movements that emerged in Hong Kong in the early 1890s. It may also help to explain why Moy Sing, James Chuey, and their consolidated Sydney lodge felt at liberty to plot a new path of civic respectability for the brotherhood from around the turn of the century.

The claim that elements of a revolutionary rural lodge in NSW were relocated to China to promote some kind of revolution appears to have some foundation. One source for the claim, Vivian Chow, enjoyed close family connections with the Hung League.[28] His mother, Jessie Mary King, was the daughter of Stephen King and Annie Lavinia Lavett who married in Grafton in 1877. Vivian recalled that his grandfather Stephen, was the second Grand Master of a rural lodge in NSW and a pioneer revolutionary in what he called the 'Revolutionary and Independence Association of Australian Chinese'. Vivian's father Chow Toong

---

[25] V. Y. Chow 1933, 'In 1850 the Revolution was Born', *United China*, vol. 1, no. 11, p. 424.

[26] 'Australia acknowledges (A compilation of press reports On the Official Historian's visit to Australia)', *United China*, vol. 1, no. 11, 1933, p. 450.

[27] V. Y. Chow 1933, 'Odyssey in the South', *United China*, vol. 1, no. 11, p. 436. The author does not say whether the original was written in English or Chinese. The parenthetic reference identifying Stephen King Jung Sao appears to be the author's since the term 'Masonic' was not employed before the 1910s.

[28] Claims to this effect can be found repeated in the articles Vivian Chow published in *United China* magazine in 1932 and 1933. See above and below for citations.

Yung is reported to have been co-leader of this Australian revolutionary party with his friend John See. During a brief visit to Sydney in October 1932, Vivian claims to have convened a meeting of 'the remnants of the Australian Chinese Independence and Revolutionary Society'.[29] At this time he was touring NSW as 'Official historian of the Chinese Masonic Lodge and Revolutionary and Independence Association of Australian Chinese' – a grandiose title which nevertheless asserts an explicit link between the later Masonic network and the little-known political association founded by his relatives five or six decades earlier.[30]

Another source for the claim that there was an Australian revolutionary society which pre-dated comparable societies in China and Hong Kong is John See's son James – better known to historians of China under the name Tse Tsan Tai. After moving to Hong Kong with his father, James played a role in founding the first revolutionary organisation in Hong Kong and subsequently co-founded the first revolutionary party with Sun Yatsen and others in that colony. James himself left a record of these events which revealed that the Australian secret society network was on intimate terms with Taiping rebels in China and with a variety of post-Taiping secret society organisations based in Hong Kong and Canton from the middle to the end of the nineteenth century. He also acknowledges in passing that his father led an Australian revolutionary party which he called the 'Chinese Independence Party of Australia'. This was presumably his own rendering of the society which Vivian Chow called the 'Revolutionary and Independence Society of Australian Chinese'.[31]

James See came into the world in Sydney on 16 May 1872 at a time when Loong Hoong Pung was still entertaining visitors at his store in Bathurst.[32] Loong belonged to the generation of James' father John who was born in Kaiping County in Guangdong Province in 1831, arrived in Australia in the late 1850s or 1860s and, with his wife Que Sam, bore six children over the decade beginning in 1870.[33] On first arriving in Sydney, John See established a business at 39

---

[29] Chow 1933, 'Odyssey in the South', p. 441.

[30] Chow 1933, 'In 1850 the Revolution was Born', p. 423.

[31] Tse Tsan Tai 1924, *The Chinese Republic: Secret History of the Revolution* (Hong Kong: South China Morning Post), p. 7. I have yet to find a source supplying a Chinese-language title.

[32] 'Australia acknowledges', p. 450.

[33] James See notes that he had three sisters and two younger brothers. See Tse 1924, *Chinese Republic*, p. 7. Four are recorded in the NSW Registry of Births Deaths and Marriages under the surname See or Ah See as follows:

1438/1870 Sydney See, Ah Father Ah, Mother Sam

1366/1872 Sydney See, Tan Hi Father Ah See, Mother Sam Que

Sussex Street under the title of the Tai Yick (*Taiyi*) Firm.[34] He later moved with his family to Northern NSW where he opened the Tse & Co general store in Grafton before finally settling in a tin-mining town not far from Inverell known as Tingha. The family was well-known on the northern tablelands of NSW under the surname Ah See. All six children were raised as Christians. The young Tse Tsan Tai was baptised James See by Anglican Bishop Greenway on 1 November 1879 in Grafton's Christ Church Cathedral, along with his elder sister Sarah and younger brothers Thomas and Samuel.[35] In 1887 John See moved with his family to Hong Kong where he lived and worked until his death in 1903.[36]

According to Vivian Chow, John See had long been a 'secret sect member' and 'Chinese Freemason' in Australia before retiring to Hong Kong.[37] Elsewhere, as we noted, Vivian Chow claimed that John See was co-leader of the Revolutionary and Independence Association with Vivian Chow's father Chow Toong Yung.[38] These claims are supported in a book James See published in Hong Kong two decades after the death of his father. In *The Chinese Republic: Secret History of the Revolution*, he painted a graphic picture of the involvement of his father's generation in a revolutionary secret organisation in Australia dating back to the 1870s which continued to maintain links with defeated leaders of the Taiping Rebellion in China well into the 1890s.

The See family became involved in insurrectionist movements against the Manchu imperial government shortly after they stepped ashore in Hong Kong. While a lad of seventeen, James joined a group of like-minded young men to plan the overthrow of the Qing Dynasty. With Yeung Ku Wan (Yang Quyun), in 1891 he formed the earliest revolutionary organisation in China, the Foo Yan Man Ser Kwong Fook Hui (*Furen wenshe guangfuhui* – Furen cultural society restoration association).[39] It was this association that later merged with Sun Yatsen's

---

12109/1876 Grafton Ah See, Thomas Father Ah See, Mother Sam

13251/1878 Grafton Ah See, Samuel Father Ah, Mother Sam

The first listed was also known as Sarah; the second was Tse Tsan Tai himself, also known as James Ah See; the third was known in Chinese as Tse Tsi-shau (Xie Zixiu).

[34] Tse 1924, *Chinese Republic*, pp. 6, 7, 24.

[35] 'Australia acknowledges', p. 450; also Chow 1933, 'Odyssey in the South', p. 444; Tse 1924, *Chinese Republic*, pp. 6, 24.

[36] Tse 1924, *Chinese Republic*, p. 7.

[37] Chow 1933, 'Odyssey in the South', pp. 443, 450.

[38] 'Early Revolutionary Crosses Great Divide', *United China*, vol. 1, no. 10, 1933, p. 402.

[39] Chow 1933, 'On Writing a History of the Chinese Revolution', p. 462. A photograph of the group dated 1891 features 10 youngish men including James See and Yeung Ku Wan seated together in the middle: Chow 1933, 'In 1850 the Revolution was Born', p. 425.

Hawaiian faction to form the Hong Kong chapter of the Revive China Society (*Xingzhonghui*). Yeung was the inaugural leader of the Hong Kong Revive China Society but within a short time surrendered the position to Sun Yatsen.

James See followed Yeung in preference to Sun, and refrained from joining Sun Yatsen's later organisation, the Revolutionary Alliance (*Tonmenghyui*), on account of his loyalty to Yeung. At the same time he maintained his Australian connections and encouraged his patron to consider visiting Australia. Yeung consented. In a letter dated 26 May 1900, Yeung Ku Wan informed Tse Tsan Tai of his plans to visit Australia over the coming year. This visit was possibly prompted by news that Liang Qichao, a leader of the rival Empire Reform Association (*Baohuanghui*), was intending to visit Australia around the same time. Liang visited Australia from October 1900 to May 1901. Yeung was less fortunate. On 10 January 1901 a gang of hired assassins broke into the school room where he was taking classes and murdered him. The assassins fled to sanctuary in imperial Canton.[40]

Although siding with Yeung Ku Wan in his competition with Sun Yatsen in Hong Kong, James See maintained independent Australian connections that were facilitated by his father's links with secret society organisations and Taiping rebels through the old Australian Masonic network. On one occasion, James recalled, a nephew of the Taiping Christian King Hong Xiuchuan called by to speak with his father John See at their home in Hong Kong. This nephew of Hong Xiuchuan was said to have trained and fought in Taiping armies in the 1850s and 1860s. He travelled under a variety of names including Hung Chun-fu, Hung Wu, and Hung Chuen-fook. On this occasion Hung called by to seek strategic advice from James' father regarding plans to mount an anti-imperial uprising in Canton. John See was by this time too frail to take part himself and encouraged his twenty-seven year old son to step forward in his place. James and his younger brother Thomas then set to work with the nephew of the Taiping leader in plotting an armed uprising in China under the guidance of the aging leader of the Revolutionary and Independence Association of Australian Chinese.

The aim of the uprising was to overthrow the imperial system and establish a modern democratic form of government in China. They certainly did not propose to restore the Ming but, significantly, nor did they propose to establish a republic. James See described the 1902 putsch as a 'commonwealth' uprising, in contrast to the 'republican' uprising organised by Sun Yatsen. He explained the difference: 'I decided to plan and organize another attempt to capture Canton and establish [a] Commonwealth Government under a 'Protector', as I was of the

---

[40] Tse 1924, *Chinese Republic*, pp. 19-20.

opinion that the 'Republican' form of government was too advanced for China and the Chinese.'[41]

Before the uprising took place, James expressed the view that the new commonwealth should be set up under 'able Christian leadership'.[42] It is not difficult to detect his Australian experience in James' revolutionary proposal to establish a 'commonwealth' (on the model of the new 'commonwealth' government of Australia) in which the Chinese people were placed under the care of able Christian 'Protectors'.

Urbanisation, consolidation, and depoliticisation

The legend of Loong Hung Pung and the history of his successors in the leadership of the Chinese Masonic network opens a rare window onto social networks operating among Chinese communities in rural Australia in the colonial period. Loong's story illustrates networking across Chinese native-place communities, networking between Chinese-Australian community leaders and European-Australian elites (as I have shown elsewhere), and networking across international boundaries of the Australian colonies, British Hong Kong, and the Chinese Empire.[43] To be sure, we have yet to estimate the role of the early lodges in facilitating labour migration to the colonies, yet to define the kinds of relationships that were maintained among rural lodges in NSW and Victoria over the period, and yet to understand how colonial Australian lodges related to others on the Pacific rim. Nevertheless the transition from the legendary era of Loong Hung Pung to the historical era of Moy Sing and James A Chuey highlights a number of important issues in Australian and Chinese social history, and invites reflection on the causes and consequences of the consolidation of scattered rural lodges into urban-based statewide lodges around the turn of the century.

As I have suggested elsewhere, archival and family records support the basic outline of legendary accounts of the founding of Chinese Masonic lodges on the western goldfields and northern tin-mines of NSW in the mid-nineteenth century under the leadership of Loong Hung Pung. The same sources help us to trace the extension of this network into a republican brotherhood based in north-eastern NSW later in the century, and to observe its further elaboration into a modern revolutionary organisation centred in Hong Kong and Canton at the turn of the twentieth century. By Vivian Chow's account this network survived, in attenuated form, through his own efforts and those of his comrades in Hong Kong, Canton and Shanghai into the 1920s and 1930s.

---

[41] ibid., p. 16.
[42] ibid., p. 18.
[43] See Fitzgerald 2005, 'Legend or History?'

By this time however the Chinese Masonic network on the eastern Australian seaboard was moving in a different direction, indicated among other things by the English title the Chinese Masonic Society impressed on the façade of its new headquarters in Mary Street. Why did it call itself the Masonic Society? In one sense the term is a cross-cultural translation – the predominant sense in which the term appeared in early English and European accounts of Chinese secret societies. Commenting on their elaborate rituals and imagined traditions in 1925, J. S. M. Ward and W. G. Stirling observed that 'like Freemasons in the West, the Hung or Triad Society seems justly entitled to claim that it is a lineal descendant of the Ancient Mysteries'. Gustav Schlegel made a similar observation four decades earlier: 'Every person who has read anything of the secret societies in China must have been struck with the resemblance between them and the Society of Freemasons.' Earlier still, in 1855, Howqua engaged in cross-cultural translation when he told the Victorian goldfields commission that the rebels who were known to Chinese miners as Hung League or Taiping rebels were 'Freemasons'. This was translation by analogy.

Analogous features of the two institutions aside, there has been little attempt to identify concrete sets of relationships that may have developed between the two autonomous networks, or to explore their wider implications for the social and political orientation of Chinese secret-society networks outside of China.[44] One exception is C. F. Yong's pioneering study of Chinese-Australian history of the period, which hints that the League's adoption of the title Chinese Masonic Society was not merely an act of translation. There were, he noted, networks of personal associations linking Chinese Masons and European Freemasonry at the time. Nevertheless the details of personal and institutional relations remain largely unexplored.[45]

In colonial Australia the relationship between the two networks was more concrete. The reorganisation of the Hung League in the 1890s and early 1900s followed closely on the consolidation of European Freemasonry as an urban-based network in Sydney in 1888, when many scattered rural and urban lodges of European Freemasonry merged to form the NSW United Grand Lodge. The Chinese brotherhood followed suit, first moving toward colony-wide consolidation in the 1890s, building offices for its state headquarters in Mary Street over the following decade, and finally proclaiming itself the headquarters of the Chinese Masonic Society of NSW.

The analogous sequence of Masonic consolidations, involving both the Chinese Masonic Society and the United Freemasons, could be regarded as fortuitous

---

[44] Gustav Schlegel [1866] 1973, *The Hung League* (Batavia; New York, NY: AMS), p. ix; J. S. M. Ward and W. G. Stirling 1925, *The Hung Society* (London: Baskerville), 3 volumes, vol. 1, p. i.

[45] Yong 1977, *New Gold Mountain*, p. 160.

were it not for a number of identifiable connections linking the two fraternal networks. Chinese-Australians were among the first people of Chinese descent in the world to gain entry to the international order of Freemasons. Some time before the successful consolidation of colonial Freemasonry, the Sydney tea merchant and teashop entrepreneur Quong Tart (Mei Guangda) was admitted into the Order of Oddfellows under the English constitution. On 8 October 1885 he was initiated to the Lodge of Tranquillity which convened at Bondi in the eastern suburbs of Sydney. Quong rose to the second degree in the Lodge of Tranquillity on 11 March 1886 and was elevated to the status of Master Mason on 12 July 1886. Quong Tart was not, to my knowledge, a member of the Hung League when he joined the Freemasons. He was however on close terms with a number of Chinese Masonic leaders and he remained an active Freemason until his death in 1903, when forty members of the fraternity accompanied his funeral procession, in full regalia, processing behind an oak coffin draped with his Master Mason's apron.[46]

By one account, Quong Tart was the third Freemason of Chinese descent to be admitted to the order anywhere in the world.[47] By the time of his death in 1903 he was far from the sole Chinese-Australian member of the Order. 'Chinese and Western' Freemasons marched side by side in his funeral cortege according to a contemporary Chinese-Australian newspaper account.[48] Others admitted into the order between his initiation in 1885 and his death in 1903 include Sun Johnson, W. R. G. Lee, and his son William Lee, in NSW, and Way Lee in South Australia – each at the same time a prominent member of the Hung League who played a role in translating its idioms and rituals into the wider English-speaking world of Federation Australia.[49]

---

[46] At the time he joined the lodge it was registered as Number 1552 under the English constitution. After the consolidation of 1888 it became Lodge 42 under the Australian constitution. G. Cumming 1995, 'Mei Quong Tart (1850–1903)', *The Masonic Historical Society of New South Wales*, no. 23, 22 May, p. 6.

[47] The first by this account was Teh Boen Keh, who was initiated in Surabaya (Java) in 1857, and the second Tsung Lai Shun who was initiated into the Hampden Lodge in Massachusetts in 1873. G. Cumming 1995, 'Mei Quong Tart'. Cumming based the claim for Quong Tart's place in the international Order upon an unpublished report issued by Right Worshipful Brother Christopher Haffner in 1995.

[48] *Guangyi huaboa* [Chinese Australian Herald], 8 August 1903. I wish to thank Guo Meifen for this reference.

[49] Way Lee was admitted to the United Tradesman's Lodge No. 4 in Adelaide in the late nineteenth century. I wish to thank Patricia Jamieson and Kevin Wong-Hoy for this reference. Sun Johnson entered Lodge Southern Cross No. 91 on 14 August 1892. Sun Johnson and William Lee both acted as English Secretaries for the Chinese Masonic Association during James Chuey's term as director.

It would be misleading to suggest that local Freemason lodges embraced Chinese-Australians as freely as they did Australians of European descent. Chinese-Australians were no more widely welcomed into the Order of Freemasons in late nineteenth and early twentieth century Australia than Chinese in colonial Asia or North America. Very few Chinese names are recorded on Australian membership rolls before the mid-twentieth century. In cases where Minute Books do refer to Chinese nominees they occasionally record blackball attempts at exclusion. Records of the inner-Sydney Wentworth Lodge record a case in 1903 when a Chinese nominee was withdrawn before his name came up for voting:

> In September [1903] a Chinese merchant was proposed, but before his separate ballot was reached his name was withdrawn, and his proposer and seconder called off, together with three other members. The interruption to the smooth working of the Lodge, which was very unpleasant, however, proved only temporary.[50]

While some lodges discriminated against nominees on racial grounds other lodges appear to have been founded to accommodate minorities. The invitation for Quong Tart to join in 1884 was issued by a Jewish lodge. Although raised by a Scottish family in rural NSW, and living in the western suburb of Ashfield while expanding his Sydney business interests, Quong Tart was initiated into a lodge that had been established with an exclusively Jewish membership in June 1875. Three years elapsed before the first non-Jewish member was admitted, in May 1878, and no more than a dozen members were admitted to the brotherhood in any one year when Quong was initiated in the 1880s.[51]

Despite these limitations on membership, invitations to join Freemason lodges were issued to some of the most prominent Hung League members in the 1890s and early 1900s. In consequence, the transformation of the Hung League into the Chinese Masonic Society over the first decade of the twentieth century came to mirror the institutional history of the NSW United Grand Lodge of Freemasons

---

I wish to thank Kuo Meifen for this information. William Lee joined a Freemason's lodge in 1903. Yong 1977, *New Gold Mountain*, p. 160.

[50] *Jubilee History of Lodge Wentworth 1881–1931* (np nd), p. 29. Archives of the United Grand Lodge of New South Wales and the Australian Capital Territory, Box 171. The minute books fail to record why the merchant's name was withdrawn. See 'The First 90 Years of Lodge Wentworth No. 89 UGL of New South Wales', p. 6. Typed Manuscript. Archives of the United Grand Lodge of New South Wales and the Australian Capital Territory, Box 171.

[51] The Grand Master who presided over his initiation was Mr. G. Gabriel. See Bro. O. U. Nickless 1961, Forward and Narrative in Two Parts of the History of the Lodge of Tranquillity No.42 UGL of NSW for the Period January 1874 to 11 May 1961. Typed Manuscript dated 11 May. Archives of the United Grand Lodge of New South Wales and the Australian Capital Territory, Box 517.

in the late 1880s and early 1890s. European Freemason lodges came together to form the NSW United Grand Lodge in the third year of Quong Tart's membership of the fraternity. Under the leadership of Moy Sing and James Chuey, rural Hung League lodges converged to form the NSW Chinese Masonic Society, and refocused their energy from the political emphasis that had characterised rural lodges associated with Loong Hung Pung, towards social, economic, and domestic political priorities related to their members' immediate concerns in colonial and federation Australia. Its leaders built a statewide organisation on a substantial urban base to mobilise support for reform of Australian laws and regulations governing Chinese immigration, for promotion of business ties between Chinese and European Australians, and for the expansion of Australian imports and exports with colonial Hong Kong and Malaya and with the treaty ports of imperial and republican China.

They also took advantage of the resources of the consolidated European network. As early as January 1896 Chinese-Australian community leaders were convening public meetings in the Sydney Freemasons Hall, and in 1901 community members gathered in the Masonic Hall to celebrate the Emperor Guangxu's birthday. Chinese Masonic leaders also made use of the hall. In November 1911, for example, Masonic leader James Chuey convened a meeting of the Young China League with leading Sydney merchant George Bew in the United Freemason's Hall.[52] As individuals, prominent Masonic members such as James Chuey held partisan political views and took part in a range of reformist and revolutionary organisations, including the Young China League and, at a later date, the Chinese Nationalist movement. From the turn of the century, however, the Chinese Masonic network no longer sponsored its own political party. It worked instead to forge links with other community organisations including European-Australian institutions and Chinese-Australian ones.

These institutional innovations were grafted onto the early foundations of rural Hung League networks long operating in NSW, in the sense that the politics of the early lodges forged regional *colonial* ties that sat alongside ties of kin and native place in China. The year of Loong Hung Pung's death falls into the earliest period for which we can find written records of pan-Chinese associations rooted on colonial Australian soil. By one account, Loong Hung Pung was laid to rest under a tombstone that recorded the gratitude of the 'Chinese Community of NSW' to their departed leader in 1874.[53] If true, this was a significant gesture. We are accustomed to thinking of Chinese immigrants as organising themselves along lines of kinship and native-place associations for mutual aid and social

---

[52] *Guangyi huaboa*, 13 January 1896; *Tung Wah Times*, 31 July 1901.

[53] J. D. Fitzgerald 1918, 'A Celestial Gentleman', in Ethel Turner (ed.), *The Australian Soldier's Gift Book* (Sydney: Voluntary Workers' Association), pp. 137-42.

advancement in the mid-nineteenth century. Most of the consolidated organisations that appeared around the Pacific rim from the mid nineteenth century were loose confederations of native place and surname associations referring to China.[54] As early as the 1870s, however, some Chinese institutions in Australia were organising regional colonial networks that were not only unrelated to native place or kinship ties in China but specifically related to their place of domicile in Australia. Those who mourned the death of Loong Hung Pung in 1874 did so through the agency of a pan-Chinese community of an Australian colony – a secret society network with an organisational locus in New South Wales.

In Memoriam

In conclusion, I would like to speculate on the significance of a number of cemetery monuments erected over this period in Victoria and Tasmania. These monuments certainly indicate pan-Chinese sentiments among immigrants in colonial Victoria and Tasmania. The question I wish to pose here is whether they also signify a 'modern' sense of China as a political state, in the Victorian case, and as a Confucian national community in the case of Tasmania. If so we may be in a position to trace a transition from revolution to respectability that parallels, monumentally, the narrative history we have been recounting of Chinese Australian history.

From the early 1870s, monumental stele began to appear in colonial Victoria bearing Chinese language inscriptions commemorating the deaths of 'elders' from 'all provinces' who were laid to rest on Australian soil. These early steles refer to the immigrants' country of birth not by the contemporary Chinese term 'Great Qing State' (*Daqingguo*) but by the modern idiom 'Chinese State' or 'China' (*Zhonghuaguo*). To the best of my knowledge these are among the earliest recorded references to the modern term for 'China' to be found on Chinese-language monuments in the world.[55] In avoiding the term for China used by the Manchu Qing dynasty we might ask whether they also challenged the legitimacy of the Great Qing State. We cannot say for certain. But a banner preserved among

---

[54] The general exception to this rule is the Chinese Masonic network. See L. Eve Armentrout Ma 1990, *Revolutionaries, Monarchists and Chinatowns: Chinese Politics in the Americas and the 1911 Revolution* (Honolulu, HI: University of Hawaii Press), and Yong Chen 2000, *Chinese San Francisco 1850–1943: A Trans-Pacific Community* (Stanford, CA: Stanford University Press).

[55] Adam McKeown has drawn my attention to the phrase *zhonghuaguo* found in documents produced in Peru some years earlier. See Chen Hansheng 1980, *Huagong chuguo shiliao huibian* [Historical materials on Chinese labourers abroad] (Beijing: Zhonghua shuju), 7 volumes, vol. 1, part 3, p. 965. It should be noted that delegates of the Qing state promoted use of the term 'zhonghua' among Chinese community organisations in San Francisco in the 1860s and 1870s. See Ma 1990, *Revolutionaries, Monarchists and Chinatown*, chapter 1; Yong Chen 2000, *Chinese San Francisco 1850–1943*, p. 72.

holdings of Chinese Masonic artifacts in the Bendigo Golden Dragon Museum suggests that the term circulated within the nineteenth century rural Hung League network. It was possibly members of the Hung League who erected these memorials in the 1870s.[56]

One of the earliest of these Victorian steles was erected in the Melbourne General Cemetery in 1873. The central column reads 'Graves of Honorable Elders from all Provinces of China' (*zhonghuaguo*). The column on the left reads 'A common offering from native villagers of the two Guangdong prefectures of Guangzhou and Zhaoqing.' The right column reads 'Erected on an auspicious day in the spring of 1873' (*Tongzhi guiyounian*). Similar steles were erected in Ballarat, Bendigo and Beechworth cemeteries over the decade, each avoiding mention of the Manchu Qing state in favour of the term 'Chinese State' and each referring to elders 'from all provinces'. The choice of words possibly reflects the development of pan-Chinese nationalism directed against the Qing but not noticeably oriented toward the restoration of the Ming, as standard histories of the Hung League would predict.

By the turn of the twentieth century, political terms of this kind were no longer to be found inscribed on cemetery monuments. Comparable steles erected in cemeteries in Northeastern Tasmania in the early 1900s refer to the 'Great Qing State' in preference to the 'Chinese State'. They also make reference to the teachings of Confucius. One memorial stele erected alongside a ceremonial oven in Moorina Cemetery in 1906, for example, bears inscriptions in Chinese and English. The Chinese reads: 'Great Qing State, Graves of honorable elders, thirty-second year of Guangxu'. The accompanying English inscription reads: 'This stone has been erected by the Chinese of Garibaldi, Argus and Moorina as a place of worship of Confusias [*sic*] religion to the departed Chinese in the Moorina Cemetery.'[57] An almost identical memorial, erected in nearby Weldborough Cemetery in 1909, begins with the Chinese expression 'Great Qing State' and ends in English with the dedication: 'This stone has been erected by the Chinese as a place of worship of Confusias [*sic*] religion to the departed Chinese and those connected with the Chinese in the Weldborough Cemetery.'[58] Such references to the Manchu Qing dynasty and to Confucianism are nowhere to be found among the earlier cemetery monuments in rural Victoria.[59] In the design of its cemetery steles, Victorian Chinese communities possibly declined

---

[56] The banner reads simply "Zhonghuaguo" (Chinese state, or China).

[57] Helen Vivian 1985, *Tasmania's Chinese Heritage: An Historical Record of Chinese Sites in North East Tasmania* (Launceston, Tasmania: Australian Heritage Commission/Queen Victoria Museum and Art Gallery), 2 volumes, vol. 1, plate 24.

[58] ibid., plate 5.

[59] They are frequently found on individual gravestones, as distinct from monumental stele.

to acknowledge the presence of the Manchu Qing Dynasty on the same grounds that Loong Hung Pung and his followers in NSW swore to 'oppose the Manchus and restore the Han people'.

These differences may indicate varying regional orientations on the part of Chinese-Australian communities in NSW and Victoria, on the one hand, and those of colonial Tasmania on the other. Given the close association between Tasmanian and Victorian Chinese communities this seems fairly unlikely. It is tempting to speculate that the disappearance of the modern term for China found on 1870s memorials in Victoria and its replacement on later memorials with references to departed elders of the great Qing state reflects a new kind of community politics that was emerging around the turn of the twentieth century – a kind of politics more in keeping with the respectable and conservative urban leadership of Moy Sing and James A Chuey, in Sydney, and their counterparts around Australia over the federation era. This was the *de*radicalised space into which Sun Yatsen and his republican nationalist revolutionaries made their move when they introduced 'modern' nationalism to Australia's Chinese communities over the period up to and succeeding the 1911 Revolution in China.

I wish to acknowledge the assistance of Cai Shaoqing, Phillip Bramble, Sophie Couchman, Mark Finnane, Jack Gregory, Kuo Mei-fen, Kok Hu Jin, Daphne Kok, Li Gongzhong and Adam McKeown in identifying sources and offering helpful criticisms and suggestions for this paper and to offer special thnaks to the Archives of the United Grand Lodge of NSW and the ACT. Research for this chapter was supported by the Australian Research Council and conducted while I was employed in the School of Social Sciences at La Trobe University.

7. 'Innocents abroad' and 'prohibited immigrants': Australians in India and Indians in Australia 1890–1910

Margaret Allen

In 1907, Eleanor Rivett MA, a young modern woman and a graduate of Melbourne University, left Australia to become a missionary for the London Missionary Society in Calcutta. As she made her way from Colombo up to Calcutta, she stopped off in Madras, and spent a day with Elsie Nicol, another Melbourne graduate. Nicol was running the YWCA hostel in Madras, where women students could stay while studying at Madras University. In following her vocation as a missionary in India, Eleanor was leaving behind her parents and her numerous siblings. But she and her brother David had made a vow, that if he won the Rhodes scholarship he would spend some time with her in India. Later in 1907, she was able to take leave and explore the northern cities of India with David on his way to Oxford. They went to Benares, Lucknow, Cawnpur, Agra, Delhi and Bombay.[1] They were, she recalled, 'the innocents abroad', but it was 'a marvellous tour'.[2]

Eleanor Rivett was the first Australian to go to north India under the auspices of the London Missionary Society and she would spend some forty years there. But neither she nor Elsie Nicol was the first Australian to work as a missionary in India. As will be discussed below, a number of Australian women and men went to India in that religious capacity. They felt drawn to travel far from their homes to take up the cause, as they saw it, of evangelising the heathen of India. As they devoted themselves to their Christian work in India, many struggled with the long separation from home and family that such a step involved. For a number, such separations were eased somewhat when members of their family and friends visited them in India. Furthermore, missionaries were able to return home on furlough. Thus the ships that serviced the routes between Australian ports and Colombo and other ports on the subcontinent, would often carry a missionary or two. Such travellers felt called and definitely entitled to travel and to stay in India for long periods of time. They engaged in many activities there, such as establishing hospitals and running schools. For Australian women missionaries, the responsibilities as administrators, teachers, preachers, nurses

---

[1] The names for India cities in use in the period being discussed, i.e. Bombay, Madras and Poona have been retained in this chapter.

[2] Eleanor Rivett 1965, *Memory Plays a Tune ... Being Recollections of India 1907–1947* (Sydney: the author), p. 10.

and doctors in the mission fields were broader than those they could have taken on in Australia. Some might claim that their religious vocation marked them off from those with a mere desire to travel and see the world, to make a career or simply experience foreign lands. But these women can be also be understood in the same framework as those studied by Angela Woollacott in *To Try Her Fortune in London*. Observing that 'the industrialization of travel and [their] ... modern ambition for education, jobs, and careers promoted [these women's] mobility'. 'The Australian girl', she suggests, came to stand for 'modernity and independence'.[3]

Also on these ships might be another figure, whom I will describe, for the purposes of summary as 'an Indian'.[4] Usually a man, the Indian traveller might have lived in India, Australia or another part of the Empire altogether. He could have been returning to Australia after a sojourn in India or a tourist seeking to enjoy the sights of Australia and other destinations. But, with the passage of the Immigration Restriction Act in the Commonwealth of Australia in 1901, such travel was limited and controlled. The Australian authorities categorised Indians, although British subjects, as 'natives of Asia', who had no automatic entitlement to travel freely between India and Australia. The Australians and the Indians had 'differential access to mobility'.[5] Although Indians were negotiating their own modernity, travelling around the world in pursuit of pleasure, greater opportunities and personal transformation, Australian government policies increasingly categorised them as people whose movements should be strictly controlled. Australians tended to represent Indians as exotic and backward. As David Walker has pointed out, Australian accounts of travel in India tended to emphasise its 'antiquity and spiritual wealth'.[6] He found in Alfred Deakin's writing on India, that 'Ancient India was readily celebrated while modern India and Indians were routinely disparaged.'[7] In the discourse of modernity, Indians

---

[3] Angela Woollacott 2001, *To Try Her Fortune in London: Australian Women, Colonialism and Modernity* (Oxford: Oxford University Press), pp. 8, 157.

[4] I use this tem in a broad and general manner to include Indian subjects of British rule and Indians living in the Princely States of India which were ruled indirectly by Britain. Of course after 1947, some of the people referred to in this paper may have been identified as Pakistanis. Australians often referred to Indians living in Australia as Afghans. It is possible that a couple of people referred to in this chapter as Indians, may have indeed been Afghans.

[5] Radhika Viyas Mongia 2003, 'Race, Nationality, Mobility: A History of the Passport', in Antoinette Burton (ed.), *After the Imperial Turn: Thinking With and Through the Nation* (Durham,. NC and London: Duke University Press), p. 211.

[6] David Walker 1999, *Anxious Nation: Australia and the Rise of Asia 1850–1939* (St Lucia: University of Queensland Press), p. 19.

[7] Walker 1999, *Anxious Nation*, p. 22. Alfred Deakin, a key figure in the moves towards federation and Prime Minister of Australia in the early twentieth century, wrote *Temple and Tomb in India*

were represented as backward, fixed and static. Woollacott has pointed out that: 'Western modernity must be viewed as having been created in a symbiotic relationship with its racially constructed others, and that racial hierarchies, including whiteness as a racial identity, have been integrally constitutive of modernity.'[8]

When the Reverend Theo B. Fischer of the Australian Churches of Christ met some of the Indian lawyers at the High Court in Madras, when on a missionary tour to India in 1912, he was clearly surprised to find that they were 'quite up in the politics of the world, acquainted with most English books of recent date, as well as standard works'.[9]

This chapter will explore the differing experiences of Australian missionaries in India in the late nineteenth and early twentieth centuries and those of Indians who also sought to travel and improve their life chances in Australia. The newly federated Commonwealth of Australia was established, in part, 'to guard ... against the dangers of Asiatic immigration'.[10] The Australian government insisted upon the creation of a white nation, which meant that the movement of Indians seeking to travel to and from Australia was strictly controlled and often forbidden.

These developments can be viewed within the broader context of the British Empire, in which the movement of British Indians was increasingly being curtailed. As British subjects, Indians posed a challenge to the governments of the settler colonies. Their status as British subjects might have meant that they could travel and settle freely, but with the growth of colonial nationalism, governments sought to maintain the power and influence of white settlers.

Following the abolition of slavery, Indians had been transported around the Empire as indentured labourers and some had elected to stay on in the colonies at the end of their term of engagement.[11] Thus there were Indian communities in South Africa, in Malaya, Fiji, in East Africa as well as in the Caribbean. By the late nineteenth century, Indians began to outnumber Europeans in the colony of Natal, which passed legislation to restrict their further immigration following

---

(Melbourne: Melville, Mullen and Slade, 1893) and *Irrigated India: An Australian View of India and Ceylon, Their Irrigation and Agriculture* (Melbourne: E. A. Petherick, 1893).

[8] Angela Woollacott 1999, 'White Colonialism and Sexual Modernity: Australian Women in the Early Twentieth Century Metropolis', in Antoinette Burton (ed.), *Gender, Sexuality and Colonial Modernities* (London: Routledge), p. 49.

[9] T. B. Fischer 1914, *A Month in India* (Melbourne: Austral Publishing Company), p. 111.

[10] Myra Willard 1923, *History of the White Australia Policy until 1920* (Melbourne: Melbourne University Press), p. 119.

[11] See Kay Saunders (ed.) 1984, *Indentured Labour in the British Empire, 1834–1920* (London: Croom Helm).

the example of an American Act of 1896 (see chapter by Lake in this collection). In 1897, the Natal government passed an act to 'prevent the importation of coolie labour from India'.[12] This used a language test to exclude those it classed as prohibited immigrants. New Zealand followed suit in 1899 and Australia in 1901.[13] Canada initially used a poll tax and shipping regulations to deter Indian immigration.[14]

The British government, while purporting to uphold the equality of British subjects across the Empire, colluded with colonial governments in their determination to discriminate against non-white British subjects. British officials suggested particular forms of words for colonial legislation that appeared not to discriminate against non-white British subjects and the Empire's Japanese allies, while making it possible for colonial and later Dominion governments to prevent the entry of Asians to their countries, to prohibit their enfranchisement and their participation in particular trades and occupations.[15] The upholding of the rights of the British subject while denying them to British Indians and other non-white British subjects was, as Radhika Mongia notes, a good example of the 'rule of colonial difference'.[16] From time to time, the Viceroy and members of the Indian Civil Service contested this double standard and voiced criticism of particular pieces of legislation such as the Australian Immigration Restriction Act. In the official correspondence, there is evidence of resentment about Australian treatment of particular Indians and a refusal to accede to Australian requests to prevent Indians departing for Australia. Natal, Australia and New

---

[12] Daniel Gorman 2002, 'Wider and Wider Still?: Racial Politics, Intra-Imperial Immigration and the Absence of Imperial Citizenship in the British Empire'. *Journal of Colonialism and Colonial History*, vol. 3, no. 3, para 30 accessed at http://muse.jhu.edu/journals/journal_of_colonialism_colonial_history/v003/ on 13 February 2003.
See also Robert Huttenback 1976, *Racism and Empire: White Settlers and Colored Immigrants in the British Self-Governing Colonies, 1830–1910* (Ithaca, NY and London: Cornell University Press), p. 139ff.

[13] Hugh Tinker 1976, *Separate and Unequal: India and Indians in the British Commonwealth 1920–1950* (London: C. Hurst and Company), p. 22.

[14] Mongia 2003, 'Race, Nationality, Mobility'.

[15] Marie de Lepervanche 1984, *Indians in a White Australia: An Account of Race, Class, and Indian Immigration to Eastern Australia* (Sydney: Allen and Unwin), pp. 56-71. There are extensive examples in National Archives (UK) Colonial Office papers CO 885/8 no. 158, CO 885/9 .no. 168, CO 886/1 nos 1-3, CO 886/2 no 10, CO 886/3 no. 19, CO 886/4 no. 21. These files comprise correspondence and papers relative to the immigration of Asiatics into the Colonies and the treatments of Asiatics in the Dominions.

[16] Mongia 2003, 'Race, Nationality, Mobility'; see also Partha Chatterjee 1993, *The Nation and its Fragments: Colonial and Postcolonial Histories* (Princeton, NJ: Princeton University Press), pp. 16-22.

Zealand had restricted immigration and Canada was anxious to do so. Eventually, however, under the guise of wartime controls, the Government of India introduced a passport system in 1915, which controlled the movement of Indians, 'requiring passports from all Indians proceeding outside India'.[17]

Mongia has focused upon debates during 1906 to 1915, around 'Canadian demands that Indians emigrating to Canada should have passports',[18] while Radhika Singha has explored the development of passport policy of the Government of India from 1911 to 1923,[19] but a transnational approach allows for a broader address to such issues, bringing together policy developments across the British Empire, at least. Lake has shown the importance of looking further, to the United States, in examining the development of ideologies and techniques to restrict non-white immigration.

Indians resident in settler colonies often campaigned vigorously against racial discrimination. In South Africa, Mahatma Gandhi was a key figure in this resistance from the 1890s and his experiences there were crucial to the later development of his political philosophy.[20] The treatment of Indians overseas was of continuing concern to the Indian nationalist movement in the early twentieth century. In 1901, Gandhi was instrumental in getting the Indian National Congress to pass a resolution on the rights of Indians in South Africa.[21] G. K. Gokhale and the Servants of India Society in Poona and H. S. Polak and the Indians Overseas Association, based in London, as well as numerous Indians across the Empire, kept these issues on the nationalist agenda.[22] The distinctions made between the white and non-white subjects of the Empire and, in particular, the denial of Dominion status to India continued to be condemned by Indian leaders in the interwar years.[23]

While Indians were campaigning for the protection of their rights as British subjects, Australians were able to move about freely and work and settle in all parts of the Empire, as Australian missionaries did in India. To discuss the missionary activity of Australians in India requires the examination of the work of a number of different Christian denominations, which before and well after

---

[17] Mongia 2003, 'Race, Nationality, Mobility', p. 210.

[18] ibid., p. 196.

[19] Radhika Singha 2005, Exceptions to the Law, and Exceptional Laws: The Regulation of Mobility in Colonial India 1911–1923, unpublished paper presented to 20th International Congress of Historical Sciences, University of New South Wales, 7 July.

[20] See Robert Huttenback 1971, *Gandhi in South Africa: British Imperialism and the Indian Question, 1860–1914* (Ithaca, NY and London: Cornell University Press).

[21] Tinker 1976, *Separate and Unequal*, p. 23.

[22] ibid., p. 24; see also B. Chaturvedi collection in Indian National Archives (New Delhi).

[23] Tinker 1976, *Separate and Unequal*.

Federation, were organised on a colonial and then state basis. In 1882, the South Australian Baptist Missionary Society sent Ellen Arnold and Marie Gilbert to do *zenana* work in Faridpur, West Bengal, where they established the South Australian mission. A number of other Australians from the various colonies followed in their footsteps. Between 1882 and 1913, the Australian Baptist Mission Societies sent fifty-four women and sixteen men to the field in Bengal.[24] The Reverend Silas Mead of Flinders Street Baptist Church in Adelaide was a strong promoter of the Baptist mission movement and has been dubbed the 'father of Australian Baptist missions'.[25] From 1892, his son Dr. Cecil Mead and his wife, Alice served as medical missionaries at Faridpur.

In the south of India, the Presbyterian Women's Missionary Association (PWMA) of New South Wales supported the Church of Scotland Zenana Mission with Mary MacLean the first PWMA missionary to arrive in 1891. A few years later, the PWMA took over the mission at Sholingur, just north of Madras. Mary MacLean founded a school there and worked there for twenty years.[26]

Mission work in India was the goal for a number of dedicated young Australian women. In the early twentieth century, many students at Australia's fledgling universities supported the Missionary Settlement for University Women (MSUW) and its work with educated and higher caste women in India. The MSUW, which set up a settlement and then a hostel for women students in Bombay, had been established by women from Newnham, Girton and Somerville Colleges in Oxford and Cambridge. Their identity as university women was central to the organisation, which attracted strong interest from students in Australia, who heard about it from the networks of Empire. A Melbourne graduate, Susie Williams, came to know of the MSUW while she was a student at Newnham College, Oxford. She wrote home to her friends, also graduates from Melbourne University, and soon there were branches established at the universities in Melbourne, Sydney and Adelaide.[27]

---

[24] See Ros [sic] Gooden 'We Trust Them to Establish the Work': Significant Roles of Early Australian Baptist Women in Overseas Mission, 1864–1913', in Mark Hutchinson and Geoff Treloar (eds) 1998, *This Gospel Shall be Preached: Essays on the Australian Contribution to World Mission* (Sydney: The Centre for the Study of Australian Christianity), pp. 126-46; and Margaret Allen 2000, '"White Already to Harvest": South Australian Women Missionaries in India', *Feminist Review*, vol. 65, no. 1, pp. 92-107.

[25] Rosalind Gooden 1994, 'Silas Mead Baptist Missions Motivator', *Our Yesterdays*, vol. 2, pp. 67-95.

[26] Janet West 1997, *Daughters of Freedom: A History of Women in the Australian Church* (Sutherland, NSW: Albatross), pp. 207-8.

[27] British Library Oriental and India Office Collection (OIOC) Mss Eur f 186/128 Missionary Society for University Women (MSUW) Annual Report 1900, p. 35.

In 1903, Katie Fell, with her sister and their mother, Lady Helen Fell, stopped off in Bombay on their way back from a European tour. Katie had graduated with an Arts degree from Sydney University, where she had become involved in the Student Christian Movement. Inspired by its leader, John Mott, with his message about the evangelisation of the world, she developed a particular interest in the MSUW. In London, its leaders had persuaded her to spend some time in Bombay and she remained there for six months, the first Australian to be based there. Other Australian women later came to work at the settlement and the associated YWCA hostels in Madras and Calcutta. Elsie Nicol had come to India under the auspices of the MSUW and soon after was asked to run the YWCA hostel at Madras, on behalf of both organisations. There she came to love the young Indian women with whom she worked, one of whom, Nallemma Williams, a medical student from Ceylon, became a special friend and her bridesmaid, when she married in Madras, in 1909.[28] Nicol supported Nallemma Williams' selection as a delegate to the YWCA world conference in Paris in 1903. Australian supporters of the MSUW could follow the activities of the settlers, which were reported at length in various other missionary publications.

These women were accustomed to the idea of travel and service abroad in the missionary cause. India was an important site of Christian missionary endeavour and for Australian Christians, who sought to become missionaries, India was an important venue. In 1895, Charles Reeve, an experienced evangelist from Tasmania, established the Poona and Indian Village Mission (PIVM) in Poona.[29] He travelled regularly to England, Scotland, New Zealand and Australia to recruit missionaries and to raise funds. A number of Australian men and women subsequently joined this mission, including Amy Parsons, a young Adelaide woman, who had initially gone to Faridpur in East Bengal in 1888 under the auspices of the South Australian Baptist Mission Society. In this, she followed in the footsteps of Ellen Arnold and Marie Gilbert, who had been the first missionaries there in 1882.[30] But back in Adelaide on furlough in 1894, she was taken by Charles Reeve's message and joined the PIVM, where she served from many years. She continued to travel back and forth to Australia, only finally retiring to Australia in the late 1940s. Having spent virtually all her adult life in India, it is not surprising that she described India as 'The Land of My Adoption'.[31]

---

[28] OIOC MSS/Eur f 186/142 MSUW Quarterly Newsletter no. 40 Jan 1909, p. 7.

[29] I am very grateful to Rachel Human (Kew, Victoria), Gillian Watch Whittall (Queensland) and Elisabeth Wilson (Hobart) for sharing information about Charles Reeve with me.

[30] See Allen 2000, '"White Already to Harvest"'.

[31] A. Parsons 1920, 'Back to the Land of My Adoption', *White Already to Harvest*, vol. 25, no. 3, p. 59.

The PIVM and other missions depended on the railways and protection of the British Empire. They could count on the support of the British forces should their preaching prove offensive to Indians, when, for example, they campaigned at holy sites on special religious occasions. From 1905, the PIVM missionaries started going to Hindu holy places at Pandharpur, near Poona, at the time of the *jutras*. When these missionaries were attacked in 1908, British authorities arrived to protect them and their mission. Twenty-six Indian men and boys were arrested, tried, found guilty and sentenced variously to rigorous imprisonment and whipping.[32]

While Australian women missionaries sought to impart a Christian education to those in the settlements, many Indians in the late nineteenth century sought to enhance their education by travelling across the world to Europe and America. Although Hindus were concerned about travelling across 'the black waters', a steady stream of students made their way to British universities.[33] Moreover, Christian converts went to recruit more to the mission field. Others just wanted to see more of the world and to experience new places and see new people. Some Indian travellers published accounts of their travels.[34] One such was Hajee Mahomed, who made extensive tours around the world between 1886 and 1887 and again between 1893 and 1895. He was a man of Empire, Indian born and in business in Cape Town. In the introduction to his book, he explained why he published an account of his travels: 'My principal object in publishing these pages is to give some idea, however faint and crude, to my countrymen, and particularly to my Mahomedan brethren, that beyond the narrow bounds of their home, there lies a world of joy and beauty.'[35]

On his second tour, he spent some time in Melbourne, Hobart and Sydney and was quite taken with the night life of Melbourne: 'On Saturday night, Melbourne, as is the case with large European cities, was gay and brilliant with illuminations and crowds of pleasure seekers going to theatres, concert and restaurants. I wandered about in amazement and wonder till a late hour.'[36] He enjoyed the

---

[32] SIM Archives, North Carolina, USA. Poona and Inland Village Mission Records Box 5 Pandarharpur Station Diary 1908–1909 includes Report in *Bombay Guardian*, 10 October 1908.

[33] Shompa Lahiri 2000, *Indians in Britain: Anglo-India Encounters, Race and Identity 1880–1930* (London: Frank Cass), pp. 5 and 21-9.

[34] Antoinette Burton 1996, 'Making a Spectacle of Empire: Indian Travellers In Fin-de-Siècle London', *History Workshop Journal*, no. 42, p. 128. See also *Pandita Rambai's American Encounter: The Peoples of the United States*, translated and edited by Meera Kosambi 2003, (Bloomington, IN: Indiana University Press).

[35] H. S. S. Mahomed 1895, *Journal of My Tours around the World, 1886–1887 and 1893–1895* (Bombay: Duftur Ashkra Oil Engine Press), p. vii.

[36] ibid., p. 62.

sights in the Dandenongs and through his imperial connections was able to visit the Observatory. A Cape Town friend, settled in Melbourne, introduced him to the superintendent, Mr. Ellery, who explained to him 'some of the wonders of the starry world'.[37] He then went north, where he enjoyed the beauty of Sydney, 'superior to Melbourne in its natural loveliness'.[38] In Hobart he saw some business opportunities: 'I believe that if some enterprising countrymen of mine were to open a business in Indian cloth Japanese curiosities and Cutch [sic] and Delhi metal and art works, they are likely to do well.'[39] Generally, he found the colonists he met kind and polite. But he also noted the difficulties encountered by poor hawkers from Bengal, Kashmir and the Sind: 'These traders appeared to be quite a harmless lot, working hard for their daily bread. They are perfectly innocent of English and do not know how very black they are painted by the jealousy and prejudice of writers in the Australian journals.'[40]

A number of Indian men had arrived in Australia from the mid-nineteenth century, and often took work as hawkers or labourers. Some arrived from elsewhere in the Empire. Otim Singh, for example, had worked as a 'supervisor in a large tobacco-plantation on Sumatra, on behalf of an English firm' where he, reportedly, had '200 coolies under his control'.[41] He returned to his home in the Punjab, where he purchased some land, but the call of distant lands caught him once more and he set sail for Batavia (Jakarta) to visit his brother, before arriving in Melbourne in 1890. He worked as an itinerant hawker in Victoria and later in South Australia, where he established a store and a prosperous business which he ran until his death in 1927.[42]

Otim Singh was one of many Indians living in Australia at the end of the nineteenth century when the Australian colonies began to legislate to restrict the entry of Indians and other 'Asiatics'. In New South Wales, for example, after an attempt to exclude Asians by name was 'reserved' by the Colonial Office, the Coloured Races Restriction and Regulation Bill, utilising the 'Natal formula', was passed in 1897. Aliens, including Indians, had thenceforth to enter their names on an Aliens Register and around ninety Indians did so in Sydney between 1899 and 1902.[43] They were required to pay two shillings and sixpence for this privilege. Acts to restrict Asian immigration were also passed in Western

---

[37] ibid., p. 64.
[38] ibid., p. 76.
[39] ibid., p. 66.
[40] ibid., p. 78.
[41] H. T. Burgess 1909, *Cyclopedia of South Australia* (Adelaide: Cyclopedia Company), vol. 2, p. 1019.
[42] *Kangaroo Island Courier*, 10 December 1927, p. 2.
[43] National Archives of Australia (NAA) Series SP 822/10 Aliens' Register (Sydney) 1898–1902.

Australia, Tasmania and Victoria.[44] At the time of federation, in 1901, one estimate calculated the number of Indians in Australia at 7637.[45] The Immigration Restriction Act of 1901, as noted earlier, classified Indians as 'natives of Asia' who could only enter Australia if they could pass a 'dictation test' in a European language, administered in such a manner as to exclude them. In the years following the passing of the Immigration Restriction Act, the number of Indians in Australia declined to around 3698 by 1911.[46]

Initially, after 1901, it became virtually impossible for any Indian to come to Australia, except some who had lived in Australia previously. It was possible for those already resident in Australia to gain a Domicile certificate and, after 1905, a Certificate of Exemption from the Dictation Test (CEDT). This operated like a passport, which allowed the holder to re-enter Australia within three years. It carried two photographs of the holder, a profile as well as full-face view and a handprint. It was possible for holders of such certificates to apply for extensions and some were able to stay away from Australia for twelve or more years before returning. But not all Indians who had resided in Australia were accorded the right to re-enter.

Marie de Lepervanche has argued that in the earliest years of federation, the definition of 'domicile' was very narrow, so that many who had lived for years in Australia were not granted a 'certificate of domicile'. Generally, those who had some capital in Australia were more likely to be allowed to return than those who had very little.[47] After 1903, it seems that 'applications for domicile were generally approved if evidence of good character and five years' residence was produced'.[48] In order to establish their worth, local police officers were required to make a check on the applicant for a Domicile certificate, or after 1905, a CEDT. Thus, in 1903, the Walgett police made enquiries about Burket Ali Khan, who applied for a certificate of domicile, as he wished to go to India for 'about three years or less, attending private business'. He had been in Australia since 1895 and was a storekeeper in partnership with Curam Bux, Nabob Khan and Omar Khan at Comborah near Walgett. Although the police reported that Burket Ali Khan was 'not the owner of any land and his share in the business is not worth over £25', he was granted a certificate. The police report noted that they 'knew nothing against his character'.[49]

---

[44] de Lepervanche 1984, *Indians in a White Australia*, pp. 51-5.

[45] Palfreeman, in de Lepervanche 1984, *Indians in a White Australia*, p. 24.

[46] de Lepervanche 1984, *Indians in a White Australia*, p. 24.

[47] ibid., p. 57.

[48] ibid.

[49] NAA Collector of Customs, Sydney Series SP 42/1 Correspondence Relating to Immigration Restriction and Passports 1898–1948 C1903/5965 re Burket Ali Khan.

Thus Indians who left Australia had to undergo quite rigorous scrutiny in order to be able to return to Australia. Their applications were accompanied by references, often from employers or people with whom they had done business, in which the referees acknowledged knowing the applicants for some time and testified to their good character. Often the police made a visit to the referees to get confirmation that the photograph on the application was that of the person for whom they had vouched.

Most Indians in Australia were men and they found it difficult if not impossible to bring wives from India. In 1904, Hushnak Singh, a domestic servant of Narrabeen applied for 'a certificate of naturalization'. A Punjabi, he had been in Australia since 1898. He was, he wrote, 'a British subject' and formerly 'a trooper in 6th Bengal Lancer[s] Prince of Wales [Regiment]'. He planned to make a brief trip to India to marry and wanted the necessary documentation to enable him to bring his bride back to Australia. The Department of External Affairs informed him that naturalisation was unnecessary as he was a British subject. His intended bride, however 'would be deemed a prohibited immigrant'. The Secretary Attlee Hunt advised, 'the Lady will have to pass the Education Test which may be imposed in any European language'.[50] It is not known what happened to Hushnak Singh and his bride, but it was very difficult for British Indians to bring their families to Australia.[51]

Until 1904, only Indians formerly resident in Australia and able to get a certificate of domicile were able to enter Australia. However, in 1905, following negotiations with the Government of India the regulations were relaxed and amended to allow for the visits and temporary stays of tourists, students and *bona fide* merchants. The British authorities in India were required to issue passports, for visits to Australia, to those eligible under the revised regulations. The passport specifically devised for this purpose detailed the traveller's name and that of his father, given in both English and the vernacular. Information on this form also included the traveller's caste or clan, residence – detailing town or village and district or state – profession, age and, for male travellers only, a description of distinctive marks. A full description of the purpose of the visit, its probable

---

[50] NAA Department of External Affairs Series A1 Correspondence Files, 1904/2531 Hushnak Singh Naturalization.

[51] Huttenback notes that while under the IRA 1901, an immigrant's wife and minor children could enter Australia, this section was suspended in March 1903 and deleted in the amended act of 1905. Huttenback 1976, *Racism and Empire,* p. 308, note 72. De Lepervanche suggests that from 1906 Indian residents could bring their wives over for six months each year. Certainly from April 1919, resident Indians could bring their wives and minor children to live with them in Australia; see A. T. Yarwood 1964, *Asian Migration to Australia: The Background to Exclusion 1896–1923* (Melbourne: Melbourne University Press), p. 135.

duration, the port of embarkation and the names, ages and relationships of members of the family accompanying the applicant were also to be given. This document and the accuracy of the information on it had to be vouched for and endorsed by a magistrate or political officer in India.[52]

Article 14 of the amended Act worked to deter shippers from bringing prohibited immigrants to Australian ports. Huttenback notes: 'It required the master or owner of any vessel bringing a prohibited immigrant to the Commonwealth to return him whence he came at no cost to the state and to recompense the Government of Australia for any expenses incurred in the interim.' Shipping companies thus became extremely cautious in deciding whether to allow Indians to embark for Australia. In 1908, when Syed Iran Shah Sahid attempted to travel to Australia to bring back 'an aged relative who had settled there' he failed to secure a passage, although he had the required passport. He travelled four times to Colombo from Madras, but discovered that 'the steamer companies there refuse to book any natives of India to Australia unless they hold a pass from the Australian government allowing them to land'.[53] Similarly, Ghulam Jan, who planned to visit Australia 'to search for a brother who has not been heard of for many years'. was also denied a passage by a shipping company at Colombo.[54] Further information had to be sent to the various shipping companies to explain the new arrangements for Indians with a legitimate passport allowing them to visit Australia.

Once Indian travellers landed in Australia, there was still a possibility of deportation. Ghulam Jan and the servant who had accompanied him ran into trouble shortly after their arrival in Australia in 1908. The West Australian police alleged that they were 'imposters', 'cadgers' and 'undesirables' and they were deported. This was despite the fact that a number of Ghulam Jan's 'countrymen and co-religionists' in Perth signed a memorial testifying that

> all can speak of the excellent character he has maintained during his sojourn in this city and the high esteem he is held in by all who have the pleasure of meeting him. We further wish to add that the Syed has been fortunate in his search, and found his brother in Port Hedland (W.A.) for which, and only purpose, he [The Syed] has visited this country.[55]

---

[52] NAA Series A1 1925/27045 Admission of Indians, Cingalese [Sinhalese] and Burmese Merchants, students and tourist travellers on passports.

[53] ibid. Acting Chief Secretary of Madras Government to Secretary Government of India 13 November 1908.

[54] ibid. Agent to Governor General, Baluchistan to Secretary to Governor General, Simla 8 May 1908.

[55] Indian National Archives, (New Delhi) Foreign Department General A Proceedings April 1909, numbers 36-8.

Indians had protested against the Australian policies since the late nineteenth century. In 1898, Indian traders in Melbourne had sent a Memorial to the Government of India protesting against the Victorian colony's Immigration Restriction Bill and in the following year, 'Certain Sikhs resident in WA' sent a petition 'complaining of their disabilities under recent legislation in that colony'. Such protests continued after 1901. Merchants in an Indian business in Melbourne wrote to the press in 1902 in relation to the Immigration Restriction Act. They were seeking to get five Indians into the country to work in their business: 'the Act is operating very harshly upon us, and is likely to bring about results inimical to the interests of Australia and to the good feeling existing between fellow British subjects of two shades of colour.'[56] They warned of a boycott, or on the part of the Mohammedans, a 'jehad' just as they had done, they said, in regard to Natal when it introduced immigration restrictions. They advised that the National Congress of India 'have already taken the matter up, and may be expected to pass some resolution on the matter early in the coming year'.[57]

Indians across the Empire became more aware of Australian policies in 1905 when Mool Chand was deported. He was an Indian civil servant from Lahore who arrived in Perth on a visit in 1904. Having previously worked on the railways in India, in Uganda and in the civil service of British North Borneo, he was an experienced man of Empire, able to travel around to take up work. When he was discovered working in a Perth business owned by a fellow countryman, Inder Singh, however, he was summarily deported. This led to a storm of protest from the Indian community in Western Australia and their supporters. Mool Chand instructed a Perth solicitor to institute action for damages for false imprisonment and illegal deportation against the Collector of Customs. He also stated his intentions to institute proceedings against Alfred Deakin, the Australian Prime Minister.[58]

When the Reverend Theo. Fischer of the Church of Christ was visiting missions in India, he was challenged about Australian policies: 'An official to whom we spoke in one place could not understand why Australia, which claimed to be a Christian country, would not admit him, for instance, to Australian shores.'[59]

---

[56] *Register*, Adelaide 22 December 1902, p. 3.

[57] ibid., 22 December 1902, p. 3; see also A. M. Zaidi , compiler, 1987–, *INC* [Indian National Congress]: *The Glorious Tradition 1885–1920* (New Delhi: Indian Institute of Applied Political Research), vol. 1, pp. 234-5.

[58] NAA Department of External Affairs Series A1 Correspondence Files, 1908/11468 Deportation of Mool Chand 1905–8. In the event, Mool Chand did not pursue these actions.

[59] Fischer 1914, *A Month in India*, p. 111.

Indian public opinion was often incensed by Australian immigration policies and Indians began to ask why, when they were being treated so badly by the Australian government, that Australian citizens could still enter India freely and take up jobs and establish businesses there. In late August 1905, three Indian doctors arrived in Perth. While they acknowledged that they had proper papers and did not have 'much difficulty' in landing in Australia, they were shocked to note that they were listed on their ship's papers as 'prohibited immigrants'.[60] They contrasted the cordial welcome they had received in England, with the efforts to debar them when they were merely making a short visit to Australia. Australian doctors visiting India, in contrast, were 'allowed every freedom'.[61] Furthermore, they would be 'free to come and go and given every help in the pursuit and investigations of their studies'. Certainly, Australian doctors visiting India were not required to carry special exemptions, nor were they on 'mustered up like sheep to pass an inspection' and subject to a penalty of £100 per head for their safe removal.[62]

While Australians – as white British subjects – enjoyed the freedom to travel to and work and spread the Christian gospel in India, the White Australia Policy effectively debarred Indians from the enjoyment of reciprocal rights in Australia. The mobility of modernity was reserved for those deemed white.

---

[60] NAA Department of External Affairs Series A1 Correspondence Files, 1908/11468 Deportation of Mool Chand 1905–8, clipping from *Perth Herald*, 29 August 1905.

[61] A number of Australian doctors worked in India at this time. Some were missionaries while others were hired by the Indian authorities to work as 'plague doctors' giving inoculations and helping to overcome plague epidemics. Dr R. Hornabrook was one of the Australian doctors who worked in this capacity in India in 1902–3. See Margaret Allen, forthcoming 2006, 'Through Colonial Spectacles', in Kate Douglas et al. (eds), *Journeying and Journalling*.

[62] Allen, forthcoming 2006, 'Through Colonial Spectacles'.

8. Postwar British emigrants and the 'transnational moment': exemplars of a 'mobility of modernity'?

A. James Hammerton

By definition all migration which involves border crossings might be said to be transnational. The truism is so obvious that it's arguable that simply affixing the 'transnational' label does not tell us anything new about meanings of migration, in terms of either collective identities or individual and group experience. Social historians of migration for years have, in effect, written transnational histories, recounting, in Oscar Handlin's classic formulation, the epic stories of the uprooted and the transplanted, their stories of trauma, alienation and vindication in two countries, and subsequently the continuing contacts and networking of family members and communities between, at least, two countries.[1] These were quintessentially transnational experiences.

So it seems legitimate to ask how much the addition of the term 'transnational' to migration history brings in the way of explanatory power or theoretical illumination. 'Migration as Transnational Interaction', the title of one recent article on the subject, seems on the surface to signify a quite straightforward process, but it is in this sense a tautology, since all migration since the formation of nation states has involved transnational interaction.[2] Migration historians have thus perhaps felt less urgency to articulate explicitly transnational perspectives while others have been challenging histories based on narrow frameworks determined by the unitary nation state.[3] While it is true that the history of migration policy and demography has conventionally been written within frameworks of the nation state and state formation, whether of the sending or receiving nations, in recent times migration historians have criticised and superseded this approach. Some have pointed to ways in which the modern ubiquity of global migration challenges the myths surrounding the grand master

---

[1] Oscar Handlin 1951, *The Uprooted: The Epic Story of the Great Migrations that Made the American People* (Boston, MA: Atlantic-Little).

[2] Loretta Baldassar 1995, 'Migration as Transnational Interaction: Italy Revisited', *ConVivio*, vol. 1, no. 2, pp. 114-26.

[3] See, for example, the deliberations of the American historians who began to debate movement away from narrow national perspectives in American history a decade ago. *Journal of American History, The Nation and Beyond, A Special Issue*: 'Transnational Perspectives on United States History', December 1999, vol. 86, no. 3.

narrative of the culturally homogeneous and assimilating nation state.[4] Indeed, writing on migrant life experience, on family and community networks and on individual trajectories of return migration, which has dominated recent research, rarely works within traditional assumptions of the assimilating nation state. So one might suggest that migration history, at least, has only in part been 'handmaiden to the nation-state', one of the guiding assumptions driving the turn to transnational perspectives. Nevertheless, there remains a useful purpose in exploring the broad spectrum between different modes of migration history, from the national to transnational, and the ways these are expressed in different aspects of migration. To paraphrase Richard White, some aspects of migration history lend themselves to national historical perspectives, and some demand a global or transnational approach.[5]

These reflections arise from a shift in my own work from the study of one form of migration history to another, specifically from traditional 'migrations of austerity', broadly conceived, to more recent 'migrations of prosperity', in both cases from the perspective of migrant experience and memory and the meanings migrants make of them. Most of the migration histories still written today are, unsurprisingly, those of austerity and dislocation, since prosperity remains a minority and recent, though increasing, stimulus for migration, most obvious in population movement from developed countries in the latter decades of the twentieth century. The differences reflect variations in traditional 'push-pull' models of migration, although for the later twentieth century such models are too simplistic to explain the complexities of modern mobility.

My explicit focus on post World War II British migration to countries of the 'Old Commonwealth' illustrates this trajectory from migrations of austerity to prosperity. Between the 1940s and 1960s Australia's 'Ten Pound Poms', about one million of them (and a similar number to Canada), were driven overwhelmingly by forces of austerity.[6] Their migrations were in the classic mould of permanent transfer from one nation state to another, in subsidised schemes driven powerfully by national interests and policies in the sending and receiving countries. The large movement (sometimes, controversially, defined

---

[4] Rina Benmayor and Andor Skotnes 1994, 'Some Reflections on Migration and Identity', in Rina Benmayor and Andor Skotnes (eds), *Migration and Identity* (Oxford: Oxford University Press), pp. 5-6.

[5] Richard White 1999, 'The Nationalization of Nature', *Journal of American History*, vol. 86, no. 3, pp. 976-7, 986.

[6] A. James Hammerton and Alistair Thomson 2005, *'Ten Pound Poms': Australia's Invisible Migrants* (Manchester: Manchester University Press).

as a 'diaspora')[7] was part of a larger set of postwar global population movements, but it was also framed and is best understood by its unique characteristics. The austerity migrations of the first postwar British generation, while not comparable to the conditions on the European continent which produced ten million refugees or 'Displaced Persons', were stimulated nevertheless by common conditions of postwar dislocation, of shortage and rationing – of food, consumer goods and housing. Their migration was thus deeply traditional, having much in common with the mass migrations of their nineteenth century ancestors. But these migrants – appropriately labelled 'invisible' because of their historiographical neglect and relative low profile as migrants in receiving societies – were privileged by the imperial heritage which shaped their mobility. A common language, 'British subject' status, the frequent official, and preferential, recognition of their occupational qualifications and the general presumption of a British 'foundational culture' in the new country made for an experience which one would expect to be significantly different, certainly easier, from that of most other postwar migrants carrying burdens like language, deep cultural differences and profound marginalisation.

This was a perception often shared by British migrants themselves, at least before their arrival. Many of them observed that they regarded their migration as a move simply 'from one part of Britain to another' – a reason often invoked for not considering the United States.[8] In the early postwar years in Australia the common currency of a British passport and British subject status made this virtually true, so that the sense of not even crossing an international boundary (as opposed, emphatically, to an unanticipated cultural boundary after arrival) was shared by most. At the outset, at least, they did not see their migration as a transnational experience so much as a translocal one, comparable in some ways to a move from Bradford to London. In these ways postwar British migrants continued to be beneficiaries of the 'colonial dividend', and this postcolonial advantage is what most distinguished them from their non-English speaking counterparts.

The British-Australian understanding of a virtually borderless movement within a postcolonial 'British World' chimed well with official views of postwar Australian and British migration policy and its ethnic goals. Arthur Calwell's well known preference for the 'British and Nordic races as first priority'

---

[7] See, for example, Stephen Constantine 2003, 'British Emigration to the Empire-Commonwealth since 1880: From Overseas Settlement to Diaspora?', *Journal of Imperial and Commonwealth History*, no. 31, pp. 16-35; Eric Richards 2004, *Britannia's Children: Emigration from England, Scotland, Wales and Ireland Since 1600* (London: Hambledon and London).

[8] These were the precise words used, among many others, by Ron Penn, a British migrant to Sydney in 1947; Hammerton and Thomson 2005, *'Ten Pound Poms'*, pp. 325-31.

underlined a general consensus about the need to maintain Australia's fundamental British character. The Menzies Liberals continued the policy seamlessly, echoed in Immigration Minister Harold Holt's declaration that 'this is a British community, and we want to keep it a British community, living under British standards and by the methods and ideals of British Parliamentary democracy'.[9] Government advertising effectively propagated these policies and assumptions. A 1959 Australia House publication assured its readers that the half million Britons who had emigrated since the war had found a 'British Way of Life' among Australians 'who are predominantly of British Isles stock'. In British Australia migrants could expect to join a familiar culture with the added advantage of superior living standards, enhanced opportunities for home ownership, good education and a sunny outdoor life far removed from Britain's oppressive climate.[10] In their expectations, at least, migrants demonstrated that they were reassured by propaganda which virtually declared that their migration would be borderless. Recalling their decision to leave in 1959, for example, English migrants Maureen and John Butts agreed that they could not have contemplated moving to a 'foreign country' like the United States, but their deeply held patriotism was unchallenged by a move to Australia. John recalled that 'we didn't think about it as a foreign country either … There was an association with English people that you were going to that you … felt comfortable with. Yes, yes.'[11]

As is usual in migrant experience, however, the living out of migrant lives in the new country departed from the anticipation. Most of the British migrants of the 1950s and 1960s moved in nuclear family groups and left close kin behind with limited opportunities for revived contacts, and it is here that the notion of the 'transnational family' – sustained kinship communication across borders to the point of dependence and emotional expectation – becomes useful for understanding how the dominant stories of these 'invisible migrants' echoed those of migrants from other backgrounds. Their move to Australia, arguably to a greater degree than for their Canadian counterparts, involved a sharp and seemingly final break with family members left behind. This was often recalled in precise descriptions of a rich network of extended family who gathered together on the train platform or the ship to bid that vividly remembered final farewell. A Welsh woman, Maureen Carter, recalls:

---

[9] Reg Appleyard with Alison Ray and Allan Segal 1988, *The Ten Pound Immigrants* (London: Boxtree), pp. 10, 28.

[10] Chief Migration Officer, Australia House 1959, *Australia Invites You* (London); Hammerton and Thomson 2005, *'Ten Pound Poms'*, p. 37.

[11] Interview, Maureen and John Butts, Perth, Western Australia, 27 March 2000, La Trobe University migration archive (LTU), no. LU 0134.

There must have been hundreds of people on that railway station, all singing, 'We'll keep a Welcome in the Hillside'! It brings tears to my eyes now! And, one of the lines is, 'We'll kiss away each hour of hiraeth [homesickness/longing in Welsh], when you come home again to Wales'! And I, I, I still crack up when I think of it. And I just had that feeling for so long, well it seemed like so long, when I first came.[12]

One response to this loss of kin networks was to set about and valorise the creation of a new family network in Australia, palpably evident in the photograph displays of grandchildren and other new family at home at the time of interviews. The Australian family reunion on the twentieth or thirtieth anniversary of arrival could be a vivid ritual marker of that celebration of the new family. Another response, especially in later years, three or four decades after migration, was to revive contact with lost kin and neighbourhoods back 'home', which can involve the virtual creation of a transnational identity in later life, through frequent return visits and reverse visits, the cultivation of extensive and regular correspondence and, more recently, email exchanges. That is, what was structurally a simple matter of individualist relocation, and a sharp break with family, could give rise to a longer-term cultivation of transnational family links. But over time we can discern different degrees of transnational interaction.

Life history sources like autobiographical writings and oral testimony help to convey the nature and effects of this transnational interaction. Pat Drohan's story illustrates the process.[13] Pat was single and twenty-four when she emigrated from Wolverhampton in 1958, with prearranged secretarial work in Ballarat, Victoria. She set out as a classic 'sojourner', intent on an adventurous two-year working holiday, but left behind a large, close-knit and convivial family, none of whom ever emigrated. She was one of those thousands of young single people, fairly comfortably employed in Britain, who in a sense 'piggy backed' on a subsidised migration scheme aimed primarily at young fertile families. Her plans shifted dramatically when, before the end of her two years, she met and married an Australian husband and settled in Ballarat. At the time it did not matter to Pat that marriage to an Australian set her on an unanticipated course to permanent Australian residence. But it did mark the beginning of her long struggle to maintain family links, intensified for her by the fact that she left behind a close twin sister. In the early years much of her life in Australia was defined by being apart from her family, especially during critical moments like childbirth. Lacking physical contact, over the years she relied on the telephone for the contact which eluded her. Her heartfelt words on the subject

---

[12] Interview, Maureen Carter, Sydney, 9 July 1998, LTU, LU 0157.

[13] Interview, Pat Drohan, Ballarat, 13 August 1998, LTU, LU 0262.

betray the emotional depth and family bond which survived the long years apart.

> And over the years the family, with the phone calls and that, they know the time difference and all that, and I've always said to them: 'If anything happens at home, you are, you are to call me, you're to *tell* me; I don't care when. Including...'. And they say: 'We *always* include you, Pat, whatever we do, you're always included in what we do, we ring you when...', 'cause I've missed weddings, I've missed births, but I think the worst are the deaths ... but I just couldn't describe what it was like, to know Mum had gone, and you, you don't know what to do, there's no-one to speak to, just nobody. And then, the calls in the middle of the night, I'll sit up and take the call, I'd, my sons lived at home then and the, my sister died suddenly, with an aneurism ... and what, what do you do? Where do you go? ... And I didn't wake my husband, and it's no good waking my sons, and I sat there crying, and, you can't talk, you can't go round, you can't do anything.

From 1973 (after 15 years) Pat was able to begin making return visits, mostly with her husband, to the family in Wolverhampton. These visits became a stimulus for an increasing sense of ambivalence in her attitude to her emigration, encompassing the idea that she has become closer to the family than before leaving. She was struck by the way her family confirmed her development of independence in Australia, especially in relation to her twin sister, with whom her earlier identity had been submerged. 'When I went back, after 15 years, the family said: "My word, you've changed!" ... They said I'd, I'd become so much more assertive and outspoken ... And I said: "Well you know", I said: "When you go out somewhere that's so far away from home, and you're on your own, you haven't got anybody to, to stand up and speak for you".'

In effect Pat re-fashioned her English identity in her later years through being away from family, through contact and return visits. Reflecting about the interview, in which she began to explore some of these feelings in deeper ways than before, she admitted 'I'm more English now than I was when I left!' As the years have passed and her family have aged, the realisation of distance and frequent farewells has brought a new poignancy to her mobility.

> My family are now getting old, we are all thinning in, in numbers ... And I ... although it's unspoken, it's there, but, we're, we're all thinking: 'When will the next visit be, will there *be* another one, and who'll be missing...?' And that, that's a fact of life! Somebody *will* be missing – it might even be me ... And so you have to make the most of every opportunity.

While there is evidence here of a gradual generational weakening of transnational family links over time, even as the emotional burden they bear strengthens, there is also stark evidence of the fashioning, in later life, of a transnational identity deeply attached to family and hyper-conscious of loss – in essence a migrant identity – which is a characteristic feature of that first generation of postwar British migrants; it was shared, to a degree, by postwar migrants from other backgrounds like the Italians from San Fior in Perth, written about by Loretta Baldassar, who juggle their loyalty to family and place through return visits and serial relocation.[14]

Pat Drohan began her travels as an intentional sojourner, and many like her managed to continue their travels without being interrupted – or hijacked! – by marriage. They provide a rather different illustration of the evolving nature of 'transnational interaction' for British migrants, and underline ways in which it was informed by its postcolonial shadow. These itinerants of the 1950s bear some resemblance to the sojourning mentality of today's highly mobile backpackers; they are their precursors in a sense, and a prophetically significant by-product of the assisted passage scheme – the ultimate transnationals. Eunice Gardner chronicled her adventures in an aptly titled volume, *The World at Our Feet: The Story of Two Women Who Adventured Halfway Across the Globe*, published in 1957.[15] Leaving Kent alone on the ten-pound passage in the early 1950s, Eunice, a hairdresser, soon met her English companion, Diana Williams. The pair worked in Sydney, hitch hiked around Australia, complete with Union Jacks on their rucksacks, and encountered a succession of like-minded single British itinerants on the move. Eunice's illustrated 'memories of Australia', including a 'Central Australian bush native' and 'making a boomerang from a solid log', hinted at their comfortable though stereotypical engagement with local populations.[16] Otherness thus served the time-worn purpose of picture postcard memory. Their adventures continued on the overland journey home through India, Afghanistan, Iran, Iraq, Turkey and Europe, the increasingly popular itinerary of budget-conscious young travellers. In Afghanistan, with the advantage of British embassy contact, the hairdresser from Maidstone danced with the King's nephew at an 'International Club' party, and narrowly evaded having to be escorted by him the next day while wearing a bhurkha.[17] These sojourners palpably claimed the benefits of Empire and a relatively politically docile Third World rendered their global travel relatively safe; like their

---

[14] Loretta Baldassar 2001, *Visits Home: Migration Experiences Between Italy and Australia* (Melbourne: Melbourne University Press).

[15] Eunice Gardner 1957, *The World at Our Feet: The Story of Two Women Who Adventured Halfway Across the Globe* (London: W. H. Allen).

[16] ibid., illustrations, pp. 64-5.

[17] ibid., p. 177.

nineteenth century world traveller forebears they engaged easily, although from less of a position of clear authority and superiority, with people of other races. The 'world at our feet' was symbolically illustrated for them by their wave on the cover – in actuality a wave at a Malayan pearl cutter in Broome, WA. Eunice had never contemplated permanent migration; her travels were motivated by what she described as 'the wander bug', a notion which set her apart from her friends at home, but it took an assisted migration scheme for her, and Diana, to realise their mobility.

We can see here how, over time, the postwar scheme's embodiment of a migration of austerity progressively took on features of the more modern version of the West's postcolonial migration of prosperity; this was underlined by the large return rate of British migrants generally – ranging over time from 20 per cent to 30 per cent.[18] By the 1980s, with the cessation of subsidised passages and new entrance rules, British migrants to Australia were losing their traditional privilege of access, but they also enjoyed easier mobility and were more easily open to 'serial migration' between countries of the 'Old Commonwealth', as well as return migration.[19] Commentators by the mid 1960s were convinced that Western migration was beginning to reveal new characteristics. Most of these are obvious to us now. The half-century after the war coincided with the dawning and consolidation of the jet age, when what had been until recently a momentous and not easily reversible journey across the world, for most became an investment in recreational globe-trotting. The process was reinforced by corporate employment practices which encouraged staff mobility. British migrants, with transnational links and associations with the 'Old Commonwealth' still fresh, were among the first to benefit from this; besides contemplating a return to Britain after an unsettling spell in the new country, they often remained open to re-migration back to their original destination, even from far distant Australia (a more difficult proposition than the so-called '$1000 cure' back from Canada). Anthony Richmond, the Canadian migration sociologist, described these migrants in 1967 as 'transilients', reflecting the nature of modern urban industrial societies 'whose populations are increasingly mobile, both geographically and socially'. Unlike earlier migrations their movements implied no inadequacy on the part of either country since there was an international market for their skills. These modern migrants 'enjoy travel for its own sake, they find little difficulty making friends wherever they go, and they lack strong family or community ties that might compel them to become sedentary'.[20] The British, of course, were not

---

[18] Hammerton and Thomson 2005, *'Ten Pound Poms'*, pp. 264-5.

[19] ibid., pp. 264-98. I am currently researching the increased British propensity to 'serial migration' since the 1960s.

[20] Anthony H. Richmond 1967, *Post-War Immigrants in Canada* (Toronto: University of Toronto Press), p. 252.

alone in enjoying the benefits of the new mobility, but in their easy access to the old 'British world' they continued to enjoy the benefits of the colonial dividend. And as the fiction of 'moving from one part of Britain to another' became harder to sustain, these serial migrants became more willing to include the United States among their migrant destinations.

According to this view then, the 1960s, the crucial 'transnational moment' in migration, witnessed some fundamental transformations in patterns of Western migration in the direction of a 'mobility of modernity'. This was not just an increased predilection towards the youthful and carefree backpacking of sojourners like Eunice and Diana. For the British it brought more complex patterns of 'transnational family' contact, which in one way or another has always been a product of migration. The sheer scale of physical family movement, once cheaper air travel began to free up mobility, could involve a staggeringly complex set of international family links. One such revealing case is Doug Benson, who first went to Australia at nineteen with his parents and five siblings in 1961. As a young man enjoying the greater freedoms of the 1960s he soon left his family, travelled Australia and the world, and returned to South Australia with a Scottish girl friend who he married in 1967. Homesick for Britain, they returned in 1969 to Somerset where they settled and raised a family, often playing host to other visiting family members, the British headquarters of the mobile Bensons. Doug's description of wider family movements since captures the dizzying moves of his wider family, more reminiscent, perhaps, of migrant cultures like those from the Mediterranean more known for chain migration practices in extended families.

> My wife has never been back to Australia, but I have been twice for about a month each time – firstly just before my father died in 1980, then again in 1992.
>
> Several members of the large family that originally emigrated in 1961 have subsequently been somewhat unsettled. My parents, brothers and sister have all moved around a lot. My middle brother went back to Britain in 1970; he returned to Australia a few years later, has been back here again for a couple of years but is now resident in South Australia. My sister married a Scotsman in Australia, then they went to live in Scotland in 1970. They divorced in 1982; she returned to Australia for a couple of years around 10 years ago, but returned again to Scotland where she still lives. My parents and two youngest brothers returned to England in 1971, but my parents could not settle and went back to Australia with my youngest brother after 2 years. They returned to Britain again 3 years later, but went back to Australia again in 1979. My father died the following year and my mother, usually accompanied by one of her sons, has lived on and off in both Australia and Britain ever

since. At the age of 83, she is now living in England but hoping to return to Australia, where she has three sons and four grandchildren, at the end of this year ...

As for my own feelings about emigration to Australia, I can say that overall I view it as a positive experience, in fact a turning point of my life. If we had not gone to Australia as a family, our lives would no doubt have turned out completely differently ... The biggest negative result is that as a family we are spread between Britain and Australia and have not seen very much of each other, especially the youngest generation.[21]

It is undoubtedly true that the kind of shifts in the 1960s pointed to by commentators like Richmond signified some deep transformations in migration in the Western world, best understood as a move from migrations of austerity to migrations of prosperity. By the 1980s these patterns had become ingrained, and there is plenty of evidence to demonstrate the depth and extent of the way that 'transnational moment' of the 1960s marked a fundamental divide in migration practices. It is worth remembering, though, that historians are concerned not only with 'fundamental divides' but also with continuities and the ways that major shifts are prefigured in earlier experience. We know, for example, that nineteenth century assisted migration to Australia was accompanied by a substantial element of return and itinerant migration among colonial migrants, not least among single women domestic servants.[22] But it was the mid twentieth century before these minority practices became a prominent trend. In this sense the first generation of postwar British migrants were, from the late 1940s, precursors of the mobility of modernity, embodying what became more characteristic of Western migration from the later 1960s.

The life history of Jackie Smith, a woman who now lives in Toronto, and whose migration experience spans the two generations, points the way.[23] On the surface she is a perfect illustration of Richmond's 'transilient', freely traversing continents. In 1959, at the age of thirteen, she and her parents left a rich South London network of working-class neighbours and extended family for Adelaide. She subsequently trained as a nurse, travelled extensively through Europe, back to Australia, then to Africa, married a Canadian (briefly) and eventually settled in Canada, with a young son, where she went to University, became a successful journalist and settled with a Jewish American. A precursor of the late twentieth century 'serial migrant' in every respect, her geographical mobility was matched by her occupational mobility. Yet the modern form of Jackie's life story belies

---

[21] Douglas Benson, written account, University of Sussex migration archive, US B10.

[22] Jan Gothard 2001, *Blue China: Single Female Migration to Colonial Australia* (Carlton, Vic.: Melbourne University Press), pp. 207-8.

[23] Interview, Jackie Smith, Toronto, 1 July 2000, LTU, LU CS50.

the apparent modernity of her ease of movement and adaptability. The eve of her family's London departure was clouded by a bitter quarrel between her mother and her sisters over an inheritance, so the ritual emotional farewells at the station or ship were replaced by a gloomy and subdued nuclear family departure. For Jackie this family estrangement was compounded by the total loss of all connection with wider family, community and friends, which she had enjoyed in London. Her sense of that permanent loss was crystallised for her by the dramatic moment of departure:

> And, so there was this huge problem. And we were going on this six-week voyage. We *knew* we would probably never return, because we didn't have the *money* to come back, you know, you had to go for two years, and we didn't have money, and there was no-one to say goodbye to there, so we took the train, from London ... down to Southampton.

The fracture in family relations was compounded in Australia by the sensory shock of their new environment. Jackie likened the new outer suburb of Elizabeth, physically and figuratively, to a desert: 'There was nothing there. It was dust storms, right? The hellish heat, dust storms, this house with cracks, not a lot of money.' The memories of her early years are dominated by a sense of recollected alienation which recurs in migrant stories of their 'shock of the new'. At school her Englishness became a liability, as she and her brother tried to evade the discrimination that newly arrived 'poms' experienced alongside non-English speakers.

Jackie remembered her early years in Australia as desperately unhappy ones, as her memories of close-knit family intimacy in London yielded to recollections of a dysfunctional and isolated nuclear family in Adelaide and idealisation of the lost network of close relations in London. It is reflected in the extent to which the past continued to govern her attitude to festivities:

> And it was very unhappy. You know, Christmas, that was the end of Christmas, like, for years afterwards, around Christmas, I would totally – I still have difficulty with Christmases. I mean, now I live with a Jewish person, we celebrate Christmas, right, I have a big Christmas party every year. I have all kinds of people over; I make Christmas for my son ... So Christmas to me became a huge thing, because in England I had this family Christmas where, you know, everybody got together and it was a real celebration. We went to Australia, there was no more family Christmas. There was no more family, no more family Christmas.

Although Jackie eventually overcame her culture shock in Australia and developed a deep affection for the country, as well as pride in an Australian rather than a Canadian identity – she spoke, in familiar Australian inflection, of her attachment to 'the land' – the emotional scars of those early years of alienation were enduring. They drove her first into therapy, then into an urge to reconnect with English survivors of her extended family, although she was disappointed both with the old family as well as the old country: 'I would never want to live in England, and I am so grateful that my parents emigrated.' The frequent disillusion with the idealised homeland decades after leaving is often accompanied by disappointment with close family connections in this way. Significantly, it coexists with a seemingly contradictory conviction that migration is unnatural and emotionally traumatic, in conflict with a 'sense of belonging' to family networks:

> I think people don't understand it. They don't understand; they think you come here, you know, and you speak the language, and they don't understand the profound internal effects … the sense of belonging … you know, the profound effect of getting on a boat, right? At a very young age … and going to the ends of the earth … you don't know who you are.

From reluctant and traumatised child migrant, to rootless and itinerant young single, to sophisticated and cosmopolitan serial migrant traversing the 'old Empire', but with a lifelong yearning for enduring 'belonging' to deep family networks, Jackie Smith's life story embodies both traditional and modern modes of migration. For the British the ease of movement which has enabled them to be in the forefront of modern modes of mobility, like Jackie's, has been facilitated by the continuing 'colonial dividend' of prior settlement. But such apparent privileges do not necessarily make for any less painful personal experiences of migration, with ongoing effects on subjective constructions of identity. The stories glimpsed here hint at the multiple ways in which single families can exhibit different aspects of migration simultaneously – permanent one-way migration, serial migration and return migration, all of them carrying their own burdens of personal pain and alienation alongside celebration. The same complexity and contradiction applies to time span; just as we can find precursors of the 'mobility of modernity' among British migrants of the 1950s, like Eunice Gardner, many of their 1980s successors have more in common with traditional permanent settler migrants of the 1950s, or for that matter the 1850s. The 'transnational moment', in this sense, has been a much more drawn out process than imagined by sociologists in the 1960s.

Modernity, Film and Romance

9. 'Films as foreign offices': transnationalism at Paramount in the twenties and early thirties

Desley Deacon

Film scholar Miriam Hansen argues that American mainstream cinema developed a 'global vernacular' – what she calls elsewhere 'an international modernist idiom on a mass basis' - whose transnational appeal derived from diverse domestic traditions, discourses, and interests, including those of the cosmopolitan Hollywood community. 'Hollywood did not just circulate images and sounds', she argues, 'it produced and globalized a new sensorium; it constituted ... new subjectivities and subjects.'[1] Although Hansen refers to the 'cosmopolitan Hollywood community', American mainstream cinema was created as much in New York as in Hollywood during the 1920s and early 1930s, when the American film industry consolidated its global reach.[2] This chapter examines some of the ways in which the New York office of Famous Players-Lasky (Paramount), America's leading producer and distributor of films during the 1920s, consciously fostered 'cosmopolitanism' or 'transnationalism'.[3]

Walter Wanger, Paramount's New York-based general manager of production in the 1920s and early 1930s, had a very clear idea of film's international role from the beginning of his career. 'While the representatives of the nations of the earth sit in conference at Washington searching for formulas which ... will guarantee to the world everlasting peace', the 27-year-old Wanger wrote in the London *Daily Mail* in December 1921, 'the great masses of those nations are meeting daily or nightly ... in kinema houses to see films that will eventually render Washington conferences unnecessary.'

> Universal peace will come only when there is between all nations and all peoples universal acquaintanceship. And by means of the moving

---

[1] Miriam Hansen 1999, 'The Mass Production of the Senses: Classical Cinema as Vernacular Modernism', *Modernism/Modernity*, vol. 6, no. 2, pp. 59-77; reprinted in Linda Williams and Christine Gledhill (eds) 2000, *Reinventing Film Studies* (London: Edward Arnold).

[2] For global reach see Victoria de Grazia 1989, 'Mass Culture and Sovereignty: The American Challenge to European Cinemas, 1920–1960', *Journal of Modern History*, vol. 61, no. 1, pp. 53-87.

[3] For FPL's dominance of domestic production and distribution see Matthew Bernstein 2000, *Walter Wanger: Hollywood Independent* (Minneapolis, MN: University of Minnesota Press), [Berkeley, CA: University of California Press, 1994], pp. 42-3. In 1926 FPL's New York studios made 40 per cent of their films. See Bernstein 2000, *Walter Wanger*, p. 60.

picture we are gaining a knowledge of what the rest of the world knows, what it eats, and, what is more important, *how* it eats; what it wears and, what is of greater importance *how* it wears it ... The written word, the spoken word, have failed to accomplish in a big way what the kine is now accomplishing for the very good and simple and true reason that ... seeing is believing ... *Nations have never known each other as thoroughly as they are now coming to know each other by means of the moving picture* ... heretofore knowledge has been the possession of the few and the Foreign Office; but henceforth the Foreign Offices of the world will be the picture houses of the world. For they offer the best means of producing greater world knowledge, world acquaintanceship, and hence, world peace.[4]

Walter Wanger (1894–1968) was, in December 1921, a theatre manager in London. But he had worked briefly, the previous year, as assistant to Jesse Lasky, vice-president for production, then as general manager of production at Famous Players-Lasky based in New York; and he returned to that position in July 1924, where he oversaw all FPL productions, selecting story properties, scouting talent, and supervising the company's studios at Astoria, Long Island, on the West Coast, and overseas in London, Paris and Bombay.[5]

Wanger's faith in cinema's 'foreign office' role stemmed most immediately from his experience in the Great War, when he served first of all as Secretary of the Recruiting Committee of New York mayor John Mitchel's Committee on National Defense, which oversaw all propaganda in the city 'on a scientific basis under a system similar to that evolved in England', then in the Signal Corps, which used aviation to collect intelligence, and finally in the Rome office of the Committee on Public Information (CPI).[6] Led by political scientist Charles Merriam, this office attempted to persuade 'as many [of the Italian] people as possible, in as vivid a way as possible' to continue their war efforts. Wanger edited and distributed newsreels and films that he was convinced were 'tremendously' influential in swaying the feelings of the Italian people. As his

---

[4] Walter Wanger 1921, 'Films as Foreign Offices', *Daily Mail* (London), 10 December, p. 6, quoted in Bernstein 2000, *Walter Wanger*, pp. 37-8. Italics in original.

[5] Matthew Bernstein 2000, 'Wanger, Walter', *American National Biography Online* (American Council of Learned Societies: Oxford University Press). For overseas studios see Jesse L. Lasky 1920, 'Future Productions of Famous Players to Prove Value of Sound Organization', *Moving Picture World*, vol. 12, June, p. 1469; and Jesse Lasky with Dan Weldon 1957, *I Blow My Own Horn* (New York, NY: Doubleday), pp. 131-2.

[6] 'City Leads Nation in Recruiting Work. Mayor's Committee Takes Over All Propaganda for Army, Navy, and Marine Corps', *New York Times*, 9 April 1917, p. 6, quoted in Bernstein 2000, *Walter Wanger*, pp. 30-1.

biographer Matthew Bernstein put it, Wanger's experience at the CPI provided him with 'a crash course in shaping public opinion' and the conviction of 'the international scope of the movies' potential influence'.[7]

Wanger developed his conviction that more effective, up-to-date forms of diplomacy were essential in the immediate aftermath of the war when he served as an aide to Wilson adviser James T. Shotwell at the Paris Peace Conference. He did briefly consider a career in the Foreign Service and he used the foreign service analogy all his life, referring to movies as '120,000 American Ambassadors' in an article in the journal *Foreign Affairs* in October 1939.[8]

Walter Wanger was applying to cinema, in 1921, a pervasive idea among young American intellectuals concerning the connection between transnationalism, or cosmopolitanism, and world peace. Born in San Francisco in 1894 into a wealthy German Jewish family, his aunts Carrie, Ettie and Florine Stettheimer were accomplished artists and writers who formed one of New York's most interesting avant-garde salons. His sister Beatrice was a modern dancer based in Paris. As a child he went regularly to Europe with his family; and after his father died in 1905 they lived for two years in Switzerland, then settled in Manhattan, where he was part of his family's wealthy, cultured, cosmopolitan world. During his years at Dartmouth College from 1911 to 1915 he saw the Abbey Theatre on tour in New York, attended Max Reinhardt productions in Berlin and Ballets Russes productions in Paris. He became familiar with the New Stagecraft pioneered by Gordon Craig.[9]

Eagerly gathering anything that was new and original, no matter what its provenance, under the inspiration of Diaghilev, Wanger was also no doubt open to the ideas of his contemporary Randolph Bourne, who articulated a new code for the young intelligentsia in his 'Trans-National America', published in the *Atlantic Monthly* in July 1916. A response to the hysteria about 'hyphenated Americans' fuelled by Woodrow Wilson's preparedness speech in December 1915 and congressional debate on the preparedness bill in March 1916, Bourne's article advocated a fluid and dynamic approach to culture and argued that: 'In

---

[7] Bernstein 2000, *Walter Wanger*, pp. 33-4.

[8] Walter Wanger 1929, '120,000 Ambassadors', *Foreign Affairs*, December, cited in Bernstein 2000, *Walter Wanger*, pp. 35, 139. For contemporary commentary see Virginia Wright 1939, 'Cinematter', *Los Angeles Daily News*, 14 October.

[9] Bernstein 2000, *Walter Wanger*, pp. 3-22. For Florine Stettheimer see Barbara J. Bloemink, 'Crystal Flowers, Pink Candy Hearts and Tinsel Creation: The Subversive Femininity of Florine Stettheimer', in Bridget Elliott and Janice Helland (eds) 2003, *Women Artists and the Decorative Arts 1880–1935: The Gender of Ornament* (Burlington, VT: Ashgate), pp. 197-218; and 2000, 'Stettheimer, Florine', *American National Biography Online* (American Council of Learned Societies: Oxford University Press).

a world which has dreamed of internationalism, we find that we have all unawares been building up the first international nation.'

> America is already the world-federation in miniature, the continent where for the first time in history has been achieved that miracle of hope, the peaceful living side by side, with character substantially preserved, of the most heterogeneous peoples under the sun ... It is for the American of the younger generation to accept this cosmopolitanism, and carry it along with self-conscious and fruitful purpose.[10]

In an address to the Harvard Menorah Society in December 1916 he elaborated on this further in a way that was particularly pertinent to the Jewish-American Wanger: The only thing that kept American culture from aggressive nationalism was the 'hyphenate', Bourne argued. Accordingly the task was to find a way to a 'cultural self-consciousness' that was pluralistic enough to avoid 'the price of terrible like-mindedness'. In Bourne's opinion, the cosmopolitanism of Jewish Americans (such as Horace Kallen, Walter Lippmann and Louis Brandeis) were concrete examples of the way the hyphenate American could help turn America into the first international nation.[11]

Accompanying this cosmopolitan vision for Bourne was a sophisticated 'modern' approach to sexual relations, articulated most effectively by his friend, the feminist anthropologist Elsie Clews Parsons. For Bourne and Parsons, being modern involved the avoidance of classificatory thinking, whether of nation or of sex. The urge to classify, fear of social change, and structures of social control are closely related, Parsons contended in her *Social Rule* in 1916. 'Social categories are an unparalleled means of gratifying the will to power. The classified individual may be held in subjection in ways the unclassified escapes.' As a feminist, Parsons called, therefore, for 'the declassification of women as women, the recognition of women as human beings or personalities ... The *new woman* means the woman not yet classified, perhaps not classifiable'; and as a pacifist she called, as Randolph Bourne did, for a diminution of national consciousness and the encouragement of a transnational perspective.[12]

---

[10] Randolph Bourne 1916, 'Trans-National America ', *Atlantic Monthly*, July, pp. 86-97.

[11] Randolph Bourne 1916, 'The Jew and Trans-National America', *Menorah Journal*, December, pp. 277-84; reprinted in Carl Resek (ed.) 1965, *War and the Intellectuals* (New York, NY: Harper Torchbooks), pp. 124-33. See Desley Deacon 1997, *Elsie Clews Parsons: Inventing Modern Life* (Chicago, IL: University of Chicago Press), pp. 165-89, for the influence of this feminist anthropologist on Bourne's thinking.

[12] Elsie Clews Parsons 1916, *Social Rule: A Study of the Will to Power* (New York, NY: G. P. Putnam's Sons), pp. 2, 54-5. See also Parsons 1915, *Social Freedom: A Study of the Conflicts between Social Classifications and Personality* (New York, NY: G. P. Putnam's Sons).

After Wanger returned to Famous Players-Lasky in 1924, his career was devoted to reconciling making a profit with the production of 'greater world knowledge, world acquaintanceship, and hence, world peace'. He did this in several ways: through his support of films with a strong documentary component; by setting films in foreign locales; after sound was introduced in 1927, by making simultaneous versions in other languages, either for a large United States minority audience such as Spanish speakers, or for foreign markets; and by developing a cosmopolitan, transatlantic style that was not identifiable as American, French, German, or British, though it borrowed elements from each of these.

Wanger's project to encourage 'world acquaintanceship' through film was supported by Jesse Lasky (1880–1958), the vice-president for production who had snapped up this debonair young entrepreneur in 1920 after meeting him at a dinner party.[13] In 1920 Famous Players-Lasky was expanding its production activities worldwide, with studios in New York, Hollywood, London and Bombay.[14] After a brief period as Lasky's personal assistant, Wanger was appointed general manager of production, with control over the company's far-flung production units from his base in New York.[15] Apart from Wanger's organisational vision, Lasky was impressed by Wanger's cosmopolitanism. Here was a man of the world, Lasky decided, who could ensure that the details of Famous Player-Lasky films were faithful to life, whether they portrayed events in American history, everyday life on a Pacific island, or the manners and morals of New York upper-class society.

The best of Famous Player-Lasky films already did this. In an interview with Louella Parsons in January 1922, the young Ernst Lubitsch, fresh from Germany, expressed great admiration for the care taken by the studio with 'the little things', giving as an example their 1921 film *Forbidden Fruit*.[16] By the time Wanger had returned to Famous Players-Lasky in July 1924, Lasky had produced *The Covered Wagon* (1923), which told the story of the wagon trains that crossed the continent in 1848–1849 in such convincing detail that the *New York Times* applauded the idea of the film being preserved in the Smithsonian Institution as an historical

---

[13] Lasky 1957, *I Blow My Own Horn*, pp. 133, 173-5, 196-7; Bernstein 2000, *Walter Wanger*, pp. 41-2.

[14] Lasky 1920, 'Future Productions of Famous Players to Prove Value of Sound Organization'.

[15] 'Walter F. Wanger Now General Manager of Production of Famous Players-Lasky', *Moving Picture World*, 13 November 1920, p. 236; 'Famous Players Sign Wanger as Special Representative', *Moving Picture World*, 1 May 1920, p. 678; 'Jesse Lasky Appoints Walter Wagner [sic] to Position of F.P.-L. Production Head', *Moving Picture World*, 12 June 1920, p. 1448.

[16] Ernst Lubitsch 1922, Interview with Louella Parsons, *New York Telegraph*, 1 January.

record of the event.[17] *North of 36* (1924), the highly documentary story of a cattle drive by a female rancher across Texas in the 1870s, was in production.[18] Even more adventurously, he was also backing a second film, *Moana* (1926), by documentary pioneer Robert Flaherty, whose *Nanook of the North*, about the daily life of an Inuit hunter and his family, had captured his imagination when it was released to considerable acclaim in 1922.[19]

Soon after Wanger's return to Famous Players-Lasky in 1924, he and Lasky began their association with Merian Cooper (1893–1973) and Ernest Schoedsack (1893–1979). These two young adventurers are best known for the enormously successful *King Kong* (1933). But in 1924 they had filmed, with Marguerite Harrison (1879–1967), the annual migration of the Baktiari people from the Persian gulf over the snow-clad Zardeh Kuh mountains to the grassy plains where they spent the summer months.[20] They were attempting to market their film to the educational market in New York when Lasky saw it at a private dinner party

---

[17] 'Screen. Film as Nation's Historical Record', *New York Times*, 25 March 1923, p. X3. See also Lasky 1957, *I Blow My Own Horn*, pp. 159-64; 'The Screen. A Movie of the Prairies', *New York Times*, 17 March 1923, p. 9; 'Story of a Great Film', *New York Times*, 16 March 1924, p. X5.

[18] Mordaunt Hall 1924, 'The Screen. *North of 36*', *New York Times*, 8 December, p. 23; Charles S. Sewell 1924, 'Newest Reviews and Comments: "North of 36"', *Moving Picture World*, 13 December, p. 625.

[19] Lasky 1957, *I Blow My Own Horn*, pp. 187-8; 'The Screen. *Nanook of the North*', *New York Times*, 12 June 1922, p. 18; Fritz Tidden 1922, '"Nanook of the North": An Epic of the Eskimo Produced by Robert J. Flaherty, F.R.G.S., and Released by Pathe', *Moving Picture World*, 24 June, p. 735; Mordaunt Hall 1927, '"Nanook" Still a Masterpiece', *New York Times*, 20 February, p. X7; Rex Ingram 1927, 'Art Advantages of the European Scene', *Theatre Magazine*, p. 24. For *Moana* see 'Flaherty to Film Samoan Islanders. Producer of a Notable Picture Showing Life of the Eskimo Sails Tomorrow', *New York Times*, 11 April 1923, p. 36; '"Nanook" Producer Finds Samoan "Mary"', *New York Times*, 6 January 1924. p. X5; '"Nanook" Producer Here with Samoan Film Study', *New York Times*, 1 March 1925, p. X5; 'The Screen. *Moana*', *New York Times*, 8 February 1926, p. 24; *New York Times*, 8 Feb 1926, p. 8; *Variety*, 10 Feb 1926, p. 40; *Film Daily*, 21 February 1926; Forsyth Hardy 1979, *John Grierson: A Documentary Biography* (London: Faber and Faber), pp. 41-3. For Robert Flaherty's work see Arthur Calder-Marshall 1963, *The Innocent Eye: The Life of Robert J. Flaherty* (New York, NY: Harcourt, Brace & World).

[20] Lasky 1957, *I Blow My Own Horn*, pp. 188-9; Merian C. Cooper 1924, 'Barefoot Nation Migrates Through Snow to Find Food', *New York Times*, 31 August, p. X14. See Kevin Brownlow 1979, 'Grass', in *The War, the West, and the Wilderness* (New York, NY: Alfred A. Knopf), pp. 515-29; Orville Goldner and George E. Turner 1975, *The Making of King Kong: The Story Behind a Film Classic* (South Brunswick, NY: A. S. Barnes), pp. 26-8; Rudy Behlmer 1966, 'Merian C. Cooper is the Kind of Creative Showman Today's Movies Badly Need', *Films in Review*, vol. 18, no. 1, pp. 17-34; Paul M. Jensen 2000, 'Cooper, Merian Coldwell', *American National Biography Online* (American Council of Learned Societies: Oxford University Press).

and acquired it for Paramount in January 1925.[21] The *New York Times* acclaimed this 'Persian "Covered Wagon"' as a 'remarkable' film that contained 'drama which is trenchant and stirring'.[22] When it was premiered before a celebrity audience in March 1925, Mordaunt Hall, again in the *Times*, called it 'instructive and compelling', filled with drama and 'captivating comedy' despite its lack of a conventional story.[23] Lasky and Wanger immediately commissioned another film from Cooper and Schoedsack, who set off for Siam (modern-day Thailand) to make what was becoming known as a 'natural drama' – a film that constructs a story, usually of a family, using native actors and animals in their natural setting.[24] *Chang*, which featured tiger hunts and an elephant stampede, was hailed as 'vivid' and 'thrilling' when it was released in April 1927. Richard Watts, in the New York *Herald Tribune*, considered it had 'some of the most thrilling moments any dramatic form has been able to encompass'. Cooper and Schoedsack are shrewd showmen, Watts observed, 'who have not been content to rely merely on the bald camera journey through the Siamese jungle'. Instead they had produced a film 'in which comedy and drama are mingled with a showman's conscious skill', and the whole is put together with 'high technical skill'. 'The film has many of the admirable uses of tempo that *Potemkin* and *The Big Parade* employed to such effect', Watts concludes. 'In addition, it is filled with pictorial beauty and photographed superbly.'[25] *Chang* received critical acclaim from all over the world, film historian Kevin Brownlow tells us, as well as one of the first Academy Award nominations.[26]

Wanger and Lasky were responsible for several other 'natural dramas' before they were dismissed from what was by then Paramount in 1931 and 1932 respectively: *The Vanishing American* (1926), made on location in Monument

---

[21] Brownlow 1979, *The War, the West, and the Wilderness*, pp. 528-9.

[22] 'Persian Tribes Filmed on Brave Mountain Trudge', *New York Times*, 8 March 1925, p. X3.

[23] *Grass: A Nation's Battle for Life* (Famous Players-Lasky Paramount, 1925), New York premiere, 30 Mar 1925; 'Grinding Out Entertainment for the Millions', *New York Times*, 29 March 1925, p. X5; Mordaunt Hall 1925, 'The Screen. A Persian Epic', *New York Times*, 31 March, p. 17; *New York Times*, 12 April 1925, p. RPA2 (photo). See also *Film Daily*, 12 April 1925, p. 8; *Life*, 4 Jun 1925, p. 35.

[24] *Chang* (Paramount Famous Lasky, 1927), New York premiere, 29 April 1927; release 3 September 1927. See 'Thrills of Making Jungle Film', *New York Times*, 10 April 1927, p. X7; *Film Daily*, 17 April 1927, p. 8; *New York Times*, 30 April 1927, p. 25; *Variety*, 4 May 1927, p. 20; *Photoplay*, June 1927, p. 20; '*Chang*', in Brownlow 1979, *The War, the West, and the Wilderness*, pp. 529-39.

[25] Richard Watts, quoted in Behlmer 1966, 'Merian C. Cooper', p. 22, in Brownlow 1979, *The War, the West, and the Wilderness*, p. 539. See also Mordaunt Hall 1927, 'The Screen. Thrilling Jungle Study', *New York Times*, 30 April, p. 25.

[26] Brownlow 1979, *The War, the West, and the Wilderness*, p. 539.

Valley and the Betatakin Cliff Dwellings, as the *New York Times* put it, 'with infinite pains';[27] *Redskin* (1929), filmed on the Navajo reservation in north-eastern Arizona about 'the conflict of the modern red man, educated at the white man's schools, seeking to fit himself into the present-day scheme of life';[28] *The Silent Enemy* (1930), a reconstruction of the Ojibwa people's struggle for food in the time before European settlement;[29] *Rango* (1931), made by Ernest Schoedsack in Sumatra;[30] *With Byrd at the South Pole* (1930);[31] and *Tabu* (1931) directed by F. W. Murnau and produced by Robert Flaherty in Tahiti, with 'only native-born South Sea islanders [and] a few half-castes and Chinese', according to the film's opening credits.[32] Most extraordinary of all, and the most successful, according to both contemporary and modern sources, was *Stark Love* (1927), a film about gender relations among the isolated mountain people of North Carolina. Produced by Karl Brown, who had been the cameraman on *The Covered Wagon*, *Stark Love* used untrained actors from the region to make what Kevin Brownlow calls 'one of the most unusual films ever made in America'.[33] As Mordaunt Hall wrote in the *New York Times*:

> By adhering closely to his subject and scorning to permit any stereotyped movie spasms to interfere with its natural trend, Mr Brown reveals a feeling akin to that of Robert J. Flaherty in 'Nanook of the North' and 'Moana of the South Seas' ... This is another notch on the production gun of Famous Players-Lasky.[34]

---

[27] See 'The Vanishing American', in Brownlow 1979, *The War, the West, and the Wilderness*, pp. 344-8; Mordaunt Hall 1925, 'The Screen. The American Indian', *New York Times*, 16 October, p. 18; *Moving Picture World*, 24 October 1925, p. 652; Ralph and Natasha Friar 1972, *The Only Good Indian... The Hollywood Gospel* (New York, NY: Drama Book Specialists), p. 133.

[28] 'Mr. Dix's Color Film', *New York Times*, 10 February 1929, p. 117; 'Redskin', in Brownlow 1979, *The War, the West, and the Wilderness*, pp. 348-50.

[29] 'The Silent Enemy', in Brownlow 1979, *The War, the West, and the Wilderness*, pp. 545-60; Mordaunt Hall 1930, 'The Screen. Indian Hunters of Old', *New York Times*, 20 May, p. 36.

[30] '"Rango", A Tiger Film', *New York Times*, 1 January 1931, p. X6.

[31] *With Byrd at the South Pole* (Paramount-Publix, 1930), New York premiere, 19 June 1930. See *Film Daily*, 22 June 1930; *New York Times*, 20 June 1930, p. 6; *Variety*, 25 June 1930, p. 109.

[32] American Film Institute Catalogue.

[33] 'Stark Love', in Brownlow 1979, *The War, the West, and the Wilderness*, pp. 499-507; 'Primitive Mountaineers Filmed in Native Nooks', *New York Times*, 20 February 1927, p. X6; 'Where Man Is Vile. "Stark Love" a Realistic Reproduction of Life of Mountaineers', *New York Times*, 6 March 1927, p. X7.

[34] Mordaunt Hall 1927, 'The Screen. Primitive Mountaineers', *New York Times*, 28 February, p. 22. See also Edward Kern, Film and Photo League 1934, 'Reviving Distinguished Films', Letter to the editor, *New York Times*, 16 December, p. X4.

Lasky's and Wanger's documentary sense was not confined to American history and what newspaper commentators referred to as 'primitive' cultures.[35] Based in New York, and closely associated, economically and personally, with the worlds they depicted, they encouraged the production of films dealing with 'modern' New York manners and morals, especially the mixture of society, show business and journalism that was creating a sophisticated transatlantic culture. This was especially the case after July 1926, when B. P. Schulberg was appointed associate manager in charge of production in the company's Hollywood studio. Although Wanger was still technically in charge of production in both studios, Schulberg's immediate success at the box office placed the two coasts in competition with each other, and Wanger, the 'European-oriented American', concentrated on a studio style described by his biographer as embodying 'the sophisticated tone and look rooted in continental dramas and fashions as exemplified by the work of directors Lubitsch and Josef von Sternberg'.[36] Wanger's competitive advantage was enhanced in 1928 with the introduction of sound, when his close links with Broadway gave him ready access to actors with acceptable voices.[37] Over the next few years he signed up actors, directors and writers who came to epitomise New York and transatlantic sophistication: actresses Jeanne Eagels, Claudette Colbert, Kay Francis, Ruth Chatterton, Miriam Hopkins, and Tallulah Bankhead; actors Maurice Chevalier, Frederic March, Walter Huston and Herbert Marshall; directors George Cukor, Rouben Mamoulian, and Robert Florey; writers Noel Coward, Preston Sturges, and Donald Ogden Stewart; and those exemplars of sophisticated comedy, the Marx Brothers.[38] From 1929 to 1931 Paramount's New York studio was known for its

---

[35] Many other films had a strong documentary flavour. Richard Koszarski calls *The Canadian* (1926) 'one of finest of silent films about modern life in remote farming communities'; Koszarski 1983, *The Astoria Studio and Its Fabulous Films: A Picture History with 227 Stills and Photographs*. With a Foreword by Rochelle Slovin. (New York, NY: Dover), pp. 44-5. Published in association with the Astoria Motion Picture and Television Foundation.

[36] Bernstein 2000, *Walter Wanger*, pp. 60-1.

[37] Paramount's first all-talking picture, *Interference*, starring Clive Brook, Doris Kenyon and William Powell, premiered in New York 16 November 1928 and went on general release 5 January 1929. See *Variety*, 30 April 1930, p. 11 for Astoria's use of plays.

[38] Bernstein 2000, *Walter Wanger*, pp. 63-5. For Kay Francis see *Gentlemen of the Press*, with Walter Huston May 1929; *Dangerous Curves*, July 1929; *The Marriage Playground*, with Fredric March, December 1929; *Behind the Make-Up*, January 1930 and *Street of Chance*, February 1930, both with William Powell; *The Virtuous Sin*, with Walter Huston, November 1930; *Scandal Sheet*, January 1931; *The Vice Squad*, May 1931; *Ladies' Man*, with William Powell and Carole Lombard, 1931. For Miriam Hopkins: *Fast and Loose*, November 1930. Fredric March: *The Royal Family of Broadway*, December 1930. *Man of the World*, William Powell and Carole Lombard's first film together, March 1931. Wanger's most memorable production during his tenure at Paramount was Rouben Mamoulian's

'sophisticated' films, the best of which dealt intelligently with modern gender roles and sexual mores.[39] Producers ought to be encouraged to make more such intelligent films, Mordaunt Hall wrote in the *New York Times* of Ruth Chatterton's December 1929 *The Laughing Lady*, which dealt with rape, divorce and hypocrisy in New York's high society.[40] 'They are real people', he wrote of the characters played by Claudette Colbert and Ginger Rogers in *Young Man of Manhattan* in April 1930, 'persons who are engaging in something of a battle with life.'[41]

Ernst Lubitsch's appointment as supervising producer at the New York studio in August 1930 confirmed Paramount's commitment to 'the sophisticated and indoor types of story'.[42] *Ladies' Man*, with William Powell, Kay Francis and Carole Lombard, was 'intelligent' and had 'comparatively grown-up dialogue', Mordaunt Hall wrote in May 1931;[43] and 'London's favorite American actress', Tallulah Bankhead, made her talking film debut that same month 'with considerable distinction' in *Tarnished Lady*, written by leading playwright of modern New York life, Donald Ogden Stewart, and directed by George Cukor.[44] Many of these films were produced simultaneously in foreign languages.

---

innovative musical *Applause*, October 1929. The Marx Brothers premiered in *The Cocoanuts*, with Kay Francis, May 1929; their *Animal Crackers*, September 1930, featured William Saulter's moderne setting; see Koszarski 1983, *Astoria*, pp. 68-9.

[39] *Variety*, 11 September 1929, p. 18; 4 April 1930, p. 4; 13 August 1930, p. 2; 20 August 1930; 25 March 1931, p. 4. For an account of this genre see Mick LaSalle 2000, *Complicated Women: Sex and Power on Pre-Code Hollywood* (New York: St Martin's Press).

[40] Mordaunt Hall 1930, 'Love And The Lawyer. Excellent Entertainment Afforded by the Film of "The Laughing Lady"', *New York Times*, 12 January 12, p. 114, cited in Koszarski 1983, *Astoria*, p. 64. Before Wanger's dismissal Chatterton also appeared in *The Doctor's Secret*, January 1929; *The Dummy*, with Frederic March, March 1929; *Charming Sinners*, August 1929; *Sarah and Son*, with Fredric March, March 1930; *Anybody's Woman*, August 1930; *The Right To Love*, December 1930; *Unfaithful*, March 1931; and *The Magnificent Lie*, July 1931.

[41] Mordaunt Hall 1930, *New York Times*, 27 April, p. 121. For *Young Man of Manhattan*, April 1930, see Koszarski 1983, *Astoria*, pp. 66-7. Colbert's other films of the period are *The Hole in the Wall*, April 1929; *The Lady Lies*, with Walter Huston, September 1929; *The Big Pond*, with Maurice Chevalier, May 1930; *Manslaughter*, with Fredric March, July 1930; *Honor Among Lovers*, February 1931; *Another Man's Wife*, with Fredric March and Ginger Rogers; *Secrets of a Secretary*, with Herbert Marshall, September 1931; and *The Smiling Lieutenant*, May 1931.

[42] *Variety*, 10 September 1930, p. 3; 1 October 1930, p. 2; 1 April 1931, p. 7. See Bernstein 2000, *Walter Wanger*, p. 66.

[43] Mordaunt Hall 1931, 'The Screen. A Lesson in Golf. A Fashionable Rogue', *New York Times*, 1 May, p. 34.

[44] Bankhead's other films at the New York studio were *My Sin*, October 1931, and *The Cheat*, November 1931, both made after Wanger's dismissal.

(French-speaking Claudette Colbert was particularly useful for this.) And from 1930 to 1933 Paramount produced French, Spanish, Swedish, German, Italian, Polish, Czech, Portuguese, Hungarian, and Romanian versions at its Joinville Studios outside Paris.[45]

But Paramount's distribution wing had never liked either the 'natural dramas' or the sophisticated New York stories, which did not play well to American regional audiences.[46] As the Depression started to bite, Wanger and Lasky found themselves under attack. In November 1930 Wanger told an undergraduate audience at his old college, Dartmouth, of the choice Paramount faced between 'more sophisticated and somewhat philosophical pictures like "Holiday"' (the Philip Barry play opposing old and new values in love and money) and 'hokum' with clearcut morality and 'heart interest', such as the current hit, *Common Clay*.[47] As he put it at the end of his life, the films he promoted at the New York studio were 'a sensation in New York, but in Kansas City, they didn't know what [they were] all about'.[48]

From 1930 to 1931 Paramount's net income dropped from $25 million to $8.7 million. In an attempt to stave off bankruptcy, distribution head Sidney Kent was appointed general manager. In May 1931 he shut down the New York studio and replaced Wanger by former newsreel director Emanuel Cohen, who was more amenable to the dictates of the distributors and exhibitors. By November 1931 Schulberg could tell *Variety* that Paramount was moving away from 'sophisticated' stories in favour of 'good old hoke tales with broader sales

---

[45] Harry Waldman 1998, *Paramount in Paris: 300 Films Produced at the Joinville Studios, 1930–1933, with Credits and Biographies* (Lanham, MD: Scarecrow Press).

[46] See 'Inside Stuff on Pictures', *Variety*, 26 March 1924, p. 22.

[47] Bernstein 2000, *Walter Wanger*, p. 67.

[48] Interview with Walter Wanger, in Bernard Rosenberg and Harry Silverstein 1970, *The Real Tinsel* (London: Macmillan), pp. 80-99, especially p. 83; quoted in Bernstein 2000, *Walter Wanger*, p. 68.

appeal'.[49] The following April, Jesse Lasky was given three months leave of absence, and in September 1932 *Time* magazine announced, 'Lasky Out'.[50]

Wanger's and Lasky's determination to 'get the details right' and to educate the public about the varieties of the world's cultures, whether among the Eskimos of northern Canada or the modern sophisticates of New York, brought them into conflict with the distribution wing of Paramount as it lost its position as industry leader to MGM and the upstart Warners in the early 1930s. But their influence remained, even at Paramount, where Ernst Lubitsch perfected the transatlantic comedy of manners in the delightful *Trouble in Paradise* in 1932, starring Wanger protegees Miriam Hopkins, Kay Francis and Herbert Marshall in the sort of rich, luminous setting that became Paramount's house style in the 1930s; in the unconventional threesome of Fredric March, Gary Cooper and Miriam Hopkins in *Design for Living* (1933); and in the tangled sexual and financial plots of Carole Lombard and Fred MacMurray in *Hands Across the Table* (1935).[51]

Their support for 'natural dramas' had its most direct influence in Britain and Canada through their association with documentary pioneer John Grierson. In 1925 Grierson (1898–1972) took up a Rockefeller Foundation fellowship at the University of Chicago, where he was supervised by Wanger's former chief

---

[49] 'Sophisticated Stories Out. Hoke for Par', *Variety*, 17 November 1931, p. 3; quoted in Bernstein 2000, *Walter Wanger*, p. 69. For Wanger's dismissal see *Variety*, 23 June 1931, p. 4; 'Par's Story Council in New York on Toes', *Variety*, 6 October 1931, p. 2. For Sidney Kent's appointment see *Variety*, 27 May 1931, p. 5. For Cohen see 'Manny Cohen Going into Al Par Film Productions', *Variety*, 29 September 1931, p. 5; 'No Personnel Changes looked for in Par-Pub Through Chicago Group', *Variety*, 3 November 1931, p. 5; 'Cohen Favors Unit System for Par', *Variety*, 17 November 1931, p. 2; 'Schulberg Proposal Changed by Zukor', *Variety*, 24 November 1931, p. 5; 'Paramount Names Seven Associates for Unit System', *Variety*, 28 November 1931, p. 13; 'Orders for Further Cuts by P-P Unofficially Aimed at Another 20%', *Variety*, 8 December 1931, p. 5; 'Cohen Set as Zukor's Par Studio Contact', *Variety*, 15 December 1931, p. 5; 'Sidney Kent Abruptly Leaves Paramount Publix, No Plans Yet', *Motion Picture Herald*, 23 January 1932, p. 13; 'Emanuel Cohen and Schaeffer Take New Posts at Paramount', *Motion Picture Herald*, 30 January 1932, p. 20; 'Katz' Studio Influence', *Variety*, 9 February 1932, p. 3; 'Keough Secretary for Paramount', *Motion Picture Herald*, 9 February 1932, p. 9. See also Peter Baxter 1993, *Just Watch! Sternberg, Paramount and America* (London: British Film Institute), pp. 39-41, 80-1.

[50] 'Adolph Zukor Tells Stockholders Story of the Paramount of Today', *Motion Picture Herald*, 30 April 1932, p. 20; 'Lasky Out', *Time*, 26 September 1932, p. 26. See Baxter 1993, *Just Watch!*, p. 45; Lasky 1957, *I Blow My Own Horn*, pp. 242-4.

[51] Scott Eyman 2000, *Laughter in Paradise* (Baltimore, MD: Johns Hopkins University Press), pp. 189-96, 205-12, 225-32. Lubitsch was named production head of Paramount in place of Emanuel Cohen on 4 February 1935. He was replaced by William Le Baron 24 January 1936; see Eyman 2000, *Laughter in Paradise*, pp. 237-9.

Professor Charles Merriam.[52] When Grierson visited New York in July 1925 he and Wanger found much in common. Both agreed that movies had a duty to educate the public by interpreting the contemporary scene in an entertaining fashion.[53] Wanger gave Grierson access to Paramount's distribution and exhibition reports for his study of the impact of movies on the immigrant audience's perceptions of current events, paid him a retainer to analyse film technique and production methods, and engaged him to lecture at the Paramount Theatre Managers Training School on 'The Conditions of Popular Appeal'.[54] Grierson popularised his ideas in articles in the *New York Sun* and the *Herald Tribune* and drew on his Paramount studies for a series of articles in *Motion Picture News* at the end of 1926. Film 'belongs to the strange and primitive animal with lusts in its body and dreams in its eyes which we call the mob', he wrote; but it 'belongs to the people as no other social institution that has ever appeared in the world before. It is the only genuinely democratic institution that has ever appeared on a world wide scale.'[55] The Eisenstein film *Potemkin*, for which Grierson helped write the English titles, provided the evidence he needed that film 'could be an adult and positive force in the world'.[56] In a review of Famous Players-Lasky's *Moana* in 1926, he invented the word 'documentary'.[57]

When Grierson returned to Britain in 1927 and began his distinguished career as the father of documentary film making at the Empire Marketing Board, he included *Grass*, *Moana* and *The Covered Wagon* in the program he mounted at the Imperial Institute cinema to persuade members of the Board of the educative and persuasive potential of film.[58] Grierson's first film for the Board, *Drifters* (1929), about herring fishing off Scotland, was 'rapturously received by the sophisticated audience' when it was shown at the London Film Society with Eisenstein's *Potemkin*. It had 'more real art than the much-belauded Russian picture', in the opinion of the *Birmingham Post*.[59] Grierson built on this success

---

[52] Bernstein 2000, *Walter Wanger*, p. 407. For Grierson in the US see Hardy 1979, *John Grierson*, pp. 31-44.

[53] John Grierson, speaking at awards ceremony of the Academy of Motion Pictures Arts and Sciences (of which Walter Wanger was president), 1942, quoted in Hardy 1979, *John Grierson*, p. 36.

[54] John Grierson, address to Paramount Theatre Managers School, reported in *Exhibitors Herald*, 26 September 1925, in Hardy 1979, *John Grierson*, p. 39.

[55] John Grierson 1926, *Motion Picture News*, 20 November to 18 December, cited in Hardy 1979, *John Grierson*, p. 36. See also p. 38.

[56] Hardy 1979, *John Grierson*, pp. 40-1. For *Potemkin*, see Mordaunt Hall 1926, 'An Old Russian Mutiny', *New York Times*, 6 December, p. 28.

[57] John Grierson 1926, *'Moana'*, *New York Sun*, 8 February.

[58] Hardy 1979, *John Grierson*, pp. 44-6.

[59] ibid., pp. 54-5.

by establishing a small school of documentary film-makers, attracting such talented young men and women as Basil Wright, Arthur Elton, Paul Rotha, Edgar Anstey, Marion Grierson and Evelyn Spice. With his faith in film as a new way of teaching citizenship, Grierson built the documentary movement in Britain with public money, first at the Empire Marketing Board, where he commissioned Robert Flaherty, of *Nanook* and *Moana* fame, to make a film about the English countryside that became *Industrial Britain*, then at the General Post office, where his unit made the classic *Night Mail*, with text in verse by W. H. Auden. In 1938 and 1939 he advised the Canadian, New Zealand and Australian governments on setting up national film units, and served from 1939 as Canadian film commissioner. From 1948 to 1951 he was controller of the film operations of the British Central Office of Information. In 1942, during Wanger's presidency of the Academy of Motion Picture Arts and Sciences, Grierson was invited to present the first Academy Award for documentary. In his speech, Grierson pointed out that his first discussions of the theories and purposes of the documentary film movement had been with Wanger almost twenty years before. As he recalled:

> At that time some of us thought the Hollywood film ... was unnecessarily out of touch with the social realities ... We saw the growing complexity of modern affairs; and we thought that if our half-bewildered, half-frivolous generation did not master events, it was not unlikely that events would master us. We saw the enormous power of the film medium and believed it had the very special public duty to interpret the contemporary scene ... we were at first called a bunch of intellectuals and propagandists and told that the documentary idea had nothing to do with entertainment.[60]

Paying tribute to Wanger, Flaherty, Schoedsack and Cooper, among other pioneers of the documentary, he pointed out that 'Without each and all of them, we would not today be celebrating the relative maturity of the documentary film.'[61]

Wanger continued to pursue his belief in the educative role of film through a variety of jobs after his dismissal from Paramount. Hired by the low-budget Columbia to give 'class' to its products, he produced *The Bitter Tea of General Yen* (1932), starring his Paramount protegee Barbara Stanwyck as an American missionary who falls in love with a Chinese warlord; *Washington Merry-Go-Round* (1932), an expose of presidential politics that prefigures Capra's 1939 *Mr Smith*

---

[60] John Grierson, address at the 14th Annual Awards Ceremony, Academy of Motion Picture Arts and Sciences, Biltmore Hotel, Hollywood, 26 February 1942, quoted in Hardy 1979, *John Grierson*, pp. 36-7.

[61] ibid., p. 124.

Goes to Washington; and *Night Mayor* (1932), which did the same for New York City politics.[62] At MGM he produced *Gabriel Over the White House* (1933), a critique of American democracy that used newsreel footage and realistic recreations of White House interiors and starred his Paramount discovery Walter Huston, and the historical drama, *Queen Christina* (1934), arguably Garbo's greatest film.[63] As a semi-independent, he again focused on political corruption in *The President Vanishes* (1935); and he revealed the world of the mental institution in *Private Worlds* (1935), featuring his Paramount protegee Claudette Colbert, now a major star.[64] At United Artists he produced *Blockade* (1938), a controversial film about the Spanish Civil War coauthored by Lewis Milestone with Group Theatre playwright Clifford Odets; John Ford's *Stagecoach* (1939), which brought the western back to the status it enjoyed with *The Covered Wagon* (and grossed nearly a million dollars in 1939); and Alfred Hitchcock's *Foreign Correspondent* (1940), which, as Wanger's biographer put it, dealt in a compelling way with the European conflict without propagandising directly.[65] In 1940 he joined forces again with Merian Cooper, who was now in partnership with John Ford in Argosy Pictures, on the strongly documentary *Eagle Squadron* (1942), about the American pilots who joined the British Air Force early in 1940.[66] The project, which was taken over by Ernest Schoedsack in 1941 when Cooper joined the Army Signal Corps, foundered at first on difficulties with their British collaborators and distributors' resistance to a picture 'made in England with an English cast'. But when it was finally completed in 1942 by Wanger's new employer, Universal, he considered it 'the perfect Hollywood accomplishment – please the masses and serve the country at the same time'.[67]

[62] See Bernstein 2000, *Walter Wanger*, pp. 75-81.

[63] ibid., pp. 81-9.

[64] ibid., pp. 93-105.

[65] ibid., pp. 114-50; pp. 158-63, especially p. 161.

[66] Since making *Chang* in 1927 Cooper and Shoedsack had filmed footage for *Four Feathers* (1929) in the Sudan and Tanganyika; in 1927 Cooper invested his earnings in aviation stocks that led him to be elected a director of PanAm, Western Airlines, General Aviation and other commercial airlines; from 1931 to 1933 he and Schoedsack made *King Kong* (1933) for RKO, where he became David Selznick's executive assistant and succeeded him as executive vice-president in charge of production in 1933; after suffering a heart attack in 1933, he spent a year in Europe and returned to produce *She* (1935) and *The Last Days of Pompeii* (1935). In 1935 he became executive producer for Pioneer Pictures, which merged with Selznick-International in 1936. In 1937 he formed Argosy Pictures with John Ford to make *Stagecoach* (1939) and *The Long Voyage Home* (1940). From 1937 to 1941 he also produced for MGM.

[67] Bernstein 2000, *Walter Wanger*, pp. 169-71, especially p. 170; pp. 178-84, especially p. 184. Wanger served as chief of staff to General Whitehead in the New Guinea invasion and deputy chief of staff for all Air Force units in the Pacific. After *Chang* (1927) Schoedsack made *Rango* (1931) in the

After the war, with ambitions of appealing to a 'world audience', Wanger joined the new British-American company Eagle-Lion; but his block-busting *Joan of Arc* (1948), starring Ingrid Bergman, was a resounding failure, perhaps because he conceived it as a 'spiritual outrider for the Marshall Plan'.[68] For the rest of his career, his best work was what he described as 'adult realism'. In 1947 he produced *Smash-Up* (about alcoholism) and *The Lost Moment* (based on Henry James's *The Aspern Papers*) for Universal-International.[69] In 1954, after serving a four-month sentence for wounding the man he accused of being his wife's lover two years earlier, he made the complex prison film, *Riot in Cell Block II*. In 1958 he produced *I Want to Live!* the story of Barbara Graham, who was executed for murder at San Quentin in 1955, starring his protegee Susan Hayward – the film that best exemplifies, according to his biographer, the combination of naturalism, message and entertainment he strove for throughout his career.[70] Screenwriter Dudley Nicholls wrote him admiringly, 'Your film doesn't say one syllable pro or con, and yet it could be the one thing that would stop capital punishment.' 'The only real propaganda against evil is the truth', he went on, 'just the cold reality, saying "here it is boys, and you're part of it too, sitting out there".'[71]

Always an articulate promoter of his ideas about film, the controversy over attempts to censor parts of *Blockade* led Wanger to help form the Conference on Freedom of the Screen to fight censorship of films. As he told the inaugural meeting

> Let me advise you with complete honesty that the issue is far greater than the success or failure of the film *Blockade* ... It is not *Blockade* they are fighting against but the fact that if *Blockade* is a success, a flood of stronger films will appear and the films will not only talk but say something.[72]

Sumatran jungles; shot material in India for *Lives of a Bengal Lancer* in 1931; directed *King Kong* (1933) with Cooper; directed *The Most Dangerous Game* for Cooper at RKO with Irving Pichel in 1933; directed *Son of Kong* (RKO 1933) and *The Last Days of Pompeii* (RKO 1935). He severely damaged his eyes during World War II and was incapacitated, but directed Cooper's *Mighty Joe Young* in 1949. See Behlmer 1966, 'Merian C. Cooper', and Goldner and Turner 1975, *King Kong*.

[68] Bernstein 2000, *Walter Wanger*, pp. 224-33, especially pp. 233; pp. 237-46; letter from Wanger to George Marshall, 1948, quoted on p. 11.

[69] Bernstein 2000, *Walter Wanger*, pp. 217, 232-6.

[70] For Wanger's shooting of Jennings Lang see Bernstein 2000, *Walter Wanger*, pp. 273-8; for *Riot in Cell Block II*, pp. 282-301; for *I Want to Live*, pp. 322-39.

[71] Quoted in Bernstein 2000, *Walter Wanger*, p. 336.

[72] 'Freedom of the Films', *Daily People's World*, 6 August 1938, p. 2, quoted in Bernstein 2000, *Walter Wanger*, p. 137. For censorship issue and Wanger's role see pp. 136-43.

As president of the Academy of Motion Pictures from 1939 to 1945, Wanger used his position to promote what he considered the beneficial role of film in modern society, and was much sought after to participate in conferences and media discussions of censorship and popular culture.[73] Writing to Office of War Information Domestic Branch chief Gardner Cowles in 1942, he argued for 'a campaign to make the average American realize how miserably uninformed he is so that it will become unpopular to be an escapist and popular to seek information'. '"To be a strong nation is to be an informed one"', he urged, quoting a favourite line from Thomas Jefferson.[74] Until his death in 1968, he promoted film as the best way to inform the nation. 'I really wanted to see our work become a respected calling', he told Bernard Rosenberg and Harry Silverman shortly before his death. 'I thought it was almost as important as the State Department.'[75]

Walter Wanger was, in his own words, a 'practical dreamer' who shared with Jesse Lasky, Merian Cooper, Ernest Schoedsack, Robert Flaherty and John Grierson a vision of the power and potential of film to help build a better world.[76] Their successes were varied and partial. Flaherty remained the 'pure' artist, honoured by the Museum of Modern Art but living in shabby rooms at the Hotel Chelsea.[77] Grierson became the prisoner of the bureaucratic entities he had been responsible for creating.[78] Cooper and Schoedsack saw their work filming in East Africa and the Sudan reduced to 'local colour' in *The Four Feathers* (1929) and they parodied their earlier selves in the enormously successful *King Kong* (1933). But as John Ford's partner in Argosy Films, Cooper oversaw the production of some of the best westerns ever made: *Fort Apache* (1948), *She Wore a Yellow Ribbon* (1949) and *Rio Grande* (1950), and as part of C. V. Whitney Productions, *The Searchers* (1956).[79] Lasky never regained the influence he lost in 1932 when he was sacked from Paramount. He died in 1958 without bringing to fruition his last 'pet project' – to produce a film called 'The Big Brass Band' to honor 'the nine million kids who spend their spare time practicing on their instruments instead of running with juvenile gangs, making music instead of

---

[73] Bernstein 2000, *Walter Wanger*, pp. 139-42, 176-8.

[74] ibid., p. 177.

[75] Rosenberg and Silverstein 1970, *The Real Tinsel*, p. 92, quoted in Bernstein 2000, *Walter Wanger*, p. 365.

[76] For 'practical dreamer' see *The Dartmouth*, 1930, quoted in Bernstein 2000, *Walter Wanger*, p. 395.

[77] Calder-Marshall 1963, *Innocent Eye*, pp. 240-1.

[78] Hardy 1979, *Grierson*, pp. 164-79.

[79] Jensen 2000, 'Cooper, Merian Coldwell'.

mischief'.[80] Wanger struggled throughout his life to reconcile his ideals with the demands of mass entertainment, and he never lost faith that this was possible.

Wanger had no doubt that the films he made helped create Hansen's 'new global sensorium'. 'There is no argument on the influence of pictures', he stated flatly in 1945. 'They have influenced interior decoration, style, life, language, everything as a matter of fact.'[81] As head of production of Famous Players-Lasky in the 1920s and early 1930s, and in his role as semi-independent maverick until his death in 1968, he was an important, and articulate, producer of the 'global vernacular' Hansen speaks about. Produced in New York as much as in Hollywood, this 'global vernacular' drew on the 'traditions, discourses, and interests' – to quote Hansen – of Wanger and his circle, whose hybrid, transatlantic culture and wartime experiences made them lifelong adherents of the idea of transnationalism disseminated by New York intellectuals and pacifists such as Randolph Bourne and Elsie Clews Parsons.

---

[80] Donna M. Paananen 2000, 'Lasky, Jesse Louis', *American National Biography Online* (American Council of Learned Societies: Oxford University Press).
[81] Walter Wanger, 1945.

10. Modern nomads and national film history: the multi-continental career of J. D. Williams

Jill Julius Matthews

In its technology, production, marketing and reception, film has been both modern and global from its very beginnings in the late nineteenth century. So there are strong empirical and epistemological claims for a transnational approach to its history. But, paradoxically, most film histories have been decidedly focused on the notion of national culture and industry. In this chapter, while I will make a case for film history to broaden out and at least establish the transnational context for their national stories, I will also explain my pessimism that this approach will not be widely adopted.

My account begins with the story of a neglected film pioneer – the story of both the pioneer and the neglect. James Dixon ('Jaydee') Williams was a 'pushful American',[1] whose adventures in the film trade across three continents in the early decades of the twentieth century make him a prime subject for transnational treatment, as much for the historiographic complexities of his story as for the bravura of his performance.

Not much is known of Williams' early years. Variously calling him James or John or J. D., American histories assert he was born in West Virginia in the late 1870s.[2] On leaving school, he worked first in live theatre, selling tickets and later playing house-organ. He then set himself up as a travelling picture showman and from around 1897 until 1908 he took his show back and forth across the continent, ending up in the north-west, where he established a number of storefront picture houses in Spokane, Seattle, and in Vancouver. Exhibition history is very much the poor cousin of production history, so Williams' early career is barely mentioned in either American or Canadian historiographies.[3]

---

[1] 'Colonial Pictures, Limited', *Theatre*, 1 July 1910, p. 22.

[2] Terry Ramsaye 1986 [1926], *A Million and One Nights: A History of the Motion Picture Through 1926* (New York, NY: Touchstone), p. 679; Gertrude Jobes 1966, *Motion Picture Empire* (Hamden, CT: Archon), pp. 53-4; 'James D. Williams', 4 September 1934, *Variety Obituaries, 1929–1938*. He is called John D. Williams by Benjamin B. Hampton 1970 [1931], *History of the American Film Industry: From Its Beginnings to 1931* (New York, NY: Dover), p. 176; and by Allan Ellenberger 1998–99, 'A History of First National Pictures', *Films of the Golden Age*, vol. 15, Winter.

[3] Peter Morris 1978, *Embattled Shadows: A History of Canadian Cinema 1895–1939* (Montreal: McGill-Queen's University Press), p. 322, fn. 142.

As the shape of the fledgling film business changed, J. D. sought new territory. He looked out across the Pacific and determined to try his luck in Sydney. At this point, his story is taken up within Australian film historiography where he is variously identified as Canadian or American.[4] In 1909 he arrived in Australia alone; or with Leon Phillips;[5] or with 'a small party of Americans'.[6] He came with a nickelodeon collection of 'old films and junk pictures',[7] a few hundred pounds capital,[8] and 'Yankee ideas of expansion'.[9] His new career began in Sydney sideshows, selling kewpie dolls on canes. It was a surprisingly successful venture that soon had him employing a retinue of sales boys both in Sydney and in Brisbane where he also hawked films of Jack Johnson's heavyweight championship fights. Within a year he had moved from outdoor to indoor amusements. In 1910, he acquired a theatre at the busy downmarket end of Sydney's George Street that he transformed in the American style – luxury for the masses. Most importantly, he introduced modern scientific management to the theatre's operations, developing the continuous picture show. At the Colonial Theatre No. 1, then across the road at the Colonial No. 2 (later the Empress), he sold cheap seats for a film show that lasted about an hour and a half, and was screened continuously from 11am to 11pm. Here, in the words of his publicist, 'people of all classes could find regular and frequent enjoyment at prices that would not make their pleasure a drain on their resources'.[10] Until then, '[t]he great mass of people had not been catered for, and [J. D.] propose[d] to make

---

[4] Williams is identified as a Canadian by: Ina Bertrand and Diane Collins 1981, *Government and Film in Australia* (Sydney: Currency Press), p. 15; Ruth Megaw 1968, 'American Influence on Australian Cinema Management 1896–1923', *Journal of the Royal Australian Historical Society*, June 1968, reprinted in Albert Moran and Tom O'Regan (eds) 1985, *An Australian Film Reader* (Sydney: Currency Press), p. 26; Katharine Brisbane (ed.) 1991, *Entertaining Australia: An Illustrated History* (Sydney: Currency Press), p. 158; and Diane Collins, 'Shopfronts and Picture Showmen: Film Exhibition in the 1920s', in James Sabine (ed.) 1995, *A Century of Australian Cinema* (Sydney: Mandarin), p. 34. He is identified as American by Diane Collins 1987, *Hollywood Down Under: Australians at the Movies 1896 to the Present Day* (Sydney: Angus & Robertson), p. 9.

[5] 'The Romance of a Great Industry', *Film Weekly*, 16 December 1926, p. 32.

[6] Greater J. D. Williams Amusement Co., Publicity Department, *A Story of Success*, Sydney, n.d. [1912].

[7] Ramsaye 1986, *A Million and One Nights*, pp. 679-80.

[8] C. A. Jeffries 1912, 'The Gold Bug', *Lone Hand*, 1 March, p. xxxviii.

[9] Franklyn Barrett, quoted in Isadore Brodsky 1963, *Sydney Takes the Stage* (Sydney: Old Sydney Free Press), p. 80.

[10] C. A. Jeffries 1911, 'The Greater J. D. Williams Banyan Tree. The Astounding Development of the Photo-Play Industry', *Lone Hand*, 1 July, p. 275.

money by catering for them'.[11] By early 1912, J. D. claimed his picture theatres were patronised by 60 000 people weekly.[12]

J. D. had a passionate commitment to the possibilities of the new medium. It 'heralded the dawn of a new era in the social life of the people – the inauguration of a new and as yet untried system of relaxation, and rest, and instruction, and entertainment.'[13] The picture business would enter 'into more intimate relation with daily life' and 'to a large extent supplant the evening newspaper'. But it was 'in the education department that cinematography is bound to make its next greatest and most important movement', teaching youngsters about their country and leaving an historical record 'of the great events of our time for the benefit of those who come after us'.[14] After a whirlwind tour of the United States, England and Europe, he returned to Sydney in late 1911 with a scheme to realise this vision.

> [I]t is my intention to regulate the [picture] shows, and put them on a high and sound basis, and this is to be accomplished by placing the film-renting business in the hands of a few people. The principle we intend to adopt is similar to that followed in the theatrical business; and it is the only way to conduct an enterprise successfully. In America the film business is in the hands of two different concerns. Something similar is to be adopted throughout England on January 1, the managers of the various enterprises having come to an agreement to work under one head. It is the same principle that I intend introducing in Australia. It will mean the proper and effectual control of the business, it will raise the standard, keep out the penny shows, and prevent film 'duping' that is, making and copying and using pictures without authority ... I intend to open in all the large cities on an elaborate scale.[15]

Williams' commercial strategies set the standard for corporate empire building for the next two decades in Australia and his feats were the stuff of tall tales among film-men in New York and Hollywood.[16] In December 1910, he consolidated his holdings into the Greater J. D. Williams Amusement Co. Ltd,

---

[11] Jeffries 1912, 'The Gold Bug', p. xxxviii.
[12] Advertisement for Lyric and Colonial Theatres, *Footlights*, vol. 5, no. 31, 3 January 1912.
[13] Greater J. D. Williams Amusement Co., Publicity Department, *A Story of Success*, [1912].
[14] Jeffries 1911, 'Banyan Tree', p. 284.
[15] 'What Australia Needs. Lessons from America', *Sydney Morning Herald*, 26 December 1911, p. 4.
[16] Jobes 1966, *Motion Picture Empire*, pp. 53-4.

with a capital of £200 000.[17] Besides his Sydney theatres,[18] this company controlled a circuit of fifteen picture theatres in Melbourne, Brisbane, Perth and New Zealand. It ran five film exchanges, had agents in London and America and a distribution outlet in China.[19] While the general opinion of film historians is that J. D. 'contributed very little to the creative side of local activity',[20] in 1912 he set up his own camera crews to cover dramatic events across eastern Australia for the first Australian newsreel, *Williams' Weekly News*. Later, in 1916, he formed an independent syndicate with Stanley Crick and John C. Jones to finance the wartime feature, *The Martyrdom of Nurse Cavell* (1916), and the historical saga, *The Mutiny on the Bounty* (1916).[21]

In this early period at least, moving pictures were not insulated from the rest of the amusement business, as implied by most film historians.[22] A jump into another historiography reveals J. D. as the champion of a wide sweep of popular entertainment. His earliest sideshow enterprise is mentioned only in passing, but in 1911 and 1912, when the film historians have him building and opening the Melba and Britannia Theatres in Melbourne, popular amusement and local historians identify him as the great impresario of Luna Park at St Kilda.[23] Directly

---

[17] Greater J. D. Williams Amusement Co., Publicity Department, *A Story of Success*, [1912].

[18] Capitol, Empress, Lyric, and Crystal Palace Theatres.

[19] *Theatre*, 1 September 1910, p. 13, cited in Ina Bertrand and William D. Rout, 'The Big Bad Combine', in Albert Moran and Tom O'Regan (eds) 1989, *The Australian Screen* (Melbourne: Penguin), p. 6.

[20] Eric Reade 1970, *Australian Silent Films. A Pictorial History 1896–1929* (Melbourne: Lansdowne), pp. 53, 58, 61; John Tulloch 1981, *Legends on the Screen: The Narrative Film on the Screen 1919–1929* (Sydney: Currency), p. 155.

[21] *The Martyrdom of Nurse Cavell*, directed by John Gavin and C. Post Mason, produced by Australasian Famous Features Company, 1916; *The Mutiny on the Bounty*, directed by Raymond Longford, produced by Crick and Jones, 1916: see Andrew Pike and Ross Cooper 1998, *Australian Film 1900–1977: A Guide to Feature Film Production*, 2nd edition (Melbourne: Oxford University Press), pp. 59-60, 64.

[22] But see, Anne Bittner, 'Spectacle and Narrative Aspects of the Relationship Between Live Performance and Film in Australia in the 1920s', in Jeff Doyle, Bill van der Heide and Susan Cowan (eds) 1998, *Our Selection On: Writings on Cinemas' Histories* (Canberra: National Film and Sound Archive/Australia Defence Force Academy), pp. 61-72; Vanessa Toulmin and Simon Popple (eds) 2000, *Visual Delights: The Popular and Projected Image in the Nineteenth Century* (Trowbridge: Flicks Books).

[23] Anna Moo 1991, 'Luna Park', http://home.vicnet.net.au/~hsosk/articles/Luna_Park.htm (Aug 2003); Robert Lashmore 2004, 'Melbourne Luna Park's Ghost Train', http://www.elvision.com/tunneloflaffs/ghosttrain/gtindex.html; Australian Heritage Database, 'Luna Park', http://www.deh.gov.au/cgi-bin/ahdb/search.pl (March 2005).

emulating its namesake on Coney Island, Luna Park was built by a largely American team of amusement park designers and technicians.[24] J. D.'s partner, Leon Phillips, with his two brothers, took over the enterprise after its spectacular opening in December 1912. J. D.'s fascination with Coney Island as the pinnacle of integrated entertainment had already been given form in Sydney. At the June 1912 opening of the second largest[25] and most lavish of the Williams' theatres, the Crystal Palace Theatre and amusement complex,[26] a *Sydney Morning Herald* reporter described it as 'a kind of miniature Coney Island transferred, as if by the Slaves of the Lamp, to Sydney, and fitted with all sorts of means of amusement'.[27] Beyond the world of cinema and amusement parks, J. D. also had interests in motorbike and motorcar racing and sales, and revived track-bicycle racing, introducing both Sydney and Melbourne to the American sport of six-day racing in 1912.[28] As his publicist recorded: 'The object of the democratic-minded J. D. W. is to revolutionise the motor and motor-bike trade, just as he has revolutionised the photo-play business, and make motors popular and cheap.'[29]

J. D. Williams' empire was built in a world of cutthroat competition, of constant manoeuvring to undermine rivals and to advance one's own position. J. D. understood that the future belonged to the efficient and the consolidated: the whole film business should be in the hands of only a few well-conducted enterprises. But a well-conducted enterprise was not easy to create or sustain. Throughout the period, 1910 to 1913, he faced disunion in the control and management of his own company and sharp competition in the field. Emerging on top after an intricate play of mergers, takeovers and court cases, in 1913 he engineered an amalgamation with his chief competitors and became the dominant

---

[24] The consulting engineer was T. H. Eslick.

[25] The Britannia Theatre in Melbourne, with 1200 seats, was at the time the largest in the world.

[26] The complex contained a picture theatre, dance hall, wintergarden café, slot-machine amusement arcade, novelty photography hall, gymnasium, and professional child-care centre: Greater J. D. Williams Amusement Co., Publicity Department, *A Story of Success*, [1912]; Katharine Brisbane (ed.) 1991, *Entertaining Australia*, p. 166; Ross Thorne, Les Tod and Kevin Cork 1996, *Movie Theatre Heritage Register for New South Wales 1896–1996* (Sydney: Department of Architecture, University of Sydney), p. 37.

[27] *Sydney Morning Herald*, 24 June 1912, p. 3, quoted in Ross Thorne 1981, *Cinemas of Australia via USA* (Sydney: Architecture Department, Sydney University), p. 115.

[28] 'Romance of a Great Industry', p. 32; Terry O'Brien 1985, *The Greater Union Story* (Sydney: The Greater Union Organisation), pp. 12, 23; Reade 1970, *Australian Silent Films*, pp. 68-72; Jeffries 1911, 'Banyan Tree', pp. 275-84.

[29] Jeffries 1912, 'Gold Bug', p. xxxviii.

partner in what was called 'the Combine'.[30] This was a distribution and exhibition company known as Union Theatres/Australasian Films, which stood as a colossus astride the Sydney moving picture field with a capital of well over £1 000 000. As with all his enterprises, J. D. did not manage the new company, but left it to others. His publicist explained the system 1912:

> He creates a company, which is an organization, to do a certain work. He creates the machine, chooses a man or men to run it, and then he leaves it to them. Auditors keep a check on them, and the balance-sheet tells him at a glance how the machine is working. If the results are not good, the man who made the machine calls around to see why it isn't doing the work it was designed for.[31]

This machine worked well and Union Theatres dominated the national field for decades, and still exists in a hybrid form today.

In 1912, following the opening of the spectacular Crystal Palace, the leading theatrical magazine *Footlights* had proclaimed J. D., 'the greatest showman that Australia has ever seen', and anointed him the 'Napoleon of Amusements'.[32] It declared that, 'The present generation sound his praise, and by posterity, he cannot be forgotten.'[33] Its prediction was, however, vain. Within a year, the fabulous J. D. Williams disappeared from the pages of Australian film history. The contemporary papers and later historians simply abandon this hero and turn to others. There is some mention of more travels in America; there are hints of a 'very spectacular crash'.[34] Then silence.

But Williams was irrepressible. Australian historiography might forget him, but he did not abandon his dreams to be and make the biggest and best. So we need to turn our attention from Australian to American film historiography, which picks up the story from 1916. What happened before that date is left rather vague. Benjamin Hampton, for example, off-handedly introduces Williams as 'a West Virginian who had been selling and exhibiting American films in various parts of the world for a number of years'.[35] In these American works, the story of J. D. begins anew. Terry Ramsaye, presents the rebirth boldly:

> The exhibitors were coming! Their lances gleamed in the starlight and their eyes lusted for treasure.

---

[30] 'Romance of a Great Industry', pp. 32, 34; John Tulloch 1982, *Australian Cinema. Industry, Narrative and Meaning* (Sydney: Allen & Unwin), p. 63.

[31] Jeffries 1912, 'Gold Bug', p. xl.

[32] *Footlights*, vol. 6, no. 3, 12 June 1912; 19 June 1912.

[33] *Footlights*, 19 June 1912.

[34] Brodsky 1963, *Sydney Takes the Stage*, p. 82.

[35] Hampton 1970, *History of the American Film Industry*, p. 176.

The leader of that menacing column had risen out of the sea and the other end of the world. J. D. Williams, former assistant treasurer of the Parkersburg opera house, was home again from Australia, looking for something to do.[36]

He found plenty. First he set up a national distribution company based in New York. From there he locked horns with Adolph Zukor's Paramount company, which had become a commanding force in the film business through its control of the most popular stars and the most profitable pictures. With Thomas L. Tally, J. D. co-founded First National Exhibitors' Circuit in 1917 and became its general manager.[37] The American histories make much of the industry politics and machinations of First National in combat with the other industry giants: 'The moves were intricate, rapid and continuous.'[38] But they make no mention of J. D.'s earlier and similar battles to create the Combine in Sydney.

First National was 'essentially a national organization of states rights franchisees',[39] but J. D. soon developed it into a production/exhibition Combine and one of the most powerful film companies in the country for many years.[40] The first contract he signed was with Charlie Chaplin, paying over a million dollars for eight two-reel pictures a year. The second was with Mary Pickford. Always cosmopolitan, he 'created a motion picture sensation in the United States'[41] when he introduced the first postwar German picture on to the First National circuit, Ernst Lubitsch's *Madame Dubarry* (retitled for commercial reasons as *Passion*).[42]

There is a photograph from 1922 showing J. D. as a foundation member of the most important regulatory agency for the film industry for the next half century, the Motion Picture Producers and Distributors of America.[43] He is sitting next

---

[36] Ramsaye 1986, *A Million and One Nights*, p. 789.

[37] Jobes 1966, *Motion Picture Empire*, p. 159.

[38] Ramsaye 1986, *A Million and One Nights*, p. 793.

[39] Richard Koszarski 1994, *History of American Cinema*, volume 3: *An Evening's Entertainment. The Age of the Silent Feature Picture 1915–1928* (Berkeley, CA: University of California Press), p. 72.

[40] Andrew Higson 1999, 'Polyglot Films for an International Market', in Andrew Higson and Richard Maltby (eds), *'Film Europe' and 'Film America': Cinema, Commerce and Cultural Exchange 1920–1939* (Exeter: University of Exeter Press), p. 276.

[41] Thomas J. Saunders 1994, *Hollywood in Berlin: American Cinema and Weimar Germany* (Berkeley, CA: University of California Press), p. 60.

[42] *Madame Dubarry* (US title: *Passion*), directed by Ernst Lubitsch, produced by Union, 1919; 'James D. Williams', 4 September 1934, *Variety Obituaries, 1929–1938*.

[43] Reproduced in Hampton 1970, *History of the American Film Industry*, Plate 75.

to the soon-to-become Movie Czar, Will Hays. In that same year, *Motion Picture News* listed him as one of the twelve greatest people of the motion picture industry.[44] Twelve years later, his *Variety* obituary noted the innovation that First National originally represented: 'Had Williams been more of an executive and less the promoter he might have revolutionized the industry's set-up.'[45]

In late 1922, J. D. was pushed to resign as general manager of First National over policy differences. At this point he drops out of American film history. His demotion also affected his standing within that history, which is largely an account of the winners and their success stories. So Williams is treated as somehow present, but unimportant, simply one wheeling dealer among many. The industry histories give no explanation for his innovative projects, no indication of his vision of moving pictures as anything other than commodities. There is no discussion of his ideals or motivation.

From 1922, the trail again goes cold, except for the minor mention that in 1925 he set up Ritz-Carlton Pictures. That company made only one picture, *Cobra*[46] with Rudolph Valentino. But when J. D. disappears from the American historiography, he resurfaces in yet another. From 1925, he is remade as a British film producer. As if born anew, his American past is only vaguely recognised by British film historians, encapsulated in the brief statements that he 'was known for his grandiose schemes on both sides of the Atlantic' – but not of the Pacific – and that 'he had already been beaten in the battle of the American film giants before coming to this country'.[47] Such language implies the inflated ambition of a mere 'pushful American', rather than the persistence of the democratic vision that was first expressed in his Australian days: to provide the broad public with 'absolutely the pick of the world's very best things in the moving-picture line' at 'the minimum rates'.[48]

Rachel Low in her magisterial *The History of British Film*, mentions in passing that J. D. Williams was a director in the British public company Stoll Picture Productions, registered in 1920,[49] but she gives no explanation nor mentions him again until 1925, when he established and became managing director of British National Pictures. He initially signed up leading American star Dorothy Gish and British director Herbert Wilcox for three British pictures, followed by

---

[44] 'Screen. The Greatest', 31 December 1922, in *New York Times Encyclopedia of Film 1896–1928*.

[45] *Variety Obituaries* 1929–38, 4 September 1934.

[46] *Cobra*, directed by Joseph Henabery, produced by Ritz-Carlton, 1925.

[47] Rachael Low 1971, *The History of the British Film 1918–1929* (London: George Allen & Unwin), p. 177. Andrew Higson devotes 12 lines to Williams' earlier career: Higson 1999, 'Polyglot Films', p. 274.

[48] 'The J. D. Williams Amusement Co.', *Theatre*, 1 September 1910, p. 13.

[49] Low 1971, *History of the British Film 1918–1929*, p. 123.

contracts with German director E. A. Dupont and the up-and-coming Alfred Hitchcock. To fund his films he made 'remarkable' deals for financial backing from the United States giants Paramount and Famous Players-Lasky. In 1926, he bought a forty-acre site and began to develop a film city, or huge super-studio – a British Hollywood – at Elstree.[50]

His aim in these projects seems to have been the same as it had been fourteen years earlier in Australia: to foster the possibilities of film as the pre-eminent modern medium of 'relaxation, and rest, and instruction, and entertainment'.[51] Now, in England, his project was not to exhibit, but to make quality films that would compete with the best that Hollywood could offer in technical polish, but that also reflected 'the very Soul of England'.[52] That Soul, he asserted, lay in English drama, not in its landscapes. His long-term plan was to rationalise the highly fragmented British film industry and develop the size of the available market in order to finance quality production.[53] Again, this plan was already present in his Australian days: 'the ambitious mind of Mr. Williams cannot see why, if we can produce good films in Australia, we should not send them all over the world.'[54] For a third time, he put the strategy of the Combine into play, but British historians have not recognised his accumulated experience.

In part, this was because his experience was not enough to win the game. In 1927, he fell out with the other backers of British National Pictures, who took over the company and the studio, creating an even bigger company, British International Pictures.[55] J. D. faded away, again. In 1928, he popped back up, in America, floating World Wide Pictures Corporation, an international distribution organisation which attempted to break into the parochialism of the American market, handling thirty or forty European pictures a year.[56] In his own words, what he proposed was 'a film conversation between nations instead of the present Hollywood monologue'.[57] Almost the last reference I have found to J. D. places him in Canada in 1931, where he picked up a film abandoned by Paramount because it didn't fit its formula. He distributed *The Viking* internationally, establishing it as one of the keystones of Canadian cinema.[58]

[50] ibid., p. 176; Higson 1999, 'Polyglot Films', pp. 274-8.
[51] Jeffries 1911, 'Banyan Tree', p. 284.
[52] Document 14: J. D. Williams 1999, 'Two Keys to the American Market', in Higson and Maltby, *'Film Europe' and 'Film America'*, p. 389.
[53] ibid., pp. 387-9.
[54] Jeffries 1911, 'Banyan Tree', pp. 280, 282.
[55] Low 1971, *History of the British Film 1918–1929*, pp. 177, 186.
[56] ibid., p. 188; Higson 1999, 'Polyglot Films', p. 277.
[57] Williams 1999, 'Two Keys', p. 392.
[58] Morris 1978, *Embattled Shadows*, pp. 321-2.

Between 1926 and 1929, J. D. elaborated on his vision of a transnational film industry in a series of speeches and articles, proposing schemes, 'either to establish British cinema as a force to be reckoned with on the world stage, or to develop a pan-European film industry'.[59] He developed a scheme for multi-language film production.[60] He proposed the formation of an Academy of Motion Pictures with a teaching staff, preferably attached to Oxford or Cambridge University.[61] Behind all these schemes was not just the desire for profit, although that certainly mattered. He was committed to the making, distribution and exhibition of quality pictures rather than genre films because he still nurtured the ambition for films that he had propounded in Sydney in 1910. Sixteen years later, in England, J. D. wrote the preface to one of the first books to address film seriously and theoretically, Gerard Fort Buckle's, *The Mind and the Film: A Treatise on the Psychological Factors in Film*.[62] In it, he reflected on the power of the cinema:

> Never before, in the history of the world has there existed an instrument even remotely approaching in influence the motion picture as we know it. There has never before existed any means by which the genius of a people could be expressed and presented dramatically to all other peoples … Because of its power the film should be taken seriously. It is a great weapon. It should be greatly used. It cannot be greatly used unless it is established as an art.[63]

Making quality pictures took huge amounts of money, which could only be provided by a world market. But, in turn, quality pictures would realise their full power and destiny within such world market.

In 1934 James Dixon Williams died in New York. After a number of years in Canada, seven years in Australia, and five years in England, his eleven paragraph obituary in *Variety* devoted a mere half paragraph to his activities in Australia, and another half paragraph to his time in England. In the later film histories of each of the four countries in which he played a significant part, his moment there is acknowledged. But what happened before or after, where he came from and where he went, and what experience and influence he carried from one

---

[59] Higson 1999, 'Polyglot Films', p. 277.

[60] *Bioscope*, May 29, June 19, 1929, cited in Low 1971, *History of the British Film 1918–1929*, p. 227; Higson 1999, 'Polyglot Films', pp. 289-10.

[61] *Bioscope*, 24 April, 1929, p. 15, cited in Low 1971, *History of the British Film 1918–1929*, pp. 36-7.

[62] Gerard Fort Buckle 1926, *The Mind and the Film: A Treatise on the Psychological Factors in Film* (London: George Routledge & Sons); Low 1971, *History of the British Film 1918–1929*, pp. 20-5.

[63] Buckle 1926, *The Mind and the Film*, pp. xii-iii.

country to the others, all is ignored or dealt with through anecdote and supposition.

My title for this chapter hails J. D. Williams as a nomad. I do not use this term to invoke Deleuze and Guattari's appropriation of it as a certain mode of critical inquiry.[64] Rather, I am impressed by John Brinkerhoff Jackson's discussion of the verb '*To dwell* [which] like the verb *to abide* simply means to pause, to stay put for a length of time; it implies that we will eventually move on.'[65] Film historians, like most others, have been seduced into thinking that staying still is the normal condition, rather than being a mere moment's pause. They have defined their subjects in terms of an identity, especially a national identity, which is the quality of a stationary people in a bounded space, rather than understanding them as mobile and multi-dimensional, as nomadic. Just as the physiological phenomenon of persistence of vision makes possible the movement of moving pictures, so too does the social phenomenon of persistence of memory make possible the fiction of the unity of personality and group identity, and the stability of place. In memory, the people we have met do not change, but stay as they were and belong where they were.

It is these fictions that are at the heart of national historiographies, most particularly for my purpose, national film histories. These histories inevitably constitute their subjects through an appeal to national identity and pride. So, how is transnational history to engage with the tyranny of the national? How is it to constitute its subject so that it is coherent, has epistemological legitimacy, and will gain acceptance from publishers and the reading public?

One answer is to adopt the mode of biography. In biography, the fiction of the continuous self, if not the unitary self, provides the coherence of the subject. Biography allows the transnational historian to prise their subject out of the death grip of the national. There are plenty of deracinated officials and entrepreneurs and proselytisers roaming across the empires of the world. The chief problem, apart from the fiction of coherent identity, is whether one's person is already or can be made interesting enough to attract a readership. Celebrity or notoriety helps. In the case of film history, this is provided by stardom. Directors are sometimes granted celebrity status (for example, Cecil B. deMille and Alfred Hitchcock), but never producers, distributors or exhibitors.

A second answer is a model of analysis based in economic history, dealing with the global movement of goods, services, and people. Immigration history also fits this model, as does the history of disease. It is the preferred approach of

---

[64] Gilles Deleuze and Felix Guattari 1987, *A Thousand Plateaus*, translator Brian Massumi (Minneapolis, MN: University of Minnesota Press).

[65] John Brinkerhoff Jackson 1984, 'The Moveable Dwelling and How it Came to America', in his *Discovering the Vernacular Landscape* (New Haven, CT: Yale University Press), p. 91.

World History and is much employed in the history of globalisation. The subject here is already constituted, or can be shown empirically to be constituted, by its inter- or multinational connections. The connections between J. D. Williams' organisational projects in each of his four nations have not been noticed before, but I doubt there will be much resistance to the idea. But nor will there be much interest.

The international dominance of the American film industry since the Great War has meant historical focus is chiefly on American expansion, a sort of imperial history, whether viewed from Hollywood as metropolis or from a specific colonised province. Often conceptualised as the threat of Americanisation to national culture, movement is followed one-way along a single track, from the centre to the provinces.[66] Very rarely do historians look at the continuous and multi-directional flow of people, technology and ideas around the whole circuit, treating America as simply another province, or perhaps as several provinces. The 'Hollywood monologue', in Williams' phrase, is film history orthodoxy. Nonetheless, there is here a recognisable field for transnational history, which has been developed by writers such as Kristin Thompson, Ruth Vasey, Richard Maltby and Andrew Higson.[67]

In terms of readership, unfortunately, the place of economic and more particularly business history in the hierarchy of historical genres is pretty low. Its status is linked to that of its subjects – the middlemen, the profit-takers who are neither producers nor creators nor end-users, and who suffer the curious prejudice against trade. Historians have typically shared this prejudice. In addition, many present-day historians as well as their readers see globalisation as the enemy of the producers and workers of the national culture and they turn their backs on business history.

A third model for a transnational approach to film history derives from the dual nature of moving pictures, as both commodities and cultural products. Certainly, film culture and its audience can easily be shown to have been transnational from the beginning. But there is very limited enthusiasm for a transnational approach to culture, and I cannot see that changing soon. Cultural nationalism was dominant throughout the entire twentieth century and remains so in the

---

[66] e.g., Victoria de Grazia 1989, 'Mass Culture and Sovereignty: The American Challenge to European Cinemas 1920–1960', *Journal of Modern History,* vol. 61, no. 1, pp. 53-87; David W. Ellwood and Rob Kroes (eds) 1994, *Hollywood in Europe. Experiences of Cultural Hegemony* (Amsterdam: VU University Press); Saunders 1994, *Hollywood in Berlin*.

[67] Kristin Thompson 1985, *Exporting Entertainment: America in the World Film Market 1907–1934* (London: BFI); Ruth Vasey 1997, *The World According to Hollywood 1918–1939* (Exeter: University of Exeter Press); Andrew Higson and Richard Maltby (eds) 1999, *'Film Europe' and 'Film America': Cinema, Commerce and Cultural Exchange 1920–1939* (Exeter: University of Exeter Press).

twenty-first. It has been fuelled by reaction to global modernity and to American economic monopoly of popular culture. Cultural nationalists everywhere have championed local culture, particularly locally made pictures that represent an idealised, often pre-modern, essential, unitary, national character. As J. D. Williams wrote in 1926:

> The desire to see fine films made in Britain is, I hope, very laudable, since I possess it and am now in process of putting it into practice; but I think it is unfortunate that this very important movement should in some way have attracted to itself the Little Englander.[68]

The history of such cultural nationalism and its imagery is complex and much studied. For my purposes here, I want only to stress its longevity in Australia, as elsewhere. It took on new life in the 1960s and 1970s, when the film renaissance changed the content of the imagery but not its significance. Like the term Little Englander, its equivalent, White Australian, no longer has currency, but similarly exclusive and protective concepts of national identity still prevail and are democratically spread throughout the broad reading public. That readership, and its close relation the movie-going audience, is acknowledged to be cosmopolitan and to have great curiosity and catholic taste. International books and films are eagerly consumed. But when the subject matter is Australia, different standards and values seem to come into play. There is something sacrosanct about certain aspects of culture, as with sport and foreign policy, that triggers the protective, exclusive, mutual embrace; that constitutes a settled 'us' against the nomadic hordes of 'them'. And film history as a genre has been seduced, or recruited, to tell that story. Most film historians continue to hold a strong allegiance to cultural nationalism, and hold the transnational elements in their accounts to be alien intrusions. The central purpose of their histories is to write into existence an authentically and uniquely national film culture. Foreign influences on that history, like foreign films from the archive, must be repatriated.

So, regrettably, I must conclude that, although there are strong empirical and epistemological arguments for a transnational film history, there are even stronger political investments in keeping film history national – even nationalist. Both the economic and the cultural sub-genres share these investments, although the history of film as culture is most thoroughly in thrall. National film history is an account of moving pictures with the pause button stuck, and histories of film culture's transnational nomads find little welcome. This inhospitable outlook will not change until the larger political discourse changes.

---

[68] Williams 1999, 'Two Keys', p. 387.

11. The Americanisation of romantic love in Australia

Hsu-Ming Teo

This chapter explores the transnational influence of consumer capitalism on the culture of romantic love in Australia during the twentieth century, particularly as it has been manifested through advertising. I want to utilise Benedict Anderson's well-known argument about how print capitalism created the 'imagined community' of the nation to argue that if the circulation of texts throughout society can foster feelings of nationalism,[1] they can also create or affect emotional experiences of romantic love.[2]

These ideas and expectations take root across national boundaries precisely because love is often assumed to be self-evidently universal; an unchanging part of the human condition, reaching beyond the boundaries of a specific nation or culture. Particular notions and practices of romantic love have become increasingly transnational because of the global reach of Anglophone culture, fostered by the prevalence of the English language throughout the former British empire and reinforced when hegemonic American popular culture piggybacked on this colonial legacy to find new markets for products and practices of romantic consumption in Anglophone societies.

The widespread use of English makes national boundaries porous because whoever controls the means to disseminate ideas widely – especially ideas about love that are generally considered 'natural' and universal rather than socially constructed – can affect other societies' ideas, expectations, and, hence, emotional experiences of romantic love. Thus the transnational influences on Australian romantic love occur through the global circulation of Anglophone print and visual culture, and the global spread of the American practice of romanticising commodities, inextricably linking experiences of romantic love to consumption.

This chapter begins with a brief sketch of the changing culture of romantic love in the United States of America throughout the nineteenth and twentieth century. It then charts how, through consumer capitalism, a particular conception of romantic love which had its genesis in affluent white middle-class America has

---

[1] My thanks to Marilyn Lake for her editorial feedback.
Benedict Anderson 1991 [1983], *Imagined Communities: Reflections on the Origin and Spread of Nationalism*, 2nd edition (London: Verso), pp. 6, 46.
[2] For a discussion of how discourse transforms desire into 'romantic love', see Jack Goody 1998, *Food and Love: A Cultural History of East and West* (London and New York: Verso), pp. 109-19. Also, Catherine Belsey 1994, *Desire: Love Stories in Western Culture* (Oxford: Blackwell), p. 81.

become transnational, influencing the way Australian women, in particular, conceived of romance especially in the mid-twentieth century. Of course it may be argued that the culture of romantic love in Australia has always been transnational because non-indigenous Australians began as 'transplanted Britons', and this British heritage has had deep and long-lasting influences in mainstream Australian culture.[3]

It should be noted, however, that this inherited culture of romantic love was not necessarily consonant with the national boundaries of the imperial metropole. John Gillis's work on romantic love in Britain, for example, demonstrates the fragmented nature of romantic rituals and attempts at intimacy throughout the British Isles where different regions and classes were concerned. Gillis argued that although certain ideals of romantic love might have been widely shared in the nineteenth and twentieth centuries, its practical outworking differed significantly between classes and generations, with, for instance, homosocial developments in some regional working-class young adult cultures forming a barrier against emotional intimacy and mutual understanding or sympathy between the sexes.[4]

This is a timely reminder to Australian historians belonging to an older imperial historiographical tradition that insists on first knowing British in order to understand Australian history,[5] or to those who would write transnational Australian history, that, as Antoinette Burton has warned, in drawing connections between cultural or other traditions, the reified nation can still creep in through the backdoor:[6] vide discussions (even in this chapter) of 'British' or 'American' cultural influences in Australia when these are hardly monolithic or cohesive

---

[3] For discussions of the Britishness of Australian society and culture see, for example, Stuart Ward and Deryck Schreuder (eds) forthcoming 2006, *The Oxford History of the British Empire: Australia* (Oxford: Oxford University Press); Tara Brabazon 2000, *Tracking the Jack: A Retracing of the Antipodes* (Sydney: University of New South Wales Press); Hsu-Ming Teo 2004, 'The Britishness of Australian Popular Fiction', in Kate Darian-Smith, Patricia Grimshaw, Kiera Lindsey and Stuart Macintyre (eds), *Exploring the British World: Identity – Cultural Production – Institutions* (Melbourne: RMIT Publishing), pp. 721-47.

[4] John R. Gillis 1985, *For Better, For Worse: British Marriages, 1600 to the Present* (New York, NY: Oxford University Press), pp. 258-9.

[5] See Ann Curthoys' discussion of W. K. Hancock and J. A. La Nauze in 'We've Just Started Making National Histories, and You Want Us to Stop Already?', in Antoinette Burton (ed.) 2003, *After the Imperial Turn: Thinking With and Through the Nation* (London and Durham, NC: Duke University Press), pp. 72-4.

[6] Antoinette Burton 2003, 'Introduction: On the Inadequacy and the Indispensability of the Nation', in Burton (ed.), *After the Imperial Turn*, p. 8.

cultures within their own geographical boundaries.[7] Even the homogeneity in ideas of romantic love spread by print capitalism through mass-market publications – magazines, advertisements and genre novels – manifested class and gender differences, and did not necessarily translate into a common lived experience of love. In the same way, the mainstream 'American' culture of romantic love could exclude or subsume differences in class, geographical regions, ethnic origins, educational and/or religious background.[8] Nonetheless, there is still a case to be made that a specific commercialised mass-market romantic culture, produced by American corporations and globally disseminated throughout the twentieth century, has become transnational in its reach. I argue in this chapter that Australian popular culture demonstrates transnational influences in its representation of romantic love, increasingly instituting white, educated middle-class Americans as authorities on romantic love by importing or reprinting American advice columns, articles, lectures and advertisements in magazines and self-help books. In the interwar years, Americans jostled alongside traditional British authorities on love and marriage; by the postwar period Americans had won the war of romantic expertise in Australia.

The culture of romantic love in the United States

The United States of America has one of the most well-documented histories of romantic love over the nineteenth and twentieth centuries. Ellen K. Rothman, Karen Lystra, Steven Seidman, Francesca Cancian, David Shumway and Eva Illouz, among many others, have examined diaries, love letters, medical journals, etiquette and advice manuals, magazines, popular literature and film to chart the changes in American understandings of romantic love.[9] Generally speaking,

---

[7] See, for example, the discussion of British people in James Jupp, 'The Making of the Anglo-Australian', James Jupp (ed.) 2001, *The Australian People: An Encyclopedia of the Nation, Its People and Their Origins* (Melbourne: Australian National University and Cambridge University Press); also L. Brockliss and D. Eastwood (eds) 1997, *A Union of Multiple Identities: The British Isles, c.1750–1850* (Manchester: Manchester University Press); and Marjorie Morgan 2001, *National Identities and Travel in the Victorian Britain* (Houndmills: Palgrave).

[8] Steven Seidman, for example, takes particular care to limit his discussion of romantic love to non-immigrant white middle-class Americans in the north-eastern United States. See Steven Seidman 1991, *Romantic Longings: Love in America, 1830–1980* (New York, NY and London: Routledge), p. 4.

[9] Ellen K. Rothman 1987, *With Hands and Hearts: A History of Courtship in America* (Cambridge, MA: Harvard University Press); Karen Lystra 1989, *Searching the Heart: Women, Men and Romantic Love in Nineteenth-Century America* (New York, NY and Oxford: Oxford University Press); Francesca M. Cancian 1987, *Love in America: Gender and Self-Development* (Cambridge: Cambridge University Press); David R. Shumway 2003, *Modern Love: Romance, Intimacy and the Marriage Crisis* (New

this body of work identifies two significant and interrelated broad changes in the culture of romantic love that affected emotional experiences of love. Firstly, in the nineteenth century Americans understood romantic love as an intensely private, spiritual experience – exalted to the point where romantic love practically became a new religion in itself.[10] The ultimate aim of romantic love was the complete disclosure of the individual self to the beloved in order to achieve intimacy in marriage.[11] By the early twentieth century, this had changed to a secularised notion of love that conceived it as inseparable from sexuality, pleasure and consumption.[12] Marriage or long-term partnership was no longer the ultimate fulfilment of love; rather, happiness and the experience of 'romance' became goals in themselves.

Secondly, the ritualised forms of romantic gender relations changed from nineteenth-century courtship to the twentieth-century practice of dating. Courtship took place in the private sphere and was controlled by the woman, who, in order to assure her security and happiness in marriage, placed obstacles in the relationship to test the love, patience, and faithfulness or loyalty of her suitor. Men occasionally tested women's affections as well. Therefore pain, endurance and the postponement of pleasure was an expected and accepted part of the experience of romantic love as well as the more pleasurable emotions.[13] The practice of dating turned this upside down. Dating replaced courtship among middle-class white Americans between 1870 and 1920. It was controlled by men who took women 'out' and 'bought' them a good time. Dating depended on practices of consumption and new technologies of transport and mass-market entertainment – the car, dance halls, movie theatres, restaurants, and the nascent hotel and tourism industries.[14] It taught men and women to commodify each other as well as the experience of 'romance', which was increasingly separated from 'love'.[15]

By the early twentieth century, therefore, romance had acquired an exchange value in dating, one which was reinforced by advertising which romanticised as well as glamorised consumer goods, so much so that romance eventually came to refer to consumption practices – gifts of chocolates, corsages, candlelight

---

York, NY: New York University Press); and Eva Illouz 1997, *Consuming the Romantic Utopia: Love and the Cultural Contradiction of Capitalism* (Berkeley, CA: University of California Press).

[10] Lystra 1989, *Searching the Heart*, p. 249.

[11] ibid., pp. 31-9.

[12] See Illouz's main argument in her 1997, *Consuming the Romantic Utopia*.

[13] Lystra 1989, *Searching the Heart*, pp. 9-10.

[14] Rothman 1987, *With Hands and Hearts*, pp. 289-94; Illouz 1997, *Consuming the Romantic Utopia*, pp. 54-6.

[15] Illouz 1997, *Consuming the Romantic Utopia*, p. 35.

dinners, cruises at sunsets, romantic holidays – rather than to the disclosure of feelings, as was the case in the nineteenth century. Where working-class women were concerned, sexual favours were often expected and dispensed in return for dating, but this was not necessarily the case among the middle-classes who took for granted gift-giving and consumption practices on dates.[16] Nevertheless, as the twentieth century wore on, sexual activity became part of dating, not because it was expected or because it had been 'bought', but because consumption reinforced the message that dating was about sensual pleasure and the goal of romance was feelings of happiness.[17]

Dating thus inverted the understanding and goals of nineteenth-century romantic love, which was experienced through the rituals of courtship and which viewed marriage as its inevitable goal. Where courtship encouraged patience and a focus on the future and surveillance by others – family members as well as the community – dating was immediate, focused on the present and comparatively free of social surveillance and control. It took place in 'islands of privacy' in the public sphere, rather than in the private sphere.[18] It had a secular, consumerist understanding of love rather than a spiritual one. Where expensive gifts had been looked on suspiciously in the nineteenth century, and personal gifts such as a lock of hair, a sketch portrait of the beloved, or hand-made cards were favoured instead, by the early twentieth century, gift-giving had become an expected part of the expression of romantic love. Dating was controlled by men rather than by women. It was focused on consumption rather than production (that is, marriage and the production of family). It was hedonistic in that pleasure was the goal, and pain was increasingly an unacceptable part of the experience of romantic love. And above all, the same limited script of romantic consumption was widely broadcast and reinforced by advertising, films, romance novels and magazines which commodified romance and romanticised commodities – especially what Eva Illouz has called 'ego expressive' commodities such as shampoo, perfume, deodorant and cosmetics.[19]

The promotion of consumerism through advertising directly impacts emotional states and our sense of well-being because, as Peter Stearns has observed, people stake 'a real portion of their personal identities and their quest for meaning – even their emotional satisfaction – on the search for and acquisition of goods'.[20] The aim of advertising and consumer capitalism is to foster an increased sense

---

[16] ibid., pp. 59-61.
[17] Seidman 1991, *Romantic Longings*, p. 4.
[18] Illouz 1997, *Consuming the Romantic Utopia*, p. 56.
[19] ibid., p. 37.
[20] Peter N. Stearns 1997, 'Stages of Consumerism: Recent Work on the Issues of Periodization', *Journal of Modern History*, vol. 69, no.1, p. 105.

of yearning, the feeling 'that one's life cannot be complete without this or that acquisition'.[21] Stearns argued that the coincidence of mass literacy and new print technology leading to dramatic changes in advertising in the 1890s, transformed the way Americans expressed their emotions. Not only did the look of commercial advertising become more visually arresting or appealing – dull newsprint gave way to 'screaming headlines, illustrations, and lavish use of color'[22] – but the style of advertising copy changed from a matter-of-fact description of content, durability and price to an appeal to the senses and emotions as products became associated with pleasure and sensuality.[23]

By the turn of the century, Americans had not only been socialised into consumption from a very young age, they had also imbibed the notion that emotions could be expressed and/or managed through consumption. For example, in the 1880s 'American girls were able to buy caskets and mourning clothes for dolls, to train in the proper expressions of Victorian grief', while children were increasingly given gifts to ameliorate jealousy upon the birth of a sibling or as emotional substitutes for fathers who were now working longer hours.[24] Inevitably, feelings of love and experiences of romance became inextricably intertwined with the consumption of commodities and services, fostered, as Seidman noted, by giant corporations grabbing local as well as non-local mass markets in the first two decades of the twentieth century.[25] Illouz, too, argued that:

> At the turn of the century, cultural entrepreneurs and established industries began promoting commodity-centered definitions of romance to further their own economic interests … Since then, consumption and romantic emotions have progressively merged, each shrouding the other in a mystical halo. Commodities have now penetrated the romantic bond so deeply that they have become the invisible and unacknowledged spirit reigning over romantic encounters.[26]

Early twentieth century advertising featured romantic couples who are 'made-up, well dressed, and expensively bejewelled',[27] engaged in acts of consumption such as dancing, dining at an expensive restaurant, drinking at sophisticated cocktail lounges or bars, going to the theatre or movies, on holiday at 'romantic' destinations and so forth. These have become clichéd images of romance, yet,

[21] ibid., p. 105.
[22] ibid., p. 110.
[23] ibid.
[24] ibid., p. 111.
[25] Seidman 1991, *Romantic Longings*, p. 67.
[26] Illouz 1997, *Consuming the Romantic Utopia*, p. 11.
[27] ibid., p. 37.

as Illouz's cross-class interviews in the 1990s demonstrate, they still have resonance and meaning for large sections of American society.[28] American practices of romantic consumption became increasingly widespread in the twentieth century because of the transnational reach of American capitalism – the export of its consumer goods and cultural products, and the adoption or imitation of American advertising and marketing strategies in other countries.

The culture of romantic love in nineteenth-century Australia

The culture of romantic love in nineteenth-century Australia shared many similarities to that in the United States, Canada and Britain.[29] Romantic love was an emotional, moral, physical and spiritual attraction believed to be a necessary prerequisite to courtship, with companionate marriage as its ideal goal. It was bound up in class consciousness and the demonstration of 'gentlemanly' or 'ladylike' behaviour.[30] Love was supposed to have an ennobling, morally and spiritually uplifting effect, especially upon the male lover. This notion was both a result of the greater spiritualisation of love in the nineteenth century as well as being part of a wider nineteenth-century belief in progress and perfectibility in all aspects of society, including love and moral character. Physical attraction was enhanced by a lover's 'character' and shared moral and/or religious values.[31] Yet while physical attraction was important and lovers wrote of their yearning for contact, kisses and embraces, the focus of courtship was on the mutual and exclusive disclosure of the self. This process was understood to be the very foundation of romantic intimacy.

In sharing their 'essence' with each other, it was expected that romantic love might produce great unhappiness, bitterness and despair as well as ecstasy and a feeling of empathy and completeness. Because marriage was taken for granted as the sole aim and fulfilment of romantic love, almost everything that accompanied married life could potentially be interpreted as an aspect of romantic love. Thus some lovers wrote that they did not necessarily expect love to produce constant happiness after marriage because they distinguished between the

---

[28] ibid., pp. 112-52, 247-87.

[29] See above references for the United States and Britain. See Peter Ward 1990, *Courtship, Love, and Marriage in Nineteenth-Century English Canada* (Montreal and Kingston: McGill-Queen's University Press). For Australia, see Hsu-Ming Teo 2005, 'Love Writes: Gender and Romantic Love in Australian Love Letters, 1860–1960', *Australian Feminist Studies*, vol. 20, no. 48, November 2005, pp. 343-61.

[30] See Penny Russell 1988, 'For Better and for Worse: Love, Power and Sexuality and Upper-Class Marriages in Melbourne, 1960–1880', *Australian Feminist Studies*, nos 7/8, Summer, pp. 11-26. Also, Marilyn Lake 1990, 'Female Desires: The Meaning of World War II', *Australian Historical Studies*, vol. 24, no. 5, p. 271.

[31] Katie Holmes 1995, *Spaces in her Day: Australian Women's Diaries, 1920s-1930s* (Sydney: Allen and Unwin), p. 4.

emotional elation and physical thrill of 'infatuation' in courtship and the steadier, more mundane serenity of married love in which bouts of boredom or apathy might well be expected in the cycles of domestic life.[32]

Much of this was similar to white middle-class British as well as American culture. However, there were a few crucial differences between the United States and Australia. Unlike nineteenth-century American lovers who viewed romantic love as something highly mystical or mysterious,[33] Australians generally tended to have more concrete and prosaic ideas about love. This was partly due to the fact that, unlike American culture, romantic love was not sacralised in Australian culture. The rhetoric of romantic love among Australians was never as intense, sublime or spiritualised as in the United States, neither was romance transformed into a new religion in Australia. Moreover, throughout the nineteenth and twentieth centuries, where the private correspondence among Australians reveal an eloquence of emotional feelings, the public rhetoric of romantic love has been characterised by awkwardness, self-deprecation and even bathos, in stark contrast to public romantic rhetoric in the United States.

These differences in the rhetoric of romantic love are still recognisable today, but in other respects, Australians have come to develop an increasingly American understanding of romantic consumption as a critical expression of love. This is demonstrated in an article, 'Money Can Buy You Love', in the *Sydney Morning Herald* on 14 February 2005, which argued that 'Valentine's Day ... has become less about intimacy than the grand, expensive gesture: the jewellery, the mink coat, the impromptu hot air balloon ride'.[34] In this article, RMIT marketing lecturer Con Stavros observed that:

> Marketing has turned Valentine's Day into the celebration that it is ... If you go back even a decade, people used to just exchange private cards and have some kind of romantic [dinner]. These days the gift has to be public, conspicuous – people [at work] ask each other: 'What did you get?'[35]

The practice of romantic consumption may have become more extravagant in conspicuous ways at the beginning of the twenty-first century, yet this was something which developed in unevenly gendered ways in the first half of the twentieth century as consumer culture in Australia became Americanised.

---

[32] Teo 2005, 'Love Writes'.

[33] Lystra 1989, *Searching the Heart*, p. 6.

[34] Alan Mascarenhas 2005, 'Money Can Buy You Love', *Sydney Morning Herald*, 14 February, viewed on-line at http://www.smh.com.au/news/National/Money-can-buy-you-love/2005/02/13/1108229857401.html on 14 February 2005.

[35] Quoted in Mascarenhas 2005, 'Money Can Buy You Love'.

The romanticisation of consumption in Australia

The historiography of consumer culture in Australia has focused largely on women and domesticity rather than romance, with Marilyn Lake's work on the sexualisation of femininity and romanticisation of advertisements in women's magazines of the 1930s being one of the few exceptions.[36] Nevertheless the extant body of work on consumerism establishes a number of important findings, the most significant of which are the gendered nature of advertising, and the sophistication of Australian women where the consumption of personal and household goods was concerned. Consumer goods were advertised in distinctly gendered ways, catering to the gendered division in shopping activities whereby, for most of the twentieth century, men 'made the majority of decision for motor mowers and electric shavers – items considered men's products. They also made the majority of decisions for bottled wines and spirits, radios, radiograms, record players and television sets'.[37] On the whole, women shopped for men's 'ego expressive' products – shirts, soaps, shampoos – for most of the twentieth century.

Meanwhile, advertisements for consumer goods bought by men tended to emphasise nationalism and men's identities as workers – collective identities, rather than individual ones. Robert Crawford has demonstrated how, until the end of the 1950s, items of personal or leisure consumption for men were advertised with images of factories: products as diverse as beer, Berger Paints, Dunlop rubber, Boomerang whisky, Australian oil and General Motors-Holden cars.[38] These images also emphasised men's social and economic role as producers. It was not until the late 1950s/early 1960s that advertising directed at Australian men shifted its focus to them as consumers. Although men's ego-expressive products such as fragrances and powders were available during the 1930s, advertisements targeted women, who were urged to buy these products for Australian men to enhance their physical attractiveness and sex appeal.[39]

Mark Swiencicki has argued that the historiography of consumption in the United States has privileged women and entrenched them as primary consumers throughout the nineteenth and twentieth century. Swiencicki contended that if the consumption of services as well as goods was taken into account, American

---

[36] Lake 1990, 'Female Desires', pp. 269-74.

[37] *Who Decides? – A Study of the Buying Habits of Australian Men and Women*, commissioned by the Readers Digest Association Pty Ltd (Melbourne, 1961).

[38] Robert Crawford 2003, 'Manufacturing Identities: Industrial Representations of Australia in Press Advertisements, 1900–69', *Labour History*, no. 84, pp. 21-46, viewed on-line 14 December 2004 at: http://historycooperative.press.uiuc.edu/journals/lab/84/crawford.html

[39] Marilyn Lake 1992, 'The Desire for a Yank: Sexual Relations between Australian Women and American Servicemen during World War II', *Journal of the History of Sexuality*, vol. 2, no. 4, p. 630.

men can be demonstrated to have consumed at least twice as much as women between the period 1880 to 1930.[40] The same may have been true of Australian men. It may be that men were as avid consumers of goods and services as women, or even more so. Nevertheless, the point remains that in advertising material, these consumer practices were not romanticised and entwined with relationships, or infused with emotions of intimacy. The same could not be said to be true of advertising aimed at Australian women in the first half of the twentieth century.

Historical scholarship on Australian consumerism has linked practices of consumption to the sexualisation of women's bodies in advertising in the 1920s. Rosemary Pringle, for example, argued that it was during this time that '"Girlie" pictures began to appear in such newspapers as *Truth*, *Smith's Weekly* and the *Labour Daily*', while 'advertisers linked sexuality to the emotionalisation of housework and the establishment of private life as the place where we "find our real selves".'[41] The timing is significant because, as Ann Stephen's work on the marketing of soap during the interwar years demonstrated, this was the period when American magazines and American companies began to penetrate the hitherto impregnable British market for women's consumer goods. Stephen's work makes clear the link between the circulation of American women's magazines in Australia and the glamour of American products for women, demonstrating that by the time the American company Palmolive entered the Australian market in 1921, in direct competition to the British soap company Lever,

> the quality of 'Americanness' already exerted a strong appeal on local audiences. This attraction was not difficult to understand, for Australian magazines, like their British counterparts could not compete with the scale and lavish colour of the two most popular US imports, the *Saturday Evening Post* and the *Ladies Home Journal*.[42]

Moreover, as Jill Matthews has noted, the association of global American commerce with exciting modernity and Hollywood glamour contributed to the attractiveness of the American brand.[43]

---

[40] Mark A. Swiencicki 1998, 'Consuming Brotherhood: Men's Culture, Style and Recreation as Consumer Culture, 1880-1930', *Journal of Social History*, vol. 31, no. 4, pp. 773-809.

[41] Rosemary Pringle, 'Women and Consumer Capitalism', in Cora V. Baldock and Bettina Cass (eds) 1988, *Women, Social Welfare and the State in Australia* (Sydney: Allen and Unwin), p. 97.

[42] Ann Stephen 2003, 'Selling Soap: Domestic Work and Consumerism', *Labour History*, no. 61, p. 63.

[43] Jill Julius Matthews 2005, *Dance Hall & Picture Palace: Sydney's Romance with Modernity* (Sydney: Currency Press), pp. 7-11.

The interwar years were in some ways a culturally hybrid moment for advertising in Australian women's magazines, when visual layouts based on American magazines were accompanied by advertising copy with a 'British' flavour.[44] Increasingly the visual style of Australian women's magazine advertisements became more American, sometimes brazenly copied with minor adjustments to 'Australianise' the image.[45] The impetus towards Americanisation in Australian advertising styles and images thus occurred during the interwar years and was driven by the perception of American women's modernity and the glamour of romantic consumption. This was reinforced by the gradual penetration of American beauty products into the Australian market during the 1930s, advertised through images of romantic consumption.[46]

The association of goods and romantic love was not new in Australian culture; by the outbreak of World War I, the Richmond Furnishing Company's advertisements in the Melbourne-based *Table Talk* magazine had already made this connection. Text advertisements for the company's wares and its store address were embedded in short love stories, play tableaux and letters purporting to be from mothers advising their daughters on marriage. What was new in the interwar years, however, was the expansion of advertisements for female ego-expressive products associated with beauty and romance in the 1920s, and, by the 1930s, youthful 'sex appeal'.[47]

In the early twentieth century, advertisements for domestic products – Horlicks malted milk, dress patterns and accessories, sewing machines, chocolate laxettes for the management of the family's health – were more numerous than advertisements for shampoos, perfumes or cosmetics. The visual image was also significantly different. Advertisements for ego-expressive products in *The Australian Women's Weekly*[48] before World War I were black and white line drawings with a preponderance of informative text over pictures. The emphasis was on health and hygiene. For example, beautiful hair was a sign of good health rather than sexual allure. Whatever the subtext might have been, beauty was advertised for its own sake rather than in the context of overt romantic encounters.

---

[44] Stephen 2003, 'Selling Soap', p. 63.

[45] ibid., pp. 65, 67.

[46] Kathy Peiss 2002, 'Educating the Eye of the Beholder. American Cosmetics Abroad', *Daedalus*, vol. 131, no. 4, pp. 101-9. Viewed on-line 15 December 2004 at: http://www.highbeam.com/library/doc3.asp?DOCID=1G1:94144191&num=6&ctrlInfo=Round9c%3AProd%3ASR%3AResult&ao=1

[47] Lake 1990, 'Female Desires', p. 271.

[48] The pre-Australian Consolidated Press publication which ran from 16 November 1912 to 30 April 1921 and continued as *Home Budget* in 1922.

This began to change in the 1920s, when advertisements for ego-expressive products were set within the context of romantic love and marriage. The contrast between British and American advertising styles and techniques during this period is clearly demonstrated in the rivalry between Lever and Palmolive. In contrast to Lever's soap advertisements in Australian women's magazines, which emphasised imperial themes of racial whiteness and hygiene even in the 1920s, the American company Palmolive focused entirely on female beauty, youth and romance, telling them to: '*Live* Your Romances! *Keep* that Schoolgirl Complexion!' The advertisement went on to advise women that

> *BEAUTY, Charm, Youth* may not be the fundamentals of romance, but they help. Practically every reader of a 'best seller' pictures the heroine as being possessed of those attributes. To *live* one's romances to-day, one stays young as long as she can, makes herself as *naturally attractive* as she can and trusts the rest to her womanly intelligence.

This advertisement, which first ran in women's magazines in the United States and was later carried by *The Australian Women's Weekly* and *Table Talk*, established a nexus between women, beauty, youth, romantic love and consumption – of 'best selling' romance novels and films as well as soap. Other companies followed suit in hawking glamorous or luxurious romance with beauty products. Thus a 1922 advertisement for Icilma face cream in *Table Talk* featured a sketch of an elegantly dressed woman standing on a balcony in front of open French doors leading into a ballroom where couples are dancing. She is powdering her nose while a man stands attentively behind her, and the caption underneath reads: 'Her Complexion won his attention.'

Kissproof lipstick ran advertisements in *Table Talk* in 1930 featuring a cartoon drawing of two young women talking in front of a mirror while one applied lipstick. The modernity of these women is conveyed by their bobbed and shingled hair, sports jackets, and the golf club one is carrying under her arm. The caption, part of the conversation between the two 'flappers', reads:

> There's no doubt about it, dear, that Kissproof Lipstick you told me about is magic, pure and simple! I'm getting so popular – just a glorious time! Kissproof Lipstick makes my lips so small and, er, you know, so – inviting! And the way it stays on, no matter what happens!

With this and other lipstick advertisements in the 1930s and 1940s promising 'seductive' and 'provocatively appealing' lips, femininity, as Lake argued, 'was beginning to cast off its passivity as the logic of the incitement to pleasure took its course'.[49] Liz Conor has further commented upon young women's dynamic sense of 'self-mastery' or agency in presenting a 'modern' appearance through

---

[49] Lake 1990, 'Female Desires', p. 274.

clothes as well as cosmetics: 'perhaps for the first time in the West, modern women understood self-display to be part of the quest for mobility, self-determination, and sexual identity'[50] – an identity fashioned in part from the images of screen stars in American romantic movies, to which young Australian women made up seventy per cent of the audience.[51]

The Americanisation of Australian women's magazines during the interwar years in terms of the promotion of romantic consumption such as dancing and dining out, as well as the romanticisation of ego-expressive commodities, was accompanied by the Americanisation of expertise on romantic love, but not without a certain measure of initial scepticism and sardonic commentary. In a 1924 issue of *Table Talk*, the social column 'What People are Saying and Doing' featured a short article on 'Love and Millions', an ironic report on how:

> An attractive stranger, Miss Alfaretta Hallam, from America, of course, is lecturing in Sydney on many popular subjects including our old friend, 'Love, Courtship, and Matrimony,' only, being a modern and an American, she disguised it as 'Practical Psychology.'[52]

This was among the first of many articles linking American expertise to romantic love as well as the psychologisation of the self. Moreover, the metaphors used by Alfaretta Hallam – the 'business of marriage', the 'training' involved in relationships, the idea that choosing a husband is like choosing a career – all emphasised the intertwining of romantic love with commerce and the market. The Australian reviewer recognised this and ended the short article with a dig at the American association between the professionalisation of love and money. Hallam's next lecture tour, the article concluded, was 'How to Make a Million Honestly'.

As with advertisements, a struggle between 'British' and 'American' styles and authority is evident in *Table Talk* magazine during the late 1920s and early 1930s. In 1926, *Table Talk* – which was always obsessed with romance, marriage and domestic harmony – ran a series on 'The New Wife'. Among the 'experts' it summoned to discuss and give advice on happy marriages were English and Australian social hostesses. A similar series subsequently featured in 1930, 'Making a Success of Marriage', again featured female society leaders from Adelaide, Melbourne and Sydney, but not from England. In the same year, however, *Table Talk* commissioned an article by the American writer Rupert Hughes on 'What is True Love?' Hughes's expertise arose from his reputation

---

[50] Liz Conor 2004, *The Spectacular Modern Woman: Feminine Visibility in the 1920s* (Bloomington, IN: Indiana University Press), p. 29.

[51] Conor 2004, *The Spectacular Modern Woman*, pp. 78-100.

[52] *Table Talk*, 31 July, no page number.

as a novelist and was described by the magazine as 'one who has, by his outspokenness and common sense views, set all America talking'.[53] The Thirties saw reprints in *Table Talk* of American articles on love, romance and marriage by Kathleen Norris – 'America's Foremost Magazine Writer' – as well as an increasing number of articles on Hollywood romances, divorces, and happy marriages. By 1936, the magazine turned to Eleanor Roosevelt to assure readers that 'A Wage-Earning Wife Does Not Cause Divorce'.[54]

British – and occasionally European – contributors continued to be featured as 'experts' on love, romance and marriage, but only if they were novelists, psychologists or philosophers: Bertrand Russell, A. A. Milne and Evelyn Waugh among them. Yet it was evident that the widespread influence of American dating rituals and practices of romantic consumption had also reached Britain. The English writer Alan Kennington, whose articles on relationships were sometimes reprinted in *Table Talk*, wrote a piece titled 'Should Girls Go Dutch?' and explained that '"Going Dutch" is an American expression, origin unknown'.[55] He opined that it was a common practice among Europeans and, presumably, Americans, but rarer in England. Kennington's article indicates anxieties in the United Kingdom as well as in Australia over the growing practice of romantic consumption and the concomitant commodification of love inherent in 'American' practices of dating. Although the article seemed to be directed towards the lower middle classes whose romantic consumption was constrained by low wages, the pen and ink illustration that accompanied the article depicted the impossibly idealised image of glamorous, romantic dating among the wealthy – the man in white tie and tails, his arms around an elegantly dressed woman with a fur stole, both of them outside an up-market theatre.

These articles, still photos of glamorous film stars in romantic poses, and advertisements in women's magazines accustomed Australian women to the idea of romantic consumption. They were calculated to provoke yearnings for beauty, youth, romance, luxurious ego-expressive products, and the experience of 'romantic' activities or services in the process of what Illouz has called 'consuming the romantic utopia'. By contrast, very few (if any) or these romanticised images appeared in Australian men's magazines, either in advertisements or as illustrations accompanying articles. It was not that men's magazines were uninterested in romance, marriage or relationships. When *Man: The Australian Magazine for Men* was launched in December 1936, the inaugural editorial proclaimed that the magazine would 'cater as completely as possible

---

[53] Rupert Hughes 1930, 'What is True Love?', *Table Talk*, 18 December, p. 40.

[54] Eleanor Roosevelt 1936, 'A Wage-Earning Wife Does Not Cause Divorce', *Table Talk*, 19 November, pp. 6-7.

[55] Alan Kennington 1936, 'Should Girls Go Dutch?', *Table Talk*, 24 September, p. 7.

for the varied monthly reading requirements of the average male'. Moreover, it would feature '90% the work of Australian writers' and '100% Australian artists'.[56] Among the articles on fiction, business, current affairs and sports, however, were the occasional pieces on romance and marriage. The Australian writer Gilbert Anstruther wrote several articles on the subject between 1937 and 1942, such as 'Are Husbands Worth While?'[57] or 'I Know About Love'.[58] Austin Roberts analysed love and jealousy in the psychology section, while Browning Thompson did the same in the sociology column. Between the late 1930s and the late 1950s, other male authors pitched in with articles on 'Marriage and Morals of the Future', 'Why Husbands Leave Home', 'Husbands Who Hate Women', 'How to – Where to – And Why You Shouldn't – Be Unfaithful', and 'How to Get Along With Women'. Not until the late 1940s, however, did *Man* feature advertisements for ego-expressive products set within a romantic context. An advertisement for Ingram's shaving cream in 1947 featured a cartoonish picture of a man climbing over a balustrade at night – presumably invoking the figure of Romeo – and a woman stroking his smooth chin. The caption was joking in tone and clumsy in text:

> Question: To what did Helen of Troy owe her fascination? The face that launched a thousand ships must have had something more than the usual complement of eyes and things. INGRAM'S, on the other hand, has launched a thousand faces. A million, maybe …

Another advertisement for 'Be-Tall' shoes in April 1957 showed the illustration of a blissfully smiling woman clasping a man's shoulder as he towers over her. The caption read: 'Tall men get the plums.' Be-Tall shoes were spruiked as 'amazing height-increasing shoes' which 'help you grow almost 2 inches taller instantly', promising an increase not only in height, but also in poise and the confidence, presumably, to go after and 'get the plums'. Such advertisements of romanticised commodities were few and far between in Australian men's magazines, and there was something slightly awkward about them.

It was not until American magazines such as *Playboy* were imported during the late 1960s that Australian men were introduced to a culture of romanticised (and, of course, sexualised) consumption for all sorts of products. For example, an advertisement for Renault's Le Car had a photo of a woman sitting on top of the car, held in the close embrace of a man, while the caption referred to the 'passion' of driving. An American advertisement for Hennessy in the 1990s showed a

---

[56] Editorial 1936, *Man: The Australian Magazine for Men*, December.

[57] Gilbert Anstruther 1937, 'Are Husbands Worth While?', *Man: The Australian Magazine for Men*, February, pp. 32, 86, 87.

[58] Gilbert Anstruther 1937, 'I Know About Love', *Man: The Australian Magazine for Men*, November, pp. 60, 62.

woman's ecstatic, upturned face as a man kisses her. The caption read: 'If you've ever been kissed you already know the feeling of Cognac Hennessy.' Interestingly enough where transnational ideas of romance are concerned, the couple are framed by the carved arches of a stone colonnade, vaguely suggestive of Europe. In this American advertisement romance is Europeanised, generic 'Europe' signifying luxurious romantic moments and classy destinations. *Playboy* notoriously commodified women's bodies and sexuality, but it also commodified romance, as with John Stack's 1980 article, 'We'll Take Romance!' Accompanying suggestions for romantic moments were thoroughly entwined with luxury consumption:

> A light and sexy Lillet with a twist of orange or lemon is our choice for a romantic aperitif ... For any occasion that seems extra-special, we recommend California Chandon, but nighttime is the right time for Cognac. Delamain (which runs from $22 to $100) is for foreplay, afterplay, and serious fooling around.
>
> Investment acumen and sentiment *do* mix. Buy each other gifts that will last: lithographs, Oriental silk flowers, inlaid boxes, photographs, leather-bound books or first editions, cognac, fine stationery, personally blended scents, pottery, season tickets (to the ballet, symphony, theatre or even hockey), museum membership, dancing (or self-defense) lessons, antiques (such as handmade quilts, bits of embroidery, old china). Or a pair of sexy black pajamas.
>
> Getting away even for a weekend is a terrific way to renew your relationship and take time off from professional stress at the same time. If you live in the country, try some bright lights/big city sight-seeing ... If, like most of us, you live in the city, look for an intimate country inn that you can make your own ...[59]

My point here is that although Australian men's magazines carried articles about marriage and romantic relationships, romantic consumption did not feature widely until after World War II – and then it was introduced to Australia via imported American men's magazines and advertising techniques copied from the Americans. In the first half of the twentieth century, therefore, there was a gender disjunction where ideas of romance and courtship or dating were concerned. This came to a head during World War II.

World War II and gendered romantic consumption

As several scholars have noted, World War II saw a widespread condemnation of, and moral panic surrounding, young Australian women's relations with

---

[59] John Stack 1980, 'We'll Take Romance!', *Playboy*, September, pp. 91-7.

American soldiers.⁶⁰ This was in part a backlash against modern young Australian women's Americanised conceptions of consumerist dating and romantic love.⁶¹ The attitude of conservative media institutions and transnational corporations was highly contradictory in this regard. Despite the fact that *The Australian Women's Weekly* carried wartime advertisements emphasising the importance of consuming beauty products – such as the Pond's 'Lips' advertisement declaring: 'She's doing a job of national importance, but she doesn't forget the importance of looking lovely for *him*' – Lyn Finch noted that the *Weekly* ran a campaign implying that the presence of American troops exacerbated 'consumerist-driven dating practices', thereby not only subverting 'normal and correct gender relations' but also

> simultaneously undermining the British character of Australian culture. While the practices and assumptions associated with courtship were conceptualised as productive and patriotic, dating was stigmatised as non-productive and neither patriotic, nationalistic, pro-Empire nor, indeed, moral.⁶²

Finch suggested that the 'competing constructions of courtship or, to be more precise, the difference between courtship and dating, lay at the centre of much of the moral panic about relations between American men and Australian women and girls'.⁶³

But it was possibly more than that. I want to propose that, as Marilyn Lake has suggested about contemporary understandings of the sexualisation of femininity in the 1930s and especially during World War II,⁶⁴ there was a gender and age disjunction in understandings of romantic love at this time, when some women, through their consumption of magazines and familiarity with commodified images of romantic love, might have been more in tune with American men's conception of gendered self-display, dating and romantic love than with

---

⁶⁰ Michael Sturma 1989, 'Loving the Alien: The Underside of Relations Between American Servicemen and Australian Women in Queensland, 1942–1945', *Journal of Australian Studies*, no. 24, pp. 4, 15-16; Gail Reekie 1985, 'War Sexuality and Feminism: Perth Women's Organisations, 1938–1945', *Australian Historical Studies*, vol. 21, no. 85, pp. 576-91; Lake 1992, 'The Desire for a Yank', p. 625.

⁶¹ Lake 1992, 'The Desire for a Yank', pp. 625-6; Lyn Finch Press 1995, 'Consuming Passions: Romance and Consumerism During World War II', in Joy Damousi and Marilyn Lake (eds), *Gender and War: Australians at War in the Twentieth Century*, (Melbourne: Cambridge University), pp. 105-16)

⁶² Finch 1995, 'Consuming Passions', pp. 106-7.

⁶³ ibid., p. 110.

⁶⁴ Lake 1990, 'Female Desires', pp. 268, 279.

Australian men's.⁶⁵ I am by no means arguing that love relationships did not develop between Australian women and men at this time, or that ideas of romantic love were reducible to romantic consumption; clearly, they were not, as the Australian War Memorial's very moving collection of love letters written by Australian soldiers to their wives and girlfriends attests.⁶⁶ What I am arguing, however, is that for some women, the initial process of 'falling in love' depended not only on sexual attraction and liking, but that these increasingly took place within a context of Americanised romantic consumption.

This can be demonstrated, for example, in gift-giving. In the nineteenth century, the types of gifts acceptable between courting couples were those of personal sentiment and little monetary value: hand-made cards, portraits, locks of hair, flowers, cakes, books of poetry or songbooks compiled by one of the lovers.⁶⁷ More expensive presents were acceptable only after the couple were engaged. In the mid-1880s, *Australian Etiquette* declared that the man could then give his fiancée 'small presents from time to time, until they are married, but if she has any scruples about accepting them, he can send her flowers, which are at all times acceptable'.⁶⁸ Yet even at the turn of the century, gifts could indicate the purchase of a woman as a man's property, as the following excerpt written by a young man to his fiancée indicates:

> I shall be able to get something nice for your birth-day this year. Perhaps the last present it [unclear] be my lot to bestow upon you or perhaps the forerunner of very many more if you become my property. Hope you will say what you would like, anything but jewelry, I will get for you.⁶⁹

The American culture of romantic consumption inverted traditional reticence over expensive gift giving because within the culture of romantic consumption, and especially in a culture where, as was argued above, emotions can be conveyed

---

⁶⁵ It is no doubt true that, as Michael Sturma (1989, 'Loving the Alien', pp. 3-17) has argued, many American men did not share such notions of romantic consumption and were not only sexually aggressive, but also economically exploitative of Australian women. Nevertheless, what I'm concerned with here is the idea of the romantic gift-giving American – uniformed and homogenised in the Australian female imagination, as Lake as suggested – that many women entertained. See Lake 1992, 'The Desire for a Yank', pp. 631-3.

⁶⁶ See also the section on World War II in Teo 2005, 'Love Writes'.

⁶⁷ See, for example, Blackburn family papers, MS 1528, Box 1760/1 (b), La Trobe Library; Broughton family papers, MLMSS 6250, Mitchell Library; Fry family papers, ML MSS 1159, add-on 2076/Box 1 and 2076/Box 4, Mitchell Library; and Gant family papers, MS 3711, Box 13023, La Trobe Library.

⁶⁸ *Australian Etiquette, or the Rules and Usages of the Best Society in the Australasian Colonies, together with Their Sports, Pastimes, Games, and Amusements* (Melbourne: People's Publishing Company, 1885), p. 198.

⁶⁹ Gant family papers, MS 3711, Box 13023, La Trobe Library.

and managed through consumption, romantic love was increasingly expressed through gift giving. Admittedly, the mere receipt of a gift was no proof of the giver's devotion, but the understanding of romantic love was transformed to a point where it was difficult, if not impossible, to declare love for someone without giving costly gifts at some stage, or engaging in frequent romantic consumption. American men were already in the habit of romantic consumption by the early twentieth century and, as Finch recognised, during World War II, gifts 'were integral to dating for American men and usually had no connotations of buying a woman'.[70]

Jill Matthews' study of young working women's leisure practices in Sydney during the 1910s and 1920s suggested that 'modern' young men were paying for 'modern' young women's cinema-going and dancing within either a heterosocial or romantic context: 'a woman who let a man pay for her to go to the pictures or to a dance was no longer necessarily a kept woman.'[71] Nevertheless, more traditional Australian men and older Australian women still believed a young woman had been 'bought' even if her process of romantic dating led to love and marriage with an American man.[72] One of the most extreme condemnations of romantic consumption during the war came from Reverend James Duhig, Catholic Archbishop of Brisbane, who asserted that: 'many girls associating with Allied soldiers have shown a spirit of greed and selfishness that does little credit to Australian womanhood.'[73]

Hollywood films as well as ego-expressive advertisements spruiking romantic consumption and the commodification of the modern, sexualised self played an important role in mediating romantic relations between modern Australian women and American soldiers. As Liz Conor has demonstrated, young women in the interwar years were accustomed to fashioning themselves as both creative subjects as well as commodified objects of the public gaze. Managing one's modern feminine appearance was achieved via film and advertising. 'Identifying with advertising promised romance; but romance was about being subject to the same intense scrutiny and appraisal as the commodity image, and this required self-surveillance.'[74] This practice of self-commodification – packaging

---

[70] Finch 1995, 'Consuming Passions', p. 112. See also Lake 1990, 'Female Desires', p. 275.

[71] Matthews 2005, *Dance Hall & Picture Palace*, p. 91.

[72] That this fantasy was still a goal of romantic liaisons is demonstrated by the number of applications to marry American servicemen lodged with the Registrar's Office – four in the first ten days of US troop arrivals, and a total of between 12 000-15 000 contracted marriages. See Lake 1992, 'The Desire for a Yank', p. 624, and Sturma 1989, 'Loving the Alien', p. 3.

[73] Cited in John Costello 1985, *Love, Sex & War: Changing Values, 1939–45* (London: Collins), p. 326.

[74] Conor 2004, *The Spectacular Modern Woman*, p. 116.

oneself in youthful, modern and sexually attractive ways which privileged visual effects – was also directed towards men.

Lake has argued that, during the war years, young women objectified and commodified the 'Yank' ('they were different, they were anonymous, one stood for all the rest, any one would do')[75] because they had been trained by Hollywood films to code 'American men as lovers, as sexual, and as objects to be looked at'.[76] Like these young women, American soldiers also appear to have been in the habit of managing their visual effects in a distinctly modern way.[77] Thus young Australian women again shared with American soldiers the modern practice of commodified self-display that not only located the sexual and aesthetic management of their bodies within a capitalist exchange economy, but that also meshed with consumerist practices of romance: gifts of silk stockings, flowers, a way with words that was inspired or adapted from Hollywood films – 'She's just like a baby Betty Grable', for instance.[78]

There is no doubt that Australian men practised consumerist dating with the women they were courting, going to the movies, dances, and on picnics. Where gift-giving was concerned, however, some letters suggest that it was women who were in a better position to give gifts and send parcels to Australian soldiers, especially to those stationed away from major urban centres.[79] Some Australian soldiers had financial constraints; others simply had no idea of what gifts to shop for, as with the soldier who wrote in all sincerity:

> I don't like accepting any further gifts from you especially when I'm so thankless in this way. I haven't given you a single thing in return yet. I've been to town a few times & window shopped but have not found anything to suit my fancy but I don't know want to appear thoughtless so you must tell me what you would like as a memento.[80]

---

[75] Lake 1992, 'The Desire for a Yank', p. 627.

[76] ibid., p. 629.

[77] See ibid., p. 628, for articles in the Australian press urging Australian men to pay similar attention to their appearance; to imitate American men's attention to their uniforms, angle of hat, position of garters, etc.

[78] ibid., p. 631; Costello 1985, *Love, Sex & War*, p. 312.

[79] See references to gifts received by women – either wives or girlfriends – in the letters of Sergeant Michael Billings, PR00610, Australian War Memorial; papers of Pte Albert Gerrard, PR03111, Australian War Memorial; letters of Flying Officer Ralph James, PR00661, Australian War Memorial; letters of Trooper Andrew Pirie, PR00602, Australian War Memorial.

[80] Letters of Trooper Andrew Pirie, PR00602, Australian War Memorial.

While the woman showed a confidence in gift-giving, which was obviously something she was used to, the man was clearly unaccustomed to this way of relating romantically.

Significantly, it was only after American magazines began to be imported to Australia in the postwar years, and the style of Australian advertising directed at men changed to a focus on them as consumers, that love letters from Australian men demonstrate the same notion of commodified romance that Australian women had become familiar with earlier in the century. Letters from Australian men written during the Vietnam War, for instance, are concerned with shopping and gift-giving in a way which would have been most surprising during World War II.[81] These Vietnam soldiers not only bought gifts for women, they were confident and decisive in what they wanted to give.

Conclusion

Thus the gender and age disjunction relating to romantic consumption gradually disappeared in the postwar years as Australian men also became orientated to romantic consumption through American-style films, magazines, advertisements and the advent of generic self-help books with their inevitable relationship case studies[82] which now made the verbal culture of American romantic love – previously confined to women's magazines and romance novels – available to men, couched in the language of psychologists and stamped with the masculine authority of 'scientists'.

With the popularisation of self-help books, another layer was added to the Western discourse of romantic love: the search for 'intimacy' replaced 'passion' as the Holy Grail of romantic love.[83] 'Intimacy' – understood as the absence of loneliness, a 'deep communication, friendship, and sharing that will last beyond the passion of new love' – promised to cut through the Gordian knot of consumerism and romantic love in the West, offering a 'refuge from the social fragmentation of late capitalism'.[84] But the route towards intimacy was 'communication', its gateway the consumption of self-help books and its guides the American authors who traversed the world selling their new gospel of hope.

The most successful of these at the end of the twentieth century was, of course, John Gray, whose *Men Are From Mars, Women Are From Venus: A Practical*

---

[81] For example, see the Papers of Lance Corporal A. D. O'Connor, PR 88/75, Australian War Memorial; papers of Private Laurence Hoppner, PR00047, Australian War Memorial; papers of Private Manfred Bohn, PR00745, Australian War Memorial; papers of Corporal Ronald James Kelly, PR87/195, Australian War Memorial.

[82] Shumway 2003, *Modern Love*, p. 149.

[83] ibid., pp. 141, 27.

[84] ibid., p. 27.

Guide for Improving Communication and Getting What You Want in Your Relationships (1993) sold over six million copies in the United States alone and was translated into more than forty languages worldwide, thereby claiming to be 'the highest selling commercial book in the 1990s next to The Bible'.[85] Gray's book was published in Australia in 1993 and HarperCollins Australia has kept it in print ever since, branding it a 'modern classic'. As late as 2000, *Mars and Venus* was selling over 20 000 copies a year in Australia, earning it a place on the annual 'bestseller' list.[86] Sales figures do not, of course, tell us anything about reader reception or whether Australians have embraced and put into practice the tenets of romantic relationships to be found in such books. Indeed, such self-help material might be read as a new genre of consolation rather than as revelations about romantic relationships.[87] The point, however, is that these discourses on romantic relationships have become transnational, not necessarily because of their intrinsic worth, but because they are marketed transnationally in what Karen S. Falling Buzzard has argued is a global process of 'brand marketing' that, for instance, sold John Gray as 'the Coca-Cola of self help'.[88]

It is these American techniques of marketing and advertising, more than anything else, that have established the American dominance of romantic love – whether it be as expertise or entertainment – in Australia through the course of the twentieth century. By the century's end, the culture of romantic love, not just in Australia but right throughout the English-speaking world, had become transnational, shaped by new technologies and communications systems as well as advanced consumer capitalism, fed by transnational publishing and media corporations, and sophisticated methods of marketing and international distribution. As Illouz observed, 'emotions are influenced and even shaped by the volatile "stuff" of culture: norms, language, stereotypes, metaphors, symbols', which means they are also 'subject to the twin influence of the economic and political spheres'.[89] As one cultural narrative of romantic love becomes increasingly hegemonic worldwide through the American-dominated global economy, there is less and less common knowledge or understanding of alternative cultures or expressions of love.

---

[85] Mars Venus Franchise web site, http://www.marsvenuscoaching.com/franchise-opportunity.html, accessed 16 February 2005.

[86] Australian Publishers Association, '2000 Public Survey', viewed on-line on 16 February 2005 at: http://publishers.asn.au/emplibrary/ACF4E53.pdf

[87] See Shumway's argument about self-help books in his 2003, *Modern Love*, pp. 133-187.

[88] Karen S. Falling Buzzard 2002, 'The Coca Cola of Self Help: The Branding of John Gray's *Men Are From Mars, Women Are From Venus*', *Journal of Popular Culture*, vol. 35, no. 4, pp. 89-102.

[89] Illouz 1997, *Consuming the Romantic Utopia*, p. 3.

Transnational Racial Politics

12. Transcultural/transnational interaction and influences on Aboriginal Australia

John Maynard

The influence of Marcus Garvey's Black Nationalist movement on the mobilisation for Aboriginal self-determination in the 1920s remains little known in the dominant Australian historical interpretation. Scholars in Australia have given scant regard to the interconnections between Aboriginal people and international relations, and have focused their examination of race relations on those between black and white. In particular, their studies of external influences on movements for Aboriginal self-determination have focused on white Christian and humanitarian influences. Given the reality of globalisation and tense international relations, it is timely to explore the historical, political, cultural and economic relationships between Aboriginal people and other oppressed groups throughout the twentieth century. This chapter outlines my own journey, exploring Aboriginal and international connections and the subsequent transcultural focus of my work.

A transnational/transcultural approach to the study of Australian history marks a shift in direction. Ann Curthoys recently pointed out Australian history has unfortunately 'become more isolated and inward looking' due to the limitations of the traditional framework of national history. Curthoys among others has called for a move towards 'transnational history' looking at networks of influence and interconnection that transcend the nation.[1] A transcultural approach adds another dimension to postcolonial critique in deconstructing the Eurocentric enclosures of the past – which not only created the Third World but also defined the cultures confined within for the West.[2] Analysing international black 'connection, flow, hybridity and syncretism' reveals and alters our understanding and offers a new direction.[3]

---

[1] Ann Curthoys 2003, 'Cultural History and the Nation', in Hsu-Ming Teo and Richard White (eds), *Cultural History in Australia* (Sydney: University of New South Wales Press), pp. 28-9.

[2] Benita Parry 1999, 'Resistance Theory/Theorising Resistance, or Two Cheers for Nativism', in Frances Baker, Peter Hulme, and Margaret Iverson (eds) *Colonial Discourse/Postcolonial Theory*, (Manchester: Manchester University Press), p. 172.

[3] Elaine Baldwin et al. 2004, *Introducing Cultural Studies* (Edinburgh: Pearson Education Limited), p. 179.

We might consider the monumental work of Paul Gilroy, whose work has sought to examine transatlantic black movement and connections, and whose concept of the 'Black Atlantic' leads us to 'think outside the fixed and misleading boundary lines of nation states'.[4][5] The maritime migration of people and ideas was instrumental not only in the passing of goods but also, in Elaine Baldwin's words, of 'the political struggles that flowed back and forth across the ocean'.[6] Gilroy's work, Baldwin suggests, considers 'the global spread of black people which has resulted from a series of forced and voluntary migrations' arguing that this 'binds together the black people of Africa, the Americas, the Caribbean and Europe in a long history of intercultural connection'.[7]

These developments in transcultural history importantly tie in with the perceptive Indigenous insight as put by Marcia Langton a decade ago, when she stressed the need of breaking out of traditional ties of white Anglo understanding:

> Let's forget about this psychotic debate we keep having with white Australia and let's start talking to Asians and people from Eastern Europe and Africa and so on and South America and talk about something else for a change. Let's do some films about genocide. How about us and the Timorese get together … How about us and the Cambodians get together, you know? That'd be so much more interesting and we could bring our experiences as human beings together you know, having been victims of human tragedies.[8]

My work is all about looking outside of the national box and examining these international connections of influence. I have, for example, been exploring similarities of experience between Gandhi and the Indian National Congress and early Aboriginal activism and found similar experiences of oppression and response.[9]

---

[4] ibid., p. 161.

[5] Peter Linebaugh 1982, 'All the Atlantic Mountains Shook', *Labour/ Le Travailleur*, vol. 10, Fall, pp. 87-121; Marcus Rediker 1987, *Between the Devil and the Deep Blue Sea: Merchant Seamen, Pirates, and the Anglo-American Maritime World, 1700–1750* (Cambridge: Cambridge University Press); Peter Linebaugh and Marcus Rediker 2000, *The Many Headed Hydra: Sailors, Slaves, Commoners, and the Hidden History of the Revolutionary Atlantic* (Boston, MA: Beacon Press).

[6] Baldwin et al. 2004, *Introducing Cultural Studies*, p. 176.

[7] ibid., p. 177.

[8] Transcribed and quoted in Stephen Muecke 1998, 'Cultural Activism, Indigenous Australia, 1972–1994', in Kuan-Hsing Chen (ed.), *Trajectories: Inter-Asia Cultural Studies* (London: Routledge), pp. 229-313, quoted passage on pp. 308-9.

[9] John Maynard 2004, 'Be the change that you want to see': The awakening of cultural nationalism – Gandhi, Garvey and the AAPA, paper to conference on Gandhi, Non-Violence and Modernity 2-3 September at The Australian National University.

A transcultural approach extends the study of Aboriginal history beyond national borders and beyond studies of the British empire, and seeks to place Aboriginal history and culture in a global perspective. Two years ago in Boston at the 'Asians Through Time and Space' conference I heard Professor Ron Richardson, head of African American Studies at Boston University, describe the importance of recognising that 'all cultures are hybrid and have been influenced by their interactions with different cultures, sometimes through interactions at a distance'.[10] Richardson spoke of 'transcultural studies', a method that 'views history as a global web of connections between cultures, rather than strictly focusing [in his case] on the black American experience ... [but] exploring how African-Americans have influenced and been influenced by other cultures and global trends.'[11] Such insights hold great significance in the scope and direction of my work, particularly examining African American historical influence and contact with Aboriginal people. My aim is to ensure that an Aboriginal presence in this global network of black connection and experience is not missed.

Aboriginal Australians and African worldwide politics

The move to a transcultural focus and understanding in my work was in the first instance more a matter of good fortune than any direct planning. In 1996 I was awarded the Aboriginal History Stanner Fellowship, and I have no hesitation in stating that this award was fundamental in everything I have achieved since. I was made a Visiting Fellow at the Australian National University with the history department and spent six months travelling around New South Wales researching my grandfather Fred Maynard's involvement with the rise of the Australian Aboriginal Progressive Association (AAPA) in 1924. I spent a lot of time in archives, and conducting oral interviews with family members and other people who were connected in some way with the beginning of the AAPA. The finished product of my research was an article published in *Aboriginal History*.[12]

My family had in its possession an old family photograph depicting a group of black men, including my grandfather. It was thought to be a photo of the Australian Aboriginal Progressive Association conference in Sydney, but in the course of my research an uncle in western New South Wales challenged this. He was adamant that it was in fact a much earlier organisation and that the tall black man wearing a beige suit in the back of the photo was famous African/American boxing champion Jack Johnson. I was incredulous! I studied the photograph with a magnifying glass and as I collected images of Jack Johnson

---

[10] *B.U. Bridge*, Boston University Community's Weekly Newspaper, 5 April 2002.

[11] *Boston Globe*, 10 February 2002.

[12] John Maynard 1997, 'Fred Maynard and the Australian Aboriginal Progressive Association (AAPA): One God, One Aim, One Destiny', *Aboriginal History*, vol. 21, pp. 1–13.

from various published sources concluded that he was in fact correct. But what did it all mean? My uncle added that the meeting depicted in the photograph had something to do with grandfather setting up a black shipping line! I was staggered to say the least and quite frankly a little perplexed. As I began to uncover more information, I found that he was largely correct, although he had confused Jack Johnson with later events. As I was to discover, my grandfather developed connections to Marcus Garvey's Universal Negro Improvement Association, which did in fact establish a Black Star Line shipping company in the 1920s in America.

At the time I could not expand the research any further, as I spent the next two years of my life just getting on and off planes and recording oral interviews in many Aboriginal community locations around the continent, in my role as a researcher with Aboriginal and Islander Health with the faculty of Medical Sciences at the University of Newcastle.[13] It was not until late 1998 that I was once more able to venture back to the archives, and particularly newspaper sources, to look for links or connections between my grandfather and Jack Johnson. I was rewarded immensely for the hours upon hours I spent going through newspapers of 1907 and 1908, eventually finding a reference to a farewell to Jack Johnson held in Sydney in 1907.[14] This was the event depicted in the photograph – a large gathering of black men, including not only my grandfather Fred Maynard, and Jack Johnson, but also Peter Felix, a West Indian boxer who fought Johnson during his visit. So, that initial interview with an old uncle about the APAA was responsible for leading me to a host of sources linking the early Aboriginal political movement and Black American influence and inspiration. In the end it led even further, to the uncovering of conclusive links between the AAPA in Australia and Garvey's massive international organisation in the United States.

The 1960s and 1970s witnessed prominent interaction, influence and connections between Aboriginal Australia and the African American experience in the United States. The 'Freedom Ride' of 1965 led by Charles Perkins acknowledged the influence of the Martin Luther King civil rights movement in the United States.[15] There were numerous other examples of international black connections with, and influences on, Aboriginal political activism in this period. In 1972 Paul Coe stated 'Black Power in Australia is a policy of self-assertion, self identity'.

> It is our policy, at least as far as we in the city are concerned ... to endeavour to encourage Black Culture, the relearning, the reinstating of

---

[13] Multimedia CD Rom 'Healing Our Way – Aboriginal Perspectives on Aboriginal Health' Project – Aboriginal and Islander Health – University of Newcastle.

[14] *The Referee*, 13 March 1907.

[15] Curthoys 2003, 'Cultural History and the Nation', pp. 2-3.

black culture wherever it is possible ... The Afro-American culture, as far as the majority of blacks in Sydney are concerned, is the answer to a lot of black problems because this is the international culture of the black people.[16]

In a similar vein Scott Robinson argued that the 'Black American experience was the most profound exogenous influence on Aboriginal political activism in the 1960s'.[17]

No less a voice than the incomparable Malcolm X perceptively commented on the obscured and oppressed position of Aboriginal Australians in 1965: 'The [A]boriginal Australian isn't even permitted to get into a position where he can make his voice heard in any way, shape or form. But I don't think that situation will last much longer.'[18]

What Malcolm X did not know was that an Aboriginal political voice had been active, constant and outspoken against prejudice and oppression for decades and that there had been a substantial and sustained international black influence in that process. As Malcolm X himself wrote:

> Just as racism has become an international thing, the fight against it is also becoming international. Those who were the victims of it and were kept apart from each other are beginning to compare notes. They are beginning to find that it doesn't stem from their country alone. It is international. We intend to fight it internationally.[19]

Malcolm X was proposing in fact not something new but more of a tradition of united opposition by oppressed groups around the world, the history of which had been forgotten. Marcus Garvey, the leader of the Universal Negro Improvement Association, formed first in Jamaica, then (in 1916) in the United States, becoming what is recognised today as the biggest black political movement ever assembled in the United States, had expressed similar sentiments over forty years earlier:

> Everywhere the black man is beginning to do his own thinking, to demand more participation in his own government, more economic justice, and better living conditions. The Universal Negro Improvement Association during the past five years has blazed the trail for him, and he is following the trail. We do not think he will turn back. He has

---

[16] G. Pryor 1988, 'Aboriginal Australians', in Ray Willis et al. (eds) *Issues in Australian History* (Melbourne: Longman Cheshire), p. 412.

[17] Max Griffiths 1995, *Aboriginal Affairs: A Short History* (Sydney: Kangaroo Press), p. 114.

[18] Malcolm X 2001, *The Final Speeches* (New York, NY: Pathfinder), p. 71.

[19] ibid.

nothing to lose and everything to gain by pushing forward, whatever the obstacles he may encounter.[20]

The UNIA founded by Garvey spread rapidly around the world in the late 1910s, and hundreds of branches of the organisation were formed. As George Frederickson writes: Garvey and his platform 'struck a response chord in the hearts and minds of black people from an astonishing variety of social and cultural backgrounds throughout the world.'[21] A Federal Bureau of Investigation report on Garvey and his activities in 1919 reveals the unease over his far-reaching message. 'Garvey's office on 135th Str. is sort of a clearing house for all international radical agitators, including Mexicans, South Americans, Spaniards, in fact black and yellow from all parts of the globe who radiate around Garvey.'[22] Garvey was able to achieve a worldwide network of information by sending out agents to spread his message. Important for my story is the fact that many of these agents were seamen.[23] Legendary Vietnamese freedom fighter Ho Chi Minh was just one who was influenced by Garvey and his doctrine.[24] As a young man Ho had been a seaman 'and he once spent a few months in New York. Garvey and the Universal Negro Improvement Association (UNIA) movement interested him greatly and he regularly attended UNIA meetings.'[25]

At the height of its power in the mid 1920s the UNIA had successfully established chapters in 41 countries, including a branch in Australia. As in many other places, the word had been spread to Australia by seamen, who encountered wharf labourers in Sydney, some of whom were Aboriginal young men later to become political leaders. In fact the connection between Aboriginal dockworkers and other cultures on Australian wharves had been ongoing for quite sometime.[26] As Tony Martin has written:

---

[20] *The Negro World*, 20 September 1924.

[21] George Fredrickson 1995, *Black Liberation: A Comparative History of Black Ideologies in the United States and South Africa* (New York, NY: Oxford University Press), p. 152.

[22] Robert Hill (ed.) 1983, *The Marcus Garvey and Universal Negro Improvement Association Papers Vol. 1* (Berkeley, CA: University of California), p. 495.

[23] Tony Martin 1983, *Marcus Garvey – Hero: A First Biography* (Dover, MA: Majority Press), p. 86.

[24] ibid., p. 65.

[25] ibid.

[26] See Maynard forthcoming 2005, '"In the Interests of Our People": The Influence of Garveyism on the Rise of Australian Aboriginal Political Activism', *Aboriginal History*; Maynard 2003, 'Vision, Voice and Influence: The Rise of the Australian Aboriginal Progressive Association', *Australian Historical Studies*, vol. 34, no. 121, pp. 91-105.

The Sydney, Australia UNIA branch was undoubtedly the furthest from Harlem. It illustrated how, in those days before even the widespread use of radio, Garvey and the UNIA were nevertheless able to draw communities from practically all over the world together into a single organization with a single aim. [27]

In August 1920, the UNIA held the first of a number of highly successful international conventions and over 25 000 members gathered at Madison Square Garden in New York to hear Garvey speak. Members from UNIA branches across the globe 'attended from places as far apart as Australia, Africa and North America'.[28] This small note offers a tantalising scenario – who were the noted Australian delegates present at that convention? One is left to ponder the impact this experience would have had on these people on returning to Australia. Could they have been future members or office bearers of the AAPA? We do know that some members of the Sydney branch of the UNIA would later hold high-ranking positions in the AAPA.[29]

This new knowledge of international connections between Aboriginal activists and Marcus Garvey's UNIA challenges established historical belief that Aboriginal activism originated in the 1930s as a result of the interaction of Aboriginal activists with white men and women imbued with strong British Christian, humanist and Marxist traditions. That there could have been international black interaction with and influence on Aboriginal political thought prior to World War II has been unthinkable in recent analyses that do not venture outside the confines of national history.

Aboriginal contacts with non-Europeans

The challenge posed by these findings to entrenched orthodoxy is not confined to the impact of African American political ideology during the 1920s and 1960s. The interaction and connection between Aboriginal people and other cultures has a very long history that needs to be explored in greater detail and recognised.

Western thought for a great part of the twentieth century was instrumental in establishing the misconception that Aboriginal culture was static and locked at the stone age of development. In recent decades this convenient myth has been overturned. Aboriginal culture was never static but evolving, adapting and changing through the exchange of goods and technology along well-established trade routes. These exchanges were not confined to the Australian continent. The most notable early visitors were the Macassans from the Dutch East Indies (present day Indonesia), who for hundreds of years visited northern Australia

---

[27] Martin 1983, *Marcus Garvey – Hero*, p. 99.
[28] ibid., p. 42.
[29] See Maynard forthcoming 2005, 'In the Interests of Our People'.

for the trepang (sea slug), an expensive delicacy which they sent in vast quantities to China.[30] Aboriginal people gained work as crewmen on these boats, which raises the probability that some Aboriginal people may have ventured far from these shores many centuries ago, certainly as far as China. One can only imagine the impact made when these early Aboriginal sailors finally returned to their own communities. Other visitors who may have contributed subtle changes to Aboriginal life included the Dutch, Portuguese, French and Chinese.

The British invasion and occupation of the Australian continent in 1788 signalled the onset of large-scale interaction between Aboriginal peoples and other nationalities. From the outset Aboriginal people made contact with black convicts and sailors as well as Europeans. One important early connection was through one sailor of the First Fleet, who was probably a Native American Indian. When the devastation of disease impacted upon the local Aboriginal population of the Sydney region in the winter of 1789 the 'Native American' sailor took it upon himself to visit and attempt to comfort two seriously ill Aboriginal children. Some may ask why he took this direction. I think the answer is obvious he cared and had empathy and compassion for the Aboriginal experience that he was witness to, and it undoubtedly drew parallels to the experience of his own people in the United States. Sadly this Native American man contracted smallpox himself and was the only recorded casualty amongst the first fleet.[31]

The British for their part immediately began a process of taking Aboriginal people back to Britain (which reflected an ongoing process of European conquest and domination – to publicly display the vanquished), first as curiosities and later as examples of the fine efforts of Christian civilising. In December 1792 Bennelong and a young man Yemmurrawannie accompanied Governor Arthur Phillip to England (as well as four kangaroos and 'other peculiar animals'). Bennelong returned to Australia in 1795 with new governor John Hunter (Yemmurrawannie died of a respiratory infection in 1794 and was buried at Eltham in England). English King George III formally expressed his desire to the new governor that 'not another native should be brought home from New South Wales'.[32] The King's wishes went unheeded and there were further Aboriginal

---

[30] Paul Kiem and Michael Smithson 2001, *Colonial and Contact History* (Melbourne: Longman), p. 190; D. J. Mulvaney 1989, *Encounters in Place: Outsiders and Aboriginal Australians 1606 – 1905* (Brisbane: University of Queensland Press), p. 22.

[31] David Collins, *An Account of the English Colony in New South Wales, with Remarks on the Dispositions, Customs, Manners, etc, of the Native Inhabitants of that Country*, vol. 1, edited by Brian Fletcher 1975, in association with the Royal Australian Historical Society (Sydney: A. H. and A. W. Reed), p. 54.

[32] Isabel McBryde 1989, *Guests of the Governor* (Sydney: Friends of the First Government House Site), p. 29.

travellers, including the man Moowat'tin or Daniel who acted as a guide and specimen collector to the botanist Caley. Caley brought Moowat'tin to England to help with identifying his specimens but also asserted the advantages of this being a 'means of bringing them [the natives] over to our customs much sooner'. What started as a trickle in the late eighteenth century built to a steady flow throughout the nineteenth century of Aboriginal people journeying to other places around the globe. It was not an Aboriginal choice, in many instances. Roslyn Poignant's recent book *Professional Savages* highlights the sad story of a group of Northern Queensland Aborigines shipped to the United States to appear in dime museums, fairgrounds and circuses all over America and Europe.[33] These circus performers were followed in future decades by Aboriginal cricketers, boxers, footballers and horsemen.

Connections between Aboriginal people and other cultures on the docks of Australian harbours have been an important and previously neglected link to the outside world and warrant further studies. As an example of this dockland cultural connection, John Askew in 1852 recorded the natural inclination and gravitation of visiting Maori to the local Aboriginal people. Askew recorded his adventures and experiences as a steerage passenger in the Australian colony noting that eleven of the crew on the ship to New Zealand were Maori. Whilst berthed in Newcastle the Maori crew left the ship and walked the streets and docks of Newcastle. He noted not only his own but also the bewilderment of the local populace at the Maori appearance:

> The Maories [sic] all came into the city that night, and their singular appearance attracted much attention. They were strapping young fellows. Some grotesquely tattooed; one or two had ear-rings of a peculiar kind of sharks teeth suspended by a piece of ribbon from their ears. [34]

Askew records a cultural exchange between the Maori visitors and the local Aboriginal people within the town.

> After strolling about the place for a considerable time, they mustered in front of James Hannel's, to look at a group of black fellows and gins, who were dancing a corrobory [sic] ... No sooner had they ended, than the Maories commenced their terrible war song. Squatting themselves down, with their legs crossed in the oriental fashion, they began by making a noise not unlike the snorting of an 'iron horse', heard half a mile off.

---

[33] Roslyn Poignant 2004, *Professional Savages: Captive Lives and Western Spectacle* (Sydney: University of New South Wales Press), front cover.

[34] J. Askew 1857, *A Voyage to Australia and New Zealand* (London: Simkin, Marshall), pp. 292-3 (available in the Archives, Auchmuty Library, University of Newcastle).

This noise was accompanied by violent gestures, and the rapid motion of their hands through the air.

As they became more excited, their eyes rolled in a frenzy, and their heads turned from one side to the other. And at every turn they sent forth roars the most piercingly savage and demonical that I ever heard from human beings. When the song was finished, one of them went round with his cap and made a collection. After the collection was secured, they all started to their feet, gave a tremendous yell, ran down to the ship and divided the spoil.[35]

Askew unknowingly has recorded a Maori performance of the Haka. Today acknowledged and celebrated around the world as the national performance of New Zealand, most notably through the pre-match ritual of the New Zealand All-Blacks. Disturbingly, Aboriginal cultural performance through corroboree has never attained either nationally or internationally the same due recognition.

Aboriginal Australians and international travel

It is also important to note that not all of the interaction between Aboriginal people and other cultures took place on these shores and that not all Aboriginal people who left Australia did so against their wishes. In fact analysing the reasons why some chose voluntarily to venture overseas may yield important insight on future Aboriginal directives.

One intriguing recent revelation is through the academic work of Terry Foenander in the United States. His search at the National Archives in Washington, DC, on details of the background of naval personnel who served in the Union Navy during the Civil War has revealed some interesting and bizarre finds. Foenander's research assistant 'located the names of at least six Union naval personnel whom, it would seem to this author, were original natives of Australia and New Zealand'.[36] Foenander's revelation raises the intriguing question 'did a small number of Australian Aborigines and New Zealand Maoris serve in the Union Navy during the Civil War?' Foenander is 'of the opinion that there would most certainly have been some who served as mariners, and some of these mariners would have been in the US at the start of the war, or later, enabling them to enlist in the services.'[37] If Foenander's find proves correct

---

[35] ibid., pp. 292-3.

[36] T. Foenander 2000, *Australasian Natives in the Union Navy*, February 8, http://home.ozconnect.net/tfoen/anz.html accessed 8/28/2005.

[37] Foenander 2000, *Australasian Natives in the Union* Navy. A short description of these men follows without solving the mystery:

John Jackson, ordinary seaman, enlisted at Boston on February 25, 1862; born in Australia; aged 28 at enlistment; personal description shows eyes and hair as black and complexion

one is struck by the impact that these men would have made when and if they returned to Australia.

One Aboriginal international traveller we know something about was Anthony Martin Fernando, born in northern New South Wales in 1864.[38] Despite being removed at an early age from his family, Fernando refused to bow and initiated a lifetime struggle against colonial domination. He drew strength from his Aboriginal cultural identification. Frustration with the inequality of Aboriginal existence and the failure of British law to uphold Aboriginal objection was responsible for him gaining work as a boilerman on a ship to Europe. Whether Fernando left Australia with a plan already in place to take the message of Aboriginal inequality to an international audience is not clear. However, his experience in Europe instilled and invigorated his opposition to the treatment of Aboriginal people in Australia. Having survived the Great War he appears in 1921 attempting to gain an audience with the Pope. He was refused on the grounds that he did not possess internationally recognised papers of identification. He was not to be daunted and moved to Switzerland and attempted to garner the support of the Swiss government to an innovative directive on Aboriginal affairs. As Heather Goodall tells us, he outlined a proposal that was

> somewhat similar to the native state concept which was to develop some years later in Australia. The latter idea was that a reserve be created in Arnhem Land which would eventually become self-governing and achieve statehood at some far-off time in the future. Fernando's proposal was more radical: he was suggesting an autonomous area in northern Australia where Aboriginal people's independence and their safety would

---

as negro (Rendezvous Reports, Volume 19, page 92). Barry Crompton of Melbourne, Australia provided further details from the Massachusetts rosters, indicating that Jackson enlisted at Hyannis, Massachusetts; served on the receiving ship USS Ohio; and is listed as deceased, March 24, 1862, aboard the Ohio.

Michael Kendy, ordinary seaman, enlisted June 10, 1864, for 3 years, at New Bedford, aged 21; born Australia; personal description shows black eyes, woolly hair and Negro complexion (Rendezvous Reports, Volume 34, page 405).

Albert McDermott, seaman, enlisted October 20, 1862, for 1 year, at New York, aged 23; born Australia; personal description shows black eyes, fuzzy hair and yellow complexion. (Muster rolls occasionally show African American servicemen with yellow complexions) (Rendezvous Reports Volume 32, page 466).

Antonio Miles, native of Australia, described as mulatto; previous occupation mariner, enlisted at age 23 in the Union Navy.

[38] Heather Goodall 1988, 'Aboriginal Calls for Justice', *Aboriginal Law Bulletin*, vol. 2, no. 3, p. 4.

be guaranteed by an international power under the control of the League of Nations.[39]

Again Fernando was rebuffed; a man of lesser courage and strength must surely have buckled. He took to the streets of Milan and London carrying placards and handing out pamphlets highlighting the ill-treatment of Aboriginal people in Australia. He was gaoled in Italy by Mussolini 'as an enemy of an ally of fascist Italy'. He was interned without a trial for many months before eventual deportation to Britain. He instigated a one-man campaign against Australia 'picketing Australia House. He covered himself with toy skeletons and pointed to them as he called out to passers by: "This is what they are doing to my people in Australia".'[40] Severely embarrassed, the Australian authorities attempted to sweep him under the carpet. He was arrested on numerous occasions and they even instigated an attempt to have him put in a mental asylum, in what was, as Goodall states, 'a well-known tactic of political repression'. The doctors refused to certify him, one of them writing: 'he holds strong views about the manner in which his people are treated, but that is a sign not of insanity but of an unusually strong mind.'[41]

Fernando refused to be intimidated by anyone. In 1929 he appeared before the court in London after pulling a gun on a white man 'who had abused him because he was black'. He utilised the platform and moment to vent his anger once more at the powers that be:

> 'I have pleaded my people's cause since 1887', he declared, 'I have seen whites in Australia go unpunished for murdering and ill-treating Aborigines. I have been boycotted everywhere. Look at my rags. All I hear is "Go away, black man" but it is all Tommy rot to say we are savages. Whites have shot, slowly starved and hanged us!'[42]

In Fernando's eyes if the British needed an example of savagery they needed to look no further than the mirror. For over two decades Fernando had waged a one-man campaign of unrelenting protest; as late as 1938 he was still in the news. Once more in court now aged seventy-four, he remained unbowed, 'We are despised and rejected, but it is the black people who keep this country in all its greatness'.[43] Fernando died shortly after this court appearance and as Goodall reverently describes, he had maintained 'his struggle against enormous odds, alone but unfailingly presenting his peoples case on the other side of the world,

---

[39] ibid.
[40] ibid.
[41] ibid.
[42] ibid.
[43] ibid., p. 5.

in the heart of the land of the colonisers'.[44] What Fernando sadly was not to know was that his efforts and sacrifice in challenging the foundations of Empire itself did not go unnoticed. As Goodall tell us, 'Aboriginal activists like Pearl Gibbs back in New South Wales hungrily clipped the press accounts of his words, taking them for inspiration for their own campaign'. Fiona Paisley has also shed new light on the remarkable and courageous Anthony Martin Fernando.[45]

Aboriginal women sometimes left Australia too. An Aboriginal missionary, born at Pialba in Queensland, Mrs Charles Aurora, was described by an old missionary friend Elizabeth McKenzie Hatton as a 'woman carrying a high standard of Christian character – a clever, refined, and educated woman, she has been used to help in the translation of the scriptures in the language of the Solomon Islands.'[46] In 1921 and after fourteen years service in the Solomon Islands she returned to Queensland and was 'shocked to find, in this Christian land of ours, so little being done for her own people and the half caste girls'.[47] She was so distressed by the conditions she witnessed she travelled to Melbourne beseeching McKenzie Hatton to 'go back and help her to rescue these young and helpless girls'.[48] In unleashing the determined McKenzie Hatton on a collision course with government authority Mrs Charles Aurora could well be said to have played no small part in the rise of Aboriginal political mobilisation some three years later. McKenzie Hatton would prove one of the most astute and courageous allies of Aboriginal rights to surface in the early decades of the twentieth century.[49]

The freedom of international travel and its impact on Mrs Charles Aurora and Anthony Fernando can be contrasted with the tight and restrictive controls of movement exerted over the Aboriginal population within Australia during those years. Tom Lacey, later to be treasurer of the Australian Aboriginal Progressive Association 1924 to 1928, revealed those very restrictions to an international audience when he penned a letter to Amy Jacques Garvey – wife of Marcus Garvey in 1924:

> We have a bit of trouble to see some of our people, as the missionaries have got the most of them, and we have great difficulty in reaching them. The authorities won't allow us to see them unless we can give them (the Aboriginal Board) a clear explanation of what we want them for.[50]

---

[44] ibid.

[45] Fiona Paisley 2001, 'Into Self-imposed Exile', *Griffith Review*, vol. 2, no. 4.

[46] McKenzie Hatton, 1921 - The National Archives AI/15 21/6686.

[47] Hatton, 1921.

[48] Hatton, 1921.

[49] *The Negro World*, 2 August 1924.

[50] ibid.

Lacey recognised the negative long-term effect of confinement on missions and reserves for the Aboriginal population. The authorities 'have got their minds so much doped that they think they can never become a people', he wrote.

International travel gave Aboriginal people a much broader perspective of events and made them aware that others around the globe had shared similar tragedy under the weight of colonisation. Certainly they were given the courage to challenge the notions of inferiority they were expected to accept. Many recognised the importance of maintaining or re-establishing strength from their own cultural identity and history. This sense of identity and history was very much at the forefront of Marcus Garvey's platform, and later W. E. B Du Bois and Frantz Fanon. As Robert Young has argued, both Du Bois and Fanon moved away from analysing the 'psychological effects of domination and disempowerment plotted in the terms of Hegelian consciousness, to increasingly radical social and political demands for empowerment and self determination'.[51] This was the very platform and directive taken up by the Aboriginal movement in Sydney during the mid 1920s.[52]

This chapter has traced how I myself became interested in transnational/transcultural history, and some of the approaches it suggests to a reworking of Australian Aboriginal history. There is a great opportunity for broader awareness and understanding of Aboriginal history to a degree previously beyond the wildest imagination. There are so many areas that could be explored – for instance the impact on Aboriginal activism of Aboriginal servicemen and women returning from fighting overseas in the Boer War, World War I, World War II, Korea and Vietnam. My aim here is simply to highlight a long tradition of international interaction between Aboriginal people and many differing groups, in the hope of inspiring others to pursue these most unlikely areas of study.

---

[51] Robert Young 2001, *Postcolonialism: An Historical Introduction* (Oxford: Blackwell Publishers), p. 221.

[52] Maynard, 'Vision, Voice and Influence', pp. 91-105; Maynard 2003, 'Australian History: Lifting Haze or Descending Fog', *Aboriginal History*, vol. 27, pp. 139-45.

13. From Mississippi to Melbourne via Natal: the invention of the literacy test as a technology of racial exclusion

Marilyn Lake

> 'Wave upon wave, each with increasing virulence, is dashing this new religion of whiteness on the shores of our time.' W. E. B. Du Bois, 'The Souls of White Folk', *Independent*, 1910.

'This new religion of whiteness'

In 1910, in an article first published in the New York journal the *Independent*, called 'The Souls of White Folk', the Black American historian, W. E. B. Du Bois wrote about his perception of a sudden change in the world, indeed the emergence of a 'new religion': 'the world in a sudden emotional conversion, has discovered that it is white, and, by that token, wonderful'.[1] In noting that 'white folk' had suddenly 'become painfully conscious of their whiteness', Du Bois was pointing to the emergence of a new subjective mode of identification that crossed national borders, an identification as white men. That same year Du Bois helped establish the journal, *The Crisis*, to combat 'race prejudice'. 'It takes its name', declared the first editorial, 'from the fact that the editors believe that this is a critical time in the history of the advancement of man'.[2]

As an historian, Du Bois wanted to emphasise the historical novelty of what he witnessed, especially the emergence of a new 'personal' sense of self:

> The discovery of personal whiteness among the world's peoples is a very modern thing – a nineteenth and twentieth century matter, indeed. The ancient world would have laughed at such a distinction. The middle age regarded it with mild curiosity, and even up into the eighteenth century we were hammering our national manikins into one great Universal Man with fine frenzy which ignored color and race as well as birth. Today we have changed all that…

He also noted white men's proprietary claims, likening the intermittent outbursts of rage among white folks to the tantrums of possessive children, who refused to share their candy. When applied to the relations between the different races

---

[1] W. E. B. Du Bois 1910, 'The Souls of White Folk', *Independent*, 18 August, p. 339; this essay was re-published in a revised form in W. E. B. Du Bois 1920, *Darkwater* (New York, NY: Harcourt, Brace and Howe).

[2] *The Crisis A Record of the Darker Races*, Editorial, vol. 1, 1910, p. 10.

of the world, however, the message seemed rather more ominous: 'whiteness is the ownership of the earth, forever and ever, Amen!' A new global movement was in the ascendancy. 'Wave upon wave, each with increasing virulence, is dashing this new religion of whiteness on the shores of our time'. That nations were coming to believe in it, wrote Du Bois, was 'manifest daily'.[3]

In seeking to explain the rise of this 'inexplicable phenomenon', Du Bois noted the political claims to equality that were beginning to be made by colonised and coloured peoples around the world: 'Do we sense somnolent writhings in black Africa, or angry groans in India, or triumphant "Banzais" in Japan? "To your tents, O Israel!" these nations are not white. Build warships and heft the "Big Stick"'.[4] In 1908, United States President Theodore Roosevelt (the author of the diplomacy 'Speak Softly and Carry a Big Stick') had sent the United States Naval Fleet on a tour of the Pacific, its ill-concealed intention to intimidate the Japanese, whose challenge to the United States over its restrictive immigration policy and the Californian policy of segregated schooling had led to a crisis in relations between the two naval powers, their 'Gentlemen's Agreement' of 1907, notwithstanding.

In seeking to explain the 'new fanaticism' that was taking hold, Du Bois insisted on the transnational nature of, and response to, the movement for racial equality:

> when the black man begins to dispute the white man's title to certain alleged bequests of the Father's in wage and position, authority and training; and when his attitude toward charity is sullen anger, rather than humble jollity; when he insists on his human right to swagger and swear and waste – then the spell is suddenly broken and the philanthropist is apt to be ready to believe that negroes are impudent, that the South is right, and that Japan wants to fight us'.[5]

As Du Bois noted, the proclamation of 'white men's countries' was a defensive reaction to the mobility and mobilisations of colonised and coloured peoples around the world. The global migrations of the late nineteenth century provide the crucial historical context for claims to racial equality that were often expressed as equal rights of mobility.

In his influential book *Imagined Communities*, Benedict Anderson defined nations as 'imagined communities' in the sense that they were composed of individuals who, though they might never meet face to face, came to identify with their compatriots and believed themselves to hold certain values, myths and outlooks in common. At the core of this process of identification was the cultural and

---

[3] Du Bois 1910, 'Souls of White Folk', p. 339.
[4] ibid., p. 340.
[5] ibid.

historical imagination, its key instruments the novel and newspaper. Anderson stressed the affective as well as the imaginary dimension of national identification which he imagined as 'fraternal'. [6]

Paradoxically, one outcome of Anderson's argument has been to naturalise the nation as *the* imagined community of the modern age, an effect that has obscured what Du Bois saw so clearly in 1910: the ascendancy of racial identifications and the emergence of an imagined community of white men that was transnational in its reach, drawing together the self-styled 'white men' of southern Africa, north America and Australasia in what Theodore Roosevelt liked to call a condition of 'fellow feeling'.[7] In this context, the designation 'white men' referred to those of 'Anglo-Saxon' descent or 'English-speaking peoples' who shared what Roosevelt in *The Winning of the West* called the same 'race history', which began, following E. A. Freeman, with the 'great Teutonic wanderings'.[8]

White men were thought to have a genius, not just for self-government, but also for colonisation. The settlement of the continents of Australia and America, Roosevelt argued, were key events in world history: 'We cannot rate too highly the importance of their acquisition', he wrote. 'Their successful settlement was a feat which by comparison utterly dwarfs all the European wars of the last two centuries.'[9] Clearly, the 'manhood' espoused by white men was a racialised as well as gendered condition.[10]

Just two years before the publication of Du Bois' essay on the 'Souls of White Folk' in the New York *Independent*, the same journal had featured a long report by W. R. Charlton, a Sydney journalist, of the effusive welcome offered by Australians to the visiting American Fleet, white men rapturously greeting fellow white men from across the Pacific. On arrival in Sydney, Rear Admiral Sperry told his hosts he spoke to them 'as white man to white men, and, I may add, to "very white men"'.[11] Charlton's article celebrated the new alliance between the 'Republic and the Commonwealth': 'It is delightful to us to say – whether it be delusion, half-truth or the truth-absolute – that the Americans are our kinsmen,

---

[6] Benedict Anderson 1991, *Imagined Communities: Reflections on the Origins and Spread of Nationalism*, revised edition (London: Verso).

[7] See Theodore Roosevelt 1902, 'Fellow Feeling as a Political Factor', in Roosevelt, *The Strenuous Life: Essays and Addresses* (London: Grant Richards), pp. 71-87.

[8] Theodore Roosevelt 1889, *Winning of the West*, vol. 1 (New York, NY: Putnam's), pp. 4-5.

[9] Roosevelt 1889, *Winning of the West*, p. 14.

[10] Marilyn Lake 2003, 'On Being a White Man, Australia, circa 1900', in Hsu-Ming Teo and Richard White (eds), *Cultural History in Australia* (Sydney: University of New South Wales Press); Gail Bedermann 1995, *Manliness and Civilisation: A Cultural History of Gender and Race in the United States, 1880–1917* (Chicago, IL: Chicago University Press).

[11] *Age*, 27 August 1908.

blood of our blood, bone of our bone, and one with us in our ideals of the brotherhood of man.'[12]

In recent scholarship, the investigation of 'whiteness' has emerged as a productive new field of historical enquiry, but most studies have conceptualised their subject within a national frame of analysis, charting national dynamics and histories. When overseas ideas are identified as important they are usually conceptualised as external influences shaping a national experience rather than as constituting transnational knowledge.[13] Yet, as Du Bois saw clearly, the emergence of this 'new religion' of whiteness was a transnational phenomenon and all the more powerful for that. It produced in turn its own powerful solidarities of resistance. One commentator writing in *Fortnightly Review*, in 1907, worried that the new solidarity of white men and their claim to monopoly of four continents, would drive Chinese and Indians into an unprecedented pan-Asiatic alliance led by the Japanese that would ultimately see the eclipse of Western civilisation.[14]

White men, meanwhile, whether in the United States, Canada, Australia, New Zealand, South Africa, Rhodesia or Kenya, looked to each other for sympathy and support, for ideas and practical instruction. They exchanged knowledge and know-how, in particular the uses of the census, the literacy test and the passport as key technologies in building and defending white men's countries.[15] This chapter looks at the deployment of the literacy test as an instrument of

---

[12] W. R. Charlton 1908, 'The Australian Welcome to the Fleet', *Independent*, vol. LXV, no. 3123, 8 October, p. 815.

[13] On 'whiteness' see, for example, Ruth Frankenberg 1993, *White Women, Race Matters: The Social Construction of Whiteness* (Minneapolis, MN: University of Minnesota Press); David Roediger 1994, *Wages of Whiteness: Race and the Making of the American Working Class* (London: Verso); Matthew Frye Jacobsen 1999, *Whiteness of a Different Color: European Immigrants and the Alchemy of Race* (Cambridge, MA: Harvard University Press); Aileen Moreton-Robinson 2000, *Talkin' Up to the White Woman: Indigenous Women and Feminism* (St Lucia: University of Queensland Press); on the influence of external ideas on national formations see, for example, Russell McGregor 1989, *Imagined Destinies Aboriginal Australians and the Doomed Race Theory, 1880–1939* (Melbourne: Melbourne University Press).

[14] *Fortnightly Review*, 1 February 1908.

[15] On the census see Marilyn Lake 2004, 'The White Man under Siege: New Histories of Race in the Nineteenth Century and the Advent of White Australia', *History Workshop Journal*, vol. 58, pp. 41-62; Tony Ballantyne 2002, 'Empire, Knowledge and Culture: From Proto-Globalization to Modern Globalization', in Anthony Hopkins (ed.), *Globalization in World History* (London: Pimlico); and Margo J. Anderson 1988, *The American Census : A Social History* (New Haven, CT: Yale University Press); on passports see Radhika Viyas Mongia 2003, 'Race, Nationality, Mobility: A History of the Passport', in Antoinette Burton (ed.), *After the Imperial Turn: Thinking with and through the Nation* (Durham, NC and London: Duke University Press).

racial exclusion and its circulation between the United States, South Africa and Australia. It also charts the concomitant racialisation of a diversity of national groups, including Africans, Americans, Australians, Indians, Japanese, Hungarians and Italians in a process that produced dichotomous categories of white and non-white, subsuming earlier multiple classifications.

The targets of the literacy test changed as did its specifications, from the requirement to write one's name, to demonstration of the comprehension of the constitution, to the ability to fill out an application form in English to a dictation test in any European language. Beginning with Mississippi in 1890, the deployment of a literacy test for racial purposes was a key aspect of the transnational process noticed by Du Bois: the constitution of 'whiteness' as the basis of both personal identity and transnational political community. Literacy was used to patrol racial borders (electoral as well as national) within and between nations, and in the process literacy became code for whiteness.

While a number of Australian historians have noted that the infamous Australian dictation test of 1901 followed the precedent of Natal in 1897, they have not noticed that the Natal legislation explicitly emulated an American Act of 1896 – passed at the behest of the Boston-based Immigration Restriction League, but which, as it happened, was vetoed by President Grover Cleveland. The United States example was all important, but the British imperial frame of analysis adopted by most historians of Australia has diverted attention from the importance of American experience to white colonials. Both in Australia and South Africa, white men looked to the example of the country they liked to call 'the great republic'.

And they looked to American history lessons more generally. The main lesson they imbibed from nineteenth century American history was the impossibility of a multi-racial democracy and the most influential source for this understanding was James Bryce's magisterial *The American Commonwealth*, first published in 1888 and re-published in a new and expanded third edition in 1893, that included two chapters on 'The South Since the War' and 'The Present and Future of the Negro'. The 'negro question', said Bryce, was 'the capital question in national as well as state politics'.[16] Moreover, 'the problem was a new one in history, for the relations of the ruling and subject races of Europe and Asia supply no parallel to it.'[17]

At Oxford University, Bryce had been a student of the pre-eminent race historian of the nineteenth century and leading proponent of Anglo-Saxonism, E. A. Freeman, whose work was also much admired both in the United States and

---

[16] James Bryce 1893, *The American Commonwealth*, third and revised edition (London and New York, NY: Macmillan), p. 510.

[17] ibid., p. 514.

Australia. Bryce was not so committed as his mentor to racial determinism, but following his extended visits to the United States in the 1880s he, too, became convinced of the unfitness of non-whites for self-government.[18] 'Emancipation found them utterly ignorant', he wrote of American Blacks in 1888, 'and the grant of suffrage found them as unfit for political rights as any population could be.'[19]

Bryce was a key transnational educator on the subject of history, nation and race. He played a crucial role in circulating knowledge about the 'failed experiment' of racial equality ushered in by Radical Reconstruction following the Civil War, when the passage of the 14th and 15th Amendments to the Constitution guaranteed the 'equal protection' of the law to 'all persons born or naturalized in the United States' and that prevented States from denying the right to vote on grounds of race or colour. Hailed by Liberal Republican Carl Schurz as 'the great Constitutional Revolution', in Bryce's account, Radical Reconstruction was a ghastly mistake, leading to terrible violence on the part of whites accompanied by 'revolting cruelty'.[20]

As Hugh Tulloch has observed:

> His summary of slavery and reconstruction classically stated the Gilded Age orthodoxy which was developed more fully in the historical works of such friends as C. F. Adams Jr, James Ford Rhodes, Woodrow Wilson, John W. Burgess and W. A. Dunning: 'Such a Saturnalia of robbery and jobbery has seldom been seen in any civilised country, and certainly never before under the forms of free self-government'.[21]

Wendell Phillips Garrison, on the other hand, writing in the *Nation*, regretted that Bryce had thrown 'the weight of his humane authority into the white scale' and Bryce drew further criticism from old English friends, including A. V. Dicey.[22]

In Australia, however, *The American Commonwealth* commanded a faithful following, where it was taken up in the 1890s as the 'bible' or 'great textbook' by colonial leaders engaged in the work of drawing up a new federal

---

[18] Lake 2004, 'The White Man under Siege', pp. 54-5.

[19] James Bryce 1888, *The American Commonwealth*, vol. 3 (London and New York, NY: Macmillan), p. 92.

[20] On Carl Schurz, see Eric Foner, *The Story of American Freedom* (New York, NY and London: W. W. Norton & Co.), p. 106.

[21] Hugh Tulloch 1988, *James Bryce's American Commonwealth: the Anglo-American Background* (Woodbridge, Suffolk: Boydell Press), p. 195.

[22] Review 1895, *New York Nation*, 31 January, pp. 86-8; Tulloch 1988, *Bryce's American Commonwealth*, pp. 197-8.

constitution.[23] In South Africa, too, as John Cell, in his study of the origins of segregation in South Africa and the importance of the American example, has noted, Bryce became the accepted authority on American race relations among English-speaking white men.[24]

The Mississippi precedent: the education test of 1890

In *The American Commonwealth*, Bryce canvassed possible solutions to the Negro problem, including the feasibility of deporting Blacks – all eight million – to Africa. He also drew attention to the Mississippi legislation of 1890, which for the first time used an 'education test' to exclude otherwise qualified Black voters from the electoral roll. Prevented by the 14th and 15th Amendments from disenfranchising Blacks on the grounds of race, the southern state of Mississippi led the way among self-styled white men's countries in deploying an education test – in this case a comprehension test – to achieve racial exclusion. The law required that to be registered a voter 'shall be able to read any section of the Constitution, or be able to understand the same when read to him, or to give a reasonable interpretation thereof'.

The requirement that voters demonstrate a degree of literacy was not itself new. The importance of literacy and education to the exercise of self-government was central to republican understandings of citizenship in the United States, as Matt Jacobsen has pointed out and, it was the northern states of Connecticut (1855) and Massachusetts (1857) that first stipulated that electors should be able to read the Constitution. Massachusetts also required that electors be able to write their names.

The 1890 Constitutional Convention of Mississippi marked a new departure, however, in the recommendation of an education test as a means to effect racial discrimination. The Supreme Court of Mississippi commented on the ways in which Blacks' racial characteristics rendered them unfit to exercise the suffrage:

> Within the field of permissible action under the limitations proposed by the Federal Constitution, the Convention swept the field of expedients to obstruct the exercise of suffrage by the Negro race. By reasons of its previous condition of servitude and dependency, this race had acquired

---

[23] J. A. LaNauze, *The Making of the Australian Constitution*, quoted in Marilyn Lake 2003, 'White Man's Country: The Trans-National History of a Trans-National Project', *Australian Historical Studies*, vol. 34, no. 122, p. 358.

[24] John W. Cell 1982, *The Highest Stage of White Supremacy: The Origins of Segregation in South Africa and the American South* (New York, NY: Cambridge University Press), p. 23.

or accentuated certain peculiarities of habit, temperament, and of character, which clearly distinguished it as a race from the whites.[25]

Although not ostensibly discriminatory, the educational test permitted race distinctions in several ways, as Gilbert Stephenson observed in his 1910 study of *Race Distinctions in American Law* :

> In the first place, registration officers may give a difficult passage of the Constitution to a Negro, and a very easy passage to a white person, or vice versa. He may permit a halting reading by one and require fluent reading by the other. He may let illegible scratching on paper suffice for the signature of one and require of the other a legible handwriting. But race discriminations in such cases rest with the officers; they do not have their basis in the law itself.[26]

Other southern states followed suit: South Carolina in 1895, Louisiana in 1898, North Carolina in 1900, Alabama in 1901, Virginia in 1901, and Georgia in 1908. The legislation had the desired effect, as Stephenson reported:

> In one county in Mississippi, with a population of about 8,000 whites and 11,700 Negroes in 1900, there were only twenty-five or thirty qualified Negro voters in 1908, the rest being disqualified, it is said, on the educational test. In another county, with 30,000 Negroes, only about 175 were registered voters ... As a general rule, taking the country at large, about one person in five is a male of voting age. In Iowa four out of five possible voters have actually voted in the last four elections; in Georgia, a State of nearly the same population, the proportion is one to six ... These figures show that the ratio of actual voters to total population in the Southern States is astoundingly smaller than in other States.[27]

In *The American Commonwealth*, Bryce observed that the strategy of racial exclusion in Mississippi had proven so effective, that it had recommended itself to 'a British colony where the presence of a large coloured population has posed a problem not dissimilar to that we have been examining'.[28] At his suggestion, the Cape Colony in South Africa followed the Mississippi precedent in its Franchise and Ballot Act of 1892, which for the first time applied an education test as well as a property test to further restrict the number of non-whites who could vote there.

---

[25] Gilbert Thomas Stephenson 1910, *Race Distinctions in American Law* (New York, NY and London: Appleton and Co.), p. 295.

[26] ibid., pp. 303-4.

[27] ibid., pp. 320-1.

[28] Bryce 1893, *American Commonwealth*, p. 511.

A literacy test to restrict immigration to the United States

The decade of the 1890s in the United States – as in Australia and South Africa – saw growing demands that the government further restrict immigration to exclude undesirable races. In the case of the United States it was the vast numbers who were entering the country that began to cause alarm as well as the changing complexion of immigrants. Italians, Hungarians, Poles and other allegedly ignorant and illiterate European peoples – 'removed from us in race and blood' – began to be targeted for exclusion.[29]

In 1790, the United States had restricted naturalised citizenship to 'all free white persons who have or shall migrate into the United States'.[30] Clearly, the legislation was racially discriminatory, but as Jacobsen points out the law also proved to be radically 'inclusive':

> What is too easily missed from our vantage point, however, is the staggering inclusivity of the 1790 naturalization law. It was this law's unquestioned use of the word 'white' that allowed for the massive European migrations of the nineteenth century, beginning with the Famine Migration from Ireland, and ultimately including the 48ers from Germany, the Scandinavian pioneers, and then successive waves of East European Jews, Italians, Greeks, Poles, Ruthenians, Slovenians, Magyars, Ukrainians, Lithuanians – none of whom the framers [of the constitution] had ever envisioned swelling the polity of the new nation when they crafted its rules for naturalization.[31]

It was these groups on whom American immigration reformers focused in the 1890s, opening up in the process the categories of 'white' and 'non-white' for re-definition. Many southern and eastern Europeans began to be considered not quite white enough for Anglo-Saxon America.[32]

The Chinese had been excluded by name in United States legislation of 1882. Now on the east coast, especially in Massachusetts, attention was focused on other undesirable 'races' who allegedly threatened the American standard of living and system of government. In two articles in the *North American Review*, in 1891, Boston Anglo-Saxonist and Republican Congressman Henry Cabot Lodge made the point that 'the immigration of those races which had thus far built up the United States, and which are related to each other either by blood or language

---

[29] Henry Cabot Lodge 1891, 'Lynch Law and Unrestricted Immigration', in *North American Review*, vol. 152, no. 414, p. 611.

[30] Jacobsen 1999, *Whiteness of a Different Color*, p. 22.

[31] ibid., p. 40.

[32] ibid., pp. 43-60.

or both was declining, while the immigration of races totally alien to them was increasing'.[33]

In the first article, in January, he used consular reports to show that immigration was 'making its greatest relative increase from races most alien to the body of American people and from the lowest and most illiterate classes among those races'.[34] He pointed in particular to the rise in the number of Hungarian Slovacs who, according to the American consul in Budapest, had 'so many items in common with the Chinese' in that they were prey to drug addictions of various kinds (alcohol not opium) and their low standard of living was undermining the 'white labourer's wages'.[35] It was time, Lodge argued, to 'discriminate against illiteracy':

> It is a truism to say that one of the greatest dangers to our free government is ignorance ... We spend millions annually in educating our children that they may be fit to be citizens and rulers of the Republic. We are ready to educate also the children who come to us from other countries; but it is not right to ask us to take annually a large body of persons who are totally illiterate ... We have the right to exclude illiterate persons from our immigration, and this test ... would in all probability shut out a large part of the undesirable portion of the present immigration.[36]

Lodge's second article in May 1891 was prompted by the lynching of eleven Italians in New Orleans and although he condemned the lawlessness of the mob, Lodge nevertheless considered there was reason for it. The local community had reason to believe the Italians were connected with the Mafia, 'offspring of conditions and of ideas wholly alien to the people of the United States', whose presence provided further evidence of 'the utter carelessness with which we treat immigration in this country'. If new restriction measures were not soon introduced – including a test of immigrants' ability to read and write – then 'race antagonisms' must surely increase.[37]

In 1894, Lodge joined other New Englanders, Prescott F. Hall, Robert DeCourcy Ward, Charles Warren and John Fiske in forming the Immigration Restriction League. As Jacobsen has observed, the 'league crystallized around the issue of a literacy test for incoming aliens' and 'race was central to the league's conception

---

[33] Lodge 1891, 'Lynch Law and Unrestricted Immigration', p. 606.

[34] Henry Cabot Lodge 1891, 'The Restriction of Immigration', *North American Review*, January, p. 32.

[35] ibid., p. 31.

[36] ibid., p. 36.

[37] Lodge 1891, 'Lynch Law and Unrestricted Immigration', p. 612.

of literacy from the beginning'.[38] Literacy was fundamental to the citizen's capacity for self-government and only Anglo-Saxons were blessed with that capacity. But arguably, just as important as the New Englanders' 'Anglo-Saxon complex' was Lodge's knowledge from State department reports that the groups he wanted to exclude – migrants from eastern and southern Europe – had very low levels of literacy.

The Immigration Restriction Bill, which required immigrants to show knowledge of reading and writing in their own language, for admission to the United States, was sponsored by Lodge in 1895 and passed in 1896. As Barbara Solomon has noted:

> An educational basis of admission seemed reasonable; the Massachusetts State Constitution already contained such a reading and writing requirement for voting. Moreover, the bill had the strategic usefulness of not discriminating against any group by name, nationality, religion or race [but] would keep out 'people we wish to exclude'.[39]

Its strategic value was immediately apparent to Joseph Chamberlain in the British Colonial Office, who was thinking about ways of preventing colonists in South Africa, Australia, New Zealand and British Columbia from passing legislation that discriminated explicitly against Chinese and Indian British subjects or Britain's Japanese allies.

In the event, the American Immigration Restriction Act of 1896 would be vetoed by President Grover Cleveland, but not before it was taken up by political leaders in Natal, who were looking for ways to stop the further immigration of Indians. In the United States, Lodge and others continued to press for immigration restriction based on a literacy test, with their political support increasingly coming from the South and the west coast, as agitation there against 'Asiatics' grew ever more strident. Twice more when immigration restriction legislation incorporating a literacy test was passed by Congress, it was vetoed by Presidents Taft and Wilson.

Founded on the American Act: Natal introduces immigration restriction

In Natal, agitation against immigrants also became vociferous in the 1890s, focused on an 'invasion' of Indian immigrants, many of whom were also accused of bringing the plague. More important than the fear of disease, however, was the prospect of their competition in employment and business and their future

---

[38] Jacobsen 1999, *Whiteness of a Different Color*, p. 77; see also Barbara Miller Solomon 1965, *Ancestors and Immigrants: A Changing New England Tradition* (New York, NY: John Wiley and Sons), pp. 59-81.

[39] Solomon 1965, *Ancestors and Immigrants*, pp. 17-18.

participation in politics for, as the Colonial Office observed sympathetically with reference to an 1894 franchise amendment, 'the Whites would never submit to being overruled by the Indian vote'.[40]

In promising to limit Indian immigration, the Natal government insisted on the political imperative of securing white man's rule:

> We have got a large unenfranchised [Black] population of roughly 500,000; we have got a European population – which in fact is the governing body as regards the whole community – roughly in numbers, 50,000; and we have got Indians who have come here at our own expense, or who have come here as a consequence of our own Immigration Laws, in round numbers nearly equal to Europeans. And we think that a large addition to the Indian population will be a cause for difficulty, not only in the present as regards competition, but also in the future as regards the political conditions of the colony.[41]

The government initially determined to follow the Australian colony of New South Wales, which had recently passed legislation extending its earlier 1888 exclusion of Chinese to 'all coloured races' regardless of their status as British subjects. However, on preparation of a similar Bill called 'A Bill to restrict the immigration of Asiatics into Natal', the government was informed that the New South Wales legislation had been 'reserved' by the Colonial Office.

Colonial Secretary Joseph Chamberlain explained to both New South Wales and Natal that these measures – and the issue of discrimination against Chinese and Indian British subjects more generally – would be discussed later that year in London when the colonial Premiers gathered to celebrate the 60th anniversary of Her Majesty Queen Victoria's accession to the throne. The invitation to join the celebrations was welcomed in Natal as a great compliment to 'the self-governing Colonies'.[42]

Clearly, explicit race-based legislation would not receive royal assent, so Natal looked to the example of the 'great Republic of America' which claimed, like themselves, 'an absolute right' 'if they think fit to place a restriction on the introduction of immigration into their country of persons who are regarded by the community as undesirable immigrants'.[43] In moving the second reading of

---

[40] Minute in response to Petition from MK Gandhi and others, re amendment to Franchise Act, CO 189, 1894, UK National Archives.

[41] Legislative Assembly Debates, Natal, 25 March 1897, CO 179/198, p. 28. UK National Archives.

[42] Legislative Council Address to Govenor, Natal, 24 March 1897, CO 179/198, UK National Archives

[43] Legislative Assembly Debates, 25 March 1897, CO 179/198, p.30.

the Immigration Restriction Bill in the Legislative Assembly, in March 1897, the Premier explained:

> The great Republic of America has found it necessary to have recourse to that restriction and I may say generally that the Bill that I now have the honour to submit to this Assembly is founded on the American Act. But it goes one step further. The American Act prohibits the immigration of ... 'persons who cannot read and write in their own language or in some other language' (these are the words of the statute) 'being of the age of sixteen and upwards'.[44]

The Premier explained further that the Natal legislation had to 'go one step further than the American Bill' because the persons whom Natal desired to exclude were 'perfectly well able to read and write in their own language'. The Natal Bill stipulated that if prospective immigrants were

> unable to satisfy the immigration officer that they can read and write in the English language in the form prescribed by the Bill – a form that will not admit of any evasion – that if persons are unable to comply with that educational test it will be competent for the Government of this country, through the proper officers, to exclude those people from forming part and parcel of this community'.[45]

The final legislation actually specified that the application must be written in 'any European language', both to avoid discouraging other European immigrants and causing offence to Britain's European allies.

Several members of the Natal Legislative Assembly had objected to the provision for a literacy test because, on the one hand, 'the wily Hindoo' could certainly circumvent such a requirement, while on the other, it would prevent otherwise excellent European colonists from immigrating to Natal. Some argued, as they would also argue in Australia, that it was more becoming to white men to speak honestly about their intentions and forget about Colonial Office objections on behalf of coloured British subjects, for 'the idea of the British subject was fading more and more every year'. It was also suggested that the American precedent was inappropriate because their legislation was thought to be directed at lower class Europeans. Rather, some politicians urged, Natal should follow her 'sister colony' of New South Wales and join them in presenting a united front to the Colonial Office on the particular matter of 'Asiatic immigration'.

In the event, the Bill 'founded on the American Act' was passed with few dissenting voices and would thence be recommended by Secretary of State Joseph Chamberlain as a model to the Australians in 1901.

---

[44] Legislative Assembly Debates, Natal, 25 March 1897, CO 179/198, pp. 30-1.

[45] Legislative Assembly Debates, Natal, 25 March 1897, CO 179/198, p. 31.

The White Australia policy

When Prime Minister Edmund Barton rose in the first federal parliament, in Melbourne, to support the measures that comprised the White Australia policy – the Immigration Restriction Bill and the Pacific Islands Labourers' Bill – he held aloft a copy of Charles Pearson's prophetic book, *National Life and Character: A Forecast*, and quoted the following passage:

> The day will come, and perhaps is not far distant, when the European observer will look round to see the globe circled with a continuous zone of the black and yellow races, no longer too weak for aggression or under tutelage, but independent, or practically so, in government, monopolising the trade of their own regions, and circumscribing the industry of the Europeans; when Chinamen and the natives of Hindustan, the states of Central and South America ... are represented by fleets in the European seas, invited to international conferences and welcomed as allies in quarrels of the civilised world. The citizens of these countries will then be taken up into the social relations of the white races, will throng the English turf or the salons of Paris, and will be admitted to inter-marriage. It is idle to say that if all this should come to pass our pride of place will not be humiliated ... We shall wake to find ourselves elbowed and hustled, and perhaps even thrust aside by peoples whom we looked down upon as servile and thought of as bound always to minister to our needs. The solitary consolation will be that the changes have been inevitable.[46]

Pearson, a former professor in modern history at King's College, London had become by the 1890s a leading Melbourne intellectual, a headmaster and journalist, a politician and educational reformer and mentor to future Prime Minister Alfred Deakin, the architect of the White Australia policy. Pearson was a progressive: he had written in support of land tax, women's rights, the Polish uprising and the Haitian revolution. His book, published by Macmillan in London and New York, in 1893, with its prediction of the decline of the white man and the rise of 'the Black and Yellow races' caused a sensation around the world.

It was reviewed at length by Theodore Roosevelt, who commended it for alerting him to the movement of 'world forces' of which he had previously been ignorant. In a personal letter, from Washington, where he was working as Civil Service Commissioner, he wrote to tell Pearson of the 'great effect' of his book:

> all our men here in Washington ... were greatly interested in what you said. In fact, I don't suppose that any book recently, unless it is Mahan's

---

[46] Quoted by Barton in House of Representatives, *Commonwealth Parliamentary Debates*, 7 August 1901, p. 3503.

'Influence of Sea Power' has excited anything like as much interest or caused so many men to feel that they had to revise their mental estimates of facts'.[47]

Roosevelt, thenceforth, would embark on a re-assertion of American racial vigour ('the strenuous life') that led to a vociferous campaign in support of national expansion and to his personal command of the Rough Riders in the Spanish–American war in Cuba.

Pearson, back in London in 1893, wrote to his friend and protégé in Melbourne, Alfred Deakin, gratified at the book's reception: 'It has been an unexpected but I think real success.' 'Hutton, Huxley, Green, Mahaffy & Simcox have been among the critics: and it has altogether been reviewed in some thirty papers.'[48] Grant Duff was an indignant reviewer, suggesting that 'the English race [would] certainly awake to its duties, when the time came, and massacre as many Chinese and Hindoos as were found superfluous'.[49] 'Can you imagine any European power setting itself to massacre 100 millions of Chinamen?' Pearson asked Deakin.[50]

The more acute of the English reviews of his book noted the significance of his change of domicile for his perspective on world forces. The London *Athenaeum* noted that Pearson's analysis of world history 'quits the beaten track of anticipation':

> His view is not purely or mainly European, nor does he regard the inferior races as hopelessly beaten in the struggle with Western civilization. The reader can indeed discern that Mr Pearson's point of view is not London or Paris, but Melbourne. He regards the march of affairs from the Australian point of view, and next to Australia what he seems to see most clearly is the growth of the Chinese power and of the native populations of Africa. In this forecast, in fact, Europe loses altogether the precedence it has always enjoyed.[51]

Residence in the New World provided a quite different perspective on world forces. Singapore, for example, in the last three decades of the nineteenth century, had suddenly become Chinese, as had much of northern Australia.

---

[47] Roosevelt to Pearson, 11 May 1894, Pearson papers, Bodleian Library, MS English letters, D190, Oxford University.

[48] Pearson to Deakin, no date, 1893 Deakin papers MS 1540/1/193; 29 March 1893, MS 1540/1/201, National Library of Australia.

[49] *Athenaeum*, 4 March 1893.

[50] Charles Pearson to Alfred Deakin, 29 March 1893, Deakin Papers, National Library of Australia, MS 1540/1/201.

[51] *Athenaeum*, 4 March 1893.

Faced with the ascendancy of coloured and colonised peoples, Pearson considered these developments to be humiliating for the white man – whose sense of self was constituted in relations of racial dominance – but historically inevitable. The proper response for the white man was to accept these changes with stoicism and manly fortitude.

Not many agreed with Pearson's stance. Australian political leaders – presiding in the 1890s over the inauguration of a new nation state – certainly could not. Encouraged by historians such as Bryce and Freeman and political theorists such as John Burgess, of Columbia University, they regarded the exclusion and expulsion of undesirable races as their primary duty as nation builders and they would confront the Colonial Office over their right to see the project through. In 1892, Pearson was moved to write to Bryce in London warning that if the British denied the Australians complete self-government in this respect, there would certainly be a Declaration of Independence within five years. The historical memory of American events loomed large.

When the Australians determined, as Barton put it, to legislate their racial identity, they had American experience in mind. 'We have only to look at the great difficulty which is being experienced in America in connexion with the greatest racial trouble ever known in the history of the world, in order to take warning and guard ourselves against similar complications', leading Liberal H. B. Higgins told the first Australian parliament in 1901.[52] Attorney-General and future Prime Minister, Alfred Deakin also pointed to the importance of American history:

> We should be false to the lessons taught us in the great republic of the west; we should be false to the never-to-be-forgotten teachings from the experience of the United States, of difficulties only partially conquered by the blood of their best and bravest; we should be absolutely blind to and unpardonably neglectful of our obligations, if we fail to lay those lessons to heart.[53]

Deakin praised those who drew up the Australian constitution (of whom he was one) for improving on the American example. He highlighted the significance of Section 51, sub-sections 26-30, in equipping Australia to deal with the problem of 'the admixture of other races':

> Our Constitution marks a distinct advance upon and difference from that of the United States, in that it contains within itself the amplest powers to deal with this difficulty in all its aspects. It is not merely a question

---

[52] House of Representatives, *Commonwealth Parliamentary Debates*, 6 September 1901, p. 4659.

[53] House of Representatives, *Commonwealth Parliamentary Debates*, 12 September 1901, p. 4806; Lake 2003 'White Man's Country'.

of invasion from the exterior. It may be a question of difficulties within our borders, already created, or a question of possible contamination of another kind. I doubt if there can be found in the list of powers with which this Parliament, on behalf of the people, is endowed – powers of legislation – a cluster more important and more far reaching in their prospect than the provisions contained in sub-sections (26) to (30) of section 51, in which the bold outline of the authority of the people of Australia for their self-protection is laid down.[54]

Whereas the United States Constitutional Amendments provided 'special inhibitions', Section 51 of the Australian Constitution made provision for 'special laws' to deal with other 'races'.

In supporting the legislation to expel the Pacific Islanders, Higgins again referred to the history of the United States:

I say that that country, more especially the Southern States, would have been ten times better off if the negroes had not been left there. There are no conditions under which degeneracy of race is so great as those which exist when a superior race and an inferior race are brought into close contact.

At issue for Higgins were the prospects of white workers:

I feel convinced that people who are used to a high standard of life – to good wages and good conditions – will not consent to labour alongside men who receive a miserable pittance and who are dealt with very much in the same way as slaves.[55]

The legislation was, according to Higgins, who would shortly become president of the Commonwealth Court of Conciliation and Arbitration, 'the most vitally important measure on the programme which the government has put before us'. He watched its course, he said, with the 'deepest anxiety'. In 1907 Higgins would use his position on the Arbitration Court to define a 'living wage' designed to secure the status of the white men as workers, whom he was always careful to define as 'civilised beings … living in a civilised community'.[56]

With the passage of the Pacific Islands Labourers Act in 1901, the Commonwealth of Australia was inaugurated in an act of racial expulsion. Australians would do what the United States – with a population of eight million Blacks – could not. For Deakin and his fellow members of parliament, the sovereignty of the people

---

[54] House of Representatives, *Commonwealth Parliamentary Debates*, 6 September 1901.

[55] House of Representatives, *Commonwealth Parliamentary Debates*, House of Representatives, 3 October 1901, pp. 6815-19.

[56] *Commonwealth Arbitration Reports*, vol. 11, 1907–08, pp. 3-4.

meant the capacity to protect their racial character. But when they spoke of the necessity of 'self-protection', they spoke not as 'Anglo-Saxons', but as 'white men'. Although neither the Pacific Islands Labourers Act nor the Immigration Restriction Act referred to race by name, their intention was clear enough. 'The two things go hand in hand', advised Attorney-General Deakin. They were 'the necessary complement of a single policy – the policy of securing a "White Australia".'

The Australian Immigration Restriction Act, following Natal and the United States, incorporated a literacy test, in this case, a dictation test, that was so framed as to give Customs Officers maximum flexibility in ensuring that all undesirable immigrants would fail. Applicants could not prepare for this test, which required them to write out, at dictation, any prescribed passage of fifty words in any European language. The American emphasis on understanding the constitution and the importance of education to citizenship had disappeared altogether. In 1908, for example, the following dictation test was given in Western Australia:

> Very many considerations lead to the conclusion that life began on sea, first as single cells, then as groups of cells held together by a secretion of mucilage, then as filaments and tissues. For a very long time low-grade marine organisms are simply hollow cylinders, through which salt water streams'.[57]

The aim in Australia was not to 'discriminate against illiteracy', as Cabot Lodge had recommended, but to discriminate against non-whites, in particular 'Asiatics' and more particularly, Japanese, as their mortified diplomatic representatives soon learned when they read the parliamentary debates. The point that caused most offence to the Japanese was that they were racialised as 'Asiatics' or worse, lumped together with all non-whites, including Kanakas and Negroes. On 3 May 1901, H. Eitaki, the Japanese Consul in Sydney wrote a note of protest to the Australian government:

> The Japanese belong to an Empire whose standard of civilization is so much higher than that of Kanakas, Negroes, Pacific Islanders, Indians or other Eastern peoples, that to refer to them in the same terms cannot but be regarded in the light of a reproach, which is hardly warranted by the fact of the shade of the national complexion ...
>
> Might I suggest, therefore, that your Government formulate some proposal which, being accepted by my Government would allow of the people of Japan being excluded from the operation of any Act which

---

[57] Myra Willard 1968, *History of the White Australia Policy to 1920*, reprint (New York, NY: Augustus M. Kelley Publishers), p. 126.

directly or indirectly imposed a tax on immigrants on the ground of colour.[58]

As the wounded Japanese realised, the literacy test was a method of 'indirect' racial discrimination. Even so, they tried to change Australian minds by pointing to the high educational standards of modern Japan, which faithfully emulated 'the most approved European methods'. Four months later, on 18 September, as the legislation was passing through the House of Representatives, Eitaki wrote again to Barton:

> In Japanese schools and other educational establishments the most approved methods are adopted, and the most important works on science, literature, art, politics, law etc which are published in Europe from time to time, are translated into Japanese for the use of students. Thus a Japanese, without being acquainted with any other language than his own, is frequently up to a very high educational standard in the most advanced branches of study, by means of a liberal use of these translations.

Why could not the Japanese language be put on the same footing as, say, 'the Turkish, the Russian, the Greek, the Polish, the Norwegian, the Austrian, or the Portuguese, or why, if an immigrant of any of the nationalities ... mentioned may be examined *in his own language* [emphasis in original], the same courtesy should not be extended to a Japanese'. The Consul advised that his government requested that his people not be marked out 'to suffer a special disability; or in other words, that they may be examined in Japanese. This can easily be provided for by adding the words "or Japanese" after the word "European"' in the legislation.[59] Despite their pained and persistent protests, in Sydney and to the Foreign Office in London, they were unable to defeat the test's binary racial logic, its division of the world into 'white' and 'non-white'.

In employing a literacy test in a European language as an instrument for racial exclusion, the Australians paid deference to Imperial sensibilities. Meeting with the colonial premiers at Queen Victoria's Jubilee, in London, in June 1897, Chamberlain impressed on them the importance of upholding the 'traditions of the empire' which made no 'distinction in favour of or against race or colour'. In the white colonies of the empire, as in the southern states of the American Union, the modern instrument of a literacy test was adopted to meet and defeat prohibitions against racial discrimination. As in South Africa, many Australian politicians, including Higgins, protested against using a cowardly subterfuge

---

[58] H. Eitaki, Consul for Japan to Prime Minister Edmund Barton, 3 May 1901, CO 418/10, UK National Archives.

[59] Eitaki to Barton, 18 September 1901, CO 418/10, National Archives, UK.

and introduced an amendment into parliament, that almost passed, calling for a straight out, manly, declaration against non-white immigration.

The Colonial Office preference for courtesy, or hypocrisy, in immigration restriction legislation prevailed, but the adoption of an American – republican – model of exclusion had an unintended consequence for the Colonial Office: the removal of the special status accorded to British subjects across racial barriers. As Charles Lucas noted perceptively in his paper 'The Self-Governing Dominions and Coloured Immigration':

> It is, I think noteworthy that Mr Chamberlain, who was in full sympathy with the self-governing communities, was especially outspoken in protesting against giving offence in the methods of exclusion and against harsh treatment of coloured British subjects, but it will be noted at the same time that the object of avoiding offence in methods of exclusion militates against giving any preference to British subjects. The principle of the Natal Act, which Mr Chamberlain accepted and recommended, is not to specify any particular race, but to exclude all who cannot write a European language ie not to distinguish in any way among non-Europeans between those who are and those who are not British subjects.[60]

And in declaring for a White Australia, that was the Australians' intention. In that same founding year of 1901, they passed legislation (the Post and Telegraph Act) that, to the intense annoyance of the British, specifically targeted non-whites for exclusion from employment on ships carrying mails: 'only white labour shall be employed in such carriage.' The Japanese again protested: the legislation contained 'the same objectionable reproach to the Japanese nation, on the ground of color, against which protests have been made on former occasions.'[61] Further legislation relating to suffrage, naturalisation, old age and invalid pensions and the maternity allowance all specified racial grounds for discrimination in the name of White Australia. The dictation test remained in immigration legislation until 1958 and lingered – oddly but symbolically – in some industrial awards (such as the Margarine Award). Australia had nailed its colours to the mast.

White Australia became, in turn, an example for others to follow in South Africa, Canada, New Zealand and the United States. In 1908, Roosevelt, as president of the United States was conspiring with Canada to bring pressure to bear on Britain to bring a complete stop to Asian immigration to white men's countries ('the Japanese must learn that they will have to keep their people in their own

---

[60] Charles Lucas, 'The Self-Governing Dominions and Coloured Immigration', pp. 52-3. CO 886/1/1, UK National Archives.

[61] Eitaki to Barton, 18 September 1901, CO 418/10, National Archives, UK.

country'). [62] In 1910, the new Union of South Africa was described by Sir Charles Lucas in the Colonial Office, with the precedent of Australia in mind, as 'a White Man's Union'.[63] A 'new religion' was indeed sweeping the world. When the American writer, Lothrop Stoddard, published *The Rising Tide of Color* in support of a eugenicist scheme of immigration restriction in the United States, he saluted the 'lusty young Anglo-Saxon communities of the Pacific' for setting an example by emblazoning across their portals the legend: "All White".' [64] 'Nothing is more striking', he wrote, 'than the instinctive and instantaneous solidarity which binds together Australians and Afrikanders, Californians and Canadians, into a "sacred union" at the mere whisper of Asiatic immigration.'[65]

Conclusion

In becoming an instrument of racial exclusion, in a world increasingly characterised by the mobility of migration and mobilisations for political rights, the literacy test consolidated understandings of 'race' in terms of a dichotomy of whiteness and non-whiteness across the world, so that not only in the United States, as John Higham has argued in *Strangers in the Land*, but in southern Africa, northern America and Australasia, 'the Negro, the Oriental and the southern European appeared more and more in a common light'.[66] In Higham's account of American 'nativism' 'race', however, belongs to others. What Du Bois saw so clearly was that the same historical processes that worked to place 'the Negro, the Oriental and the southern European' 'in a common light' were also producing 'whiteness', as both global in its power and personal in its meaning, at once the basis of transnational political identifications and a subjective sense of self. As a modern technology, the literacy test was the instrument of whiteness *par excellence*.

---

[62] Quoted in William Lyon 1959, *Mackenzie King: A Political Biography* (London: Methuen and Co.), p. 152.

[63] David Phillips 2003, 'Towards a "White Man's Union"', in John Chesterman and David Phillips (eds), *Selective Democracy: Race, Gender and the Australian Vote* (Armadale: Circa), pp. 38-49.

[64] Lothrop Stoddard 1920, *The Rising Tide of Color Against White World-Supremacy* (New York, NY: Scribner's), p. 281.

[65] ibid.

[66] John Higham 1988, *Strangers in the Land Patterns of American Nativism 1860–1925*, second edition (New Brunswick, NJ and London: Rutgers University Press), p. 173.

Postcolonial Transnationalism

14. Islam, Europe and Indian nationalism: towards a postcolonial transnationalism

Patrick Wolfe

As a comparative historian interested in race and colonialism, I sometimes find myself wondering what all the fuss is about when people advocate transnational history. Putting the definitional niceties of the term 'nation' aside for the moment and using it, in a vernacular sense, as something like 'country', both race and colonialism are inherently transnational phenomena. Confronted with the call to transnationalise, therefore, the historian of race and colonialism might well recognise how Mark Twain must have felt on discovering that he had been speaking prose all his life. Even in internal-colonial contexts, at least one of the contending parties originally came from somewhere else, a fact that continues to demarcate the relationship. As often as not, this demarcation is inscribed in the language of race. I have argued that race is a regime of difference that has served to distinguish dominant groups from groups whom they initially encountered in colonial contexts.[1] These contexts were inherently spatial, the groups involved having previously been geographically separate. Thus we might adapt Mary Douglas' celebrated dictum that dirt is matter out of place[2] to human dirt, the racialised, who are constructed as fundamentally contaminatory. It would be hard to find a construct of race that has not involved concepts of spatiality and contamination, usually in association. Hence the frequency with which the racialised are spatially segregated to hygienic ends. This principle has not been particular to the modern discourse of race, which emerged in company with colonies and nations.[3] Anti-Semitism and Islamophobia, enduring

---

[1] An earlier version of this chapter was presented to the Fourth Galway Conference on Colonialism in 2004. Thanks to Tadhg Foley. For comments and criticism, thanks to Dipesh Chakrabarty, Phillip Darby, Leela Gandhi, Peter McPhee and, especially, to my teacher, Sibnarayan Ray. Thanks also to Ann Curthoys and Marilyn Lake for their very helpful approach to editing.

Patrick Wolfe 2001, 'Land, Labor, and Difference: Elementary Structures of Race', *American Historical Review*, vol. 106, no. 3, pp. 865-905, at p. 867.

[2] Mary Douglas 1966, *Purity and Danger: An Analysis of Concepts of Pollution and Taboo* (London: Routledge & Kegan Paul).

[3] From a large literature see, e.g., Collette Guillaumin 1995, 'The Idea of Race and its Elevation to Autonomous Scientific and Legal Status', in her *Racism, Sexism, Power and Ideology* (London: Routledge), pp. 61-98; Ivan Hannaford 1996, *Race: The History of an Idea in the West* (Baltimore, MD: Johns Hopkins University Press); Kenan Malik 1996, *The Meaning of Race: Race, History and*

proto-forms of European racism, applied internally and externally respectively: to the Jew within, who characteristically 'wandered' – a spatial determination – from ghetto to ghetto, and to the Saracen, Turk or Mahomedan, who threatened – and thereby constituted – the borders of Christendom from without.

To deal with race and colonialism is, therefore, to take transnationalism (or, before the nation state, some form of transregionalism) for granted. Again, therefore, what is all the fuss about? It seems to me that transnational history's radical potential is a matter of its address. Until relatively recently, the call to transnationalism has been largely confined to historians of the United States (this is despite the fact that its principal advocate has been an Australian, Ian Tyrrell).[4] Transnational historians have critiqued the Anglocentric historiography in which the United States has figured as miraculously conceived from Puritan sources, pointing to the formative contributions of Native American, African, Spanish, French, Chinese, Irish and other nations. To this extent, transnational history is a subset of United States minority history writing or, more broadly, of history from below. Self-consciously transnational histories differ from the generality of minority accounts, however, in insisting on the migrations and other global transactions that preceded and continue to underlie minority status in United States society. The nation is not axiomatic. For transnational history – and here pan-Africanism may be seen as paradigmatic[5] – minorities have pre-United States genealogies to which space is central.

But to say that the call to transnational history has been directed to historians of the United States and not to historians of colonialism raises obvious problems. One has only to mention Native Americans or African Americans for the incoherence of the distinction to be patent. Thus the issue is not one of distinguishing between histories of colonialism on the one hand and histories of United States society on the other. It is about how and why that false distinction came to be established. What kind of exceptionalism is it that absolves United States history from – or, perhaps, enclaves it within – the global narrative of European colonialism? In promising to dismantle that solipsistic historiography,

---

Culture in Western Society (Basingstoke: Macmillan). For discussion, see my 2002 'Race and Racialisation: Some Thoughts', *Postcolonial Studies*, vol. 5, no. 1, pp. 51-62.

[4] Ian Tyrrell 1991, 'American Exceptionalism in an Age of International History', *American Historical Review*, vol. 96, no. 4, pp. 1031-55; Tyrrell 1999, 'Making Nations/Making States: American Historians in the Context of Empire', *Journal of American History*, vol. 86, December, pp. 1015-44.

[5] See, e.g., Robin D. G. Kelley 1999, '"But a Local Phase of a World Problem": Black History's Global Vision', *Journal of American History*, vol. 86, December, pp. 1054-77; Kelley 2002, 'How the West Was One: The African Diaspora and the Re-Mapping of US History', in Thomas Bender (ed.), *Rethinking American History in a Global Age* (Berkeley, CA: University of California Press), pp. 123-47.

transnational history has a radical potential that can be compared to the postcolonial project of dismantling the sovereign subjecthood of the West. For this potential to be realised, however, transnational history will have to extend its purview beyond its current, unfortunately narcissistic preoccupation with White-settler societies.[6] Accordingly, while it is refreshing that transnational history should now be establishing a foothold in Australia, whose White-settler national mythology has historical correspondences with that of the United States, we should remain mindful of the varied range of colonial social formations.

The exclusion of minority genealogies in favour of a dominant group's monopolising of the national narrative has been a commonplace of accounts of the nation since Ernest Renan's famous 1882 lecture on the forgetting that is central to nationalism.[7] This kind of selective amnesia would seem to be particularly congenial to settler-colonial nationalism. After all, settler colonialism strives for the elimination of the native in favour of an unmediated connection between the settlers and the land – hence the notion of building clone-like fragments of the mother country in the wilderness. In this fantasy, nobody else is involved, just settlers and the natural landscape. Such a situation is clearly conducive to solipsistic narratives. On this basis, it is not surprising that transnational history should be developing in settler societies.

Yet the screening-out of other contributions may well be endemic to the nation state formation itself, rather than particular to its settler-colonial variant. This consideration suggests ways in which we might widen the scope of transnational history writing. Moreover, the very distinction between European and settler societies occludes the actual histories of European state formation (think, for instance, of Norman England, the Basques in France and Spain, or the Nazi *lebensraum* in eastern Europe). In this light, one could cite the Comte de Boulainviller, in early eighteenth century France, as a metropolitan precursor to self-consciously transnational history writing. In a nice conflation of race and class, Boulainviller reduced French history to a contest between a 'race' of external conquerors, the Francs, and the native Gauls, the invaders becoming the ruling class by right of conquest.[8] In classic settler-colonial style, this

---

[6] An exception is Prasenjit Duara 2002, 'Transnationalism and the Challenge to National Histories', in Bender, *Rethinking American History*, pp. 25-46.

[7] Ernest Renan 1947–61, 'Qu'est-ce qu'une Nation?' ['What Is a Nation?'], in 'Discourses et conférences', in Renan, *Œuvres Complètes*, 10 volumes, Henriette Psichari (ed.) (Paris: Calmann-Lévy), vol. 1, pp. 117-41.

[8] Comte Henry [sic] de Boulainviller, 'Dissertation sur la Noblesse Françoise servant de preface aux memoires de la maison de Croî et Boulainviller', reproduced in André Devyver 1973, *Le Sang épuré: Les préjugés de race chez les gentilshommes français de l'Ancien Regime (1560–1720)* (Brussels: Editions de l'Université de Bruxelles), pp. 501-48. For interesting comment, see Hannah Arendt (who

involved Boulainviller in basing his own class's claim to dominance on their not being native. In settling, though, and asserting their transcendent bond to the territory of France, they became so. By contrast, European authorities in franchise colonies such as British India or the Netherlands East Indies did not, in the main, come to stay. They remained as agents of the metropolitan power, their agenda being the aggrandisement rather than the cloning of the metropolis. In such colonies, nationalist momentum came from among the ranks of the natives. They, rather than the colonisers, proclaimed an eternal bond between themselves and the land. Yet the historiography of franchise-colonial nationalisms, unlike that of settler nationalisms in dominion territories, is unproblematically transnational. There has not, for instance, been a struggle to write Indians into the history of British India to compare with the scholarly energy that had to go into finding Aborigines a place in the Australian national narrative.[9] In this light, the core issue that transnational history problematises is the core characteristic of the nation state itself: the assertion of privileged affinities between particular groups of people and particular parcels of land. Stated in these more general terms, transnational history has no necessary confinement to settler societies in the West. I wish to argue that, by adopting a transnational approach to other situations, we can contribute to the postcolonial project that Dipesh Chakrabarty has termed the provincialising of Europe.[10]

In what follows, I intend to revisit a topic that I have previously written about, only this time in a more self-consciously transnational manner. In a critique of Gayatri Spivak's 'Can the Subaltern Speak?', I noted that, for all their differences, Hindu nationalism and British colonialism had concurred over the exclusion of Indian Islam from the colonial encounter. In particular, they had shared the assumption – embarrassing for anti-colonial nationalists, affirming for their colonisers – that key features of Indian nationalist discourse were themselves a colonial endowment inherited from the European rationalist tradition. Using the example of the early nineteenth century Bengali reformer Rammohun Roy, I argued that this widely-held assumption was not only misleading but could only be maintained so long as the Indian Islamic tradition was overlooked; that key rationalist premises attributed to the European enlightenment could be found already expressed in Indian Islamic discourse, where they testified to a post-Hellenistic Arabic-language inheritance which, as a result of the translation

---

uses the alternative spelling of 'Boulainvilliers') 1944, 'Race-Thinking Before Racism', *Review of Politics*, vol. 6, no. 1, pp. 36-73, at pp. 43-6.

[9] Though this admittedly leaves the question, influentially insisted on by the *Subaltern Studies* group, of which Indians have been written about.

[10] Dipesh Chakrabarty 1992, 'Postcoloniality and the Artifice of History: Who Speaks for "Indian" Pasts?', *Representations*, vol. 37, Winter, pp. 1-26; Chakrabarty 2000, *Provincializing Europe: Postcolonial Thought and Historical Difference* (Princeton, NJ: Princeton University Press).

movement in al-Andalus, had also bolstered the European Renaissance. In returning to Islamic rationalism by way of India, colonising Europe was returning to its own repressed. Bringing a transcontinental Islamic inheritance together with Indian nationalism and British colonialism, the analysis was manifestly, albeit inadvertently, transnational (not to say transhistorical). Nonetheless, al-Andalus hardly fits the nation state category, while the 'nation' of Indian nationalism was still at a very early stage of its imagining, so the discussion was also somewhat unorthodox in transnationalist terms – as, of course, was its application to a non-Western, non-settler colonial context. Moreover, the analysis sought to decentre Islamophobia, instancing the contradictory variety of Islamophobic legacies involved in the current global malaise. On all these grounds, and trying to keep repetition to a minimum, I would now like to return to the analysis with a more informed transnational awareness, in the hope of casting some light on what might be called the creole genealogy of Western imperialism.[11]

A derivative discourse?

Opening the 1933 celebrations to commemorate the centenary of Rammohun Roy's death, the great Rabindranath Tagore was unstinting:

> Rammohun Roy inaugurated the modern age in India. He was born at a time when our country, having lost its links with the inmost truths of its being, struggled under a crushing load of unreason, in abject slavery to circumstance. In social usage, in politics, in the realm of religion and art, we had entered the zone of uncreative habit, of decadent tradition, and ceased to exercise our humanity. In this dark gloom of India's degeneration Rammohun rose up, a luminous star in the firmament of India's history with prophetic purity of vision, and unconquerable heroism of soul. He shed radiance all over the land: he rescued us from the penury of self oblivion.[12]

Tagore's[13] panegyric is in keeping with a well-established historiographical formula that unites an otherwise diverse range of scholars, both Hindu and

---

[11] I wish I could claim this phrase, which I have adapted from Richard Handler and Daniel A. Segal, 'How European Is Nationalism?', *Social Analysis*, no. 32, 1992, pp. 1-15, at p. 4.

[12] R. N. Tagore 1935, 'Presidential Address', in S.C. Chakravarti (ed.), *Commemoration Volume of the Rammohun Roy Centenary Celebrations*, 2 volumes (Calcutta), vol. *ii*, p. 3.

[13] Reference by family name (e.g., 'Tagore') is a European convention; reference by given names (e.g., 'Rammohun') is a Bengali one. With obvious exceptions, I shall generally follow the European convention (which, apart from anything else, facilitates the checking of citations). In conformity with his own practice, I use the conventionally anglophone Rammohun Roy rather than the transliteral Rammohan (or Ram Mohan) Ray.

European. Rammohun, the 'father of modern India', is seen (whether approvingly or with resentment) as a conduit between enlightened Europe and a regressive Brahmin elite, who were awakened and vitalised by his campaign to reform Hinduism. This campaign, which Rammohun conducted in English and other languages, harmonised with the ideas of European philosophers and missionaries, in particular orientalist scholars who had devoted themselves to recovering Hinduism's pristine purity from beneath the corruptions that, in their view, had accumulated over the centuries that had elapsed since its original enunciation. In its orientalist rendering, pristine Hinduism bore a distinct resemblance to the monotheism and ethical precepts of the Christian West. Thus the price of Hindu redemption was the predicament that Partha Chatterjee has termed derivativeness. 'As inaugurator of modern India, therefore, Rammohun pioneered the embarrassing irony that the emancipatory ideology with which Indian nationalism sought to mobilise an anticolonial movement was itself a colonial endowment'.[14]

In the sectarian balance, Hindu renaissance is synonymous with Muslim decline. In claiming to have recovered Hinduism's lost glories, European Orientalists abetted a Brahminical narrative in which the intervening era of Muslim rule figured as a period of darkness and decay that separated an interrupted Hindu golden age from the present. In colonising India, the British East India Company was also delivering it from Islam. Through an analysis of Rammohun's reformist creed, I hope to show that Indian nationalism's derivation anxiety required not only the humiliation of colonial conquest but also the suppression of Islamic discourse as conditions of its possibility. The historical process of nationalist self-fashioning entailed the discursive erasure of this fact. Rammohun's career occupies a crucial transitional site in this regard, since the premises that were to secure his place as founder of modern India can be found already formulated in a Muslim-addressed tract written in Persian and Arabic that this Hindu figure published in 1804, over a decade before he embarked on the anglophone career of reform on which his reputation is based, and well before he had learned enough English to have had any meaningful exposure to European ideas.

The existence of this tract, the *Tuhfat-ul Muwahhiddin* ('Gift to Monotheists'), is well enough known.[15] The problems treated in the *Tuhfat* are classical ones. Their specification and assemblage, together with the propositional protocols employed, bear the unmistakable imprints of both Judaic and Hellenistic reasoning. Contrary to Eurocentric assumptions, however, this does not entail

---

[14] Partha Chatterjee 1986, *Nationalist Thought and the Colonial World: A Derivative Discourse?* (London: Zed for the United Nations University). Quote from Patrick Wolfe 2002, 'Can the Muslim Speak? An Indebted Critique', *History and Theory*, vol. 41, no. 3, pp. 367-80, at p. 374.

[15] Rammohun Roy 1975, *Tuhfat u'l Muwahhiddin*, translator O.E. Obaide, reproduced as appendix (24 pp) in K. C. Mitter and Rammohun Roy, *Rammohun Roy and Tuhfatul Muwahhidin* [sic] (Calcutta).

that they were taken from European sources since, in addition to sharing in Christianity's Hebraic inheritance, the Islamic philosophical canon incorporates a Greek legacy which is as profound as that of the Pauline West. This chapter is not concerned with Rammohun's individual qualities but with the optic that his career provides into the historical terrain that he so conspicuously occupied. His significance is extrinsic. Focusing on the *Tuhfat* enables us to see not only that Indian nationalism (at least, in its Bengali origins) was structured by the exclusion of Islam, which is hardly news. It also enables us to see the nationalist predicament of derivativeness in a reciprocal context. For the exclusion of Islam is also foundational to Western discourse – where, too, it represents a form of derivation anxiety.

In seeking to provincialise Europe in this way, the intention is not to metropolise anywhere else but to underscore the inter-textuality of the major discourses involved. This chapter will briefly survey the community between Islamic and Western discourse, on which basis it will identify the Islamic character of the *Tuhfat* and illustrate the extent to which Rammohun's post-1815 anglophone reformist ideology continued its distinctive principles. In conclusion, the chapter will consider some of the diverse ways in which the exclusion of Islam has been reproduced and maintained in the historiography of Indian nationalism. Taking salient examples from a varied range of histories – Christian-hagiographic, Hindu-nationalist, secular-liberal, Marxist, postcolonial – we shall see how, beneath their otherwise considerable differences, these accounts agree on excluding the Islamic inheritance that Rammohun Roy brought to the enunciation of Indian (proto-) nationalist discourse.

Arabic into Latin

In al-Andalus (Iberia), in the eleventh century of the Christian era, Ibn 'Abdun warned his fellow Muslims about the activities of the translators: 'One should not sell scientific books to Jews or Christians ... since they translate these scientific books, attributing authorship to their own bishops and coreligionists when they are actually Muslim works'.[16] Since Ibn 'Abdun's time, a minority tradition of Western scholarship (including Bacon, Leibniz, Voltaire, Gibbon and Priestley) has sought to rectify the suppression of Europe's scientific, philosophical and cultural debt to the Islamic or Arab-speaking world, a debt which was incurred in al-Andalus.[17] The background to the Andalusian

---

[16] Evariste Lévi-Provençal, translator, 1947, *Séville Mussulmane au début du XIIe siècle. Le traité d'Ibn 'Abdun sur la vie urbaine et les corps de metiers* (Paris), p. 128, § 206, my trans. from the French.

[17] Wolfe 2002, 'Can the Muslim Speak?', p. 375. For substantiation, see, e.g., Maxime Rodinson, 'The Western Image and Western Studies of Islam', in Joseph Schacht, with C. E. Bosworth (ed.) 1974, *The Legacy of Islam*, 2nd edition (Oxford: Clarendon), pp. 9-62; Rodinson 1987, *Europe and*

achievement can be briefly outlined.[18] In the wake of the division of the old Roman Empire into Eastern and Western blocs that were comparatively watertight (Sicily, extending up to Naples, being an exception), a rough distribution of the cultural inheritance of classical antiquity obtained whereby, while the Eastern (Byzantine) empire maintained the scientific, philosophical, literary and cultural legacy of Greece, the Western (or 'European') empire found itself the repository of the relatively reduced inheritance of the Latin world.[19] During the momentous century or so following Muhammad's death, Islam spread outwards from the land of its origins with an unstoppable vitality that exceeded even that of imperial Rome. In the process, most of Byzantium and Sassanian Persia were taken over and their Greek philosophical and scientific learning (though not the poetry and

the Mystique of Islam, translator R. Veinus (Seattle, WA: Washington University Press). For references from the nineteenth century on, see 'Abd al-Rahman Badawi 1968, *La Transmission de la philosophie grecque au monde arabe* (Paris: J. Vrin), pp. 181-7; Francis E. Peters 1968, *Aristoteles Arabus: The Oriental Translations and Commentaries on the Aristotelian Corpus* (Leiden: Brill), pp. 1-3; J-J. Waardenburg 1963, *L'Islam dans le miroir de l'Occident* (Paris: Mouton).

[18] Alternative accounts of the general history outlined in this and the following two paragraphs can be found in Roger Collins 1995, *Early Medieval Spain. Unity in Diversity 400-1000*, 2nd edition (Basingstoke: Macmillan), pp. 144-221; Richard Fletcher 1992, *Moorish Spain* (London: Weidenfeld and Nicolson); Thomas F. Glick 1979, *Islamic and Christian Spain in the Early Middle Ages* (Princeton, NJ: Princeton University Press), pp. 19-50; Gabriel Jackson 1972, *The Making of Medieval Spain* (London: Thames and Hudson), pp. 9-70; Joseph F. O'Callaghan 1975, *A History of Medieval Spain* (Ithaca, NY: Cornell University Press), pp. 89-357; Abdulwahid Dhanun Taha 1989, *The Muslim Conquest and Settlement of North Africa and Spain* (London: Routledge); Montgomery Watt 1965, *A History of Islamic Spain* (Edinburgh: Edinburgh University Press).

[19] M-T. D'Alverny 1982, 'Translations and Translators', in Robert L. Benson and Giles Constable, with C. D. Lanham (eds), *Renaissance and Renewal in the Twelfth Century* (Cambridge, MA: Harvard University Press), pp. 433-35; Nikita Elisséeff 1986, 'Les échanges culturels entre le monde musulmane et les croisés à l'époque de Nur ad-Din b. Zanki (m. 1174)', in Vladimir P. Goss and Christine Lerzár Bornstein (eds), *The Meeting of Two Worlds. Cultural Exchange between East and West during the Period of the Crusades* (Kalamazoo, MI: Medieval Institute Publications, Western Michigan University), p. 39; J. M. Millas-Vallicrosa 1963, 'Translations of Oriental Scientific Works to the End of the Thirteenth Century', in Guy S. Métraux and François Crouzet (eds), *The Evolution of Science. Readings from the History of Mankind* (New York, NY: New American Library), pp. 128-67, at pp. 128-30; R. Southern 1962, *Western Views of Islam in the Middle Ages* (Cambridge, MA: Harvard University Press), p. 8; Richard Walzer 1945–46, 'Arabic Transmission of Greek Thought to Medieval Europe', *Bulletin of the John Rylands Library*, vol. 29, pp. 160-83, at pp. 162-8. Minor exceptions to the general rule that Greek was not translated in western Christendom for around six centuries after the death of Boethius include Irish scholars such as Eriugena (John Scotus), but their work was religious rather than scientific (for references, see J. T. Muckle 1942, 'Greek Works Translated Directly into Latin Before 1350' [pt. 1], *Mediaeval Studies*, vol. 4, pp. 33-42.)

literature)[20] translated into Arabic, usually from the Syriac or other Byzantine language into which it had earlier been translated but sometimes from the original Greek. Over the next century or so, this learning was subject to the vicissitudes of survival under the aggressively militaristic regime of the Ummayyad Caliphate, but it managed to live on in the eastern outposts of the Islamic empire, particularly in exiled Nestorian centres of learning in eastern Persia, where it was augmented with scientific (especially astronomical) and mathematical knowledge emanating from India.[21] With the ascendancy of the 'Abassid Caliphate and the shifting of the political centre of the Islamic world to Baghdad, science and philosophy were actively encouraged and magnificent libraries assembled. The exiled legacy of ancient Greece was brought to the centre of Islamic culture, where, among other things, it was enlisted to buttress Islam's dialogic armature in response to disruptive theological problems, concerning revelation, monotheism, predestination and the like, which had arisen through contact with the different faiths of the conquered peoples. To secure key elements of the Islamic tradition which were still being transmitted orally, the 'Abassid caliphs sponsored the wholesale commitment of knowledge (including the Qur'an) to Arabic script, in the course of which project, during the eighth and ninth centuries of the Christian era, most of the Greek philosophical and scientific sources available today were translated into Arabic.[22]

Somewhat prior to these latter developments – in the early eighth century A.D. – and on the north-western frontier of the Ummayyad empire, Visigothic Andalusia was conquered in a series of expeditionary raids carried out by combined forces of Arabs and Berbers and brought under the administrative control of Qayrawan, the regional headquarters of the African segment of the empire, situated in modern Tunisia. Though the Berbers had adopted Islam,

---

[20] George F. Hourani 1972, 'The Medieval Translations from Arabic to Latin Made in Spain', *The Muslim World*, vol. 62, pp. 97-114, at p. 105; Franz Rosenthal 1992, *The Classical Heritage in Islam*, E. and J. Marmorstein translators (London: Routledge), p. 10; Walzer 1945–46, 'Arabic Transmission of Greek Thought', p. 162.

[21] For a list of translators from Greek, Sanskrit and Pahlavi (Persian) into Arabic at the Nestorian college at Jundishapur, see Mehdi Khan Nakosteen 1964, *History of Islamic Origins of Western Education, A.D. 800-1350* (Boulder, CO: University of Colorado Press), pp. 24-6. See also De Lacy O'Leary 1949, *How Greek Science Passed to the Arabs* (London: Routledge and Kegan Paul), pp. 96-130; Franz Rosenthal 1990, 'On Some Epistemological and Methodological Presuppositions of al-Biruni', in Rosenthal, *Science and Medicine in Islam: A Collection of Essays* (Aldershot: Variorum, c. xi), pp. 147, 153.

[22] The Greek originals of a number of important texts are still missing, so these remain available only from the Arabic. For examples, see Badawi 1968, *La transmission de la philosophie grecque au monde arabe*, pp. 119-80; Rosenthal 1992, *Classical Heritage*, p. 12; Walzer 1945–46, 'Arabic Transmission of Greek Thought', p. 164.

they maintained cultural and linguistic separateness and continually agitated against the overlordship of the Arab minority. This antagonism continued into al-Andalus, so that, when the 'Abassids expelled the Ummayyad caliph 'Abd ar-Rahman and his followers from Damascus in 750 A.D. and moved the capital to Baghdad, the fugitive ar-Rahman sought allies amongst the disaffected Berbers, at first in Africa but finally and successfully in al-Andalus, where he established his family dynasty from Cordoba in 755 A.D.

Despite the administrative and political dividedness of the Islamic world, a comparatively high degree of logistical cohesion was maintained. Relegated to provincial status in the far west, the Ummayyad sultans[23] in Cordoba displayed an attitude toward science and learning which was markedly different from that which had characterised their predecessors in the Damascus Caliphate. They patronised the importation of intellectual and scientific (especially medical) knowledge from the eastern centre and attracted a number of polyglot Jewish intellectuals from Mesopotamia and elsewhere. In its third century (i.e. during the 10th century A.D.), the Ummayyad dynasty in al-Andalus produced two rulers, 'Abd ar-Rahman III and al-Hakam II, who successively presided over a period of extraordinarily fruitful interchange and collaboration between Muslim, Jewish and Christian intellectuals, all writing in Arabic, in Cordoba, Toledo, Seville, Granada and other centres. By this stage, whatever a scholar's religion, the language of scholarship was definitively Arabic, and Muslim faith had no necessary connection to Arab ethnicity. In following centuries, the work of translation having been effectively completed, most of the greatest developers of the Hellenic tradition (Ibn Rushd [Averroës], Ibn Sinha [Avicenna] and Ibn Maymun [Maimonides] to cite but three) took their Aristotle, their Galen and their Neoplatonism from Arabic sources and did not even know Greek. The Greek only lived in the Arabic.[24]

This was the world of learning that became available for translation into the Latin of the Western Empire as a result of conquest – or, more specifically, of the *Reconquista*, the Christian *jihad* into al-Andalus through which an emergent Europe embarked on the Crusades. It should be stressed that 'world' of learning here signifies a dynamic tradition which, far from acting as an inert or neutral transmitter, creatively and critically engaged with the Greek legacy over a long period of time, extending it, changing its emphases, reshaping it and

---

[23] They became caliphs following a declaration by 'Abd ar-Rahman III in 929 A.D.

[24] Rosenthal 1992, *Classical Heritage*, p. 12. When, in the tenth century A.D., the Byzantine emperors Constantine VII and Romanus presented 'Abd ar-Rahman III with a Greek manuscript of Dioscorides' medicine, they failed to realise, as George Hourani put it, 'that there was nobody in Andalusia who could read Ancient Greek'. Hourani 1970, 'The Early Growth of the Secular Sciences in Andalusia', *Studia Islamica*, vol. 32, pp. 143-56, at p. 151.

incorporating new elements from outside.[25] The *Reconquista* brought about a coexistence of Latin speaking (or, at least, writing) conquerors and Arabic speaking locals, generating a requirement for dialogue and, accordingly, for translations and translators.[26] From the thirteenth century on, translation into Latin was increasingly done directly from the Greek.[27] Prior to this, however, from the tenth-century translations of information concerning the astrolabe to the comprehensive alienation of knowledge that fuelled the intellectual transformation that Charles Homer Haskins termed the 'Renaissance of the twelfth century',[28] Europe (or what was to become Europe) principally derived its scientific and philosophical advancement from its exposure to the Arabic tradition. Under different circumstances, things could have been otherwise – after all, the Greek texts had theoretically been available in western Christendom all along. As Haskins again put it, however, the Latin world '*could* have got much Greek science in this way, but for the most part it *did* not'.[29]

---

[25] See, e.g.: M.-T. d'Alverny 1982, 'Translations and Translators', in R. L. Benson and G. Constable (eds), *Renaissance and Renewal in the Twelfth Century* (Oxford: Clarendon Press), pp. 421-62; Anwar Chejne 1980, 'The Role of Al-Andalus in the Movement of Ideas Between Islam and the West', in Khalil I. Semaan (ed.), *Islam and the Medieval West. Aspects of Intercultural Relations* (Albany, NY: State University of New York Press), pp. 110-33; F. Gabrieli 1970, 'The Transmission of Learning and Literary Influences to Western Europe', in Peter M. Holt, Ann K. S. Lambton and Bernard Lewis (eds), *Cambridge History of Islam*, vol. 2 (Cambridge: Cambridge University Press), pp. 851-89; Charles Homer Haskins 1924, *Studies in the History of Mediaeval Science* (Cambridge, MA: Harvard University Press), pp. 3-19; Haskins 1925, 'Arabic Science in Western Europe', *Isis*, vol. 7, pp. 478-85; Haskins 1927, *The Renaissance of the Twelfth Century* (Cambridge, MA: Harvard University Press), pp. 278-302; R. Lemay 1963, 'Dans l'Espagne du XIIe siècle: les traductions de l'arabe au latin', *Annales*, vol. 18, pp. 639-65.

[26] Chejne 1980, 'Role of Al-Andalus', pp. 117-18; Norman Daniel 1975, *The Arabs and Medieval Europe* (Beirut), pp. 263-4; Hourani 1972, 'The Medieval Translations from Arabic to Latin', p. 101; Jean Jolivet 1988, 'The Arabic Inheritance', in Peter Dronke (ed.), *A History of Twelfth-Century Western Philosophy* (Cambridge: Cambridge University Press), p. 114.

[27] Though such diffuse processes are hard to date with any degree of clarity, it seems fair to nominate the (re)capture of Constantinople in 1204 A.D. as a turning-point in the shift to translation directly from the Greek. It can be difficult to detect the use of Arabic texts where translators suppressed their reliance on them (d'Alverny 1982, 'Translations and Translators', pp. 423-4; see also George Makdisi 1976, 'Interaction Between Islam and the West', *Revue des Etudes Islamiques*, vol. 44, pp. 287-309, at p. 308).

[28] Haskins 1927, *Renaissance of the Twelfth Century*.

[29] Haskins 1925, 'Arabic Science in Western Europe', p. 485, compare Haskins 1927, *Renaissance of the Twelfth Century*, p. 301.

Some scholars have attributed the European Renaissance and (by implication at least) the bulk of global modernity beyond it to Islamic inspiration,[30] while others have dismissed such claims as emanating from naive enthusiasm, Islamic conviction or both.[31] The non-committed have occupied a surprisingly narrow stretch of middle ground.[32] Through all this, the integrity of the Islamic Other has remained robust, since almost no-one has problematised the process whereby the substantial commonalities between Islamic and Western discourse have persistently been erased in favour of a stark and mutual contrariety (a notable exception is the work of Maria Rosa Menocal).[33] Focusing on the commonalities linking Islam and the West is at least superficially at odds with the stress on otherness that runs through Edward Said's *Orientalism*. Incommensurability does not plausibly account for the intensely specific virulence that has animated Western discourse on Islam. Islam gets under – more accurately, is already under – the skin of the West. The two have never been separate after all. Not only do we share a book, but Muslims have had the blasphemous temerity to find our Saviour deficient from within and to claim that an impostor has furnished them with the remedy. Pagans, savages or barbarians are merely ignorant; they cannot

---

[30] The strongest claims have been advanced by writers who are Muslim, e.g. M. M. Sharif's reference to Muslim philosophy's role in *inter alia*, 'Bringing about the Italian Renaissance', *A History of Muslim Philosophy*, vol. 1 (Wiesbaden, 1963), p. 8; compare Nakosteen 1964, *History of Islamic Origins of Western Education*, p. 186. A number of non-Muslim Western writers have not lagged far behind them. Consider the implications of, e.g. Eugene A. Myers' assertion that the translations 'shocked Europe out of its long slumber and ignited the explosive development of the West'. Myers, 1964, *Arabic Thought and the Western World in the Golden Age of Islam* (New York, NY: Ungar), p. 78. Or Donald Campbell's 'it is owing to the [Andalusian] Omayyad Caliphs that the sciences were preserved from extinction in Europe'. Campbell 1926, *Arabian Medicine and its Influence on the Middle Ages*, 2 volumes (London: Kegan Paul & Co.), vol. 1, p. 42. Compare David C. Lindberg 1978, 'The Transmission of Greek and Arabic Learning to the West', in his (ed.), *Science in the Middle Ages* (Chicago, IL: University of Chicago Press), p. 62; De Lacy O'Leary 1922, *Arabic Thought and Its Place in History* (London: Kegan Paul), pp. 290-1; Bernard F. Reilly 1992, *The Contest of Christian and Muslim Spain 1031–1157* (Oxford: Blackwell), pp. 255-6.

[31] e.g., H. A. R. Gibb 1955–56, 'The Influence of Islamic Culture on Medieval Europe', *Bulletin of the John Rylands Library*, vol. 38, pp. 84-5.

[32] See, e.g. C. Burnett 1992, 'The Translating Activity in Medieval Spain', in Salma Khadra Jayyusi (ed.), *The Legacy of Muslim Spain* (Leiden), pp. 1036-58, at p. 1046; Daniel 1975, *The Arabs and Medieval Europe*, p. 281; Hourani 1972, 'The Medieval Translations from Arabic to Latin Made in Spain', pp. 105, 107-08; Jolivet 1988, 'The Arabic Inheritance', pp. 123-4.

[33] Mariá Rosa Menocal 1987, *The Arabic Role in Medieval Literary History: A Fogotten Heritage* (Philadelphia, PA: University of Pennsylvania Press); Menocal 2002, *The Ornament of the World: How Muslims, Jews, and Christians Created a Culture of Tolerance in Medieval Spain* (Boston, MA: Little, Brown).

blaspheme. Nor can they frustrate the coming of universal Christianity. They are safely Other. To appreciate the intensity of Western discourse on Islam, we should recognise it as not simply a species of undifferentiated Othering, but as a quite specific suppression of sameness.[34] This consideration further underlines the historical contingency of the convergence between European Islamophobia and Hindu communalism, whose history is not marked by this particularity of European discourse.

Mughal to British

In the wake of the Clive's victory at Plassey in 1757 and the subsequent transfer of the Mughal right to administer and tax (*diwani*) to the East India Company in 1765, the political and economic bases to Muslims' marginalisation were spatially correlated in a general shift whereby major foci of power and learning followed the gravitation of economic activity to the British centre.[35] The formative years of the British regime saw Muslims generally left out of the economic, political and cultural boardrooms of the colonial interchange. As a Hindu *bhadralok* (member of the urban elite) steeped in Muslim culture, Rammohun is, therefore, a transitional figure who still evinces a confluence that would be emphatically undone in later colonial discourse.

Born into a Mughal court and dying in England, Rammohun even exceeded at being transitional. In between, his career encapsulated the sea-change going on around him. After a period of youthful travelling which seems to have included some formal Islamic training at Patna,[36] he accumulated considerable wealth through commercial dealings with British interests and took on a number of financial and estate management posts with British employers, in particular John Digby. In 1815, more than ten years after the publication of the *Tuhfat*, he settled in Calcutta, where he took up the tireless and multilingual public attack on corruptions and abuses for which he was to become renowned, rapidly antagonising Hindu orthodoxy by translating sacred writ into popular and even foreign languages. On the basis of his reading of the Hindu (which, for him, meant Vedantic) canon – a monotheistic, rationalist and socially reformist

---

[34] This recognition also has the virtue of restoring the Islamic specificity to Said's *Orientalism* (New York, NY: Pantheon Books, 1978), whose unwarranted extension to all and any alterity has, in my view, robbed it of its bite.

[35] A. F. Salahuddin Ahmed 1965, *Social Ideas and Social Change in Bengal, 1818–1835* (Leiden: Brill), pp. 37-8.

[36] Dilip Kumar Biswas and Prabat Chandra Ganguli 1962, 'Supplementary Notes', to Sophia Dobson Collet [1900], *The Life and Letters of Raja Rammohun Roy*, D. K. Biswas and P. C. Ganguli (eds) (Calcutta: Sadharan Brahmo Samaj), pp. 12-13, 18; Lant Carpenter 1833, *A Review of the Labours, Opinions, and Character of Rajah Rammohun Roy in a Discourse on Occasion of Death* (London: Rowland Hunter), pp. 101-2.

construction of sacred writ that strikingly resembled that of the European Orientalists – he launched a campaign to clean up Hinduism, singling out polytheism, idolatry and *sati* (burning widows alive) for particular attention. In contrast to European critics of contemporary Hinduism, however, Rammohun was even-handed in his denunciations, applying the same standards to Christian practices as he did to Hindu or Muslim ones. In my view, the adroit switch whereby he repeatedly held British institutions accountable on their own terms represents one of the formative moments of Indian nationalism. Accordingly, while he so admired Christian teachings that he learned Greek and Hebrew in order to translate the Gospel, his resultant *Precepts of Jesus* contained only the moral and social teachings, omitting the miracles, divine incarnation and other supernatural machinations that he regarded as irrational and absurd in popular Hinduism. Consistently, rejecting the Christian Trinity and Hindu polytheism alike, he set up the first public unitarian association in the world (the Atmiya Sabha, soon to develop into the Brahmo Samaj, whose influence on the nationalist movement would be disproportionate to its numbers,[37]) to which he attracted, among others, the Scottish evangelist William Adam (who thereby became known among the European community as the second fallen Adam!). In this and many other regards, Rammohun's public career articulated the characteristically nationalist demand for Indians and Europeans to be subject to a common set of rational universal conditions.[38]

The decade that intervened between the appearance of the *Tuhfat* and the commencement of that public career has led to the *Tuhfat*'s being seen as disconnected from Rammohun's historical mission. In consequence – and much more significantly – the genealogy of Indian nationalism is disconnected from the Indian Islamic tradition. As we shall see, however, there was no rupture between the *Tuhfat* and Rammohun's later programme. The decade in question

---

[37] The first Unitarian chapel had been founded in London by Theophilus Lindsey in 1774, but propagation had been a matter of private rather than public contact (the first service, for instance, was not publicly advertised). The first Unitarian periodical (Belsham's *Monthly Repository of Theological and General Literature*) did not appear until 1806 (i.e. after the *Tuhfat*), while the first Unitarian Associations in Britain and the USA were both established in 1825 – i.e. ten years after Rammohun's Atmiya Sabha. See E. M. Wilbur 1945, *A History of Unitarianism – in Transylvania, England and America* (Boston, MA: Beacon Press), pp. 285–6; S. Lavan 1973, 'Raja Rammohun Roy and the American Unitarians: New Worlds to Conquer (1821–1874)', in Barbara Thomas and Spencer Lavan (eds), *West Bengal and Bangla Desh: Perspectives from 1972* (East Lansing, MI: Asian Studies Center, Michigan State University), p. 3. Conrad Wright dated American Unitarianism proper from 1805, the year of Henry Ware's election as Hollis Professor of Divinity at Harvard. Wright 1976 [1955], *The Beginnings of Unitarianism in America* (Hamden, CT: Archon Books), p. iii.

[38] Compare Partha Chatterjee 1993, *The Nation and Its Fragments: Colonial and Postcolonial Histories* (Princeton, NJ: Princeton University Press), p. 10.

was probably taken up with such mundane but demanding distractions as the making of money and the learning of English. Thus we turn to the *Tuhfat*.

The *Tuhfat*

Rammohun's object in the *Tuhfat* is an 'enquiry into the truth and falsehood of various religions' (p. 19), an undertaking which has had him dubbed the founder of a characteristically post-Enlightenment enterprise, the science of comparative religions.[39] Again and again, in impeccably rational-empiricist style, he opposes the dead weight of unreflective habit (fostered by those with a vested interest in the maintenance of traditional institutions) to the pristine endowment (intuition, reason, sensory experience) which affords humanity the ever-present possibility of true belief ('Oh God give me strong power for making distinction between habit and nature', p. 9). True belief is attainable 'without instruction and guidance from anyone simply by keen insight into, and deep observation of, the mysteries of nature' (p. 8). These capacities are manifest and irrepressible, as evidenced by the fact that people everywhere and at all times acknowledge 'the existence of One Being' (p. 1), even though they conceptualise that Being in different ways. Despite this, however, divergent concepts of the attributes and requirements of the One Being ('an excrescent quality', p. 1) engender sectarian conflict. In common with the *philosophes*, the *Tuhfat* attributes distortions of the truth to priestcraft, the founders of religion being the 'first class of deceivers' (p. 8), who exploit the credulity of the common people by claiming miraculous or supernatural corroboration for their missions. Once their followers have accepted illogical or impossible beliefs, the way is open for their tolerance of correspondingly baneful social practices. Pre-eminent among such illogical beliefs is idolatry, which Rammohun excoriates tirelessly. He is also concerned to discredit miracles, noting drily (p. 11) that people are less gullible when it comes to concerns more worldly than religion. Where phenomena defy human understanding (as in the cases of 'many wonderful inventions of the people of Europe and the dexterity of jugglers', p. 10) then intuition would prefer to attribute the failure to the limitations of our own understanding than to 'some impossible agency inconsistent with the law of nature' (p. 10).

Whether in the *Tuhfat* or in his later works, Rammohun's writings only make consistent sense when they are read in relation to a constant set of strategic ends. Throughout his career, his sovereign end was equating monotheism with social benefit. So far as monotheism is concerned, Rammohun's problems start with the *Tuhfat*'s founding premises. For it is either the case that acknowledgement of the One Being is universal or that illogical beliefs are producing polytheism and idolatry, but surely not both. Indeed, if it really were the case that

---

[39] Sushil Kumar De 1962, *Bengali Literature in the Nineteenth Century (1757–1857)* [*sic*] (Calcutta: Firma K. L. Mukhopadhyay), p. 548, citing Monier Williams (without reference) in support.

monotheism was general, the *Tuhfat* would not have had a problem to address. Thus the appeal to popular sagacity which underlies the claim that monotheism is generally observable is starkly at odds with the *Tuhfat*'s contemptuous reference to the '*Muquallids* or common people following that religion [idolatry] by blind imitation' (p. 5). The point is not, of course, to critique the *Tuhfat* but to show that its inconsistencies are consistently motivated by Rammohun's pedagogical ends. Where they conduce to social benefit, for instance, religious beliefs that cannot be substantiated by either observation or reason are nonetheless excused the charge of illogicality. Hence irrational beliefs in souls and after-lives are to be excused in view of the restraining fear that they exercise, whereby people 'refrain from commission of illegal deeds' (p. 7). On this basis, even the founders of religion need not all be deceivers (Rammohun, after all, was later to become one himself). It depends on whether or not their teachings conform to Rammohun's particular version of the truth. This nexus in the *Tuhfat*'s thinking – the necessary interdependence of dualistic monotheism and social welfare – lies at the heart of the difficulty that Rammohun was trying to overcome in 1804. Associated with the link between monotheism and social welfare is Rammohun's dismay at the cruelty and corruption occasioned by religious sectarianism, which anticipates the Brahmo Samaj's linking of theistic universalism with social harmony. Similarly, as noted, Rammohun's desire to refute prophecy and revelation while privileging particular canonical traditions prefigures his selective invocation of the Vedanta.

The Orientalist narrative was inherently cyclical: a golden age had given way to an era of corruption from which redemption now offered itself. Given the Edenic structuring of this narrative (innocence – fall – redemption) the extent of its distribution through Western discourse is hardly surprising. By the same token, nor is it surprising that it should also structure Islamic discourse. In bringing together questions of reason, revelation, tradition and social welfare within an Edenic framework (founding truth – distortion – return to truth) the *Tuhfat* was conforming to a pervasive model. These *Tuhfat* themes continue to preoccupy Rammohun through his post-1815 writings, where they have been held to testify to a Christian and Utilitarian influence. I am not suggesting that the later Rammohun was unaffected by imported ideas – given the extraordinary historical foment in which he found himself, this would be unthinkable. Nonetheless, a reading of the *Tuhfat* shows that the principles of his anglophone ideology were already formulated before he could have been significantly exposed to such influences. In other words, Rammohun's endorsement of foreign doctrines arose from their concordance with a position that he had previously developed rather than from their novelty. Moreover, the *Tuhfat* treats issues and themes which had been extensively discussed in Indian Islamic disputation. Rammohun's characteristic arguments were recognisably drawn from this indigenous tradition, which had been developing in India for the better part of a millennium.[40]

Quite apart from these considerations, the idea that he could have been familiar with English writings in 1804 is rendered implausible by John Digby's account of the timing of Rammohun's acquisition of English. By 1801, he 'could merely speak it well enough to be understood on the most common topics of discourse, but could not write it with any degree of correctness'.[41] His sustained study of English appears to have commenced as late as 1809, when he became Digby's *dewan* (administrative agent) in Rangpur.[42] Rammohun's own anonymous account clearly dates his acquisition of English as subsequent to the *Tuhfat* (and, incidentally, affirms the *Tuhfat* as a precursor to his engagement with Christianity):

> ...Rammohun Roy; who, although he was born a Brahmin not only renounced idolatry at a very early period of his life, but published at that time a treatise in Arabic and Persian against that system, and no sooner acquired a knowledge of English, than he made his desertion of idol worship known to the Christian world by his English publication.[43]

Rammohun's association with Fort William College from 1801 to 1804, together with commercial activities that brought him into regular contact with East India Company servants, have been held to have been adequate for imparting a familiarity with Western philosophy and ethics,[44] but his lack of an adequate command of English makes this unlikely. Moreover, Colebrooke's landmark *Essay On The Vedas*, from which Rammohun is alleged to have derived his later

---

[40] I have sketched some of this background in Wolfe 2002, 'Can the Muslim Speak?', pp. 375-7.

[41] From Digby's preface to his 1817 London edition of Rammohun's translation of the *Kena Upanishad* and *Abridgement of the Vedanta*, quoted in Collet [1900] 1962, *Life and Letters*, p. 24. See also De 1962, *Bengali Literature in the Nineteenth Century*, pp. 509-10; Rajat K. Ray 1975, 'Introduction', in V. C. Joshi (ed.), *Rammohun Roy and the Process of Modernization* (Delhi: Vikas), pp. 1-20, at p. 8.

[42] Rammohun first entered Digby's service in 1805, at Ramgarh (Biswas and Ganguli 1962, 'Supplementary Notes', p. 37). Digby himself referred to Rammohun's mastering English by perusing his (Digby's) mail, conversing and corresponding with Englishmen and reading English newspapers whilst he was Digby's *dewan* – i.e. at Rangpur. Digby's Rangpur collectorship commenced in 1809. R. P. Chanda and J. K. Majumdar 1938, *Selections from Official Letters and Documents Relating to the Life of Raja Rammohun Roy* (Calcutta: Calcutta Oriental Book Agency), vol. 1, p. 41.

[43] Rammohun here refers to himself in the third person because, as was his wont, he had adopted a pseudonym (in this case, 'A Friend to Truth', *The English Works of Raja Rammohun Roy*, 6 volumes, Kalidas Nag and Debayjoti Burman (eds) (Calcutta, 1945–51), (henceforth *English Works*), vol. v, p. 58.

[44] See the discussion of David Kopf's account (below).

enthusiasm for the Vedanta, was not published until 1805 – i.e. after the *Tuhfat*[45] – so the monotheistic and socially benign principles that he was to divine in the Vedanta were certainly not new to him. Indeed, his most intense study of Hinduism would appear to have taken place at the same time as he was mastering English – in Rangpur, after 1809, in association with Hariharananda Tirthaswami.[46] In sum, therefore, the evidence renders any significant Western input into the *Tuhfat* implausible.

I have previously indicated some of the major lines of transmission whereby, *mutatis mutandis*, the Hellenistic legacy in Islam 'was also incorporated into the Mughal theatre of Islamic civilization, where the young Rammohun, whose Brahmin father was a Mughal courtier, came to imbibe it as a central component of his polyglot education'.[47] Of particular note is al-Shahrastani's Kitab *al-milal wa'l-nihal*, which was widely read in late eighteenth-century India, together with the teachings of Shah Wali-Allah of Delhi and his son Shah Abdul-Aziz. With more specific reference to Rammohun's immediate milieu, the Persian *Dabistan Mazahib* (conference of religions), which was inspired by religious debates that had taken place at the court of the ecumenically-inclined Mughal emperor Akbar, is significant. The *Dabistan*

> was well-known among Islamic scholars in eighteenth-century Calcutta. Maulavi Nazr Ashraf of the *Sadr Diwani Adalat*, whom Rammohun would have known, edited the first printed edition of the *Dabistan*.[48] Francis Gladwyn had translated the first chapter into English in 1789.[49] The rest of the work was not translated into English until 1843, ten years after Rammohun's death (Anthony Troyer, one of the translators of the 1843 edition, had known him personally).[50] The *Dabistan* is devoted to comparative discussion of religions, including Islam, Hinduism, Judaism, Christianity and others. So far as Rammohun is concerned, the most striking section occurs towards the end of the work – in the third volume – where Akbar's *Ilahi* [personal faith] is represented by a philosopher

---

[45] Henry T. Colebrooke's book was originally published in *Asiatic Researches*, vol. 8 (1805), pp. 369-476.

[46] Ray 1975, 'Introduction', p. 8; Rachel van M. Baumer 1975, 'The Reinterpretation of Dharma in Nineteenth Century Bengal: Righteous Conduct for Man in the Modern World', in Baumer (ed.), *Aspects of Bengali History and Society* (Hawaii, HI; University Press of Hawaii), pp. 82-98, at p. 87.

[47] Wolfe 2002, 'Can the Muslim Speak?', p. 375.

[48] Ajit Kumar Ray 1976, *The Religious Ideas of Rammohun Roy* (New Delhi: Kanak Publications Books India Project), p. 22.

[49] ibid.

[50] Anthony Troyer (ed.) 1843, 'Preliminary Discourse', in *The Dabistan, or School of Manners*, David Shea and Anthony Troyer translators, 3 volumes (Paris, 1843), vol. *i*, p. 118.

who engages in disputation with, among others, a Muslim, a Christian and a Brahmin. The *Dabistan*'s philosopher thus took on adversaries almost identical to those whom Rammohun was later to engage.[51]

Whether or not Rammohun was directly indebted to the *Dabistan*, however, the point at issue is the availability of an indigenous discourse rather than his personal relationship to it.

Where intertextualities are concerned, it is difficult to nail down particular influences from within a complex and evolving world tradition with any degree of confidence. It has been asserted that the major Islamic influence on the *Tuhfat* was the Mu'tazilite school (or heresy) which flourished in Baghdad and other centres from the eighth to the eleventh centuries of the Christian era.[52] The Mu'tazilites championed the primacy of reason and freedom of the will, maintained the strictest interpretation of monotheism and denied the eternity of the Qur'an. They also insisted that their beliefs conduced to a just social order.[53] The Mu'tazilites would thus seem to present a plausible precedent for Rammohun's central contentions (though his concept of social justice was at stark variance to theirs). But there is no reason why he should have lifted his ideas from one Islamic source alone. Rather, the premises and concepts which animate the *Tuhfat* recur throughout Islamic disputation. To illustrate the manifest general influence, it is hard to avoid arbitrariness. I happen to find greater resonance between the writings of al-Razi and the *Tuhfat* than I do between the Mu'tazilites and Rammohun's text, but this is not to say that this influence was necessarily formative either. Al-Razi's attitude to knowledge was consistent with utilitarianism. He valued knowledge in proportion to its practical worth. The three means whereby he ensured the reliability of knowledge were the same as those of the *Tuhfat* – reason, intuition and authentic tradition. Consistently with this, al-Razi valued treatises on astronomy, logic, geometry and medicine more highly than sacred works, even than the Bible and the *Qur'an*.[54]

These sentiments not only recall the *Tuhfat*. They also harmonise with the controversial letter on education that Rammohun was to write to Lord Amherst nearly twenty years after the *Tuhfat* was published. In this letter, Rammohun recalled the 'sanguine hopes' that money earmarked for an educational institution would have been 'laid out in employing European gentlemen of talents and

---

[51] Wolfe 2002, 'Can the Muslim Speak?', p. 377.

[52] Cyril Glassé 1989, *The Concise Encyclopaedia of Islam* (London: Stacey International), p. 292; compare Rosenthal 1992, *Classical Heritage*, pp. 4-5.

[53] Mir Valiuddin 1963, 'Mu'tazilism', in M. M. Sharif (ed.), *A History of Muslim Philosophy*, vol. 1, pp. 199-220, at p. 200.

[54] Badawi 1968, *La transmission de la philosophie grecque*, p. 446.

education to instruct the natives of India in Mathematics, Natural Philosophy, Chemistry, Anatomy and other useful Sciences'. Since a traditional Hindu school had been chosen instead, one like those that already abounded in India to no social advantage, Rammohun complained that 'This seminary ... can only be expected to load the minds of youth with grammatical niceties and metaphysical distinctions of no practicable use to the possessors or to society.'[55] These sentiments, which are clearly in accord with the views of al-Razi and others like him, also recall the split that Partha Chatterjee has shown to haunt the articulation of Indian nationalism.[56] For Rammohun would have plenty of time for metaphysics in other contexts. But metaphysics belonged in the inner world of Indian culture and spirituality, a world that was quite separate from the outer world of material advancement that it was proper for Europeans to make available to Indians.

Al-Razi was familiar with Indian science, which he employed in his medical practice. The traffic was not one-way. Further, while al-Razi himself may not have attracted widespread support, his works were extolled by al-Buruni, whose writings on India secured him continuing attention there.[57] The correspondences multiply. Half a millennium after al-Razi, the aforementioned Shah Abdul-Aziz exhibited a split attitude to the British which also anticipated Rammohun's. As observed, Rammohun was to treat traditional Sanskritic learning as an internal Hindu matter, demanding that the British should not involve themselves with 'useless' (in material-scientific terms) metaphysical concerns but should provide a progressive Western education. Similarly, Shah Abdul-Aziz issued a *fatwah* declaring land occupied by the British to be *daru'l harb* (infidel territory)[58] whilst simultaneously permitting the study of English and extolling British achievements in arts and industry.[59] This ambivalence prefigures the division in the Indian Muslim elite, embodied in the Deoband and Aligarh schools, which

---

[55] This letter, which is inexplicably missing from *English Works* (1945–51), is quoted in Collet [1900] 1962, *Life and Letters*, p. 458.

[56] Chatterjee 1986, *Nationalist Thought and the Colonial World*; Chatterjee 1993, *Nation and Its Fragments*.

[57] Richard Walzer 1962, *Greek Into Arabic. Essays on Islamic Philosophy* (Oxford: Bruno Cassirer), p. 17; Rosenthal 1990, 'Presuppositions of al-Biruni'.

[58] *Fatawa*, vol. 1, p. 17, cited in K. A. Nizami 1971, 'Socio-Religious Movements in Indian Islam (1763–1898)', in S. T. Lokhandwalla (ed.), *Indian and Contemporary Islam (Proceedings of a Seminar)* (Simla), p. 192.

[59] *Fatawa*, vol. 1, p. 195, *Malfuzat*, p. 51, both cited in Nizami 1971, 'Socio-Religious Movements', p. 102.

corresponded to the division in Brahmo Samaj ranks that David Kopf has attributed to Rammohun's own split approach.[60]

In short, one could go on citing correspondences indefinitely. Persistence is ultimately unnecessary, however, since the *Tuhfat* itself explicitly and abundantly declares its Islamic orientation. The issue is not the *Tuhfat*'s Islamic credentials, which can hardly be doubted, but its continuity with Rammohun's anglophone campaign of reform as that was conducted in texts that he published after settling in Calcutta in 1815.

The English writings

The premises that dominate Rammohun's English writings are precisely those that had earlier dominated the *Tuhfat*. Still pairing monotheism and social utility,[61] his later publications repetitively champion reason and sensory experience as grounds for discrediting institutionalised traditions and furthering his own brand of sacred writ in a manner wholly conforming to the *Tuhfat*'s argumentation. Accordingly, while regularly citing Hindu authorities in support of his contentions, he is careful to establish that the doctrines which he associates with these authorities are both rationally sound and socially beneficial:

> I agree in the first assertion, that certain writings received by the Hindus as sacred, are the origins of the Hindu law of inheritance, but with this modification, that the writings supposed sacred are only, when consistent with sound reasoning, considered as imperative.[62]

As in the *Tuhfat*, distortions of scripture are promoted by leaders of religion, who prey on the ignorance of the populace.[63] Institutions sponsored by leaders of religion foster division and war between people, 'everlasting dissensions' being occasioned by their conflicting interpretations of original truths.[64] Not only do the leaders of religions remain the first class of deceivers, but the *Tuhfat*'s positive formula for the attainment of true belief remains the same. Thus the induction from nature whereby the *Tuhfat* argued that God's existence was inferrable by everyone is ascribed to Vyasa's position in the Vedanta, which explains 'the Supreme Being by his effects and works, without attempting to

---

[60] David Kopf 1969, *British Orientalism and the Bengal Renaissance: The Dynamics of Indian Modernization, 1773–1835* (Berkeley, CA: University of California Press); Kopf 1979, *The Brahmo Samaj and the Shaping of the Modern Indian Mind* (Princeton, NJ: Princeton University Press).

[61] The combination that Sumit Sarkar termed 'the two standards of "reason" and "social comfort" which recur so often in his works.' (Sarkar 1975, 'Rammohun Roy and the Break with the Past', in Joshi, *Rammohun Roy and the Process of Modernization*, p. 48).

[62] *English Works* (1945–51), vol. *i*, p. 20.

[63] ibid., vol. *ii*, p. 0. Compare ibid., vol. *ii*, pp. 44, 85, 88.

[64] ibid., vol. *vi*, p. 39; vol. *i*, p. 14.

define his essence'.⁶⁵ Accordingly, divine truth is not the preserve of any single creed.⁶⁶ That this rules out miracles is presupposed in the selection criteria of the *Precepts of Jesus* and explicated in the *Appeals* in their defence: 'Had his doctrines of themselves made that due impression, the aid of miracles would not have been requisite, nor had recourse to.'⁶⁷

To substantiate his claim that all religions are monotheistic, the later Rammohun returns to the *Tuhfat*'s empirical premise:

> ...in China, in Tartary, in Europe and in all other countries, where so many sects exist, all believe the object whom they adore to be the Author and Governor of the Universe; consequently, they must also acknowledge, according to their own faith, that this our worship is their own.⁶⁸

Rationally unsustainable eschatologies are excused in the English writings on grounds that are familiar from the *Tuhfat*:

> The virtues of this class [i.e. peasants or villagers] however rests chiefly upon their primitive simplicity, and a strong religious feeling which leads them to expect reward or punishment for their good or bad conduct, not only in the next world, but like the ancient Jews, also in this.⁶⁹

Similarly, Rammohun's regard for Christian ethics, the single issue around which the allegation of Western models is strongest, is expressed in the Introduction to the *Precepts of Jesus* in terms which are pure *Tuhfat*:

> a notion of the existence of a supreme superintending power, the Author and Preserver of this harmonious system ... and a due estimation of that law which teaches that man should do unto others as he would wish to be done by ... The former of these sources of satisfaction, viz, a belief in God, prevails generally; being derived either from tradition and instruction, or from attentive survey of the wonderful skill and contrivance displayed in the works of nature ... [the latter] ... moral doctrines, tending evidently to the maintenance of the peace and harmony of mankind at large, are beyond the reach of metaphysical perversion, and intelligible alike to the learned and to the unlearned.⁷⁰

Where Christianity is concerned, though Rammohun values the connection between religion and good works, he is not prepared to overlook offences for

---

⁶⁵ ibid., vol. *ii*, p. 63; compare vol. *ii*, p. 129.
⁶⁶ ibid., vol. *ii*, pp. 72, 89, 124.
⁶⁷ ibid., vol. *v*, p. 64.
⁶⁸ ibid., vol, *ii*, p. 130.
⁶⁹ ibid., vol. *iii*, p. 64.
⁷⁰ ibid., vol. *v*, pp. 3, 4.

which he criticised other religions in the *Tuhfat* .[71] Thus he condemns Christian sectarianism as well as its miracles and paradoxes.[72] In common with Muslim theologians, he asserts that Trinitarianism is a later corruption of an originally monotheistic creed, in one place attributing the origin of Islam to this corruption.[73] He compares the Inquisition and witch-burning to *sati*. In short, he holds Christianity to account on its own terms – a tactic which, as I contended above, was formative for Indian nationalism.

In this light, we need to consider why Rammohun should have chosen Christianity as a vehicle for his ideals in his English writings, especially since Islam was equally compatible with them. He testified to studying Euclid and Aristotle from Arabic sources.[74] Moreover, not only did he dress (see illustration), eat and even, it seems, marry in a Muslim manner.[75] He commended Muslims, along with Sikhs, Christians and the Kabir Panth, as renouncers of idolatry,[76] he characterised the idea that Christ personified the mercy of God as a Muslim concept,[77] he acknowledged the monotheistic purity of Islam,[78] he noted that,

---

[71] One of his more memorable critiques of the doctrine of the Trinity confirmed the *Tuhfat*'s emphasis on childhood conditioning: 'These missionary gentlemen have come out to this country in the expectation, that grown men should first give up the use of their external senses, and should profess seriously, that although the Father is ONE God and the Son is ONE God and the Holy Ghost is ONE God, yet the number of God does not exceed ONE – a doctrine which though unintelligible to others, having been imbibed by these pious men with their mothers' milk, is of course as familiar to them as the idea of the animation of the stony goddess "Kali" is to an idolatrous Hindu, by whom it has, in like manner, been acquired in infancy'. *English Works* (1945–51), vol. *ii*, p. 180; compare vol. *ii*, pp. 105, 162, 163, 183; vol. *iv*, p. 48.

[72] ibid., vol. *v*, pp. 58-9.

[73] ibid., vol. *v*, p. 62; vol. *vi*, pp. 54-5.

[74] So Rammohun informed Lant Carpenter. Mary Carpenter (ed.), *The Last Days in England of the Rajah Rammohun Roy*, 3rd edition (Calcutta, 1915), p. 2. See also Rammohun's 'Autobiographical Sketch', reproduced in Carpenter (ed.), *Last Days in England*, pp. 28-9.

[75] Most contemporary pictures of Rammohun depict him in Muslim dress (illustration from Collet [1900] 1962, *Life and Letters*, facing p. 128, see also frontispiece and illustration facing p. 360). See also Romesh Chandra Majumdar 1978, *History of Modern Bengal, Part One (1765–1905)* (Calcutta: G. Bharadwaf) , p. 54 (including diet); Salahuddin Ahmed 1965, *Social Ideas and Social Change*, p. 36. Though, by his father's arrangement, married three times in his youth to Hindu women, Rammohun seems later to have married a Muslim woman (whose name I cannot trace) by the unorthodox *shaiva* form of marriage, she being the only one of his wives to accompany him to Calcutta (De 1962, *Bengali Literature in the Nineteenth Century*, p. 504).

[76] *English Works* (1945–51), vol. *ii*, p. 89.

[77] ibid., vol. *ii*, p. 93.

[78] ibid., vol. *i*, p. 30 (where there is no mention of the Sunni/Shia divide).

in contrast to the divisions within Hinduism, Muslims observed one homogeneous and harmonious social order,[79] and, in evidence to a select committee of the British House of Commons, even suggested that there were more honest Muslim lawyers than Hindu ones.[80] In these connections, though, he was addressing a predominantly English audience, so Christianity was the appropriate strategic idiom for him to adopt. Furthermore, given the effective eclipse of Mughal rule, Islamic discourse was marginal to colonial power. In Muslim dress, Rammohun's universalism might have appealed to *munshi*s, but no-one else would have noticed. Since this is precisely the fate that had befallen the *Tuhfat*, it is no accident that he should have started to learn English a short time after its publication.[81]

Raja Rammohun Roy
After a painting by H. P. Briggs, Bristol Museum. Blocks lent by the Prabasi, Calcutta.

One could go on producing examples of the concordance between Rammohun's English writings and the *Tuhfat* but it hardly seems necessary. A difficulty in

---

[79] ibid., vol. *i*, p. 13.

[80] ibid., vol. *iii*, p. 16.

[81] It is significant that the *Tuhfat* stands out as a major work that Rammohun did not translate. This is consistent both with its intended audience being Muslim and with Rammohun's not yet knowing English (compare Sarkar 1975, 'Rammohun Roy and the Break with the Past', p. 50).

presenting this argument is that a reading of Rammohun's corpus bears it out so consistently that substantiation becomes a labouring of the obvious. Thus we turn now to the historiography, considering some salient examples of a pervasive cross-factional consensus whereby Rammohun's career has served to effect a rupture between Indian Islam and the enunciation of Indian nationalism.

Polar history writing

Traditional histories of the emergence of Indian nationalism conventionally counterpose Christian Europe to Hindu India, an exclusive pairing that admits a number of variations. The predominantly literary quality of the model of the Brahmannical/Christian encounter excludes the unlettered discourses of debt-bonded subalterns. It also effaces the generality of Muslims. In particular, the image of British foreigners taking over from Mughal foreigners suggests that Indian Muslims had somewhere to go back to. It does not matter where. Their effective disappearance is the practical outcome.

The same exclusion operates in a variety of historiographical guises. Some are obvious. It is only to be expected, for instance, that a Christian account should play down the consequence of Islam and emphasise that of Christianity. Sophie Dobson Collet's *The Life and Letters of the Raja Rammohun Roy*[82] was a pious exercise designed to demonstrate the virtues of a colonial subject to an English readership. It remains the most widely cited secondary source on Rammohun. Collet did not question the *Tuhfat*'s manifestly Islamic provenance; she simply discounted its significance for Rammohun's later career. Nonetheless, as a Unitarian convert to Trinitarian Christianity, she remained able to acknowledge that it was 'indubitable that Rammohun always retained a large amount of sympathy with Islam for the sake of its cardinal doctrine of the unity of God, and that he warmly appreciated the good which had thence resulted in counteracting Hindu idolatry'.[83]

Though a Hindu nationalist is as likely as a Christian to discount Islam, the situation is complicated by Rammohun's having a foot in two camps – how to relegate the Muslim part without jeopardising the nationalist part? This dilemma found serial realisation in the work of Romesh Chandra Majumdar, the doyen of Hindu-nationalist historians. Majumdar consistently stressed Hindu/Muslim dividedness and cast Islam as antithetical to the nationalist ('freedom') movement.[84] In keeping with this view, Majumdar divided British domination

---

[82] Collet [1900] 1962, *The Life and Letters of Raja Rammohun Roy* (London: Harold Collet), citations from 3rd edition (Calcutta: Sadharan Brahmo Samaj).

[83] Collet [1900] 1962, *Life and Letters*, p. 22.

[84] See, e.g. R. C. Majumdar 1960, *Glimpses of Bengal in the Nineteenth Century* (Calcutta: Firma K. L. Mukhopadhyay), pp. 7-9.

into two phases, a benign one (the suppression of Muslim power) and an oppressive, subsequent one. From a communal perspective such as this, it would be unthinkable that a major restatement of Hindu ethics should have sprung from Islamic precedents. Thus Rammohun must have got his ideas from the West. Majumdar did not shrink from iconoclasm; this made Rammohun the first great comprador.[85] Yet this evaluation marked an extraordinary turnabout. Ten years earlier, in his *History of the Freedom Movement in India*, Majumdar had represented Rammohun as the 'first and best representative' of the new spirit of rationalism.[86]

In a manner reminiscent of European Orientalism, the earlier Majumdar had singled out Rammohun's opposition to 'medieval' forces for particular credit, medieval and Mughal being readily interchangeable. Thus Rammohun could enlist British inspiration to rouse India from a period of medieval decay without unduly compromising the Hindu nation's credentials. Despite their incongruity, Majumdar's ambivalent versions of Rammohun consistently sustained a Hindu-nationalist agenda. Since the Mughals were no less foreign than their British conquerors, the early phase of British domination could figure as the lesser of two evils in a way that did not have to compromise nationalist memory. The contrasting depictions of Rammohun do not affect this outcome. All that changes is the periodisation: the earlier depiction makes him part of the benign phase of British rule, while, in the revised version, the same actions, displaced into its oppressive phase, become compradorship. Either way, Islam is excluded from a nationalist version of the colonial duality.

The exclusion of Islam does not require a religious basis, however. A secular dichotomy – especially the modern liberal assimilation of East/West to traditional/modern – is no less solidifying within its poles. David Kopf's bifurcated title, *British Orientalism and the Bengal Renaissance*, belies his attempts to complexify the two parties to the colonial encounter. For, although he went to considerable lengths to show how the category 'British' split up into conservative/liberal, Orientalist/Anglicist and so on (with the *bhadralok* correspondingly divided into orthodox/progressive, etc.), Kopf failed to avoid the familiar dualism of penetration and response.

From its title on, Kopf's subsequent book, *The Brahmo Samaj and the Shaping of the Modern Indian Mind*,[87] makes even grander claims for Rammohun's legacy. This book's manifest pretension is to the reconstruction of a quantity known as 'the modern Indian mind' from the evidence of a small association of Bengali

---

[85] R. C. Majumdar 1972, *On Rammohun Roy* (Calcutta: Asiatic Society).

[86] R. C. Majumdar 1962, *A History of the Freedom Movement in India*, 3 volumes (Calcutta: Firma K. L. Mukhopadhyay), vol. 1, pp. 291, 308, 312.

[87] Kopf 1979, *The Brahmo Samaj and the Shaping of the Modern Indian Mind*.

bhadralok, without regard either to the whole of Muslim society or to the rest of the Hindu population (or, for that matter, to the rest of India). In it, Kopf returns to the European division between Orientalists and Anglicists, reaffirming Rammohun's encounter with Orientalism as the model for the rest of the century (and, presumably, for the entire 'modern Indian mind').

Kopf's Orientalist-Anglicist controversy corresponds to Majumdar's chronological division of British colonialism. The era of Orientalist predominance, of which Kopf approves, accords with Majumdar's early benign period, while the ensuing Anglicist ascendancy is for both scholars a victory for racial suprematism. Regardless of their doctrinal differences, both require a division whereby British rule has an early, relatively benevolent phase, since they use this phase to graft Europe's ideological import onto a Hindu version of indigenous tradition.

The notion of colonialism having a positive initial phase is also stamped on Indian Marxism, where it has caused any number of problems. Without embarking on a resuscitation of the Asiatic Mode of Production, we should at least recall in this connection that the Marx of the *New York Daily Tribune* articles saw British incursion, for all its violent rapacity, as injecting the historical germ necessary to disrupt the stagnant balance of Indian society and let loose the dynamic tensions which would eventually propel India into the capitalist era and thence on to its own socialist revolution.[88] In conformity with this perspective (and with his Comintern line that the revolution would flow from the colonies), the pioneer Indian communist M. N. Roy contended that the iron hand of British rule provided the objective conditions for an Indian act of emancipation,[89] while Palme Dutt maintained that the 'objectively progressive' aspect of British colonialism was its destruction of village economies that had prevented people from rising above subsistence preoccupations.[90]

In a colonial context, one of the drawbacks of orthodox Marxism is that the category 'class' is blind to ethnic differences. The religious and colour-coded nature of colonial domination seems incidental.[91] Thus we should not expect that an Islamic increment should significantly affect a Marxist critique of *bhadralok* ideology. The issue is not the etymology of comprador thinking but

---

[88] 'England has to fulfil a double mission in India: one destructive, the other regenerating – the annihilation of old Asiatic society, and the laying of the material foundations of Western society in Asia...' Karl Marx, 'The Future Results of the British Rule in India', in Marx and F. Engels 1959, *The First Indian War of Independence, 1857–1859* (Moscow: Foreign Languages Publishing House), p. 30.

[89] M. N. Roy, *Indian in Transition* (Bombay, 1922).

[90] R. Palme Dutt 1940, *India To-Day* (London: Victor Gollancz).

[91] Patrick Wolfe 1997, 'Culture and Imperialism: One Hundred Years of Theory, from Marx to Postcolonialism', *American Historical Review*, vol. 102, no. 2, pp. 388-420, at p. 407.

its conformity with colonial relations of production. In a careful analysis of the material conditions of Rammohun's thought, S. N. Mukherjee did not erect the usual barrier between the *Tuhfat*, to which he attached considerable importance, and the rest of Rammohun's ideas. He also allowed the possibility of looking on Rammohun as a tantric opponent of Bengali Vaishnavism and/or as 'the last prophet of the Indo-Islamic syncretic movement carrying on the tradition of Kabir, Dara Shikoh [Akbar's son] and many others'.[92] Ultimately, however, the dual encounter – in this case, East versus West as feudal (or Asiatic) versus capitalist – was bound to eclipse such heterodox inspirations:

> Rammohun's faith in individualism was inspired by Western political philosophy, more particularly by the works of Locke and Bentham, but individualism was also part and parcel of the social, religious and economic aspirations of the Bengali middle class. Moreover, the social model of Rammohun – a competitive market society – corresponds to the social reality of Bengal in the early Nineteenth Century.[93]

I am not suggesting that Rammohun was impervious to Bentham (he was not). The point is, rather, that 'individualism' is not dependant on Bentham (read Europe). It can select other notations. For instance, Maxime Rodinson argued cogently that the Neoplatonic tradition in Islam provided a model for individualistic philosophy that was as capable as its Western-Christian counterpart of subtending an emergent local capitalism.[94] The issue is important because the one-to-one correlation between 'market society' and certain European philosophers makes individualism (among other things) impossible without European invasion. This, in turn, subordinates Indian history to the global narrative of European capitalist expansion as surely as missionary ideologues subordinated it to the coming of universal Christianity. Mukherjee's account is built on what Partha Chatterjee terms 'the condition of discursive unity':

> This condition is nothing other than the assumption that the history of Europe and the history of India are united within the same framework of universal history, the assumption that made possible the incorporation of the history of India into the history of Britain in the nineteenth century: Europe became the active subject of Indian history because Indian history was now a part of 'world history'.[95]

---

[92] S. N. Mukherjee 1974, 'The Social Implications of the Political Thought of Raja Rammohun Roy', in V. S. Sharma and V. Jha (eds), *Indian Society – Historical Probings (in Memory of D. D. Kosambi)* (New Delhi: People's Publishing House), p. 366.

[93] ibid., p. 361.

[94] Maxime Rodinson 1974, *Islam and Capitalism*, Brian Pearce translator (London: Allen Lane). See also Samir Amin 1989, *Eurocentrism*, Russell Moore translator (London: Zed), pp. 55-7.

[95] Chatterjee 1993, *Nation and Its Fragments*, pp. 32-3.

In substantially ruling out an Islamic contribution to the enunciation of colonial nationalism, however, Chatterjee himself might be seen to have subscribed to a global incorporation. In his influential postcolonial account, which merits more extended consideration, Chatterjee scrupulously and regularly registers Indian nationalism's dependence on the exclusion of Islam.[96] Yet there is a tension between this acknowledgement and the structuring of his narrative. In his account, the predicament of derivation produced a powerful dual agenda. On the one hand, Indian nationalism aspired to the technical, material and political advantages that colonialism had made available; on the other, it sought to resist the colonisers' intrusions into native life. The outcome was a division into discursive domains that resemble the public and private spheres of feminist critique. Thus outer became to inner as material to spiritual, as universal to particular, as economic to cultural and so on, a trade-off whereby nationalists' rising to the colonial bait in the domain of science, economics and statecraft was counterbalanced by an aggressive particularism, an insistence on irreducible difference in the inner-family world of Bengali language, religion and culture. For Chatterjee, this inner domain, which gave nationalism the autonomous difference from Europe that a self-conscious and self-producing national project required, was prerequisite to the development of political nationalism, conventionally dated from the founding of the Indian National Congress in 1885. This reversal of the received order of priorities enables Chatterjee to backdate the emergence of nationalism proper to the 1860s, which saw the development of a new, self-regulating internal realm of Bengali language and culture with the confidence to exclude Europeans. Though his prioritising of nationalism's inner realm enables Chatterjee to date nationalism from the aftermath of the Great Insurrection of 1857 (which the *bhadralok* had failed to support), it also instals a rupture between the preceding period of reform and the nationalist movement. Nationalist self-sufficiency is distinguished from Rammohun-style reform, which sought to regulate Bengali society by enlisting the support of the colonial masters. The problem here is that Indian Islam also lies on the other side of this rupture. Thus we should consider Chatterjee's periodisation.

As observed, what interests Chatterjee is not so much the separation of nationalism's two discursive domains as their mutual effects, the ways in which each 'has not only acted in opposition to and as a limit upon the other, but, through this process of struggle, has also shaped the emergent form of the other'.[97] This dynamic mutuality leaves behind the static pairings – traditional

---

[96] e.g. 'The idea of the singularity of national history has inevitably led to a single source of Indian tradition, namely, ancient Hindu civilization. Islam here is either the history of foreign conquest or a domesticated element of everyday popular life. The classical heritage of Islam remains external to Indian history', Chatterjee 1993, *Nation and Its Fragments*, p. 113.

[97] ibid., p. 12.

versus modern, status versus contract, feudal versus capitalist, etc. – that colonial discourse has made familiar. Thus subalternity is not simply a feudal throwback, and the nationalist elite are more than merely an incomplete version of the capitalist moderne. Rather, together and singly, in their ceaseless co-formation, they are historically specific. This interpenetration of the two poles, a Saussurian procedure inherited from Ranajit Guha, performs a crucial methodological function. It is the basis on which the *Subaltern Studies* group insists that Hindu–Muslim antagonism is not some atavistic residue from a superseded era but an active constituent of colonial modernity. This structuralist element, shared with the earlier Foucault, is conducive to abruptness of periodisation (Chatterjee terms his version of Foucault's episteme shift a 'narrative break').[98]

In before-and-after mode, Chatterjee reads Mritunjay Vidyalankar's history of India, published in Bengali in 1808, to show how the inculcation of European narrative forms modernised the historical consciousness of educated Bengalis. Mritunjay's[99] narratology, which Chatterjee memorably dubs 'entirely pre-colonial', is shown to lack the distinguishing features of the first criterion of nationalist history writing, a consciousness of the nation as historical agent and of the historian as forming part of it. Rather, the agents in Mritunjay's chronicle are gods and kings.[100] Moving forward half a century, Chatterjee then finds the requisite national agency, and historians identifying with it, in Bengali textbooks of the 1860s and 1870s:

> History was no longer the play of divine will or the fight of right against wrong; it had become merely the struggle for power. The advent of British rule was no longer a blessing of Providence. English-educated Bengalis were now speculating on the political conditions that might have made the British success possible.[101]

This is no doubt the case, but consider the following statement, which could well be the implicit referent of Chatterjee's 'blessing of Providence'. It was made by a Bengali in an appeal to the King of England in 1823, around four decades before the origin of nationalist historical consciousness as Chatterjee dates it:

> Divine Providence at last, in its abundant mercy, stirred up the English nation to break the yoke of those tyrants [the Mughals] and to receive the oppressed natives of Bengal under its protection ... your dutiful subjects consequently have not viewed the English as a body of

---

[98] ibid., p. 80.

[99] ibid.

[100] ibid., p. 84.

[101] ibid., p. 91. On pp. 88-9, this shift (the genealogy of this new history of 'the nation') is narrowed down to the period 1857–1869.

conquerors, but rather as deliverers, and look up to your Majesty not only as a Ruler, but also as a father and protector.[102]

This appeal has been taken by Majumdar to show that Rammohun, who penned it, was so anxious to celebrate the replacement of the Mughals by the British that he repudiated India's Islamic inheritance.[103] Yet it was actually a none-too-subtle serving of what his audience wanted to hear. The excerpt is part of an indignant demand that recently introduced press regulations be withdrawn. The flattering comparison between the British and the Mughals allows the regulations to be depicted as incompatible with the qualities that had enabled the British to defeat the Mughals in the first place.[104] As Rammohun's strategy unfolds, however, the self-same comparison produces the possibility that continued abuses of British power would be resisted violently. In stark contrast to Mritunjay's version of 'Divine Providence', therefore, Rammohun's conduces to anti-colonial agency on the part of Indians. The initially favourable comparison with the Mughals being agreeable to his English audience, Rammohun goes on to suggest a corollary whereby much less pleasant consequences would follow if they continued with the press regulations – consequences which conspicuously involved conscious historical agency, including the establishment of independence on the part of the subjected:

> The greater part of Hindustan having been for several centuries subject to Muhammadan rule, the civil and religious rights of its original inhabitants were consistently trampled on, and from the habitual oppression of the conquerors, a great body of their subjects in the Southern Peninsula (Dukhin), afterwards called Marhattahs, and another body in the Western parts now styled Sikhs, were at last driven to revolt; and when the Mussulman power became feeble, they ultimately succeeded in establishing their independence.[105]

As this example shows, Rammohun himself was not above tactically acquiescing in the characterisation of the Mughals as foreigners. A more important point is the extent to which his campaigning anticipates characteristics that Chatterjee confines to the second half of the nineteenth century. Moreover, might we not

---

[102] *English Works*(1945–51), vol. *iv*, pp. 11-12.

[103] Majumdar 1962, *History of the Freedom Movement*, vol. 1, p. 54.

[104] Such tactics were by no means without precedent: 'A remarkable form of cultural syncretism expressed through Persian [in eighteenth-century Mughal India] was historical writing by Hindu historians in a Muslim idiom. Ram Lal in his *al-Hind* (*The Indian Present*), 1735–36, followed Muslim convention so far as to state that the establishment of Muslim rule in India was divinely ordained and that when Shivaji, Aurangzib's Maratha antagonist, died, he departed to hell'. Peter Hardy 1972, *Muslims of British India* (Cambridge: Cambridge University Press), p. 17.

[105] *English Works* (1945–51), vol. *iv*, p. 11.

be forgiven for discerning a tacit admission on Chatterjee's part that the supposedly European-derived nationalist mode of historical memory, the one that was lacking in Mritunjay, might be found (if only we were allowed to look) in Persian and Arabic?:

> This [Mritunjay's] was the form of historical memory before the modern European modes were implanted in the minds of the educated Bengali. In Mritunjay, the specific form of this memory was one that was prevalent among the Brahman literati in eighteenth-century Bengal. What, then, was the form followed by Bengali Muslim writers? *The court chronicles of the Afghan or the Mughal nobility are not of concern here because these were never written in Bengali.*[106]

Or consider the following:

> Another source often acknowledged in the Bengali textbooks is the series called *The History of India as Told by Its Own Historians* ... these eight volumes comprise translated [into English] extracts from over 150 works, principally in Persian, covering a period from the ninth to the eighteenth centuries. It was a gigantic example of the privilege claimed by modern European scholarship to process the writings of a people supposedly devoid of historical consciousness and render into useful sources of history what otherwise could 'scarcely claim to rank higher than Annals'.[107]

The problem with this, of course, is that, having excluded Persian works from our concern, Chatterjee is not in a position then to reassimilate them to the entirely pre-colonial status that he assigns to Mritunjay. Not, that is, unless 'entirely pre-colonial' is a condition of discursive unity. Chatterjee nowhere argues, let alone shows, that Indian Islamic discourse in Persian lacked historical protocols to distinguish it from Mritunjay's epistemology.[108] The periodisation that Mritunjay's missing modernity sustains requires suppression of the counter example of Rammohun Roy, whose narratology was as nationalist, on Chatterjee's own criteria, as was his establishment of that native self-improvement organisation the Brahmo Samaj.

Despite their substantial differences, therefore, these various historical approaches agree on endorsing a recalcitrant Hindu/European binarism in which the two parties are contrapuntally homogenised. Whether or not the category 'nation'

---

[106] Chatterjee 1993, *Nation and Its Fragments*, pp. 85-6 [my emphasis].

[107] Chatterjee, *Nation and Its Fragments*, p. 100.

[108] Chatterjee (ibid., p. 86) does equate a much later Muslim writer with Vidyalankar ('There does not seem to be much difference in the mode of historical thinking'), only he makes it clear that the discourse is at a subaltern (or, at least, village) rather than elite level.

is altogether appropriate to this situation, transnational history's insistence on a wider global perspective provides a basis for unravelling such homogeneities.

Conclusion

In its connectedness to Indian Islam, the *Tuhfat* is strategically situated in two senses. First, it represents a moment when colonial discourse is not yet fully established (in Raymond Williams' sense) – an interregnum, somewhere between thesis and antithesis but still short of synthesis, when the discursive elements of the colonial regime are still emergent.[109] By identifying such moments, we can more clearly see what colonial discourse is structured to screen out. Second, it marks a space beyond the penumbra of colonial influence in which (proto-) nationalist discourse could be thought. In both respects, the case of the *Tuhfat* raises the question of the mechanisms whereby indigenous alternatives to European models became occluded.

In its various divisions – pre-nationalist period, early benign phase, etc. – the historiography touched on above has sought to quarantine an era in which Hindu and European discourses confronted each other as antithetical monoliths. The desire to graft the imported onto the local, both conceived as pristine, reflects an essentialist preoccupation with origins. Yet when it comes to origins, a Europe so riddled with transnational supplements is itself constitutionally derivative. Islamic Neoplatonism presents Europe with a formative derivation anxiety. In confronting Muslim India, Europe was also returning to its own repressed. By inscribing this return, we can begin to provincialise Europe.

---

[109] Raymond Williams 1977, *Marxism and Literature* (Oxford: Oxford University Press), pp. 115-27.

Index

Abassid Caliphate, 241, 242
Abdul-Aziz, Shah, 250, 252
Aboriginal Australians, 11, 19, 68–9. See also history
    and African worldwide politics, 197–201
    and international travel, 204–8
    and non-Europeans, 201–4
Abu-Lughod, Janet, 29, 32, 33, 40
Academy of Motion Picture Arts and Sciences, 145, 152, 155
acquaintanceship, 7, 139, 140, 143
Adam, William, 246
adda, 69–71
Addams, Jane, 7, 8
Adshead, S. A. M., 29
adult realism, 154
advertising, 171, 174–7, 179–82, 186, 189, 191, 192
Africa, 85, 223. See also West Africa
African Americans, 12, 197, 198, 201, 214, 215, 225. See also Black Atlantic; history; Mississippi precedent
Afro-American culture, 199
Afro-Eurasia, 28
al-Andalus, 237, 239, 242
Allardyce, Gilbert, 26
Allen, Margaret, 18
al-Razi, 251, 252
America. See United States
American colonies, 78, 79, 81
American Fleet, 211
American Immigration Restriction Act of 1896, 19, 219
Americanisation, 42, 168, 181, 183
'Americanness', 180
Anderson, Benedict, 171, 210, 211
Anglicists, 258, 259
Anglo-Atlantic World, 49
Anglo-Saxonism, 211, 213, 219, 226, 229
Anstruther, Gilbert, 185
anti-Semitism, 233
Arabic, 236, 238, 239–45, 249, 264
Argosy Films/Pictures, 153, 155
Armitage, David, 46, 47, 48, 49

Arnold, Ellen, 116
Asiatics, 119, 219, 226
Askew, John, 203
assisted migration schemes, 18, 126, 131, 132, 134
Atlantic history, 17, 28, 29–30, 45
    development and definition of, 46–8
    difficulties of, 48–52, 59–60
    possibilities for, 52–9, 60–1
    writings in, 49, 50, 51, 54, 55, 57–8
Atlantic world, 45, 51, 59, 60, 61. See also Atlantic history
Aurora, Mrs Charles, 207
Australia, 9, 77, 171. See also colonialism; history; White Australia policy
    British migration to, 127–36
    culture of, 169, 172
    and Indian immigration, 114, 118–24
    missionaries in India, 115–18
    and race relations, 213, 214, 219
    romantic consumption in, 179–86
    romantic love in, 171, 177–9
    secret societies in, 91
    and the United States, 187–91, 211
    J. D. Williams in, 158–62, 165, 166, 167
Australian Aboriginal Progressive Association (AAPA), 197, 198, 201, 207
Australian Baptist Mission Societies, 116
Australian Masonic Society, 93
Australian Women's Weekly, 181, 182, 187

backpackers, 131
Bailyn, Bernard, 30, 51, 52, 58
Baktiari people, film of, 144
Baldassar, Loretta, 131
Baldwin, Elaine, 196
Ballantyne, Tony, 6, 17, 19, 67
Bandler, Faith, 11
Bankhead, Tallulah, 147, 148
Baptist missionaries, 64, 65, 116
Barton, Prime Minister Edmund, 222, 224, 227
Battleship Potemkin, The, 145, 151
Bayly, C. A., 17, 35–43, 68
Bengal, 260, 263, 264
Bennelong, 202

Benson, Doug, 134
Bentham, Jeremy, 260
Bentley, Jerry H., 73
Bernstein, Matthew, 141
Bew, George, 107
biography, 167
Birth of the Modern World 1780–1914: global connections and comparisons. See Bayly, C. A.
Black Atlantic, 17, 30, 55, 196
Black Star Line shipping company, 198
Blainey, Geoffrey, 77
Blockade, 153, 154
borders, 53–4, 57, 125, 127, 128
Bose, Sugata, 31
Botany Bay, 78, 86, 88
Boulainviller, Comte de, 236, 235–6
Bourne, Randolph, 7, 141–2, 156
Boxer, C. L. R., 31
Braddick, Michael J., 49
Brahmo Samaj, 246, 248, 253, 265
Brandeis, Louis, 142
Braudel, Fernand, 29
Breen, T. H., 50
Breslaw, Elaine G., 57
Bright, Charles, 25
Brisbane, 158, 160
Britain, 40, 65, 66. See also British empire; India
    and Aboriginal Australians, 202–3
    and Atlantic history, 50, 51
    and Jamaica, 64, 67, 71
    and postcolonialism, 66–7
    and romantic consumption, 184
    romantic love in, 172
    J. D. Williams in, 164–5, 166, 167
British Columbia, 219
British East India Company, 33, 238
British Empire, 40, 65, 66, 73
    and Atlantic history, 51
    Indian movement in, 113–15
    and the White Australia policy, 227, 228
    and the writing of history, 66–7
British India, 236. See also India
British International Pictures, 165
British National Pictures, 164, 165

Brown, Karl, 146
Brownlow, Kevin, 145, 146
Bryce, James, 213–15, 216, 224
Buckle, Gerard Fort, 166
Burgess, John, 224
Burton, Antoinette, 9, 40, 42, 66, 67, 172
Bush, Barbara, 72
Bush, George W., 64
Butts, Maureen and John, 128
Buzzard, Karen S. Falling, 192

Cai Tingkai, General, 93
Calcutta, 69
Caley, George, 203
Calwell, Arthur, 127
Canada, 9, 114, 115, 132, 228
    J. D. Williams in, 157, 165, 166, 167
Cannadine, David, 39, 40, 66
Canning, Kathleen, 41
Canny, Nicholas, 30, 57
capitalism, 27n12, 72, 177, 260
    consumer, 171, 175, 192
    print, 171, 173
Caribbean, 113
Carneiro, Pablo E. DeBerredo, 26
Carter, Maureen, 128
Cell, John, 215
cemetary monuments, 108–10
censorship, 154, 155
Certificate of Exemption from the Dictation Test (CEDT), 120
Chakrabarty, Dipesh, 69–71, 236
Chamberlain, Joseph, 219, 220, 221, 227, 228
Chand, Mool, 123
Chang, 145
Chaplin, Charlie, 163
Charlotte, 86, 88
Charlton, W. R., 211
Chatterjee, Partha, 238, 252, 260–5
Chaudhuri, K. N., 31, 40
Chaunu, Pierre, 29
China, 33, 38, 39, 43, 91, 223
    reference to in Australian cemetaries, 108–10
    republican revolution, 91, 92, 95, 97, 99, 100, 101, 110. See also Taiping Rebellion

Chinese Masonic Society of New South Wales, 18
   background, 89–92
   history and legend, 92–7
   politics of, 97–103
   urbanisation, consolidation and depolitisation, 103–8
Chinese nationalist movement, 91, 107
Chinese-Australians, 91, 93, 110. See also cemetary monuments; Revolutionary and Independence Association of Australian Chinese
   and Freemasonary, 104, 105, 106, 107
   networking by, 103, 107
   radicalisation of, 97, 99
Chow Toong Yung, 97, 99
Chow, Vivian, 98, 99, 100, 101, 103
Christian, David, 40
Christianity, 246, 249, 254–6, 257. See also missionaries
Christopher, Emma, 6, 18
Chuey, James A., 95, 96, 99, 103, 107, 110
cinema. See film
civil rights movements, 11, 198
civilisations, 33. See also Western Civilisation
Civilising Subjects: Metropole and Colony in the English Imagination 1830–1867. See Hall, Catherine
class, 64, 66, 172, 173, 175, 235, 259
Cleveland, President Grover, 213, 219
Coe, Paul, 198
Cohen, Emanuel, 149
Colbert, Claudette, 147, 148, 149, 153
Cold War, 52
Collet, Sophie Dobson, 257
colonialism, 64, 66, 67, 74. See also postcolonialism
   Australian, 68, 69
   British, 70, 236, 259
   and transnational history, 234–6
   as transnational phenomenon, 233–4
colonies, 42, 50, 63, 64, 73–4
colonisation, 211
Coloured Races Restriction and Regulation Bill (1897), 119
Columbia Pictures, 152

Committee on Public Information (CPI), 140, 141
communalism, 245
comparative religion, 247
Conference on Freedom of the Screen, 154
Confucius, 109
Connecticut, 215
Conor, Liz, 183, 189
consumerism. See consumption
consumption, 174, 175, 191–2
   and romantic love, 171, 175, 176, 177, 178, 179–86
   and World War II, 187–91
convicts, 18, 77, 202. See also Limpus, Thomas
Cooper, Merian, 144, 145, 152, 153, 155
corporations, 173, 176, 187
cosmopolitanism, 18, 139, 141, 142, 143
courtship, 174, 177, 187
Covered Wagon, The, 143, 146, 151, 153
Cowles, Gardner, 155
Cox, James, 86
Crawford, Robert, 179
Crick, Stanley, 160
Crosby, Alfred W., 40
cross-cultural encounters, 27, 32
Crusades, 242
Crystal Palace Theatre, 161, 162
Cukor, George, 147, 148
cultural anthropology, 72
culture, 141, 150, 155, 157, 197. See also nationalism
   Aboriginal, 201
   Australian, 169, 172, 173, 178, 181, 187
   black, 199
   and romantic love, 192
Curthoys, Ann, 195
Curtin, Philip, 40, 54

Dabistan Mazahib, 250–1
dating, 174–5, 184, 187, 189
Davis, David Brion, 60
De Lepervanche, Marie, 120
Deacon, Desley, 6, 7, 18
Deakin, Alfred, 112, 123, 223, 224, 225, 226

Index   269

Den Keyser, 80, 81, 82, 86
Denoon, Donald, 16
derivativeness, 238, 239
Dicey, A. V., 214
dictation test, 120, 213, 226, 228. See also education test; literacy test
Digby, John, 245, 249
diplomacy, 141
discipline, 93
disease, 39, 167, 202, 219
distance, 77, 88, 130
documentary and documentary-style films, 143, 144, 147, 150, 151–2, 153
Domicile certificate, 120, 121
Douglas, Mary, 233
Drohan, Pat, 129–31
Du Bois, W. E. B., 8, 19, 208, 209–10, 211, 212, 213, 229
Dudziak, Mary, 16
Duff, Grant, 223
Duhig, Reverend James, 189
Dutt, Palme, 259

Eagle-Lion, 154
East Africa, 113
East Asia, 37
economic history, 33, 37, 40, 71, 167–8
education, 144, 159
education test, 121, 216, 215–16, 221. See also dictation test; literacy test
Eitaki, H., 226, 227
Elbourne, Elizabeth, 9
Ellinghaus, Kat, 10
Elliott, John, 46, 50, 53, 55
Eltis, David, 54
emotionalisation, 180
emotions, 176, 189, 192
empire, 39, 42, 65, 67. See also British Empire; Mongol Empire; Mughal Empire; Muslim Empire
England. See Britain
English language, 171, 211, 221, 252, 264
  and Rammohun Roy, 238, 247, 249–50, 253–7
Eurasia, 28–9, 33, 37
Eurocentrism, 24, 28, 37, 60, 195

Europe, 223, 236, 237, 239
  Aboriginal Australians in, 203
  in history, 25, 27, 32–4, 37–40, 43, 60
  and India, 257, 259, 260, 261, 262, 264, 265
  and the Islamic world, 19, 239–45, 265
  and modernity, 33, 37, 41, 42
  and postcolonial histories, 9, 71
Europeans, 31, 32, 56, 60, 61, 77
Evans, Julie, 9
exceptionalism
  American, 7, 15, 234
  European, 32, 37, 66
Eyre, Edward John, 67

Famous Players-Lasky (Paramount), 139, 140, 143, 144, 146, 151, 156, 165
Fanon, Frantz, 208
Felix, Peter, 198
Fell, Katie, 117
femininity, 179, 182, 187
feminists, 68–9, 73
Ferguson, Niall, 39, 40, 65
Fernando, Anthony Martin, 205–7
Fiji, 113
films, 143, 167–9
  and consumption, 181, 189, 190
  influence of, 139–40, 156, 166. See also Wanger, Walter
  and J. D. Williams, 159–60, 162, 163–6
Finch, Lyn, 187, 189
First Fleet, 79, 80, 81, 86–8, 202
First National Exhibitors' Circuit, 163, 164
Fischer, Reverend Theo B., 113, 123
Fitzgerald, John, 18
Flaherty, Robert, 144, 146, 152, 155
Fletcher, Joseph, 32
Foenander, Terry, 204
Forbidden Fruit, 143
forgetting, 235
France, 236
Frank, Andre Gunder, 40
Frederickson, George, 200
freedom, 52, 60
Freedom Ride, 11–13, 198
Freeman, E. A., 211, 213, 224

Freemasons, 104–7
French Annales school, 7, 29, 30
Friedman, Max Paul, 14
Frost, Mark Ravinder, 31
Furber, Holden, 31

Gandhi, Mahatma, 115, 196
Gardner, Eunice, 131–2
Garrison, Wendell Phillips, 214
Garvey, Amy Jacques, 207
Garvey, Marcus, 11, 19, 195, 198, 199–201, 208
Geggus, David P., 57
gender, 40, 55n17, 64, 68, 73, 148
   and consumption, 179, 187–91
   and romantic love, 173, 179
George III, 202
Georgia, 216
Geyer, Michael, 25
gift giving, 188–9, 190–1
Gikandi, Simon, 68
Gilbert, Marie, 116
Gillis, John, 172
Gilroy, Paul, 9, 54, 57, 196
globalisation, 36, 168, 195
Gokhale, G. K., 115
Goodall, Heather, 205, 206, 207
Goodman, David, 17
Gottschalk, Louis, 26
Gray, John, 191, 192
Greater J. D. Williams Amusement Co. Ltd, 159
Greene, Jack, 59
Grierson, John, 150–2, 155
Griffiths, Tom, 17
Grimshaw, Patricia, 9
Guha, Ranajit, 262

Hall, Catherine, 9, 17, 42, 63, 64–8, 71–2, 74
Hall, Mordaunt, 145, 146, 148
Hall, Stuart, 9
Hall, Timothy, 50
Hallam, Alfaretta, 183
Hampton, Benjamin, 162
Handlin, Oscar, 125

Hansen, Miriam, 139, 156
happiness, 174, 175, 177
Harrison, Marguerite, 144
Haskins, Charles Homer, 243
Hellenic tradition, 242
Higgins, H. B., 224, 225, 227
Higham, John, 229
Hindu India, 19, 257
Hinduism, 36, 37, 238, 246, 250, 256
Hindus, 118, 238, 253, 257, 258, 259, 265. See also Hinduism; nationalism
Hindustan, 263
history, 5, 7, 38. See also Aboriginal Australians; Atlantic history; transnational history;
   World history
   Aboriginal Australian, 12, 197, 208, 236
   Australian, 13, 16–17, 195
   Black, 8, 10–13
   of the body, 40, 41
   British imperial, 8–9
   comparative, 6, 57, 59
   cultural, 73
   feminist, 15–16
   film, 157, 160, 162, 164, 167. See also identity
   migration, 125, 126, 167
   national, 5, 8, 13–15, 19, 25, 67, 195, 201
   and the nation state, 23–4
   postcolonial, 17–18, 63–4, 68, 69, 71, 72, 73
   race relations, 16
   regional, 6
   social, 71, 73
   sub-Saharan African, 72
   white settler, 9–10
   writing of, 64, 65, 66, 72, 257–65
History of India as Told by Its Own Historians, The, 264
history wars, 12, 67
Ho Chi Minh, 200
Hodgson, Marshall S., 28–9
Hollywood, 139, 152, 156
'Hollywood monologue', 165, 168
Holt, Harold, 128

Honduras Bay, 84
Hopkins, A. G., 8–9
Hornabrook, Dr R., 124n61
Howard, Prime Minister John, 69
Howqua (Chinese interpreter), 91, 104
Hudson, John, 86
Hughes, Rupert, 184
Hung League, 89–91, 94, 99, 104, 105, 106, 107. See also Chinese Masonic Society
   and cemetary memorials, 109
Hunt, Attlee, 121
Hunter, Governor John, 202
Huttenback, Robert, 122

identity
   Aboriginal, 198, 208
   Australian, 224
   British, 50
   and film historians, 167
   and history writing, 23, 24
   and modern women, 183
   national, 169
   and nation states, 35
   and whiteness, 113, 213
   subjective constructions of, 136
   transnational, 129, 131
Illouz, Eva, 173, 175, 176, 177, 184, 192
imagined communities, 19, 35, 171, 210, 211
immigration, 90. See also migration
   Asian, 113
   Chinese, 96, 107
   to Natal, 113
   restriction, 123, 219–21, 228, 229
   into the United States, 217–19
Immigration Restriction Act in the Commonwealth of Australia (1901), 112, 114, 120, 123, 226
Immigration Restriction Bill (Australia), 222
Immigration Restriction Bill (Natal), 221
Immigration Restriction League, 213, 218
imperialism, 9, 17, 39, 53, 64, 65, 66, 73
India, 237, 238, 241. See also nationalism
   Australian attitudes towards, 112–13, 118–24

   Australians in, 18, 111–12, 115–18
   and the British Empire, 113–15, 219, 220, 236, 257, 259, 261, 263
   and Marxism, 259
   passport system (1915), 115
   and the writing of history, 257–65
Indian Civil Service, 114
Indian Islam, 19, 236, 246, 248, 257, 261, 264, 265
Indian National Congress, 115, 123, 196, 261
Indian Ocean, 28, 31–2, 33
Indians Overseas Association, 115
indigenous peoples, 9–10, 15, 55, 56, 59. See also Aboriginal Australians
individualism, 260
information, 155. See also Committee on Public Information
international relations, 195
internationalism, 142
'intimacy', 191
Islam, 238, 250, 255, 257, 258, 260. See also Indian Islam
   exclusion of, 236, 239, 257, 258, 261
   influence of, 239–45
Islamic world, 38, 43
Islamophobia, 233, 237, 245

Jackson, John Brinkerhoff, 167
Jacobsen, Matt, 215, 217, 218
Jamaica, 64, 67, 68, 71
James, C. L. R., 8, 30
Jan, Ghulam, 122
Japan, 34, 114, 210, 212
   and the White Australia policy, 226, 227, 228
Jiménez, Michael, 54
Johnson, Jack, 158, 197, 198
Johnson, Sun, 105
Jones, John C., 160
Journal of American History, 8
Journal of World History, 40, 63, 73

Kai Koon, 99
Kallen, Horace, 142
Keary, Anne, 10

Kelley, Robin, 8
Kenney, Padraic, 14
Kennington, Alan, 184
Kent, Sidney, 149
Khan, Burket Ali, 120
King, Jessie Mary, 99
King, Martin Luther, 198
kinship communication, 128–31
Klein, Bernhard, 77
Klooster, Wim, 57
Knight, Franklin W., 57
knowledge, 140, 143
Kopf, David, 253, 258–9

Lacey, Captain, 82
Lacey, Tom, 207, 208
Lake, Marilyn, 16, 19, 115, 179, 182, 187, 190
Langton, Marcia, 196
language test, 114
Lasky, Jesse, 140, 143–7, 149, 150, 155
Latin, 239–45
Latin America, 30, 50, 52n11, 56
Laughing Lady, The, 148
Lee Fook, 93
Lee, W. R. G., 105
Lee, William, 105
Lester, Alan, 9
Lever Company, 180, 182
Liang Qichao, 102
liberty, 60
Limpus, Thomas, 18, 78–9, 87, 88
    first convict voyage, 79–83
    second convict voyage, 83–6
    third convict voyage, 86–7
Linebaugh, Peter, 54, 57
Lippmann, Walter, 52, 142
Liss, Peggy, 57
literacy test, 13, 19, 213, 221, 227, 229. See also dictation test; education test
    in the United States, 217–19
Liu Daren, 97
Lodge of Tranquillity, 105
Lodge, Henry Cabot, 217–19, 226
London Missionary Society, 111
Loomba, Anita, 74

Loong Hung Pung, 94, 95, 96, 97–9, 103, 107, 108
love, 173, 174, 177, 184, 189, 192. See also romantic love
love letters, 188, 191
Lovejoy, Paul E., 57
Low, Rachel, 164
Lubitsch, Ernst, 143, 147, 148, 150, 163
Lucas, Charles, 228, 229
Luna Park, St Kilda, 160, 161

Macassans, 201, 202
Mackenthun, Gesa, 77
MacLean, Mary, 116
magazines. See also Australian Women's Weekly; Man; Table Talk
    men's, 184–6, 191
    women's, 179, 180, 181, 182, 183, 184, 188
Mahomed, Hajee, 118–19
Majumdar, Romesh Chandra, 257–8, 259, 263
Malaya, 113
Man: The Australian Magazine for Men, 185
Maori, 203, 204
marriage, 174, 177, 182, 183, 184, 185, 189
Martin, John, 81
Martin, Tony, 200
Marxism, 72, 259
Maryland, 83, 84
Massachusetts, 215, 217, 219
Matthews, Jill, 6, 13, 14, 18, 181, 189
Maynard, Fred, 197, 198
Maynard, John, 11, 15, 19
    relatives of, 197, 198
McCalman, Janet, 90
McDonnell, Michael, 6, 17
McGerr, Michael, 13
McGrath, Ann, 10
McKenzie, Kirsten, 17
McNeill, J. R., 60
McNeill, W. H., 26–8
Mead, Dr Cecil, 116
Mead, Reverend Silas, 116
Melbourne, 160, 161

Index 273

men, 70, 175. See also gender
    as consumers, 174, 179, 180, 190, 191
Menocal, Maria Rosa, 244
Menzies, Robert, 128
Mercury, 83, 84, 85, 86, 87
Merriam, Charles, 140, 151
Métis, 58
metropole, 42, 50, 63, 64, 73
Mexico, 59
MGM (Metro-Goldwyn-Meyer), 150, 153
Mignolo, Walter D., 27fn12
migration 56, 125–6, 196
    British, 18, 126–36
    mobility of, 210, 229
Milne, A. A., 184
Ming dynasty, 102, 109
missionaries, 64, 207. See also London
Missionary Society
    in India, 18, 111, 115–18
Missionary Settlement for University
Women (MSUW), 116, 117
Mississippi precedent, 19, 213, 215–16
Moana, 144, 146, 151
mobility, 73, 112, 126, 132, 210, 229
    and British migration, 127, 130, 132, 133, 134
    and modern women, 112, 183
'mobility of modernity', 18, 124, 133, 134, 136. See also mobility
modernity, 36, 37, 38, 39, 40, 41, 42, 113
    and adda, 69, 70
    and consumption, 181, 182
    and India, 112, 262, 265
    and Islam, 244
    and nationalism, 169
    in the West, 25
    and whiteness, 124
Mongia, Radhika, 114, 115
Mongol Empire, 29, 33
monotheism, 238, 247, 248, 251, 253
Moore, George, 84
Moowat'tin, 203
Morrison, Michael A., 57
Motion Picture Producers and Distributors of America, 163
moving pictures. See films

Moy Sing, John, 95, 96, 97, 99, 103, 107, 110
Mritunjay Vidyalankar, 262, 263, 264, 265
Mu'tazilite school, 251
Mughal Empire, 33, 39, 245, 250, 256, 257, 258, 263–4
Mukherjee, S. N., 260
Mulvaney, John, 202
Murnau, F. W., 146
Muslim Empire, 38
Muslim India, 19, 252, 265
Muslims, 239, 244, 245, 255, 256, 257

Naipaul, V. S., 65
Nanook of the North, 144, 146
Natal, 19, 113, 114, 123, 213, 219–21, 226
nation state, 5, 32, 235, 236
    and the writing of history, 23–4, 125, 126
nationalism, 14, 72, 235. See also transnational history
    and C. A. Bayly, 35
    and circulated texts, 171
    colonial, 23, 73, 113, 235, 236, 261
    cultural, 14, 168–9
    Hindu, 236
    Indian, 237–9, 246, 252, 255, 257, 261, 262
Native/North American Indian, 56n18, 202
New South Wales, 11, 78, 87, 88, 92, 108, 220
New York, 139, 147, 148, 149, 150, 163
New Zealand, 9, 10, 114–15, 160, 219, 228
newsreels, 140, 160
Nicol, Elsie, 111, 117
nomads, 14, 167, 169
Norris, Kathleen, 184
North America, 25, 27, 60

ocean. See sea
Orientalism, 65, 258, 259
Orientalists, 258, 259
outlaws of the Liangshan marshes, 93

Pacific Islands Labourers Act, 226
Pacific Islands Labourers' Bill, 222, 225

Padula, Alfred, 57
Pagden, Anthony, 57, 71
Paisley, Fiona, 68–9, 71, 207
Palmer, Robert R., 53, 54
Palmolive, 180, 182
Paramount, 139, 145, 147–52, 163, 165. See also Famous-Players Lasky
Paramount Theatre Managers Training School, 151
Parsons, Amy, 117
Parsons, Elsie Clews, 142, 156
Parsons, Louella, 143
peace, 139–40, 141, 143
Pearson, Charles, 222–4
Perkins, Charles, 11, 198
Persian, 238, 249, 264
Perth, 160
Petty, John, 80n10
Phillip, Governor Arthur, 87, 88, 202
Phillips, David, 9
Phillips, Leon, 158, 161
Pickford, Mary, 163
Playboy, 185, 186
pleasure, 174, 175, 176, 182
Poignant, Roslyn, 203
Polak, H. S., 115
Pomeranz, Kenneth, 37, 38, 39, 40
Poona and Indian Village Mission (PIVM), 117, 118
population movements, 126, 127
Porter, Roy, 71
postcolonialism, 42, 65, 66, 68, 72–4
Precepts of Jesus, 246, 254
Presbyterian Women's Missionary Association (PWMA) of New South Wales, 116
pride, 167
Prime, John, 80n10
Pringle, Rosemary, 180

Qing dynasty, 91, 101, 108, 109, 110
Quinn, David Beers, 30
Quong Tart, 105, 106

race, 19, 36, 209, 214, 215, 220, 233–5. See also history
    connection with empire and violence, 39
    connections to gender and class, 64, 68, 69, 72, 73
    and the literacy test, 216–18, 229
    and transnationalism, 19, 233–4
    and the White Australia policy, 222–9
race relations, 16, 67, 195, 209, 215
racial discrimination, 11, 115, 215, 216, 227. See also Australia; United States
racial equality, 210, 214
racial exclusion, 13, 215, 216, 227, 229
racism, 65, 199, 234
Radical Reconstruction, 11, 214
Ramsaye, Terry, 162
rationalism, 237, 258
Reconquista, 242–3
Rediker, Marcus, 54, 57
Reeve, Charles, 117
religion, 36, 37, 247
Renaissance, 244
Renan, Ernest, 235
respectability, 89, 90, 92, 108
Revive China Society, 97, 102
Revolutionary and Independence Association of Australian Chinese, 99, 100, 101, 102
Richardson, Professor Ron, 197
Richmond Furnishing Company, 181
Richmond, Anthony, 132, 134
Ritz-Carlton Pictures, 164
Rivett, Eleanor, 111
Roach, Joseph, 57
Roberts, Austin, 185
Robin, Libby, 17
Robinson, Scott, 199
Robinson-Gallagher thesis, 38
Rodinson, Maxime, 260
Rogers, Nicholas, 57
romance, 174–6, 178, 179, 181, 182, 184–6, 189–91
romantic love, 18, 171–3, 181–3, 187–9, 191–2
    in Australia, 171, 177–9
    in the United States, 173–7

romanticisation, 179–86
Roosevelt, Eleanor, 184
Roosevelt, President Roosevelt, 211
Roosevelt, President Theodore, 210, 211, 222, 223
Roy, M. N., 259
Roy, Rammohun, 236–9, 245–46, 257–60, 263–5
   English writings, 253–7
   and the Tuhfat, 247–53
Royal Commission on the [Australian] Constitution, 69
Royal Commission on the status of Aborigines in Western Australia, 69
Ruglass, John, 80, 82, 86
Russell, Bertrand, 184
Russia, 34

Sahid, Syed Iran, 122
Said, Edward, 9, 64, 65, 66, 67, 71n18, 244, 245n34
sailors. See seamen
Scalmer, Sean, 13
Schlegel, Gustav, 104
Schoedsack, Ernest, 144, 145, 146, 152, 153, 155
Schulberg, B. P., 147, 149
Schurz, Carl, 214
sea, 77–9, 83, 86, 88
seamen, 19, 83, 88, 200, 202
Second Fleet, 87
secret societies, 90, 91, 104, 108
See Yup native-place association, 89
See, James, 99, 100–3
See, John, 99, 100–1, 102
See, Thomas, 99, 101, 102
segregation, 11, 12, 215
Seidman, Steven, 173, 176
self-commodification, 190
self-determination, 183, 195, 208
self-government, 52, 211, 214, 215, 219, 224
Sen, Tansen, 32
Sensbach, Jon F., 58
sensuality, 176
Servants of India Society in Poona, 115

settler societies, 9–10, 17, 235, 236. See also colonialism
sexualisation, 179, 180, 187
sexuality, 40, 142, 148, 174, 175, 179, 181
Shotwell, James T., 141
Sidaway, Robert, 86
Singapore, 223
Singh, Hushnak, 121
Singh, Otim, 119
Singha, Radhika, 115
Sinha, Mrinalini, 42
slave trade, 55, 79, 80, 81, 84, 87
slavery, 60, 65, 80
Smith, Jackie, 134–6
social benefit, 247, 248. See also monotheism
social categories, 142
sojourners, 129, 131, 133
Solomon, Barbara, 219
Soons, John, 80n10
South Africa, 9, 10, 213, 215, 216, 219, 228, 229
   Indians in, 113, 115
South Asia, 33, 38, 43
South Australian Baptist Missionary Society, 116, 117
Spanish Peru, 59
Sparks, Randy J., 58
Spengler, Oswald, 25
Sperry, Rear Admiral, 211
Spivak, Gayatri, 236
Stack, John, 186
Stark Love, 146
Stasiulis, Daiva, 9
Stavros, Con, 178
Stearns, Peter, 175, 176
Stephen, Ann, 180
Stephenson, Gilbert, 216
Stettheimer, Carrrie, Ettie and Florine, 141
Stewart, Donald Ogden, 147, 148
Stirling, W. G., 104
Stoddard, Lothrop, 229
Stoll Picture Productions, 164
Subaltern Studies group, 18, 67, 71, 72, 236n9, 262
Subrahmanyam, Sanjay, 32

Sun Yatsen, 91, 97, 98, 100, 110
Swain, Shurlee, 9
Swiencicki, Mark, 180
Swift, 83, 84
Sydney, 78, 199, 200
    J. D. Williams in, 158–9, 161, 162
Sydney Freemasons Hall, 107
Sydney Masonic Hall, 89, 95, 107
Sydney Masonic Lodge, 92–4

Table Talk, 181, 182, 183–4
Taft, President William H., 219
Tagore, Rabindranath, 237
Taiping Rebellion, 94, 100, 101, 102
Tally, Thomas L., 163
Taylor, Alan, 50, 51
'Ten Pound Poms', 18, 126
Teo, Hsu-Ming, 18
Thelen, David, 8
theory, 71
    dependency, 27
    Gramscian-derived, 72
    postcolonial, 69, 71, 72
    social, 37, 43
    world systems, 7, 27, 38, 72
Third World, 26, 72
Thompson, Browning, 185
Thompson, E. P., 71
Three Principles of the People, 98
Tian Xinyuan, 97
Tock Gee, 94
Tong Wars, 89
Topik, Steven, 40
Townsend, Camilla, 54
Townsend, John, 81, 82
Toynbee, Arnold, 25, 27
transilients, 132, 134
translators, 239, 243
transnational history, 5, 19–20, 195, 234–6. See also postcolonial history
    and Aboriginal Australians, 208
    Australian, 15–17, 172
    and Black history, 10–13
    dangers of, 13–15
    definition of, 5–7
    difficulties of, 45
    and films, 168, 167–9
    historiography of, 7–10
    and migration, 125–6
    and nationalism, 167–9
    and postcolonialism, 72–4
    and the sea, 77
    and J. D. Williams, 157
    writing of, 235, 265
transnationalism, 18, 139, 141, 156, 234. See also films; transnational history
    of romantic love, 172, 192
transportation, 18, 78, 87. See also Limpus, Thomas
Tuhfat-ul Muwahhiddin, 238–9, 246, 247–53, 254–7, 260, 265
Tulloch, Hugh, 214
Turner, Ralph E., 26
Tyrrell, Ian, 7–8, 10, 17, 234

Ummayyad Caliphate, 241, 242
uniformity, 36
Union Theatres/Australasian Films, 162
Unitarianism, 246n37
United Artists, 153
United Nations Educational, Scientific and Cultural Organisation (UNESCO), 25–6
United States, 9, 34
    Aboriginal Australians in, 203
    and Atlantic history, 51, 52
    British migration to, 127, 128
    Civil War, 204
    and consumerism, 181
    film industry, 168
    historians of, 7, 8, 10
    and racial discrimination, 213, 214, 217–19
    and romantic love, 173–7, 183, 192
    soldiers, and Australian women, 187–91
    and transnational history, 8, 234–5
    and the White Australia policy, 224, 225, 226, 228
    J. D. Williams in, 157, 163–4, 165, 166, 167
    and world history, 42
United States Civil Rights movement, 12

Universal Negro Improvement Association (UNIA), 19, 198, 199–201
Universal Pictures, 153
universalism, 64, 248, 256
urbanisation, 69

Valentine's Day, 178
Vedanta, 248, 250, 253
Vietnam War, 191
violence, 39, 42
von Sternberg, Josef, 147

Wai, Reverend John Young, 92
Walcott, Derek, 77
Walker, David, 112
Wall, Governor Joseph, 80, 82
Wallerstein, Immanuel, 27n12
Walvin, James, 42
Wanger, Beatrice, 141
Wanger, Walter, 18, 139–41, 142, 143, 149, 152, 156
    films of, 143–9, 152–5
    influence of, 150–1
Ward, J. S. M., 104
Warner Brothers, 150
Watts, Richard, 145
Waugh, Evelyn, 184
Way Lee, 99, 105
Wells, H. G., 25
West, the 25, 27, 28, 32, 34, 60. See also Western Civilisation
West Africa, 79, 80, 80–2
Western Australia, 226
Western Civilisation, 25, 26, 42, 52, 212
westerns, 153, 155
White Australia Policy, 18, 124, 222–9
White, Richard, 126
whiteness, 19, 113, 182, 209–15, 229. See also identity
Williams, Diana, 131, 132
Williams, J. D., 18, 157–67, 168, 169
Williams, Nallemma, 117
Williams, Susie, 116
Williams' Weekly News, 160
Wilson, Kathleen, 42
Wilson, President Woodrow, 141, 214, 219

Wolfe, Patrick, 16, 19
women, 18, 70, 112, 142
    as consumers, 179, 180, 183, 184, 187, 190. See also dating
Wong, R. Bin, 37, 38, 39, 40, 43
Woodham, Samuel, 80, 82, 86
Woollacott, Angela, 17, 42, 112, 113
World history, 6, 7, 17, 68, 73
    and C. A. Bayly, 35–43, 68
    development of, 25–34
    and economic history, 168
World History Association, 63
World Parliament of Religions, 36
world systems theory, 7, 38, 72
World War II, 187–91
World Wide Pictures Corporation, 165

X, Malcolm, 199

Yemmurrawannie, 202
Yeung Ku Wan, 101–2
Yong, C. F., 94, 95, 96, 104
Young China League, 107
Young, Robert, 208
Yuval-Davis, Nira, 9
YWCA (Young Womens Christian Association), 117

Zook, Melinda S., 57